I0094846

Rebalancing and Sustaining Growth in China

Other titles in the China Update Book Series include:

Rebalancing and Sustaining Growth in China

Huw McKay and Ligang Song (eds)

Australian
National
University

E PRESS

社会科学文献出版社
SOCIAL SCIENCES ACADEMIC PRESS(CHINA)

ANU
E PRESS

Published by ANU E Press
The Australian National University
Canberra ACT 0200, Australia
Email: anuepress@anu.edu.au
This title is also available online at: http://epress.anu.edu.au

Co-published with SOCIAL SCIENCES ACADEMIC PRESS (CHINA) under the China Book International scheme. This scheme supports co-publication of works with international publishers.

CHINA BOOK
INTERNATIONAL

National Library of Australia Cataloguing-in-Publication entry

Title:	Rebalancing and sustaining growth in China / edited by Huw McKay and Ligang Song.
ISBN:	9781921862793 (pbk.) 9781921862809 (ebook)
Series:	China update series.
Notes:	Includes bibliographical references and index.
Subjects:	China--Economic conditions. China--Economic policy. China--Commerce.

Other Authors/Contributors:
McKay, Huw.
Song, Ligang.

Dewey Number: 330.951

All rights reserved. No part of this publication may be reproduced, stored in a retrieval system or transmitted in any form or by any means, electronic, mechanical, photocopying or otherwise, without the prior permission of the publisher.

Book design and layout by Teresa Prowse, http://www.madebyfruitcup.com

Cover image: Huw McKay

This edition © 2012 ANU E Press

Contents

Tables

Figures

Abbreviations

AO	Agricultural Output
ASEAN	Association of South-East Asian Nations
BIS	Bank for International Settlements
CBRC	China Banking Regulatory Commission
CCP	Chinese Communist Party
CDB	China Development Bank
CEO	Chief Executive Officer
CEC	China Enterprise Confederation
CES	Constant Elasticity of Substitution
CNOOC	China National Offshore Oil Corporation
CNPC	China National Petroleum Corporation
CO2	Carbon Dioxide
CPI	Consumer Price Index
CSRC	China Securities Regulatory Commission
CU	County-level Unit
DNA	Deoxyribonucleic Acid
DWUC	Direct Water Use Coefficient
EIA	Energy Information Administration
ETDAs	Economic and Technological Development Areas
ETDZs	Economic and Technological Development Zones
EM	Emerging Market
EOUs	Export Oriented Units
EPZs	Export Processing Zones
FDI	Foreign Direct Investment
FIEs	Foreign-invested Enterprises
GDP	Gross Domestic Product
GDPG	Gross Domestic Product Growth Rate
GDPP	Gross Domestic Product Per Capita
GE	Generalised Entropy
GMM	Generalised Method of Moments
GNP	Gross National Product
GRP	Gross Regional Product
GVIAO	Gross Value of Industrial and Agricultural Output

GVRSP	Gross Value of Rural Social Product
HS	Harmonised System
HTIDA	High Technology Industrial Development Area
HTIDZ	High Technology Industrial Development Zones
IBRD	International Bank for Reconstruction and Development
IEA	International Energy Agency
IMF	International Monetary Fund
IOC	International Oil Companies
LIBOR	London Interbank Offered Rate
M&As	Mergers and Acquisitions
MNCs	Multinational Corporations
MNEs	Multinational Enterprises
MOFCOM	Ministry of Commerce
MOHRSS	Ministry of Human Resources and Social Security
MSG	Monosodium Glutamate
NBS	National Bureau of Statistics
NDRC	National Development and Reform Commission
NEER	Nominal Effective Exchange Rate
NELM	New Economics of Labour Migration
NI	National Income
NOCs	National Oil Companies
NPC	National People's Congress
NPES	National Population and Employment Statistics
NVWE	Net Virtual Water Export
ODI	Outward Direct Investment
OECD	Organisation for Economic Cooperation and Development
ONGC	Oil and Natural Gas Corporation
OPEC	Organisation of Petroleum Exporting Countries
PBC	People's Bank of China
PLC	Proprietary Limited Company
QFII	Qualified Foreign Institutional Investors
QDII	Qualified Domestic Institutional Investors
R&D	Research and Development
RCA	Revealed Comparative Advantage
REER	Real Effective Exchange Rate

RHS	Rural Household Survey
RMB	Renminbi
RNAO	Rural Non-Agricultural Output
ROA	Return on Assets
RUMiCI	Rural–Urban Migration in China and Indonesia
SASAC	State-owned Assets Supervision and Administration Commission
SEZs	Special Economic Zones
SIA	Social Insurance Administration
SITC	Standard International Trade Classification
Sinopec	China Petroleum & Chemical Corporation
SMEs	Small and Medium Enterprises
SOBs	State-owned Banks
SOEs	State-owned Enterprises
SSB	State Statistical Bureau
TFP	Total Factor Productivity
TPP	Trans-Pacific Partnership
TWUC	Total Water Use Coefficient
UHS	Urban Household Survey
UMS	Urban Migrant Survey
UN	United Nations
UNCTAD	United Nations Conference on Trade and Development
US	United States
USD	United States Dollars
WDI	World Development Indicators
WTO	World Trade Organization
WR	Water Resources
WU	Water Use
YRCC	Yellow River Conservancy Commission

Contributors

Fang Cai
Institute of Population and Labour Economics, The Chinese Academy of Social Sciences, Beijing.

Tsun Se Cheong
Economics Department, School of Business, University of Western Australia, Perth.

Sylvie Démurger
Centre for National Scientific Research, University of Lyon, Lyon.

Jane Golley
Australian Centre on China in the World, The Australian National University, Canberra.

Anders C Johansson
Stockholm School of Economics, Stockholm.

Sherry Tao Kong
Research School of Economics, ANU College of Business and Economics, The Australian National University, Canberra.

Lillie Lam
Representative Office for Asia and the Pacific, Bank of International Settlements, Hong Kong.

Guonan Ma
Representative Office for Asia and the Pacific, Bank for International Settlements, Hong Kong.

Huw McKay
Westpac Bank, Sydney; Research School of Economics, The Australian National University, Canberra.

Robert N. McCauley
Monetary and Economic Department, Bank for International Settlements, Switzerland.

Qu Yue
Institute of Population and Labour Economics, The Chinese Academy of Social Sciences, Beijing.

Minjun Shi
Research Centre on Fictitious Economy and Data Science, The Chinese Academy of Sciences, Beijing.

Ligang Song
China Economy Program, Crawford School of Public Policy, The Australian National University, Canberra.

Wei Tian
Department of Applied Economics, Guanghua School of Management, Peking University, Beijing.

Rod Tyers
Economics Department, School of Business, University of Western Australia, Perth.

Bijun Wang
China Centre for Economic Research,
National School of Development,
Peking University, Beijing.

Andrew Watson
School of Social Sciences, University
of Adelaide, Adelaide.

Yanrui Wu
Economics Department, School of
Business, University of Western
Australia, Perth.

Jing Xiang
Department of Agricultural
Economics, College of Economics and
Management, Nanjing Agricultural
University, Nanjing.

Chaofeng Yang
Institute of Scientific and Technical
Information of China, Beijing.

Hong Yang
Swiss Federal Institute of Aquatic
Science and Technology, Zurich.

Miaojie Yu
China Centre for Economic Research,
National School of Development,
Peking University, Beijing.

Xiaobo Zhang
Development Strategy and
Governance Division, International
Food Policy Research Institute,
Washington DC.

ZhongXiang Zhang
East-West Centre, Honolulu.

Zhuoying Zhang
Graduate University of the Chinese
Academy of Sciences, Beijing.

Zhiyun Zhao
Institute of Scientific and Technical
Information of China, Beijing.

Funing Zhong
Department of Agricultural
Economics, College of Economics and
Management, Nanjing Agricultural
University, Nanjing.

Acknowledgments

The China Economy Program (CEP) gratefully acknowledges the financial support for the China Update 2012 provided by Rio Tinto through the Rio Tinto-ANU China Partnership, as well as the assistance provided by Dan Hyde, Luke Hurst, Luke Meehan and our colleagues at the East Asia Forum at The Australian National University.

1. Rebalancing the Chinese Economy to Sustain Long-Term Growth

Huw McKay and Ligang Song

> Meeting the challenge of the domestic restructuring to sustain growth, asserting the right to develop and not to be penalized purely for being large, while taking on increased responsibility for global balance, stability, and governance and representing the interests of less-powerful developing countries are major new mountains to climb. China's success or failure will, in any event, have a significant impact on the rest of the world.
>
> —Michael Spence (2011:198)

Introduction

The call to rebalance economic growth in China is primarily motivated by the structural problems within China as well as in its economic relations with the rest of the world. China's international payments surpluses during the first decade of the twenty-first century have corresponded with deepening domestic structural risks to China's economic growth and development. These structural challenges include the composition of growth resulting from China's dynamic internal transformation, China's trade orientation, the trajectory of resource use and carbon dioxide emissions, welfare problems of distribution and international constraints. It is thought to be necessary for China to confront these challenges now in order to put the growth path into a more sustainable trajectory in the future (Deer and Song 2012). The purpose of this year's China Update book is to examine the challenges China faces in addressing its economic imbalances and sustaining growth against a backdrop of heightened domestic and international uncertainty.

The transition from a traditional to a modern economic system entails major and often rapid structural change in economy-wide processes of industrialisation, urbanisation and agricultural transformation (Syrquin 1988). As a result of rapid structural change, transitional economic challenges arise, which can pose risks to future growth if not well managed. Rapid change can also create welfare challenges, as the institutional settings required for an equitable distribution of income might not be present. As such, the pursuit of 'balanced' economic growth is best thought of as a broad policy objective that aims to limit risks to growth and to mitigate the negative impact on welfare. It should therefore not be expressed as a particular target, such as a reduction in the current account surplus or a rise in the labour share of income. The role of policy should be to design and implement a framework that reduces distortions, encourages and rewards innovation, equalises access to education, employment, a social safety net and capital for investment, while minimising rent-seeking opportunities. The desire to achieve such an environment will create demand for institutional reforms that can facilitate these processes of structural change in the least disruptive fashion.

The enormous scale of China's aggregate imbalances—crudely summarised as the unbalanced nature of domestic expenditure—and its external payment surplus, which reflects a stark excess of saving over investment, are well known. Unbalanced domestic expenditure refers to China's high, and until recently, growing share of investment relative to consumption in the expenditure measure of gross domestic product (GDP). The external payment imbalance refers to China's current account, trade account and private financial account surpluses. While the list of Chinese economic characteristics that deserve the label 'unbalanced' is legion—including the level of the exchange rate, the urban–rural income divide, the coast–hinterland divide and asymmetries in the degree access to credit, education, social security and housing—at some level they all relate to and inform the basic macroeconomic structure and the external payments position.

Figure 1.1 China: Expenditure shares of GDP, 1978–2010 (per cent)

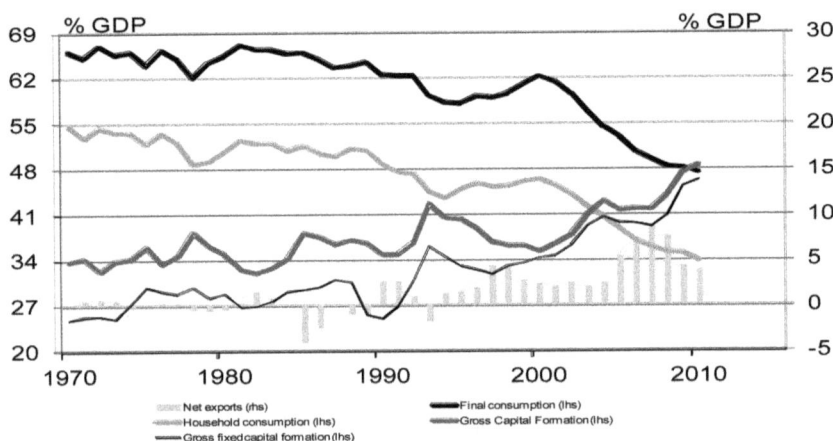

Source: CEIC data, available from <http://www.ceicdata.com/China.html>

Figure 1.1 shows the composition of China's growth by broad expenditure measures of GDP from 1978 to 2010. Three broad trends are evident: from the late 1990s there was a sharp rise in the investment share of GDP and a sharp fall in the final and household consumption shares of GDP, while the share of net exports rose sharply from a modest base after 2002. China's high investment share of GDP implies a very rapid rate of capital accumulation. China's investment share of expenditure in GDP (using gross capital formation—that is, including inventories) rose sharply from 35 to 48 per cent of GDP between 2000 and 2010, equating to a 13 percentage point rise.[1] A high investment share of expenditure in GDP is relatively common in industrialising economies, such as Japan in the 1960s and Korea in the 1970s, particularly in the early period of rapid (catch-up) economic growth (Fukumoto and Muto 2011; Knight and Wang 2011; McKay and Song 2010:Table 1, p. 6). Catch-up growth driven by rapid capital accumulation can be sustained for decades in capital-poor transitional economies with an abundant supply of labour. China's still relatively low level of income per capita and capital stock per worker, in addition to its relatively low (policy-suppressed) urbanisation rate and the relative backwardness of its central and interior provinces, argue that concentrated growth on the Chinese Mainland could potentially continue for longer than it did in its neighbours, including Chinese Taiwan and South Korea.

Nevertheless, China's investment-led growth model is coming under increasing scrutiny due to the increasingly unhelpful international environment in which it finds itself today, in addition to the sheer heft that China exercises as the world's largest manufacturing exporter, emitter and commodity consumer. Furthermore, the costs of resource-intensive growth—via high pollution and energy intensity—are becoming increasingly apparent. The low share of household consumption in total expenditure is a result of both a high marginal propensity to save and the low wage share of income at the national level (and declining real rural incomes). China has avoided a major slowdown or recession to date, but cyclical overinvestment in certain sectors has been a feature of each successive boom, especially during the recent heavy-industry and stimulus-infused housing and transport infrastructure booms of 2004–07 and 2009–10 (McKay 2011)

The sharp rise in the investment share of expenditure in China's GDP has been mirrored by a fall in the share of final consumption expenditure. Figure 1.2 shows the fall in final consumption expenditure has been led by a falling share of household consumption. Between 1979 and 2010 total household

---

1   Note that gross fixed capital formation (GFCF) has risen by slightly less than gross capital formation (GCF) over the equivalent period, which reflects a cyclical rise in inventories at the end point. A longer sample, comparing 2010 with 1994, shows that GCF rose by 8 percentage points of GDP but GFCF rose by 12 points. This reflects the fact that the increasing commercialisation and efficiency of the corporate sector have reduced the bloated inventory position that characterised the early transitional economy.

consumption expenditure fell by 13 percentage points. This fall in the share of household consumption expenditure has been led by a fall in the share of rural household consumption, which has not been offset by urban consumption growth. Across this period, the government share was low and declined from 15 to 13 per cent of final expenditure.[2] As a result, China's share of consumption expenditure remains at a relatively low level.

Figure 1.2 Final Consumption Expenditure Shares of China's GDP, 1978–2010 (per cent)

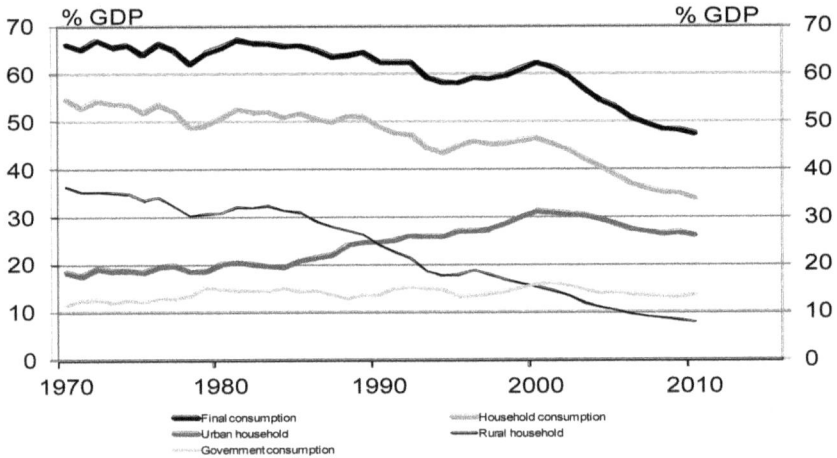

Source: CEIC data, available from <http://www.ceicdata.com/China.html>

The sharp rise in China's trade surplus between 2004 and 2008 was driven by a spectacular improvement in China's heavy machinery and transport balance, as documented by McKay and Song (2010) and shown in Figure 1.3. This offsets a widening deficit on primary products.

---

2 Note that the government share of income rose through this period, but the portion of public income allocated to capital formation rose, thus leaving public consumption at a low level. See the discussion of public savings in the chapter in this volume by Ma et al.

Figure 1.3 China's Trade Balance, Decomposed by Broad Sector, 1993–2009 (per cent)

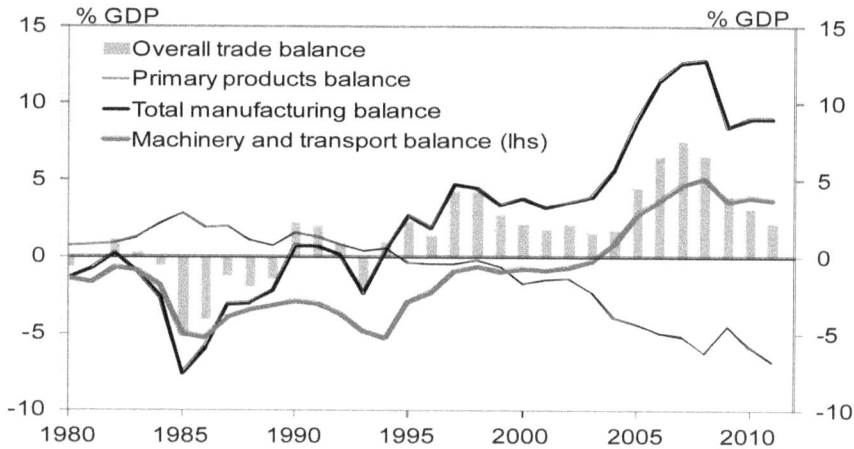

Note: Primary includes agriculture, fuel and other mineral resources.

Sources: CEIC data, available from <http://www.ceicdata.com/China.html> Updated data based on original in McKay and Song (2010).

China's total manufacturing trade balance was in net surplus from as early as 1994 but this was concentrated in lower value-added manufactures, and was initially offset by a net deficit in heavier machinery and transport sectors; however, the machinery and transport equipment balance turned to surplus and rose sharply from 2004 to 2008. This turnaround in the machinery and transport equipment balance was the result of rising investment in heavy industry in the early 2000s (Anderson 2008), which led to a sharp rise in heavy manufactured goods output, an expanding market share abroad and import substitution at home when capacity came on stream from 2004. Yet this sharp rise in output was not matched by an equivalent rise in domestic or foreign demand and, thus, the rise in market share led to falling prices, a lower rate of profit and continual deterioration of China's terms of trade (McKay and Song 2010).

Many of the challenges arising from China's structural imbalances are more or less common to transitional economies undergoing rapid growth and development. This is because the process of economic transition from a traditional to a modern economy entails a set of linked structural transformation processes such as industrialisation and urbanisation. This structural transformation is often marked by the concentrated growth of industry, a rising investment share, sharp rises in the energy intensity of production and demand for resources, and falling expenditure shares of consumption.

Nevertheless, in the case of China's economy, the legacies of its pre-reform heavy industrial structure and its institutional and policy architecture have led to a pattern of growth marked by widening imbalances that are more pronounced than those seen in other industrialisation drives, and which were not present in the initial stages of China's reform. Indeed, China's pattern of growth during the 1980s was remarkably balanced by current standards as household incomes rose on the back of a rapid growth of labour-intensive production outside the traditional state-owned sector. China's domestic expenditure and external imbalances, however, widened in the 2000s as a result of China's stalled institutional reforms in the 1990s, and this has reinforced an investment-led industrial structure, especially in heavy industrial production and real estate development. The current growth pattern highlights the opportunity costs of stalled structural reform areas such as the migration and labour market systems, vertical fiscal relations, state-owned enterprises and the financial system.

Tackling China's economic imbalances requires economic policy reform to direct a new pattern of growth, which requires a major alteration of the current industrial structure and the institutional arrangements associated with it. The key is shifting the economic environment and incentive structure within which China's economic entities operate. The rebalancing policy objectives are to raise the domestic absorptive capacity of China's economy, through raising the relative share of consumption in final expenditure, rather than by seeking to reduce the net role of exports; and to direct resources further away from the relatively inefficient into the more productive sectors of the economy through an improved market mechanism.

Three sets of market-enhancing institutional reforms are necessary: reform of the labour system, reform of the financial system and reform of the government system, particularly in regards to the local government and state-owned enterprise sectors. The interdependence of the Chinese economy with the world economy also suggests the significance of these channels for international rebalancing (Deer and Song 2012).

The effective (as opposed to spatial) urbanisation of China's migrant workers is the most effective and realistic mid-term policy strategy for rebalancing China's macroeconomy. Institutional reform can accelerate the long-run processes of migration and urbanisation in China, which would raise domestic demand and, thus, reduce both the internal and the external imbalances in China's macroeconomy, and shift the current unbalanced industrial structure. A policy of urbanising rural migrant workers by removing threshold barriers to urban residency and ensuring equal access to social housing, education, health and social protection[3] is likely to raise consumption by migrant workers (Song et al. 2010).

Moreover, the process of urbanisation requires investment in urban infrastructure (such as mass transit and utility provision) and in service industries. The effect, combined with higher domestic consumption by migrant workers, would be to raise growth and enhance structural change. Urbanising China's rural migrant workers would also help to integrate China's still segmented labour markets and provide a basis for long-term real wages to rise. Real wage gains can accelerate structural change by raising household consumption in domestic demand[4] and by providing a basis for real currency appreciation. That can help shift China's industrial structure towards the tertiary sectors, which would benefit from the broader and deeper consumption basket of the better remunerated household sector. This would have positive implications for employment and enhance many qualitative aspects of future growth.

Given the objective of rebalancing China's industrial structure, capital market reforms are necessary for China to rebalance in three related areas: the allocation of capital, the cost of capital and the link between domestic financial reform and exchange arrangements. Although China's bank-dominated financial system deepened its asset base considerably over the reform period, China's system of formal credit allocation has remained narrow, and is mainly directed to the state sector as state-owned banks (SOBs) continue to dominate the sector. China's state-owned commercial banking sector allocates capital at rates that are low relative to those prevailing in private markets or a broad indicator such as the growth rate of nominal GDP, which reinforces the wider structure of investment and expenditure imbalances.

It will be difficult to develop domestic financial markets without further liberalisation of the foreign exchange system or of financial (capital) account controls. The two spheres are mutually reinforcing, even circular (McKay 2007). The exchange rate remains the anchor for China's monetary policy and any move towards a flexible currency needs to be accompanied by a shift to a different anchor. Current efforts to build up the interbank lending market and thereby establish a benchmark short-term interest rate to serve as this anchor show

---

3 Andrew Watson's chapter in this volume advocates a centralisation of the retirement income system—a recommendation in harmony with our own thinking.

4 Another way of thinking about this relation is through unit labour costs and the wage–profit share. If workers are under-remunerated for their productivity, unit labour costs fall and profits rise. That summarises the events of the past decade. Changing the direction of these dynamics—fully remunerating (or even a period of catch-up over remuneration)—would lower profits, boost the wage share, raise consumption and possibly lower investment also, although the effect on investment is ambiguous due to differentiated sectoral effects and the altered relative price between capital and labour predicted by rising unit labour costs.

some promise. Speaking pragmatically, however, this market remains immature, liquidity remains variable and its ability to independently anchor monetary policy is a distant surmise. For now, all prescriptions for financial liberalisation must be offered within the context of the present regime apparatus.

A feasible reform would be to seek to incorporate China's large informal financial sector into the official financial system, in tandem with a removal of administrative ceilings on bank deposit rates and floor lending rates. The objective would be to create a legal sector of smaller non-bank financial lending and deposit institutions.[5] These firms would compete with the banking system to provide market-based contract terms for households and small and medium- enterprises (SMEs). Once this reform has been given some time to gain traction, targeted moves to liberalise private capital outflows could be introduced as a further market discipline on the banking system. This would have the additional benefit of increasing the loan to deposit ratios of the banks, which would increase their wholesale funding requirements, which would deepen the interbank funding market, which would increase the potency of interest rates as a monetary policy tool, and thus accommodate the required transition away from the exchange rate anchor, as ventured above; however, the circularity of the financial reform arguments again come into play. The possibility of a deterioration of bank asset quality at a time of weak asset prices and a substantial pool of legacy loans from the quasi-fiscal lending expansion of recent years argues for a prudent approach to avoid unnecessary instability. Regardless of the precise time frame, deepening the reform of the SOBs is a requisite achievement if capital allocation is to improve and contribute positively to the ultimate rebalancing goal. Recent official commentary[6] and the incorporation of interest rate liberalisation into the Twelfth Five-Year Plan offer some grounds for hope.

The current pattern of local government investment, especially its role in real estate investment, is a key element, along with the high share of investment in heavy industry, of China's cyclical macroeconomic imbalances, which have led to repeated overheating of China's economy during each phase of the investment-led boom (McKay 2011). Since fiscal reforms in 1994, the majority of government revenues have been collected by the Central Government, while local governments have remained responsible for the majority of public and social expenditure, especially on health and education (Figure 1.4). As a consequence

---

5 The recent rise of shadow banking in China indicates that this is not such a distant goal. Official data accessed via CEIC show that non-banks (and the off-balance-sheet activities of banks) made up 44 per cent of 'total social financing' in 2010, which is material. Indeed, the subsequent slowdown in non-bank finance is a major factor in the deceleration in economic activity under way in the first half of 2012.

6 Premier Wen Jiabao addressed the monopoly power of SOBs in a radio address in April, as reported in the *Asian Wall Street Journal* (2012).

of this fiscal and governmental system, not only do local governments have a powerful incentive to maximise growth, but they also have an overriding fiscal incentive to do so through driving new investments, such as in real estate, in which they have direct or indirect claims to income, rather than through raising consumption.

Figure 1.4 Revenues and Outlays by Level of Government

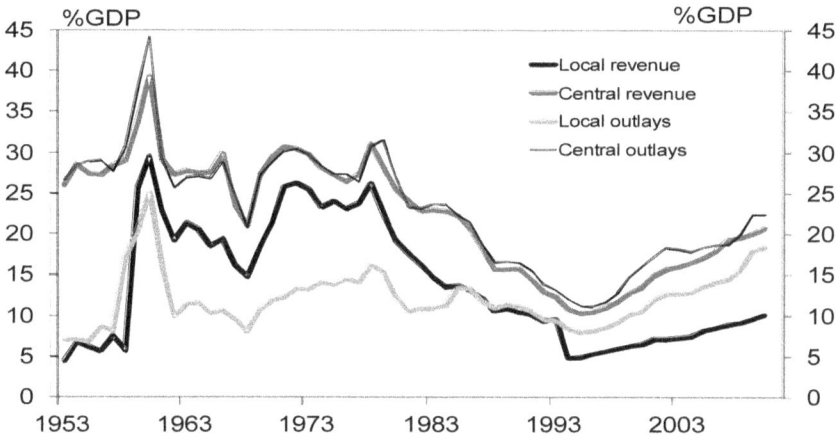

Sources: CEIC data, available from <http://www.ceicdata.com/China.html>

The current pattern of local government investment—and outlays, more broadly—could be better directed to meeting the needs of China's current urban and migrant populations by directing more expenditure to social housing and educational and social services (such as health, retirement income, transportation, unemployment insurance, public space and environmental amenity). There is much more to be done to reform the fiscal system at central and local government levels, including shifting the current land-transaction tax system to a property valuation and rates system. Reducing reliance on turnover and land sales would reduce two of the most egregious incentive distortions of the current system, while moving to a periodic valuation tax on housing would reduce investor willingness to leave property idle (untenanted), thus bringing about an effective increase in housing supply. Turning what is currently a heavily pro-cyclical revenue source (land sales) into something more closely resembling an annuity stream, would improve the sustainability of sub-national government finances in a material way. Recent moves to allow local governments to issue bonds, while cracking down on financing platforms, are useful policies but they do not attack the underlying issues.

Rebalancing China's economy also requires reform of the state-owned enterprise (SOE) sector. There are immediate and long-term term reasons for this. Although China's SOEs no longer account for the majority of output in all sectors, the SOEs remain dominant in strategic monopoly sectors (Xiao et al. 2009). State-owned enterprises have accounted for much of the sharp rise in heavy industrial profits and enterprise savings in the period since 2000. The monopoly position of China's SOEs also poses a longer-term challenge to the reform of China's industrial structure towards a more balanced trajectory. Although the non-state sector accounted for the majority of industrial output in 2007, the SOEs accounted for more than 53 per cent of non-agricultural fixed investment, while employing only 13 per cent of the total workforce (Brandt and Zhu 2010). These discrepancies reflect the capital-intensive heavy industries in which the SOEs operate. They also suggest, however, an inefficient allocation of capital across sectors, which also reflects the still large distortions in China's factor markets, which cumulatively benefit the SOE sector disproportionately (Huang and Wang 2010). Rebalancing China's economy towards domestic demand will therefore require better access to capital for the non-state enterprises, reduced barriers to entry in SOE-dominated sectors, a greater openness to foreign direct investment in those same areas, further privatisation and a greater insistence on shareholder rights regarding dividend payments. The overall opportunity costs can be further reduced or even minimised should more resources be allowed to flow into the more vibrant non-state sectors through improved factor markets. This goal cannot be achieved unless China deepens the reform of state-owned enterprises.

Investment in hard infrastructure, from telecommunications to transport, remains central to long-term growth, but there is also a clear tendency towards cyclical overinvestment in certain heavy industries, from cement and steel production to machinery and transport production. Competition and anti-trust policy is needed to more fully redistribute monopoly rents (Tyers and Lu 2008), especially in China's strategic monopoly and pillar industries. Opening up share ownership and trading could potentially redistribute savings to a wider range of investors and allow new commercial entrants, while corporate tax reform through unifying the corporate tax rate for all firms including private and foreign firms could potentially redistribute more of these savings/profits to consumers. This suggests that the task of rebalancing will also hinge on how China reforms and strengthens its regulatory system especially with respect to competition, market entry and taxation.

High rates of investment at early stages of development tend to gradually shift towards a moderately rising consumption share as the structural processes of urbanisation and industrialisation effectively mature. The familiar inverted-U shape (sometimes labelled a Kuznets curve, as in McKay 2008) present across a number of development indicators when mapped in GDP per capita space attests to this. Therefore, it is entirely reasonable to expect China's domestic absorptive capacity to rise over time; however, while a rise in China's domestic absorptive capacity will, by definition, reduce China's external surplus, this does not mean that China's current account will move immediately into deficit; indeed, twin surpluses could remain for the time being. China's current account surplus has moderated in recent years on: a) soft demand for its exports; b) rapid increases in the price of its import basket; and c) strong demand for imported resource volumes. While an element of this narrowing is evidently cyclical, and thus we should not use the absolute latest level as the 'jumping off point', it is most unlikely that the current account will ever again approach the level seen in 2007. The rough estimate of Ma et al. (Chapter 4, this volume) that the average current account will move towards 1 per cent of GDP over the coming decade is a good starting point for discussion and debate.

In any case, the pressures that are currently building will ultimately convince China to accelerate the pace of structural adjustment including the pace of liberalising its capital account with the full convertibility and 'internationalisation' of the renminbi (RMB). At the same time, China's eventual success in achieving the objective of rebalancing will also depend on how China's major trading partners seek to overcome their own structural problems. The experiences of the United States show that while a deep recession can narrow external imbalances, mitigating the fallout from a contraction in private demand via fiscal expansion can substantially reduce policy flexibility down the line. The experiences of Europe show that ageing, developed economies with inflexible labour markets and exchange rates and open capital accounts can find the task of adjusting imbalances comes with major questions of financial instability and rising sovereign risks. The Japanese story is a cautionary tale that shows that sometimes even a sharp decline in the investment share will not bring about external rebalancing. The global economy will be challenged to maintain the rate of expansion required to return balance sheets to health while demand centres and relative prices continue to shift.

Tackling China's economic imbalances necessitates economic policy reform to facilitate a more sustainable pattern of growth that will fundamentally alter China's industrial structure and its trade orientation. Rebalancing requires a strategy for removing factor price and cost distortions that have arisen from the traditional state-owned heavy industrial and governmental structures and the macro-financial architecture that supports them.

Market-enhancing institutional reforms will be central to the reduction of China's macroeconomic imbalances. The next phase of transition must be built around a strategy of reforms in four key areas: the migration and labour market system, reform of the government system (particularly local government, with an emphasis on a sustainable fiscal policy and better decision making regarding outlays), reform of the state-dominated non-financial sectors and reform of the overall financial system. Each of these strategic areas constitutes a key link in the overall path-dependent chain that constitutes China's current and future structural trajectories. Reform in these segments will have strong positive multiplier and spillover effects in a range of sub-aggregate arenas relevant to achieving greater equity (contemporary and intergenerational), balance and sustainability.

Structure of the Book

We began by stating that 'the role of policy should be to design and implement a framework that reduces distortions, encourages and rewards innovation, equalises access to education, employment, a social safety net and capital for investment, while minimising rent-seeking opportunities'. Each of the chapters in this volume tackles the issue of rebalancing. Part one comprises those works that do so directly in a broad macroeconomic framework. Part two comprises those chapters that approach imbalance from a sectoral or sub-macro perspective.

Part one begins with a chapter by Rod Tyers that styles the rebalancing imperative as the search for inward-looking growth. To frame the discussion, Tyers presents a menu of policy regimes that seems promising with regards to achieving this end. These regimes are then 'tested' via a model of the Chinese economy that emphasises the oligopoly power of large firms.

Working from a sophisticated conception of the middle-income trap—'the distinction is between the "natural" slowdown in the convergence process… and premature stagnation due to powerful vested interests'—Tyers finds that a successful turn inwards should incorporate a 'more ardent attack on oligopoly rent'. In what fashion? Tyers argues that policies of pure privatisation and industrial fragmentation offer less promise than either price regulation or foreign competition in services.

The chapter by Anders C. Johansson puts a strong case that financial repression is a root cause of both domestic and external imbalances in the Chinese economy. He argues that comprehensive financial reforms should be central to any concerted attempt to address imbalances, although he is at pains to highlight that due respect for correct sequencing must be taken into account. By discussing the apparent international and local symptoms of China's financially repressive policies in an integrated framework, Johansson builds up a convincing narrative that a multitude of superficially disparate issues can be fruitfully considered from this perspective.

In Chapter 4, Guonan Ma, Robert McCauley and Lillie Lam build on their impressive recent output on China's savings rate. The focus of this effort is the current account surplus from a savings–investment perspective, with an exchange rate overlay. A masterful review of the state of play in these areas is followed by some educated prognostication on the future course of the savings and investment shares over the coming decade, in tandem with some observations on the historical trajectory of the real exchange rate compiled under various methodologies. The authors conclude that the current account surplus is likely to narrow further in coming years, with the savings shares declining by more than the investment share, and the quite considerable historical (and future) real appreciation of the RMB the authors envisage continuing to do its work.

Chapters 5 and 6 can be considered together. Yue Que, Fang Cai and Xiaobo Zhang argue in Chapter 5 that the 'flying geese' are moving inland as rising cost pressures on the coast drive them out. In Chapter 6, Miaojie Yu and Wei Tian offer a rich and highly disaggregated view of the 'DNA' of China's processing trade, where a great many of these 'flying geese' reside. Que et al. empirically demonstrate why the push away from the coast has occurred. They show that the proportion of manufacturing activity accounted for by the coastal provinces follows an inverted-U shape, with the benefits of agglomeration initially drawing capital out of the interior, before factor prices in these densely occupied regions reached a threshold level, which was the signal to go west. Yu and Tian offer an extremely comprehensive overview of the processing trade—who, what, where, how—mining a huge database the authors created through an innovative merger of transaction and firm-level trade information. They supplement the descriptive element of the chapter with an estimate of productivity growth in the processing sector, which they conclude is lower than that of firms conducting ordinary trade.

The final chapter in part one is by Bijun Wang. Wang poses the question of whether China's outward direct investment (ODI) can contribute positively to the rebalancing issue through improving the quality of growth. She argues that this is an unanswerable question without more detailed knowledge of the motivation for and style of the ODI decision. To gain this insight, Wang presents granular data on approved transactions, suitably cleansed, arriving at a taxonomy suitable for addressing the rebalancing. To Wang, if ODI is undertaken from a resource security perspective, it removes a bottleneck in the economy *as it is presently constructed*, but it could reduce the incentive to alter the growth model in fundamental ways. If ODI is undertaken to acquire strategic assets, the implications for rebalancing are more promising, with both direct and tacit influences working to enhance the quality of growth. Efficiency-seeking ODI, which has contributed very strongly to structural change over the course of Japan's development drive, is not yet seen as a major factor driving the ODI decisions of Chinese firms.

The last two chapters of part one reflect one of the hallmarks of this volume: the recognition that disaggregated data—whether from the firm, the province, the county or the single industry—are of tremendous value in understanding macroeconomic trends in China and should not be the sole domain of sectoral experts. The chapters of part two continue in this vein, with some fascinating information presented on the spatial aspect of inequality, migration decisions, rural population and intergenerational mobility. Some of these data come from official sources; some have been created by painstaking survey work.

The issue of income inequality has become a major focus of policymakers in recent times. This volume contributes to the debate from a number of angles. In addition to the studies in part one that touch on the inequality issue in a broad macroeconomic framework, our knowledge of the spatial aspect of income inequality in China—all the way down to county level—is greatly enhanced by the results detailed in Chapter 8 by Tsun Se Cheong and Yanrui Wu. Further, in Chapter 10, Jane Golley and Sherry Kong delve into The Australian National University's Rural–Urban Migration in China and Indonesia (RUMiCI) survey database to broaden our understanding of educational access (a fundamental driver of inequality) across generations and locales.

Cheong and Wu offer a comprehensive study of the spatial distribution of income inequality. Their work is distinctive as it estimates contributions to inequality across five spatial tiers, starting at the county level. They find that intra-provincial differences in output per head—that is, differential income levels across counties in the same province—are substantial contributors to overall inequality levels. They argue that this makes the case for policy formulation to have a strong local component. Further, they find that inequality has different spatial characteristics in the hinterland (where inter-county inequality dominates) and the coastal and north-eastern regions (where intercity inequality is an additional major factor).

Golley and Kong undertake a detailed study of intergenerational patterns of educational attainment across three population segments: urban residents, rural residents and rural-to-urban migrants. They begin with a multilayered question: 'Does the persistence of educational attainment across generations reflect genetic factors, uneven opportunities or uneven returns?' They approach the question by documenting evidence of the degree of persistence/mobility in intergenerational educational achievements in the above segments. They find that the uneven nature of returns to education in urban and rural areas, a lack of investment in rural education from early childhood onwards and the segmented urban labour market skew the incentives to pursue education, particularly beyond junior high; urban residents have a strong incentive to move up the ladder, rural residents less so, with migrants somewhere in between. This reinforces and amplifies the urban–rural divide.

Chapters 9 and 11 offer new perspectives on China's rural communities and the actual and potential internal migrants within them. In Chapter 9, Sylvie Démurger delivers some compelling insights into the complex economic and social calculus that goes into the migration decision: the decision to leave home, where (how far) one should go and for how long. Her framework, which owes much to the 'new economics of labour migration', takes the household as the basic decision-making unit and the household's goal is to minimise income risk. The boundaries of the investigation are set beyond economic, landholding and geographic factors to incorporate the influence of social and family networks. Social networks are shown to be a significant influence on migration decisions that send the individual far afield, whereas it is only the presence of a family network that is significant for shorter haul migration. Chapter 11 gives an initial glimpse of a new demographic survey undertaken in a number of key migration source regions in rural China, with data collected in the winter of 2010–11. Funing Zhong and Jing Xiang offer a discussion of their sample relative to that of the official household survey, detail their methodology and collection method and give some preliminary conclusions on the basic contours of the data. Expect to hear a great deal more from this project as time goes by.

One cannot get too deep into an educated discussion of Chinese imbalances without making mention of the social safety net. Yet detailed work on this vital policy area is surprisingly scarce. Chapter 12 by Andrew Watson steps into the breach, focusing predominantly on the provision of retirement incomes in an ageing society. Watson highlights the fact that the current system is contradictory, with a geographically fluid labour market sitting uneasily alongside a geographically rigid social security infrastructure. Following a magisterial account of historical developments and the current policy position, Watson recommends the adoption of an integrated, portable, centrally funded and administered system characterised by equal access for all citizens. This chapter is highly recommended to all those who have at some stage caught themselves vaguely recommending social security reform in China without any specific notion of exactly what that might entail.

The following chapter, by Zhiyun Zhao and Chaofeng Yang, looks at China's efforts to move up the value chain and become an internationally competitive innovator, which is an important co-requisite of travelling the positive road to a more balanced economy. At the outset, the authors characterise China's high-tech industry of today as being afflicted by weak innovation capacity, low technology intensity and poor economic efficiency. They posit that with developed countries pursuing a 'technology blockade' strategy, it is vital that China builds an indigenous innovation capability, with imported technology playing a complementary role. To them, this implies that a preferential industrial policy for firms with innovative potential should be put in place. They also offer a practical suggestion for policy design that will be swiftly recognised by those who stand by the maxim 'what gets measured gets done'. They argue that quantitative targets for high-tech output at the local level should be replaced with qualitative ones that emphasise the desire for more sophisticated production. Further, they argue that competition policy should be used to reduce entry barriers (with a side note that large firms in China are less innovative than smaller ones), the Government should play a guiding role while market forces should be catalytic, while noting an inherent institutional weakness in the commercialisation of innovative ideas.

The volume concludes with two chapters dealing with China's resource endowment. Chapter 15 deals with its quest for security of energy supply while Chapter 14 looks at its struggles to maintain the quality and abundance of its water supply. In Chapter 14, Hong Yang, Zhuoying Zhang and Minjun Shi offer a timely reminder that the joint problems of water pollution and water scarcity together threaten to undermine economic growth. They highlight the fact that China's industrial structure—which makes it a net exporter of virtual water (or embodied water)—is incompatible with its status as a water-poor country. They also go below the national level to highlight that the regional distribution of economic activity places water-intensive manufacturing in water-poor locales.

The energy security issue remains an emotive one inside China and without. ZhongXiang Zhang's chapter, which concludes the volume, aims to address what he feels are the 'misconceptions and misunderstandings' surrounding energy security in both China and internationally. Coincidentally, the East–West Centre in Hawaii, one of Zhang's academic homes, seems an ideal place from which to intermediate the sometimes strident discourse. Zhang makes a number of important points. The first is that for China, energy security is really about oil security. The second is that the Strait of Malacca is the major point of strategic vulnerability for China, given it has little geopolitical leverage in the area and the disproportionate amount of its imports using this narrow body of water. He ties this reality to the Chinese perception that an 'oil blockade' of China by the West is a genuine threat; and then douses the flames by systematically dismantling this thesis. Three, he emphasises that the loans-for-oil deals between Chinese development banks, foreign oil concerns and China's own national oil companies have not been successful in reducing energy insecurity, principally because the Chinese companies have shown no clear predilection to bring the oil home for domestic consumption where prices are set below those prevailing in international markets. Further, he argues that Chinese investment is adding to global supply potential in a net sense, which benefits all consumers of oil.

References

Anderson, J., 2008, 'China's industrial investment boom and the renminbi', in M. Goldstein and N. Lardy (eds), *Debating China's Exchange Rate Policy*, Peterson Institute for International Economics, Washington, DC, pp. 61–9.

Asian Wall Street Journal, 2012, 'Chinese premier blasts banks', *Asian Wall Street Journal*, 4 April, viewed 15 May, <http://online.wsj.com/article/SB100 01424052702304750404577321762422668428.html>

Brandt, L. and Zhu, X., 2010, *Accounting for China's growth*, IZA Discussion Paper No. 4764, Institute for the Study of Labour, Bonn.

Deer, L. and Song, L., 2012, 'China's approach to rebalancing: a conceptual and policy framework', *China and World Economy*, vol. 20, no. 1, pp. 1–26.

Fukumoto, T. and Muto, I., 2011, *Rebalancing China's economic growth: some insights from Japan's experience*, Bank of Japan Working Paper Series 2011 No. E-5, Bank of Japan, Tokyo.

Huang, Y. and Wang, B., 2010, 'Cost distortions and structural imbalances in China', *China & World Economy*, vol. 18, no. 4, pp. 1–17.

Knight, J. and Wang, W., 2011, *China's macroeconomic imbalances: causes and consequences*, Bank of Finland Institute for Economies in Transition Discussion Papers No. 15, Bank of Finland, Helsinki.

McKay, H., 2007, 'Reforming China's exchange arrangements: monetary and financial sovereignty, sequencing and the foreign exchange market', in R. Garnaut and L. Song (eds), *China: Linking markets for growth*, Asia Pacific Press, Canberra, 290–315.

McKay, H., 2008, *Metal intensity in comparative historical perspective: China, North Asia, the United States & Kuznets curve*, Global Dynamic Systems Centre Working Paper 006, The Australian National University, Canberra.

McKay, H., 2011, 'China's turbulent half-decade', in L. Song and J. Golley (eds), *Rising China: Global challenges and opportunities*, ANU E Press, Canberra, pp. 9–27.

McKay, H. and Song, L., 2010, 'China as a global manufacturing powerhouse: strategic considerations and structural adjustment', *China & World Economy*, vol. 18, no. 1, pp. 1–32.

Song, L., Wu, J. and Zhang, Y., 2010, 'Urbanisation of migrant workers and expansion of domestic demand', *Social Sciences in China*, vol. 31, no. 3, pp. 194–216.

Spence, M., 2011, *The Next Convergence: The future of economic growth in a multispeed world*, University of Western Australia Press, Perth.

Syrquin, M., 1988, 'Patterns of structural change', in H. Chenery and T. N. Srinivasan (eds), *Handbook of Development Economics*, North-Holland, Amsterdam, pp. 203–73.

Tyers, R. and Lu, F., 2008, 'Competition policy, corporate saving and China's current account surplus', Working Papers in Economics and Econometrics No. 496, College of Business and Economics, The Australian National University, July.

Xiao, G., Yang, X. and Janus, A., 2009, 'State-owned enterprises in China: reform dynamics and impacts', in R. Garnaut, L. Song and W. T. Woo (eds), *China's New Place in a World in Crisis: Economic, geopolitical and environmental dimensions*, ANU E Press, Brookings Institution Press and Social Sciences Academic Press, Canberra, pp. 155–78.

2. Looking Inward for Growth

Rod Tyers[1]

Introduction

There is wide agreement outside China, and more recent concurrence inside, that China's growth will, and should, be increasingly underpinned by rising home consumption rather than exports.[2] The foreign viewpoint is notwithstanding the considerable contributions of China's export-led growth to improvements in the foreign terms of trade and to cheaper financing of investment and government spending. The dominant political force behind this view seems to be concern over declining overall economic performance, at least compared with China, comparatively high unemployment and the very visible nature of manufacturing 'offshoring'.[3]

Yet the global gains conferred by China's growth are fragile and the Chinese regime that has produced them faces potentially destabilising threats from within and without. For this reason there looms the 'middle income trap' widely ascribed to other developing regions (World Bank 2010). The poor performance of trading-partner economies clearly weighs on China's government, as does foreign political hostility to continued export-led growth. Internally, there has been a tightening of labour markets, foreshadowing a Lewis 'turning point' that would mark a natural end to export-led growth.[4] In addition, there are reasons why increased public investment and the fostering of increased

1   Funding for the research described in this chapter is from Australian Research Council Discovery Grant No. DP0557885. It was conducted in part during visits to the China Center for Economic Research (CCER) at Peking University. Special thanks are due to Feng Lu and Ling Huang at Peking University for many constructive conversations on the topic and to Peter Dixon, Yew-Kwang Ng, James Giesecke, Yuanfang Li, Miaojie Yu, Yongxiang Bu and to other participants at lively CCER and CoPS seminars. More recently, valuable comments on the latest draft have been received from Ligang Song, Huw McKay and Warwick McKibbin. Research assistance was provided by Pingkun Hsu at ANU, Liu Liu at the CCER and at the UWA Business School by Ying Zhang and Tsun Se Cheong.
2   For the foreign, and particularly the American, perspective, see Bergsten et al. (2008) and Lardy (2006, 2012). For the official Chinese line on the 'rebalancing' of its economy, including its external accounts, see Wen (2007, 2011) and Yi (2011).
3   Foreign animus towards China's economic policy regime has been further inflamed by the large current account surpluses of the past decade and the perspective of some in the West that China's political system denies basic human rights or of others that its large government and defence forces represent a strategic threat. See Tyers (forthcoming).
4   The timing of China's Lewis turning point is a subject of controversy, as suggested by the contrasts between the views expressed by Cai (2010), Garnaut (2010) and Golley and Meng (2011), which offer just a sampling of a substantial literature. There is, however, little doubt that the turning point is on its way, even if there is little agreement as to whether recent real wage rises suggest its presence.

private consumption are of considerable political value at present. The high environmental costs of China's manufacturing expansion have yet to be fully covered and there is increased income inequality associated with rents in the state-owned sector that will be politically difficult to unwind.[5] This inequality coincides with socioeconomic stratification in China's periphery, which has precipitated increased class, ethnic and regional conflicts.

Middle-income 'slowdowns' in developing countries that have heretofore grown strongly out of poverty are the subject of expanding interest (Easterly 2001; Eichengreen et al. 2011). The focus is the distinction between 'natural' slowdown in the convergence process as poorer countries approach full industrialisation, which is due to diminishing returns to physical and human capital and diminished 'catch-up' investment incentives (Lucas 2009), and premature stagnation due to powerful vested interests that oppose economic policy reforms needed for the final catch-up phase (Haber et al. 2008; Riedel 2011).[6] The sense in which the slowdown is considered a 'trap' derives from a divergence of collective interests from those of the leadership group, with the latter associated with rent extraction (corruption) that peaks at middle levels of real per capita income.

So, where are the rents and the vested interests that could retard China's future growth and does 'turning inward' exacerbate the risk of an associated slowdown? The financial sector is one location. Very high saving challenges this sector to allocate efficiently across investment opportunities. The many weaknesses in this process, stemming in part from the protection of state-owned financial institutions, have already received considerable attention (Riedel 2007; Walter and Howie 2011). Yet the potential gains from further industrial reform that reduces rents in protected corners of the economy extend well beyond the financial sector to include comparatively protected and state-owned heavy manufacturing and services. Industrial reforms have penetrated these sectors less because of their political sensitivity. If such reforms are required for inward-focused growth then there will be political difficulty achieving it. Yet such reforms offer an effective replacement of export-led growth that is also transformative of China's economic structure and its labour force.

Alternative approaches to inward-focused growth are numerous and they include, importantly, policies and institutional development to support domestic innovation and human capital accumulation. These are the engines of steady state growth, whereas in this chapter the focus is on alternatives that follow

---

5   For a discussion of the institutional and industrial reform agenda and its difficulty, see, for example, Deer and Song (2012), Riedel (2011) and Tyers and Lu (2008).

6   These issues parallel an established literature in political economy that originated with Mancur Olson (1965) and Gordon Tulloch (1967) and from which emerged the term 'eurosclerosis' to describe stagnation due to interest group conflict and rent seeking in Europe.

on from the export-led era in that they could further transform the structure of China's economy. They include expanded government and further industrial reforms, amongst which are pure privatisation, the fragmentation of state-owned enterprises (SOEs), price-cap regulation and foreign direct investment (FDI) in heavy manufacturing and services. The economic implications of changes of these types are assessed using a mathematical model of the Chinese economy that captures the behaviour of state-owned oligopolies and the impacts of further industrial reform. The greatest potential for inwardly generated growth is shown to rest, as expected, with further industrial reform in heavy manufacturing and services. The simulation results suggest the best prospects for further growth are to attack rents with tighter price-cap regulation and to advance services productivity through foreign direct investment. The first of these will be resisted by those currently enjoying the rents and the second presses against the desire on the part of China's government to protect services from foreign ownership.

The next section reviews the relative merits of export-led growth, develops the reasoning behind China's choice to turn inward and discusses the sources of internally generated transformative growth. In section three, the particular structure of China's economy is reviewed along with the associated sensitivity of its overall performance to its real exchange rate. Section four offers a description of the model used and the construction of its database. The fifth section compares inward-sourced growth scenarios and section six concludes.

The Turn Away from Export-Led Growth

Economic development is primarily about shifting the population from low labour productivity farming to urban employment where the availability of physical capital ensures higher income and more efficient access to essential services. This requires rural–urban migration and, at least initially, basic (mainly primary) education and training. These conditions supply a workforce suitable for light manufacturing. If the protection of property rights and the export infrastructure facilities are sufficient, the availability of adequately trained workers then attracts capital that is supplied from both domestic saving and foreign direct investment. In the 'East Asian model', much of the migration from rural areas goes into manufacturing, though some goes to construction and other services, which also expand.[7] In a final phase, the transition from middle level to very high real per capita income requires further education and training suited to the growth of sophisticated services.

---

7   The Indian model differs from this in that the rural to urban migration goes primarily to services, with manufacturing limited by regulatory and infrastructural constraints. See Bardhan (2010).

The Merits of Export-Led Growth

The growth in the local supply of light manufactures that occurs in the early stage in the East Asian model is more than can meet local demand. Comparative advantage in light manufacturing is realised via openness to trade, so the home labour force is transformed by exporting. As it turns out, this transformation is also beneficial to already industrialised trading partners. This is because the resulting change in the international terms of trade is positive for them: light manufactured imports are cheaper and skill-intensive durable (consumer and capital) goods, which they export, are in higher demand. Moreover, since the opening of such developing economies in this way supplies additional low-skill labour to the integrated global economy, FDI opportunities are abundant and savers in industrialised countries earn higher returns. Idiosyncratically, the East Asian model has also offered high saving households and firms that have supplied excess saving to the global economy. This has financed investment and government expenditures in the industrialised economies in ways that have enhanced their growth.[8]

The Choice to Look Inward

Variations on the East Asian model have been the dominant basis for catch-up by poorer countries and regions for more than a century (Dooley et al. 2004). Why then should the Chinese choose to 'look inward' now? The reasons are manyfold. First, it is inevitable that China will cease to depend on labour-intensive exports and move its production up the chain of sophistication in the manner of Japan, the Republic of Korea and its regions in Taiwan and Hong Kong before it. This generally coincides with a slowdown in the rate of rural to urban migration and some acceleration in the rate of rise in real wages—the 'turning point' of Lewis (1955). The ardent debate over the proximity of this turning point notwithstanding, the most carefully considered evidence suggests it could still be some way off (Cai 2010; Golley and Meng 2011). It is nonetheless true that demographic changes associated with China's One-Child Policy have accelerated it, and labour costs have indeed grown more sharply in recent years. Even though this pattern of labour-force tightening is smooth, the associated transition to slower growth can be abrupt and destructive, as in the case of Japan in the late 1980s,[9] so it is possible the Chinese Government seeks to ensure a smooth transition.

---

8 While it is true that cheaper credit has not always led to growth-enhancing expenditures in these countries, their errors in public and private expenditure patterns have not been the fault of the Asian high savers.

9 The literature on Japan's stagnation since the late 1980s is vast. See Hayashi and Prescott (2002) and Tyers (2011).

A second important reason is that growth has slowed in the regions to which China's exports are directed. This raises the prospect that the terms of trade might shift more rapidly against it if exports continue to be pushed out at the current rate, so a smaller proportion of the benefits from export-led growth would accrue to China.[10] Third is political pressure from destination regions against China's current account surpluses of the past decade, the perceived unfairness of Chinese policy and the loss of trading-partner employment in manufacturing. Political attacks on Chinese exports, and anti-Chinese xenophobia in general, are more likely when the movement of vast numbers of Chinese workers into the modern sector is perceived as being associated with the unemployment of one-tenth of those seeking work in Western Europe and the United States. This association has high-level backing in policy debates, particularly in the United States (Bernanke 2006; Krugman 2010).

The Western backlash is essentially mercantilist and much of it is directed at China's exchange rate. The perception in the United States that countries like China use 'exchange rate protection' stems from the role of the US dollar as the reserve currency and the difficulty the United States faces when a lack of competitiveness would justify a depreciation against others. In the 1980s, this ire was directed against Japan, leading to the Plaza Accord and a large and destructive appreciation of the yen (Goyal and McKinnon 2003; Hamada and Okada 2009), and ultimately to the US *Exchange Rates and International Economic Policy Coordination Act of 1988*, which formalised the United States' 'defence' against currency manipulators. Poverty and its associated low wages are seen in US policy debates as an unfair trade advantage rather than a problem that is solved by expanded trade. The fact that the underlying real exchange rate of China against the United States has appreciated substantially since 2004 and continues to appreciate seems to have been missed in the American literature (Tyers and Zhang 2011).[11]

Finally, China is constantly criticised for its lack of political rights and for its treatment of unhappy minorities such as the Tibetans and the *Hui zu*. This criticism is sometimes justified but often it stems from fear of China as a potential strategic opponent and a sense that the advocacy of additional political and religious rights might weaken it in such a competition. These external criticisms of the Chinese state and its policies, while occasionally well intentioned, are too often xenophobic and made in ignorance or disregard of the considerable benefits of Chinese growth for the West. Within China, however, inequality

---

10 This raises the prospect of 'immiserising growth', which is already hotly debated as a consequence of Chinese export expansion, at least for smaller, poorer exporters that compete with China (Bhagwati 1987).

11 While the American literature continues on this refrain, the Geithner-led US Treasury—the guardians of the 'currency manipulator' label—have increasingly tried to highlight the real exchange rate adjustment as one of the arguments behind their unwillingness to cite China. Thanks to Huw McKay for this note.

has become a major political issue and the 'turn inward', via expanded public investment, has also been justified as a means of redirecting the fruits of growth to lagging regions and to the rural sector in general (Wen 2011).

Inward Sources of Growth

Potential inward contributions to growth are numerous and they include improved policy implementation in the areas of innovation and human capital growth (Robertson 2011) as well as in the urbanisation of migrant workers (Song et al. 2010). In what follows the focus is on some particular sources of growth that are natural successors to export-led growth in that they could further transform the structure of China's economy.

Given the apparent success of China's surge in public investment during the global recession in 2008–09, the Government is surely tempted to think of expanded government activity as an inward source of future growth. And it is common for governments of developing countries to undersupply public goods that are foundations for growth. In China's case these include the facilities and regulatory institutions to support basic and higher education, transport and telecommunications infrastructure, retirement insurance, health insurance and environmental protection. Compared with other developing countries, China is in the fortunate situation of having implemented a sensible tax law in 1994 that is accessing an increasing share of all its economic activity. This means that Central Government tax revenue is rising faster than gross domestic product (GDP) and it was this that allowed the substantial increase in public investment in 2009 without a large increase in the fiscal deficit (Jia and Liu 2009).[12] So, depending on the extent of crowding out and of Ricardian equivalence amongst savers, a rise in government activity could help expand China's GDP by reducing the rate at which home income is spent on foreign assets and products and therefore bolstering aggregate demand abroad rather than at home. It is unclear, however, to what extent this expanded government activity can bring about anything but a comparatively short-term, one-off change in national output.

An important and yet untapped source of further growth is in the extension of industrial reforms to heavy manufacturing and services. State-owned firms in these sectors have been relatively protected and significant foreign ownership shares have been prevented. One consequence of this is that these firms—supplying as they do essential materials and services to an economy that

---

12 A less well-publicised reason for the modest expansion in Beijing's fiscal deficit is that the increased spending on provincial public projects was heavily financed by commercial banks and therefore associated with similarly rising deposit rates and at least implicit government guarantees. It was therefore 'off balance sheet' so far as the Federal Government was concerned. Thanks also to Huw McKay for this observation. The key implication is that private saving has financed public investment at the provincial level.

is expanding rapidly, courtesy of the more competitive light manufacturing export sector—have been extremely profitable (Lu et al. 2008). At the same time, these firms have returned little in the way of dividends to the Central Government, so their profits have not been distributed to their public owners. Instead, these profits have been reinvested. Consequently, the decision to save or consume from this component of national income has been denied households, contributing substantially to China's extraordinary saving—amounting to more than half its GDP.[13]

Substantial potential future growth lies in the redistribution of these rents, which would make Chinese intermediate products cheaper and foster overall output growth while at the same time raising private consumption. A number of approaches are possible, some of which are already being tried.

1. Pure privatisation: this would return the profits of SOEs to private households and foster consumption, raising domestic demand for China's goods and services.

2. SOE fragmentation: this would force more competition between firms and thus reduce mark-ups.

3. Tighter regulation of SOE pricing: this could, at least in theory, force firms to price at their average costs, eliminating rents altogether and reducing the price level.

These alternatives are examined in the analysis to be discussed in subsequent sections.

China's Structure, Performance and its Real Exchange Rate

The implications of a turn inward ride rather importantly on consequent changes in China's underlying real exchange rate, or its level of global competitiveness. This special sensitivity stems from its economic structure, as summarised in Table 2.1. Four patterns stand out

1. the majority of non-agricultural employment is in the export-oriented light manufacturing sector—indeed, employment in this sector exceeds that in agriculture

2. the light manufacturing sector dominates China's exports

---

13 The contribution of corporate saving to China's overall saving rate and to the current account surpluses of the past decade is examined by Kuijs (2006), Kuijs and He (2007) and Tyers and Lu (2008).

3. light manufacturing is relatively competitive—price mark-ups are low so pure or economic profits make up only a small share of total revenue

4. the SOE-dominated energy, metals and services sectors are less labour intensive and at the same time they are oligopolistic, generating substantial rents.

Table 2.1 Structure of the Chinese Economy, ca 2005[a]

Per cent	Value-added share of GDP	Share of total production employment	Share of total exports	Pure profit share of gross revenue
Agriculture	13	24	2	0
Petroleum, coal, metals	16	11	10	20
Light manufacturing	29	33	82	5
Services	42	32	6	20
Total	100	100	100	12

[a] Pure profits are calculated from national statistics estimates of accounting profits, deducting required returns to service industry specific prime rates. Here they are presented gross of tax and corporate saving and as shares of total revenue.

Source: Model database, derived from Dimaranan and McDougall (2002), and an updating of the national data to 2005.

Since exporting firms are highly competitive, generate little pure profit and carry most of the new or 'modern sector' employment, future employment performance is very sensitive to the relativities between home wages and export prices, and hence to China's real exchange rate.

Yet the inward-looking policy changes that could contribute most to enlarging China's economy all have implications for the real exchange rate. Consider, first, the case of government expansion. There are several mechanisms by which expanded government expenditure tends to appreciate the real exchange rate.

The Mundell–Fleming Effect

When financial capital is internationally mobile, even if imperfectly, increased government borrowing raises home yields and induces financial inflow (Fleming 1962; Mundell 1963). The net effect is to raise demand for home relative to (more elastically supplied) foreign products and services and hence to appreciate the real exchange rate.

The Non–Traded-Good Demand Effect

This recognises that governments concentrate their spending on non-traded services, so their expansion changes the composition of aggregate demand towards more inelastically supplied home products, driving up their relative price and hence the real exchange rate.[14]

The Oligopoly Rent Effect

Increased government spending raises home demand for home products, reducing the exported share of the average firm's output. Because foreign demand is the most elastic, this reduces the elasticity of demand faced by oligopoly firms, which then raise their mark-ups. And since these firms reside mainly in the protected heavy manufacturing and largely non-traded services sectors, such price rises appreciate the real exchange rate by raising the relative prices of non-traded services and by increasing costs faced by the competitive export sector (Tyers and Lu 2008). A way of thinking of this is that the excess profits are achieved by supplying less output so the oligopoly firms reduce productivity in the largely non-traded sectors of the economy.

In assessing fiscal expansions, the negative effect on the real exchange rate is commonly seen as being more than offset by the resulting expansion in aggregate demand. A key mechanism for this is that the increase in government dis-saving reduces the *national* saving rate, at least temporarily, requiring the failure of Ricardian equivalence. Because reduced national saving contracts the leakage of expenditure abroad, which in China takes the form of foreign reserve accumulation, the current account surplus is reduced and more Chinese expenditure falls on the home relative to the foreign economy. This has the effect of either inducing a home inflation or arresting a deflation. If the latter, it stabilises the relationship between nominal wages and the price level and hence maintains the steady-state level of employment. Tyers and Huang (2009) take just such a short-run approach to government spending in China. In this study, the focus is on transformative sources of growth that operate in the long run so the expansion of government to be considered here is long run in orientation and therefore tax financed.

Returning to the oligopoly pricing effect on the real exchange rate, the alternative of further industrial reform is also considered here. To the extent that this reduces oligopoly mark-ups it will tend to depreciate the real exchange rate and thereby preserve the competitiveness of China's export manufacturing sector.

14 De Gregorio et al. (1994) and Froot and Rogoff (1995), and more recently Galstyan and Lane (2009), recognise that boosting government expenditure appreciates the real exchange rate by this mechanism, even in the case of public investment, at least in the short run.

The further alternative of FDI in Chinese services offers increased services productivity. This also would depreciate the real exchange rate by reducing the relative price of non-traded products. To quantify the effects of these on China's overall economic performance, a complete model of the Chinese economy is offered.

An Oligopoly Model of the Chinese Economy

To capture the behaviour of the oligopolistic SOEs, a comparative static macroeconomic model of the Chinese economy is used that embodies a multi-industry structure in which all industries are treated as oligopolies, with firms in each industry supplying differentiated products and interacting on prices.[15] The model is described in detail by Tyers (2012) and in appendices to Tyers and Lu (2008). A short summary of the relevant elements is offered here.

Behavioural Underpinnings

The model has neoclassical foundations with final consumption, intermediate demand and the demands created by a capital goods sector treated as in most economy-wide models, with nested CES preferences.[16] Government expenditure is an exogenous policy variable but it is subdivided across goods and services also via nested constant elasticity of substitution (CES) systems, and government revenue stems from a tax system that includes both direct (income) taxes levied separately on labour and capital income and indirect taxes including those on consumption, imports and exports.[17] The level of total investment placing demands on the capital goods sector has Q-like behaviour, being influenced positively by home rates of return on installed capital and negatively by a financing rate obtainable from an open 'bond market' in which home and foreign bonds are differentiated to represent China's capital controls. Savings are sourced from the collective household at a constant rate and from corporations at industry-specific rates on the assumption that corporate saving (retained earnings) in SOEs depends on the magnitudes of pure (economic) profits earned. Foreign direct investment and official foreign reserve accumulation are both represented, to complete China's external financial accounts.[18]

---

15 It is a distant descendant of that by Harris (1984) and Gunasekera and Tyers (1990), though it is considerably generalised to include macroeconomic behaviour.

16 See, for example, Dixon et al. (1982).

17 Income taxes are approximated by flat rates deduced as the quotient of revenue and the tax base in each case.

18 Hereinafter the capital, financial and official sub-accounts of China's balance of payments will be referred to as the 'capital account'.

The departure from convention arises with the way production is specified to account explicitly for oligopoly. Firms in each industry supply differentiated products. They carry product-variety-specific fixed costs and interact on prices. Cobb-Douglas production technology drives variable costs so that average variable costs are constant if factor and intermediate product prices do not change but average total cost declines with output.[19] Firms charge a mark-up over average variable cost, which they choose strategically. Their capacity to push their price beyond their average variable costs without being undercut by existing competitors then determines the level of any pure profits and, in the long run, the potential for entry by new firms.

Thus, each firm in industry i is regarded as producing a unique variety of its product and it faces a downward-sloping demand curve with elasticity ε_i (< 0). The optimal mark-up is then as given in Equation 2.1.

Equation 2.1

$$m_i = \frac{p_i}{v_i} = \frac{1}{1 + \dfrac{1}{\varepsilon_i}} \qquad \forall\, i$$

In Equation 2.1, p_i is the firm's product price, v_i is its average variable cost and ε_i is the elasticity of demand it faces. Firms choose their optimal price by taking account of the price-setting behaviour of other firms. A conjectural variations parameter in industry i is then defined as the influence of any individual firm, k, on the price of firm j. For this parameter the non-collusive (Nash) oligopoly implies a zero value, while for a perfect cartel, it has the value unity. Although the level of price collusion between firms is not readily estimated, it is calibrated for each industry in China from prior knowledge of mark-ups and elasticities of demand.

Critical to the model's behaviour is that the product of each industry has exposure to five different sources of demand. The elasticity of demand faced by firms in industry i, ε_i, is therefore dependent on the elasticities of demand in these five markets, as well as the shares of the home product in each. They are final demand (F), investment demand (V), intermediate demand (I), export demand (X) and government demand (G). For industry i, the elasticity that applies to (19), above, is a composite of the elasticities of all five sources of demand (Equation 2.2).[20]

---

19 While firms are oligopolists in their product markets they have no oligopsony power as purchasers of primary factors or intermediate inputs.
20 The expressions for these elasticities are messy and voluminous. They are derived in appendices to Tyers and Lu (2008).

Equation 2.2

$$\varepsilon_i = s_i^F \varepsilon_i^F + s_i^V \varepsilon_i^V + s_i^I \varepsilon_i^I + s_i^X \varepsilon_i^X + s_i^G \varepsilon_i^G \qquad \forall i$$

In Equation 2.2, s_i^j denotes the volume share of the home product in market i for each source of demand j. These share parameters are fully endogenous in the model.

Thus, the strategic behaviour of firms, and hence the economic cost of oligopolies, is affected by collusive behaviour on the one hand and the composition of the source of demands faced by firms on the other, both of which act through the average elasticity of varietal demand. Thus, when economic shocks change the composition of demand, they also change the average elasticity of demand faced by firms. When this falls, oligopoly firms raise their mark-ups and extract increased rents. Of course, rent extraction depends on costs, and importantly on fixed costs. If there is entry into an industry, fixed costs rise with the number of firms, raising average total costs and hence the mark-up required to break even.

Model Structure

The scope of the model is detailed in Table 2.2. Factor intensities by industry and initial demand shares, elasticities and mark-ups are reported in Tables 2.3 and 2.4 respectively. The economy modelled is 'almost small', implying that it has no power to influence the border prices of its imports but its exports are differentiated from competing products abroad and hence face finite-elastic demand. The consumer price index (CPI) is constructed as a composite Cobb-Douglas–CES index of post–consumption-tax home product and post-tariff import prices, derived from the aggregate household's expenditure function. This formulation of the CPI aids in the analysis of welfare impacts. Because collective utility is also defined as a Cobb-Douglas combination of the volumes of consumption by generic product, proportional changes in overall economic welfare correspond with those in real gross national product (GNP).

Table 2.2 Model Scope

Regions	China
	Rest of world
Primary factors	Land
	Natural resources (mineral, energy deposits)
	Skilled (professional) labour
	Unskilled (production) labour
	Physical capital

Industries	Agriculture
	Metals, including steel, minerals and (non-coal) mining
	Coalmining and production
	Petroleum production and refining
	Processed agricultural products
	Electronic equipment
	Motor vehicles
	Chemical, rubber, plastic products
	Textiles
	Other manufactures
	Electricity supply and distribution
	Gas supply and distribution
	Telecommunications
	Insurance and finance
	Transport
	Construction
	Other services

Source: Aggregates of the 57-industry GTAP Version 6 database from Dimaranan and McDougall (2002).

Table 2.3 Factor Intensities by Industry[a]

	Capital	Production labour	Skilled labour	Land and natural resources
Agriculture	11	59	0	30
Metals and minerals	66	27	5	2
Coal	28	30	3	39
Petroleum	86	5	1	7
Processed agriculture	38	54	7	0
Electronic equipment	66	26	8	0
Motor vehicles	59	35	6	0
Chemical products	62	32	6	0
Textiles	40	52	7	0
Other manufactures	68	27	5	0
Electricity	69	21	11	0
Gas manufacturing and distribution	49	37	14	0
Communications	92	5	3	0
Insurance and finance	80	12	8	0
Transport	78	18	4	0
Construction	56	37	7	0
Other services	54	27	19	0

[a] These are factor shares of total value added in each industry, calculated from the database. Capital shares include pure profits. Shares sum to 100 per cent horizontally.

Source: Model database (social accounting matrix), derived from Dimaranan and McDougall (2002).

Table 2.4 Initial Demand Shares, Elasticities and Mark-ups[a]

	Demand shares (%)					Demand elasticities					Average demand elasticity	Industry mark-up[b]
	Intermediate	Final	Export	Investment	Govt	Intermediate	Final	Export	Investment	Govt		
Agriculture	53	40	4	3	0	-10.2	-28.6	-40.1	-15.6	-16.0	-18.8	1.06
Metals, minerals	84	3	10	2	1	-2.9	-4.4	-8.9	-2.8	-2.8	-3.5	1.39
Coal	61	4	33	0	2	-3.6	-6.1	-11.2	-2.4	-2.5	-6.2	1.19
Petroleum	58	12	5	14	12	-2.1	-2.8	-6.2	-2.3	-2.1	-2.4	1.69
Processed agriculture	50	34	15	0	1	-12.0	-30.8	-26.8	-16.4	-17.0	-20.7	1.05
Electronics	24	4	65	6	0	-2.7	-6.4	-9.8	-2.9	-2.9	-7.5	1.15
Motor vehicles	46	8	15	29	1	-4.8	-10.0	-16.9	-3.4	-3.7	-6.6	1.18
Chemicals	77	6	17	0	0	-3.6	-6.3	-10.4	-2.5	-2.5	-4.9	1.26
Textiles	45	11	44	0	0	-6.5	-16.9	-25.7	-10.4	-10.2	-16.1	1.07
Other manufacturing	43	5	35	16	0	-2.6	-7.1	-9.5	-4.0	-4.0	-5.5	1.22
Electricity	84	13	1	1	1	-6.4	-12.3	-21.0	-7.5	-7.7	-7.3	1.16
Gas manufacturing and distribution	50	10	0	8	32	-4.9	-7.7	-13.4	-4.8	-4.9	-5.2	1.24
Telecommunications	42	24	1	5	27	-1.7	-1.4	-5.1	-1.5	-1.7	-1.7	2.45
Finance	57	29	2	3	8	-1.8	-2.6	-6.6	-2.2	-2.2	-2.2	1.86
Transport	53	18	8	7	14	-1.3	-1.6	-5.9	-1.6	-1.5	-1.8	2.26
Construction	4	2	0	86	8	-2.5	-5.1	-12.3	-4.4	-4.0	-4.3	1.30
Other services	46	21	4	4	25	-3.4	-8.6	-11.7	-3.1	-2.8	-4.7	1.27

[a] All these variables are endogenous in the model. Initial (base) values are provided here.

[b] Industry mark-ups are the ratio of producer prices and average variable costs.

Source: Model database, derived from Dimaranan and McDougall (2002) and 2005 national statistics.

The quantity of domestically owned physical capital is fixed both in the short and the long runs, so that changes in the total capital stock affect the foreign ownership share and hence the level of income repatriated abroad. In the experiments to be presented, a long-run closure is used throughout.[21] Physical capital is homogeneous and fully mobile between industries, though claims on home and foreign capital are differentiated, so there is a wedge between the home and domestic bond yields (interest rates) that stems the differentiation of these financial assets (due, say, to the retention of inward and outward capital controls) combined with endogenous reserve management policy. All real unit factor rewards are flexible and domestic factor supplies are fixed. A fixed oligopoly structure is retained, assuming SOEs are protected from competitive entry and are prevented from exiting if losses are incurred. Consistent with China's heretofore fiscal conservatism, the base fiscal deficit is held constant with exogenous expenditure changes covered by endogenous changes in tax rates.

Comparing Alternative Regimes

To quantify the 'natural' slowdown story, the simulations commence with representations of continuing export-led growth and the Lewis turning point. Government expansion is then considered—first financed by a rise in consumption taxation and then financed by a rise in corporate taxation. Turning to industrial reform, three types are considered. First, a pure privatisation is simulated by allowing all profits of SOEs to accrue as income to the collective private household. Second, a threefold fragmentation of SOEs is tried in order to elicit more competitive pricing, and third, price-cap regulation is imposed to force mark-ups halfway to the level sufficient to cover average costs. Finally, the option of opening the services sector to additional FDI is considered and hence of fostering accelerated productivity growth in that sector. It is worth noting that, except for the last, all these scenarios ignore natural innovation and productivity improvements that would continue irrespective of the fiscal or industrial policy regime. As such, these simulations consider policy changes that could offer the major boost to China's GDP that might replace that yielded by export-led growth.

Further Export-Led Growth

Continued export-led growth is illustrated in this simulation by some representative shocks to productivity and a closure that allows rising labour supply. There is a rise in labour productivity in agriculture, to represent its capacity to continue shedding workers, and a rise in total factor productivity in

---

21 This contrasts with the results presented by Tyers and Huang (2009), which are short run in nature.

the light manufacturing export sector, to represent the effects of continued FDI into that sector. There is also an arbitrarily low increase in the real production wage, which is made exogenous for this simulation so that the supply of workers to the modern sector can grow. Workers continue to be released by agriculture, foreign capital flows in and expansion is substantial as expected. The results are shown in the first column of Table 2.5.[22]

Table 2.5 Simulated Export-Led Growth and Government Expansion Effects[a]

Per cent changes	Continued export-led growth[b]	Export-led growth beyond the Lewis turning point[c]	Government expansion G/Y up by 25%, consumption tax financed[d]	Government expansion G/Y up by 30%, company tax financed[d]
Real GDP	16.6	4.9	2.6	−1.7
Real GNP	9.3	3.9	−8.9	0.6
Real exchange rate	1.3	3.5	1.3	2.0
Exports/GDP	19.1	5.8	−7.9	−10.0
Consumption/GDP	−8.7	−2.9	−2.1	0.8
CA surplus/GDP	17.0	−3.2	−4.4	−2.4
Production employment	17.7	0.0	0.0	0.0
Real production wage	2.0[e]	7.2	−3.5	−3.3
Real skilled wage	18.4	4.1	−1.5	−0.7
Physical capital stock	19.8	5.3	−1.4	−1.5
Real home capital income[f]	−3.8	−3.2	−13.6	−7.1

[a] These simulations are all made in long-run mode—endogenous capital stock with exogenous external rate of return on excess saving and perfect mobility of workers between agriculture and the other sectors. The number of oligopoly firms is fixed, however, so that pure profits are endogenous.

[b] This simulation retains the existing policy regime and applies 4 per cent labour productivity in agriculture, to continue to release workers, and 4 per cent productivity in light manufacturing (the export sector) due to continued FDI, combined with an exogenous rise in the real production wage of just 2 per cent. Modern sector labour supply therefore rises substantially.

[c] Here the agricultural productivity rise is not imposed and the supply of production workers is fixed.

[d] These simulations represent tax-financed fiscal expansions, which raise the government spending share of GDP by one-quarter in the case of consumption tax financing and one-third in the case of capital income tax financing.

[e] In the export-led growth case the real production wage increase is an arbitrary and exogenous 2 per cent.

[f] Real home capital income is the income accruing to domestically owned capital net of tax and depreciation.

Source: Simulations of the model described in the text.

22 Real net income to home capital owners actually falls slightly. This is because total saving continues to increase under this scenario and capital controls are retained. This excess supply of saving is transferred to foreign reserves only incompletely, leaving a decline in the home bond yield.

Lewis Turning Point

Here, the same shocks are applied, except that there is no productivity gain in agriculture associated with departing workers and the closure is changed so that the supply of production labour is fixed and the real production wage is endogenous. The results are shown in the second column of Table 2.5. In this case, surplus workers are no longer available so that growth then stems from the productivity changes alone and is much reduced. The real production wage rises faster, however, and there is a reduction in the current account surplus due to a decline in pure profits in the protected sectors (in effect, a gain by workers at the expense of capital) and hence a decline in corporate saving. The current account balances because of the saving change and there is a 'natural' redistribution of the SOE rents in favour of working households. If the Government can maintain a steady policy hand during this shock, while growth will clearly slow, many of the other structural issues with the Chinese economy are corrected.

Consumption Tax-Financed Government Expansion

In the long run an expansion of government activity must be financed by taxation. Here the instrument of choice is the consumption tax. The experiment is an arbitrary increase in the government share of GDP by 25 per cent. It requires an increase in consumption tax revenue by 14 per cent of the tax base. This is a large negative shock that contracts real domestic factor income at new home prices. The results, shown in the third column of Table 2.5, confirm that home workers and home-owned capital are losers, so real GNP contracts; however, real GDP rises slightly. This is due to the retention of considerable foreign capital, the income from which is not subject to the consumption tax, and the fact that the real rate of return on capital rises in terms of foreign prices on the back of reduced real labour costs. The protected heavy manufacturing and services sectors expand in this scenario while private households and workers are worse off.

Corporate Tax-Financed Government Expansion

If the government expansion is financed from company, or capital income, tax the net effects are as shown in the final column of Table 2.5. The tax needed to expand the government share of GDP by 30 per cent turns out to be 7.7 per cent of the capital income tax base. Because corporate saving depends on profits, it declines, also contracting the current account surplus. Apart from a substantial cut in real income to home capital owners, this policy has little effect on overall real economic activity. Enlarging government, at least via tax increases, therefore offers little real long-run expansion under the assumptions of this model.[23] A key to this is the turning inward of demand under the government expansion scenarios, which reduces the export share of production and therefore the elasticity of demand facing oligopoly firms. The result is a modest but influential real appreciation in each case that is larger than would arise were there to be no oligopoly behaviour.

Pure Privatisation

The first shock simply places the majority of SOE assets in private hands, so that profits are distributed to households. The rates of corporate saving across industries are reduced until total corporate saving falls to a more normal 5 per cent of GDP.[24] Most after-tax company income then accrues to households, so it can be allocated by them to saving or consumption.[25] By itself, as indicated in the first column of Table 2.6, this reduces national saving and the current account surplus. Other than this, however, the simulation suggests that privatisation generates no substantial growth in and of itself so long as the competition facing SOEs is restricted.[26]

Fragmentation of SOEs

Here SOEs are subdivided within sectors and encouraged to compete on price. This has been a popular approach in some protected sectors, yet the simulation suggests the results are not attractive. A threefold increase in the number of oligopoly firms is imposed in the heavy manufacturing and services sectors, the effects of which are shown in the second column of Table 2.6. The problem with this approach is that, while it does induce more competitive pricing and hence lower mark-ups, each new firm carries fixed costs so the sectoral fixed-cost burden rises sufficiently for prices to rise, lower mark-ups notwithstanding. Because fixed capital is required, the capital stock increases substantially but capital returns are slashed. While production workers gain, domestic capital owners lose and no substantial growth is yielded.

---

23 A separate experiment to measure the effects of a similar expansion that is bond financed finds results that are contractionary of both GDP and GNP in real terms. This result is examined in short-run mode by Tyers and Huang (2009), who find that the usual Keynesian expansion is more than offset by oligopoly price increases and the associated real appreciation.

24 This is the scale of corporate saving in Taiwan. See Tyers and Lu (2008).

25 It is achieved by shocking down the corporate saving rate (retained earnings rate) so that discretionary corporate income accrues to households.

26 Had it been assumed that privatisation might eliminate x-inefficiency and hence raise productivity by making poor-performing firms takeover targets, a one-off growth surge might be expected from this change.

Table 2.6 Simulated Industrial Reforms and Expansion Potential[a]

Per cent	Pure privatisation of SOEs[b]	Pure splitting of SOEs: threefold fragmentation[c]	Price caps on SOE oligopolies[d]	Services-driven growth: 4% productivity
Real GDP	0.6	−12.9	28.3	15.9
Real GNP	0.8	−13.8	13.0	6.5
Real exchange rate	1.2	2.9	−8.2	−6.6
Exports/GDP	−10.6	−17.2	42.9	22.3
Consumption/GDP	13.2	17.6	−12.0	−7.0
CA surplus/GDP	−61.9	−143.3	80.4	48.7
Real production wage	−0.2	15.6	30.4	19.4
Real skilled wage	0.9	−1.6	42.1	21.8
Physical capital stock	−0.4	26.4	28.3	16.9
Real home capital income[f]	−0.7	−50.0	4.4	3.2

[a] These simulations are all made in long-run mode—endogenous capital stock with exogenous external rate of return on excess saving and perfect mobility of workers between agriculture and the other sectors. The number of oligopoly firms is fixed, however, so that pure profits are endogenous.

[b] Pure privatisation requires that all corporate income after tax should accrue to the collective private household and be split between consumption and saving at private rates.

[c] The number of firms is enlarged threefold in heavy manufacturing and services.

[d] Price caps alter the pricing formulae of oligopolistic firms, forcing them to halve their mark-ups over their average costs.

[f] Real home capital income is the income accruing to domestically owned capital net of tax and depreciation.

Source: Simulations of the model described in the text.

Tighter Price-Cap Regulation of SOEs

The results for tighter price caps on SOEs are more positive. Indeed, they suggest that substantial new growth is available from this policy option. In oligopoly industries with fixed costs, mark-ups over average variable cost are required to break even. In the simulation, price caps are imposed that would force firms to reduce their mark-ups halfway towards the level that would cover average costs. Such price-cap regulation appears to have been successful in many industrial countries and the simulation suggests that the effect in China would be to reduce costs in industries whose products are used as intermediate inputs throughout the economy and hence economic activity would be expanded substantially. As indicated in the third column of Table 2.6, the lower costs help depreciate the real exchange rate, aiding the export sector and, aside from the overall expansion it offers, it unwinds much of the income inequality of recent decades by redistributing rents and raising wages.

FDI-Induced Productivity Growth in Services

The final simulation considers the effect of a productivity improvement in services of the type that could be delivered by additional foreign investment. The results are indicated in the final column of Table 2.6. The more efficient services sector depreciates the real exchange rate, boosting rather than impairing exports and fostering overall growth. The Balassa–Samuelson hypothesis notwithstanding, there is also structural convergence of the Chinese economy with the industrialised West. The simulation yields substantially higher real wages that benefit both skilled and production workers. These represent higher costs, however, so they cause a redistribution of industrial output and exports in favour of heavier manufacturing. The Chinese economy continues to open but it is much more reliant than before on intra-industry trade with the West, in the manner of the United States and Western Europe.

The Difficult Politics of Internally Generated Growth

While the results obtained here are dependent on some strong assumptions underlying the modelling,[27] they are clear in suggesting that, for substantial further growth to be found from looking inward, China will need to combine other elements of industrial reform with a more ardent regulatory attack on oligopoly rents. This will be difficult politically, as will the other key element of further growth—namely, substantial productivity growth in the primarily state-owned services sector. Achieving this will require levels of FDI in services that parallel those in Chinese manufacturing. Heretofore, the Government has opposed foreign ownership in key services and heavy manufacturing industries, so allowing such FDI will also be very difficult politically.

Conclusion

With the impending end to export-led growth and conflicts due on the one hand to rising domestic inequality and, on the other, to recently high current account surpluses, China is in need of a further stage of transformative growth that will maintain the pace of its catch-up and address its internal and external

---

27 One such assumption is that the private household saving rate from disposable income remains constant. Those policy changes that substantially increase household disposable income, such as privatisation, could see a change in this rate, though it is not clear in which direction. A permanent income story might suggest a rise but the focus here is on the long-run steady state and in that case it is possible that households expecting a continuation of higher incomes might choose a lower rate. A fully dynamic approach, along the lines of McKibbin and Woo (2004), would help address this, though even then, the results would rely on much debated assumptions about the formation of household expectations and it is unlikely that the direction or the relative scale of the projected changes in overall performance would be altered.

conflicts. One inevitable transformation to come stems from the Lewis turning point. Its arrival will see accelerated real wage growth and hence the fruits of further growth will be less concentrated and, since this will raise the share of total income available to households, the corporate share of saving should fall. This in turn should reduce the overall saving rate and the current account surplus. It will, of course, bring with it the need for costly adjustments since, as shown in the previous section, growth will slow and the supply of new labour to the heretofore efficient and relatively competitive light manufacturing sector will gradually dry up. Moreover, the net benefits from China's growth that accrue to the global economy will also decline. Yet if, as some believe (Garnaut 2010), this transition is imminent, the silver lining it brings will be reduced political pressure from at home and abroad and hence less incentive to abandon the heretofore successful market-oriented policy regime.

But there remain the matters of sustaining the overall growth rate and of an orderly transition. As to the latter, both the Republic of Korea and Taiwan made orderly economic transitions away from dependence on the transformation of their labour forces via labour-intensive exports. Political transformations towards liberal democracy also occurred in both, commencing as their urban middle classes assumed numerical majorities. Of course, they were helped in this by the stimulus associated with China's own growth surge. Japan's initial transition was orderly, surviving the oil and commodity crises of the 1970s, but it was subsequently disrupted by policy errors during the 1980s and early 1990s. Japan's comparatively liberal democracy could not chart those waters effectively even with the growth of China on its doorstep. Now China must do so, but without the external stimulus associated with a growth surge in a large near neighbour.

As for moderating the growth slowdown, a further source of transformative growth is required to avoid a rapid and possibly disruptive slowdown. This issue is here addressed via simulations of a 17-sector model of the Chinese economy that takes explicit account of the oligopoly behaviour of SOEs and a database that captures essential economic structure—namely, a largely competitive light manufacturing export sector and oligopolistic heavy manufacturing and services sectors dominated by state-owned enterprises. The results suggest that further transformative sources of growth do exist but, to exploit them, China's government must dig deep and produce industrial reforms that reduce the rents that currently concentrate economic gains while at the same time welcoming FDI into its hitherto protected service industries. The benefits available are considerable, including not only final steps towards real per capita income convergence with the West but also reduced inequality and stronger, more externally engaged heavy industry and services.

While delivering this will be a tall order politically, China's governments since the early 1980s have faced constant political and economic challenges and they have thus far been effective. The fundamentals behind Chinese growth to date seem sound and the obstacles to continued transformation are known to the Government and its branches (*The Economist* 2011). The continuing external clamour for greater consumption is essentially xenophobic—tantamount to demands that the Chinese should invest less and have their economy perform more poorly. A strong Chinese economy and a smooth economic transition are in the global collective interest and will require that Western political pressure is restrained. At the same time, the Chinese are in a better position to learn from the Japanese experience and resist external pressure for economic policy changes that are not beneficial domestically.

Bibliography

Balistreri, E. J., Hillberry, R. H. and Rutherford, T. J., 2007, Structural estimation and solution of international trade models with heterogeneous firms, Paper presented at the Tenth Annual Conference on Global Economic Analysis, Purdue University, Lafayette, Ind., July.

Bardhan, P., 2010, *Awakening Giants, Feet of Clay: Assessing the economic rise of China and India*, Princeton University Press, Princeton, NJ.

Bergsten, C. F., Freeman, C., Lardy, N. R. and Mitchell, D. J., 2008, *China's Rise: Challenges and opportunities*, Peterson Institute for International Economics, Washington, DC.

Bernanke, B., 2006, Speech to the Chinese Academy of Social Sciences, Beijing, 15 December, <http://www.federalreserve.gov/BoardDocs/Speeches/2006/20061215>

Bhagwati, J. N., 1987, 'Immiserizing growth', in J. Eatwell, M. Milgate and P. Newman (eds), *The New Palgrave: A dictionary of economics*, Macmillan, London.

Cai, F., 2010, 'Demographic transition, demographic dividend and Lewis turning point in China', *China Economic Journal*, vol. 3, no. 2 (September), pp. 107–19.

Deer, L. and Song, L., 2012, 'China's approach to rebalancing: a conceptual and policy framework', *China & World Economy*, vol. 20, no. 1, pp. 1–26.

De Gregorio, J., Giovannini, A. and Wolf, H., 1994, 'International evidence on tradables and non-tradables inflation', *European Economic Review*, vol. 38, pp. 1225–34.

Dimaranan, B. V. and McDougall, R. A., 2002, *Global Trade, Assistance and Production: The GTAP 5 data base*, May, Center for Global Trade Analysis, Purdue University, Lafayette, Ind.

Dixon, P. B., Parmenter, B. R., Sutton, J. and Vincent, D. P., 1982, *ORANI, A Multi-Sectoral Model of the Australian Economy*, North Holland, Amsterdam.

Dooley, M. P., Folkerts-Landau, D. and Garber, P., 2004, *Direct investment, rising real wages and the absorption of excess labor in the periphery*, NBER Working Paper 10626, July, National Bureau of Economic Research, Cambridge, Mass.

Easterly, W., 2001, *The Lost Decades: Developing countries' stagnation in spite of policy reform 1980–1998*, February, The World Bank, Washington, DC.

Eichengreen, B., Park, D. and Shin, K., 2011, *When fast growing economies slow down: international evidence and implications for China*, NBER Working Paper 16919, National Bureau of Economic Research, Cambridge, Mass.

Fleming, J. M., 1962, *Domestic financial policies under fixed and under flexible exchange rates*, IMF Staff Papers Vol. 9, International Monetary Fund, Washington, DC, pp. 369–79.

Froot, K. A. and Rogoff, K., 1995, 'Perspectives on PPP and long run real exchange rates', in G. M. Grossman and K. Rogoff (eds), *Handbook of International Economics. Volume III*, Elsevier, Amsterdam.

Galstyan, V. and Lane, P. R., 2009, 'The composition of government spending and the real exchange rate', *Journal of Money, Credit and Banking*, vol. 41, no. 6, pp. 1233–49.

Garnaut, R., 2010, 'Macroeconomic implications of the turning point', *China Economic Journal*, vol. 3, no. 2 (September), pp. 181–90.

Golley, J. and Meng, X., 2011, 'Has China run out of surplus labour?', *Chinese Economic Review*, vol. 22, no. 4, pp. 555–72.

Goyal, R. and McKinnon, R. I., 2003, 'Japan's negative risk premium in interest rates: the liquidity trap and the fall in bank lending', *The World Economy*, vol. 26 (March), pp. 339–63.

Gunasekera, H. D. B. and Tyers, R., 1990, 'Imperfect competition and returns to scale in a newly industrialising economy: a general equilibrium analysis of Korean trade policy', *Journal of Development Economics*, vol. 34, pp. 223–47.

Haber, S. H., North, D. C. and Weingast, B. R., 2008, 'Introduction', in S. H. Haber, D. C. North and B. R. Weingast (eds), *Political Institutions and Financial Development*, Stanford University Press, Stanford, Calif., pp. 1–9.

Hamada, K. and Okada, Y., 2009, 'Monetary and international factors behind Japan's lost decade', *Journal of the Japanese and International Economies*, vol. 23, pp. 200–19.

Harris, R. G., 1984, 'Applied general equilibrium analysis of small open economies with scale economies and imperfect competition', *American Economic Review*, vol. 74, pp. 1016–32.

Harris, R. G, Robertson, P. E. and Xu, J., 2011, 'The international effects of China's trade and education booms', *The World Economy*, vol. 34, no. 10, pp. 1703–25.

Hayashi, F. and Prescott, E. C., 2002, 'The 1990s in Japan: a lost decade', *Review of Economic Dynamics*, vol. 5, pp. 206–35.

Jia, K. and Liu, W., 2009, *China's Fiscal Policies During the Post-Crisis Era*, Research Institute for Fiscal Science, Ministry of Finance, Beijing.

Krugman, P., 2010, 'Taking on China', *The New York Times*, 30 September.

Kuijs, L., 2006, *How will China's saving–investment balance evolve?*, Policy Research Working Paper 3958, July, The World Bank, Beijing.

Kuijs, L., 2011, 'How much will Asia slow down in a global downturn?', *Asia Pacific Economics Note*, 7 October, MF Global Hong Kong.

Kuijs, L. and He, J., 2007, *Rebalancing China's economy—modelling a policy package*, China Working Paper No. 7, September, The World Bank, Beijing.

Lardy, N. R., 2006, *Toward a consumption-driven growth path*, Policy Brief 06-6, Peterson Institute for International Economics, Washington, DC.

Lardy, N. R., 2012, *Sustaining China's Growth after the Global Financial Crisis*, January, Peterson Institute for International Economics, Washington, DC.

Lewis, W. A., 1955, *The Theory of Economic Growth*, Taylor and Francis, London.

Lu, F., Song, G., Tang, J., Zhao, H. and Liu, L., 2008, 'Profitability of Chinese firms, 1978–2006', *China Economic Journal*, vol. 1, no. 1.

Lucas, R. E., jr, 2009, 'Trade and the diffusion of the Industrial Revolution', *American Economic Journal: Macroeconomics*, vol. 1, no. 1, pp. 1–25.

Mundell, R.A., 1963. "Capital mobility and stabilisation policy under fixed and flexible exchange rates", *Canadian Journal of Economics and Political Science*, 29: 475-485.

McKibbin, W. and Woo, W. T., 2004, *The global economic impact of China's accession to the WTO*, Trade Policy Working Paper No. 3, Organisation for Economic Cooperation and Development, Paris.

Melitz, M. J., 2003, 'The impact of trade on intra-industry reallocations and aggregate industry productivity', *Econometrica*, vol. 71, no. 6, pp. 1695–725.

Olson, M., 1965, *The Logic of Collective Action: Public goods and the theory of groups*, Harvard University Press, Cambridge, Mass.

Riedel, J., 2006, *Seeing But Not Believing: Technological progress and structural change in China*, School of Advanced International Studies, Johns Hopkins University, Baltimore.

Riedel, J., 2007, 'China needs many things but not a new growth engine', *Financial Times*, [Asia edition], 21 February.

Riedel, J., 2011, *The Slowing Down of Long Term Growth in Asia: Natural causes, the middle income trap and politics*, School of Advanced International Studies, Johns Hopkins University, Baltimore.

Riedel, J., Jin, J. and Gao, J., 2007, *How China Grows: Investment, finance and reform*, Princeton University Press, Princeton, NJ, and Peking University Press, Beijing.

Robertson, P. E., 2011, 'Clash of the titans: comparing India and China', in J. Golley and L. Song (eds), *Rising China: Global challenges and opportunities*, ANU E Press, Canberra.

Song, L., Wu, J. and Zhang, Y., 2010, 'Urbanization of migrant workers and expansion of domestic demand', *Social Sciences in China*, vol. XXXI, no. 3 (August), pp. 194–216.

The Economist, 2011, 'How real is China's growth?', *The Economist*, 1 June, <http://economist.com/blogs/freeexchange/2011/05/chinas_economy>

Tulloch, G., 1967, 'The welfare costs of tariffs, monopolies, and theft', *Western Economic Journal*, vol. 5, no. 3, pp. 224–32.

Tyers, R., 2011, *Global implications of Japan's economic stagnation*, CAMA Working Paper No. 20-2011, The Australian National University, Canberra.

Tyers, R., 2012, *Looking inward for transformative growth in China*, CAMA Working Paper, The Australian National University, Canberra.

Tyers, R., forthcoming, 'The rise and robustness of economic freedoms in China', in G. Moore (ed.), *The Open Society and Its Enemies in East Asia*, Nordic Institute of Asian Studies Press, Copenhagen.

Tyers, R. and Huang, L., 2009, *Combating China's export contraction: fiscal expansion or accelerated industrial reform?*, CAMA Working Paper 2/2009, February, College of Business and Economics, The Australian National University, Canberra.

Tyers, R. and Lu, F., 2008, *Competition policy, corporate saving and China's current account surplus*, Working Papers in Economics and Econometrics No. 496, July, College of Business and Economics, The Australian National University, Canberra.

Tyers, R. and Zhang, Y., 2011, 'Appreciating the renminbi', *The World Economy*, vol. 34, no. 2 (February), pp. 265–97.

Tyers, R., Golley, J., Bu, Y. and Bain, I., 2008, 'China's economic growth and its real exchange rate', *China Economic Journal*, vol. 1, no. 2 (July), pp. 123–45.

Walter, C. E. and Howie, F. J. T., 2011, *Red Capitalism: The fragile financial foundation of China's extraordinary rise*, John Wiley & Sons, Singapore.

Wen, J., 2007, *The Conditions for China to be able to Continue to Guarantee Stable and Rapid Economic Development*, National People's Congress, Beijing, 16 March, viewed 28 October 2011, <http://www.npc.gov.cn>

Wen, J., 2011, *Report on Work of the Government*, National People's Congress, Beijing, 5 March, viewed 24 March 2011, <http://www.npc.gov.cn>

World Bank, 2010, 'Escaping the middle-income trap', in *East Asia and Pacific Economic Update 2010. Volume 2: Robust recovery, rising risks*, November, The World Bank, Washington, DC.

Yi, G., 2011, 'How China plans to strike an economic balance', *CaiXin Online*, [English], 4 February.

3. Financial Repression and China's Economic Imbalances

Anders C. Johansson

Introduction

China's impressive growth over the past three decades has come under scrutiny from both domestic and international economists. Most observers as well as the Chinese leaders themselves now agree that the economy needs to rebalance in order to sustain high levels of growth in the long run.[1] Economic imbalances such as high levels of investment and saving and low levels of consumption, external imbalances, high and increasing levels of inequality, and increasing environmental problems need to be addressed. This chapter argues that these imbalances and challenges, while pressing, are primarily symptoms rather than root causes. I propose that repressive financial policies constitute a central problem in the Chinese economic system and that comprehensive financial reforms should play an important part in any serious attempt to address current economic imbalances.

It is a well-known fact that the Chinese Government has applied severe policies of financial repression as part of its development strategy since the beginning of the reforms in the late 1970s (for example, Lardy 2008; Lu and Yao 2009). Financial repression is, however, relatively seldom tied to the increasing imbalances and challenges to continued economic development that the country is facing. One plausible reason for this is that research on financial repression has mainly focused on the direct relationship between repressive financial policies and economic development. A common finding in this research literature is that financial repression has a significant and negative effect on economic growth. To some extent, this relationship does not go hand-in-hand with the very repressive financial policies seen in China together with the strong and sustained level of China's economic development. Recent research, however, sheds new light on the relationship between financial repression and economic growth, suggesting that the relationship is nonlinear. Furthermore, and more importantly, new research on financial repression and economic imbalances highlights the fact that repressive financial policies often lead to both domestic

---

1 During a speech at the 2011 Boao Forum, President, Hu Jintao, stated that 'population, resources and the environment have put great pressure on our economic and social development, and there is [a] lack of adequate balance, coordination or sustainability in our development' (Hu 2011). Examples of scholars and policymakers stating the need for restructuring include Huang and Wang (2010), Lardy (2012), World Bank (2012) and Yao (2011).

and external economic imbalances. Governments can use financial repression to allocate limited financial resources, skew relative prices and provide capital to preferred sectors. This is perhaps especially common in developing countries, where governments often want to attract foreign investment, increase the competitiveness of the traded sector and develop domestic industrial capability (Johansson and Wang 2011).

The connection between financial repression and economic imbalances in China and its importance for sustained economic development is seldom highlighted in the literature on China's imbalances.[2] The aim of this chapter is twofold. First, I want to shed light on the forms of repressive financial policies that have been used in China over the past three decades and provide an initial discussion on how reforms can be undertaken in order to address imbalances that are threatening the economy. Second, I highlight some of the specific imbalances that are likely to be at least partly due to repressive financial policies. To fulfil these two aims, I first introduce the concept of financial repression and briefly discuss individual repressive policies in China. I then draw on recent research that connects financial repression with economic imbalances to highlight the relationship between the two in the case of China. The main point of this chapter is not to argue that financial repression constitutes the single cause of China's economic imbalances. These policies should instead be seen as part of a complex economic system that is marked by significant imbalances.

The remainder of this chapter is organised as follows. The section immediately following introduces the concept of financial repression. Section three takes a closer look at repressive financial policies in China. The fourth section discusses the relationship between financial repression and economic imbalances and places this relationship in the Chinese context. Section five discusses potential financial reforms that are likely to have a positive impact on current imbalances and section six concludes the study.

Financial Repression

The term 'financial repression' was arguably first used about 40 years ago by McKinnon (1973). He defined financial repression as policies that regulate interest rates, set high reserve requirements on bank deposits and mandatorily allocate resources in the economy. Such policies are generally used more extensively in developing countries. It is often argued that repressive financial

---

2   One important exception is Lardy (2012), who emphasises the need for the Chinese Government to undertake financial liberalisation in order for the economy to continue to grow at high levels during the next decade. The World Bank's recent report on the Chinese economy that aims to bring forward a new development strategy for China also touches on the need for financial liberalisation (World Bank 2012).

policies hinder financial development and lower the overall efficiency of the financial system. For example, Pagano (1993) finds that policies such as interest rate controls and reserve requirements limit the financial resources available for financial intermediation. A natural extension of this is the argument that financial repression holds back economic development (McKinnon 1973; Shaw 1973).[3] This is because repressive financial policies discourage saving and investment due to lower returns than in a competitive market. In an often-cited paper, Roubini and Sala-i-Martin (1992) present theoretical and empirical analyses of the negative relationship between repressive financial policies and long-term economic growth. In a related paper, King and Levine (1993) use an endogenous growth model to show that financial sector distortions reduce growth by way of limiting the rate of innovation in an economy.

It should be noted that even though there today exists a large number of theoretical and empirical studies that portray the negative link between repressive financial policies and economic growth, other studies have cast doubts on the relationship between the two. One proponent of this alternative view is Joseph Stiglitz, who argues that imperfect information might result in a need to impose financial restraints in order to uphold stability in the financial system. For example, Stiglitz (2000) attributes the increasing frequency of financial crises during the past decades to the process of financial liberalisation in developing countries. It can thus be argued that such countries are better able to manage their money supply and financial stability under policies that focus on financial restraints due to the existence of significant degrees of imperfect information (Hellmann et al. 1997, 2000; Stiglitz 1994; Stiglitz and Weiss 1981). These two seemingly opposite approaches to repressive financial policies do not, however, necessarily contradict each other. In a recent study, Huang and Wang (2011) examine the impact of financial repression on economic growth in China during the past three decades. Their findings confirm that repressive financial policies have indeed helped economic growth in China. The authors link this positive relationship to a prudent and gradual approach to liberalisation; however—and what is more important for the analysis in this chapter—their results also indicate that the impact turned from positive during the first two decades of reform to negative in the 2000s. At least in the case of China, these findings indicate that the effect of repressive financial policies on growth and its composition are dependent on the general level of development as well as the institutional setting. How repressive financial policies affect economic activity is thus dependent on the net effect of the positive and negative influences discussed here.

---

3 For a detailed and interesting review of the topic of financial development and economic growth, see Levine (2005).

Repressive Financial Policies in China

In this section, we discuss different forms of repressive financial policies in China. The repressive financial policies in China that are most often mentioned in the literature include interest rate controls, credit controls and reserve requirements; however, financial repression includes several additional policies that can be and often are used in countries around the world, including China. Here, the discussion is based on a list of different policies in an index of financial reforms developed by Abiad et al. (2008), who cover a range of potential ways to liberalise the financial sector: interest rate controls, credit controls and reserve requirements, barriers of entry and state ownership in the banking sector, capital account restrictions, regulations and supervision in the banking sector, and security market policies. The last two of these are usually not seen as typical repressive policies, but as they are directly connected to other policies of financial liberalisation or repression, we briefly discuss them as well.

Interest Rate Controls

Repressed interest rates constitute arguably the most-often cited repressive financial policy in China (for example, Lardy 2008; Lu and Yao 2009). During the period of the traditional planned economy, interest rates were deliberately kept low in order to stimulate the development of heavy industry in China. After economic reforms were initiated in 1978, artificially low interest rates remained. Basically, very low deposit rates and lending rates have resulted in an implicit tax on net lenders. As Lardy (2008) points out, since households are major net savers in China, the redistribution has to some extent been from households to corporations, but even more so to the state. Due to the fact that the state has full control over the domestic banking sector, the major beneficiaries of repressive interest rate policies have been the state-owned enterprises (SOEs); however, Chinese corporations are also large net savers. According to Lardy (2008), one of the most significant gains for the state has therefore been that the cost of sterilisation has been kept relatively low, thus allowing for a significantly undervalued renminbi during most of the past decade.

Figure 3.1 shows the real interest rate during the reform period. The very low general level of real rates of return to bank deposits is clearly visible. There are even several prolonged periods with negative real interest rates during this period.

Figure 3.1 Real Interest Rate, 1978–2011

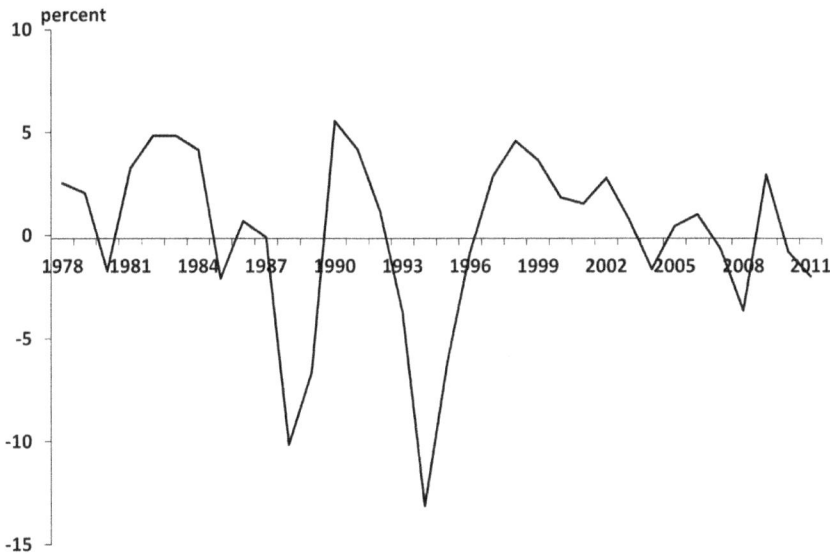

Source: Data from National Bureau of Statistics of China.

Credit Controls and Reserve Requirements

It is still common for many countries to require that a minimum share of total bank lending be given to priority sectors or companies. This is especially so in the case of China, where the banking system is generally regarded as a channel for industrial policy. Research shows that state-owned banks in China tend to favour SOEs and generally do not focus primarily on enterprise profitability (for example, Podpiera 2006; Wei and Wang 1997). A typical example of credit control and direct lending in China is the difficulty faced by private enterprises looking to obtain credit.[4] Walter and Howie (2011) argue that most of the bank lending in China goes to state-owned enterprises. Some observers are worried that this became worse during the global financial crisis, stating that much of the fiscal stimulus package introduced in 2008 resulted in an increase in directed lending. There are, however, those who take the opposite view. Lardy (2012) argues that the view that Chinese banks' main purpose is to provide funding for the Government and SOEs is 'outdated and wholly inaccurate'. Looking at lending during the global financial crisis, he shows that the growth of lending to small firms was more than twice the growth of lending to large firms and that the total amount of new lending to small firms actually surpassed that

---

4   Some solutions to this and other forms of discrimination for such firms have included disguising themselves as a state-owned or collectively owned entity ('wearing a red hat') or developing strong ties to political leaders (for example, Feng et al. 2011).

to large firms (Lardy 2012). While SOEs might be receiving less of the total lending than before, it is clear, however, that the banking system is still filled with preferential treatment to certain groups of enterprises. A growing literature on political connections shows that strong ties to leading politicians are very valuable for Chinese firms. One of the effects of political connections is preferential access to debt capital (Shih 2008). Supporting the view that the Government is still very much controlling credit, the International Monetary Fund (IMF) recently published a report claiming that the Chinese Government's role in credit allocation is partly responsible for causing a build-up of contingent liabilities and making the much needed reorientation of the financial system more difficult (IMF 2011).

Besides control over credit allocation, the Government can use reserve requirements to repress the financial system. Figure 3.2 shows the reserve requirements for Chinese banks imposed by the People's Bank of China during the reform period. While the level of required reserves was very high during the initial stage, it then came down to the 5–15 per cent interval, only to return to about 20 per cent during the past two years. Abiad et al. (2008) use 20 per cent as a threshold when determining whether reserve requirements are to be seen as excessive, suggesting that China's reserve requirement ratio is to be regarded as too high. Lardy (2012) also argues that China's reserve requirements are 'very high' and that they should be addressed in future financial reforms.

Figure 3.2 Reserve Requirements, 1978–2011

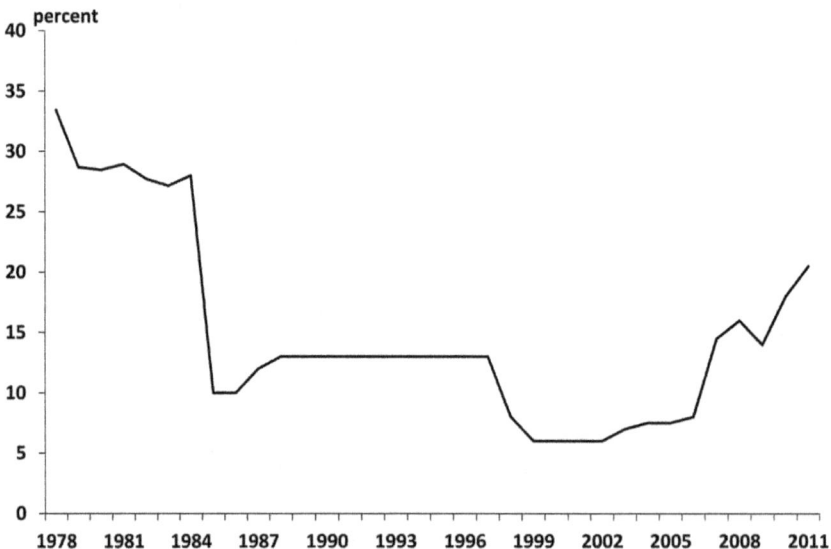

Source: Data from National Bureau of Statistics of China.

Entry Barriers and State Ownership in the Banking Sector

In China, most of the capital in the financial system is allocated through banks. As Walter and Howie (2011) point out, '[i]n China, the banks are the financial system'. Naturally, ownership of banks is the most direct way to control credit allocation in an economy. State ownership of banks is therefore an important indicator of how liberalised the financial system is. Here, it is clear that financial reforms in China have a long way to go. While China's banking sector has undergone significant reforms during the past two decades, the state still controls all the major banks. Table 3.1 shows the different banks in 2009, classified by ownership structure according to the People's Bank of China. Policy banks are fully owned by the state. The four major banks have all undergone initial public offerings, but still remain under majority state control.[5] Of the other 13 major banks classified as joint-stock commercial banks, 11 are controlled by national or local government organs. This means that the state-controlled banks hold assets of close to RMB59 trillion, corresponding to approximately 73 per cent of total bank assets in 2009.

Table 3.1 China's Banking Institutions, 2009

	Number	Share (%)	Assets (RMB trillion)	
			Amount	Share (%)
Policy banks	3	0.05	6.95	8.63
State-owned commercial banks	4	0.07	39.04	48.47
Joint-stock commercial banks, state as largest shareholder	11	0.20	12.59	15.63
Others	2	0.04	2.01	2.50
Others				
City commercial banks and credit unions	158	2.80	5.71	7.09
Rural commercial banks and credit unions	5241	93.02	8.64	10.73
Postal savings bank	1	0.02	2.70	3.35
Foreign banks	32	0.57	1.35	1.68
Non-bank institutions	182	3.23	1.55	1.92
Total	5634	100.00	80.53	100.00

Source: Data from Deng et al. (2011).

---

5   The four large commercial banks (commonly called the 'Big Four') are: Industrial and Commercial Bank of China, China Construction Bank, Agricultural Bank of China and Bank of China.

Walter and Howie (2011) argue that banks are basically used as utilities providing unlimited capital, which is then mainly channelled to state-owned enterprises. In this sense, the Chinese economic model during the past three decades has been based on a developmental state that channels funds through the banking system. This has not been without cost. It has been argued that the financial system is quite fragile and that it will need to be recapitalised on a regular basis based on current business practice (for example, Walter and Howie 2011). Reforming the banking sector in China probably constitutes one of the most difficult challenges in the effort to reform the financial sector, as it would result in a significant loss of control over capital allocation in the economy. Nevertheless, it should be seen as a key priority in the effort to secure long-term financial stability. Showing that China's leadership is aware of this problem, Prime Minister, Wen Jiabao, recently stated that the large commercial banks are making profits far too easily due to their monopoly position (Barboza 2012).

Capital Account Restrictions

Capital account restrictions are imposed to obtain greater control over the exchange rate as well as domestic credit flows. A desire to limit competition for 'captive' bank deposits is a further motivation. Typical policies related to the capital account include restrictions or taxes on inflows or outflows as well as alternative exchange rates for different forms of transactions across country borders. Without tight capital account restrictions in place, repressive financial policies such as suppressed interest rates would be much less effective.

Ever since the beginning of the economic reforms in the late 1970s, the Chinese Government has taken gradual steps to liberalise the capital account in China. Foreign direct investment was allowed to flow in early and outward direct investment has been allowed for most of the past decade; however, besides small test cases (such as the qualified foreign institutional investor, QFII, and the qualified domestic institutional investor, QDII, schemes), private portfolio flows have been kept off limits. It is not unusual for developing countries to have relatively low levels of capital account convertibility. One could therefore argue that China's policies follow those of other emerging economies. Figure 3.3 shows Chinn and Ito's (2006) index for capital account openness for the United States and a number of emerging economies. Naturally, the United States has a much higher level of capital account openness; however, even when compared with other, larger emerging economies, China exhibits a relatively low level of capital account convertibility. It is only India that shows signs of a similar low level of liberalised capital account. At the same time, there seems to be a growing consensus among Chinese policymakers that continued capital account liberalisation is desired. A recent report published by the survey and statistics department of the People's Bank of China states that it is now time to open up the capital account. The report even provides a three-step roadmap for such reform over the coming 10 years (*China Securities Journal* 2012). These signals are consistent with the trend towards internationalising the renminbi, which has gathered pace since 2010.

Figure 3.3 Capital Account Openness Index

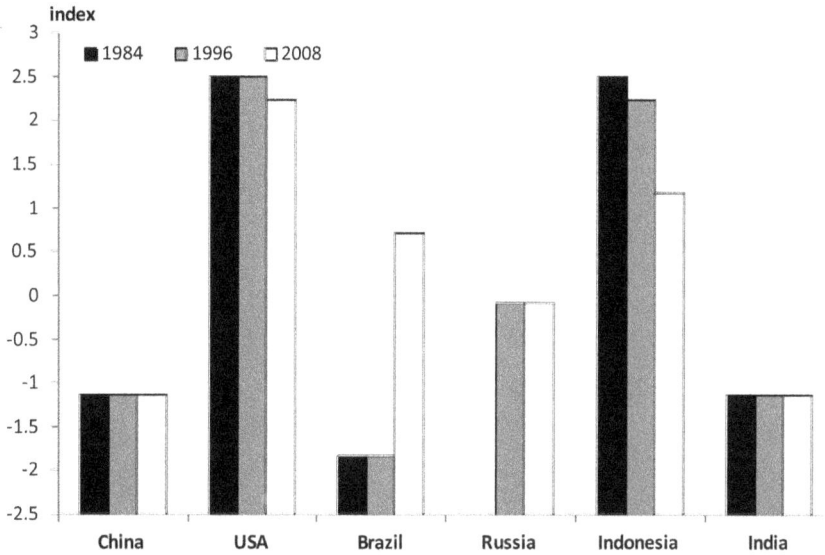

Note: The Chinn–Ito index measures a country's degree of capital account openness. The higher the index is, the higher is the degree of openness.

Source: Data from Chinn and Ito (2006); Ito and Chinn (2010).

Regulations and Supervision in the Banking Sector

Prudential regulation and supervision of banks are important for financial reforms. Not only the formal regulative framework, but also, more importantly, the actual supervisory oversight is crucial in the development of a sound and stable banking system. In the case of China, significant steps have been taken to improve the regulatory framework and the supervision of the banks. Nevertheless, as pointed out in a recent assessment by the World Bank and the IMF, the autonomy of the China Banking Regulatory Commission (CBRC) is challenged due to the fact that the banking system is used so extensively by the Government to pursue its economic policy and to facilitate a high level of credit growth (World Bank 2011).

Security Market Policy

The development of the securities market constitutes an important part of financial development. It allows for investors to further diversify their portfolio holdings and provides alternative channels for funding. The Government can carry out a range of different policies to facilitate the development of domestic securities markets, including the auctioning out of government securities, establishing debt as well as stock markets, making use of different forms of encouragement such as tax incentives, and opening up domestic capital markets to foreign investors, albeit under a quota system (Abiad et al. 2008).

While China has taken steps to develop its securities markets, it is still far from having well-functioning capital markets. The bond market especially has yet to become an important part of the financial system. While the domestic stock market has grown significantly in size over the past decade, it is still far from developing into a mature and well-functioning market. Foreign investors' access to the Chinese stock market is also still very limited; most are allowed to trade only in B-shares, which constitute a very limited share of the overall market, with a relatively small number of QFII firms able to fill an A-share quota. Most trading activities by foreign investors instead take place in Hong Kong (as well as other markets), where a large number of companies from the Mainland have listed, especially during the past decade. Furthermore, supervision of the stock market is generally considered weak and it is commonly argued that the supervisory body, the China Securities Regulatory Commission (CSRC), is in need of considerably more resources in order to function well. Even the recently appointed chairman of the CSRC, Guo Shuqing, has stated that 'insider trading, market manipulation, fraudulent listings and other illegal activities have not only seriously distorted the normal path for investors seeking returns, but have also severely harmed investor confidence and critically affected normal market functions' (Lu et al. 2012). According to a recent joint report by the World Bank and the IMF, the CSRC needs greater operational autonomy. The report also states that the commercial court, enforcement of illegal investment activities and the detection and deterrence of unfair trading practices need to be improved (World Bank 2011). There is thus still much work to be done to facilitate the development of more market-driven and market-based intermediation in China.

Financial Repression and China's Imbalances

In this section, some of the imbalances in the Chinese economy are highlighted. Each of them is then discussed within the framework of repressive financial policies in an attempt to shed light on how such policies might have played a role in the emergence of such imbalances.

Structural Imbalances

Recent research has shown that repressive financial policies are associated with structural imbalances. Typically, countries follow a similar pattern of structural change as their economy develops. Economic growth is accompanied by the gross domestic product (GDP) share of the agricultural sector falling as the GDP share of the industry sector increases. Later, the industry share of GDP decreases as the service sector expands. In countries that make use of strict, repressive financial policies, however, such policies will slow structural transformation. Johansson and Wang (2011) develop a model in which financial repression affects the balance between the industry and the service sectors. The main implication of their model of non-balanced growth is a repressed service sector relative to the industry sector. Their empirical findings on a large set of countries strongly support the theoretical framework, indicating that institutional distortions can have important consequences for a country's economic structure.

This unbalanced pattern of development is quite apparent in the case of China. Figure 3.4 depicts structural change during the reform period. While the agricultural sector follows the typical pattern of structural change seen in many other countries, the industry sector's share of GDP has remained at very high levels throughout the three decades. Given the strong focus on industry during the period before 1978, industry's share of total GDP at the beginning of the reforms was at a very high level. The fact that it has remained at this level throughout such a long period of very high economic growth indicates that the economic structure has become heavily distorted.

Figure 3.4 Sectors' Share of GDP, 1978–2008

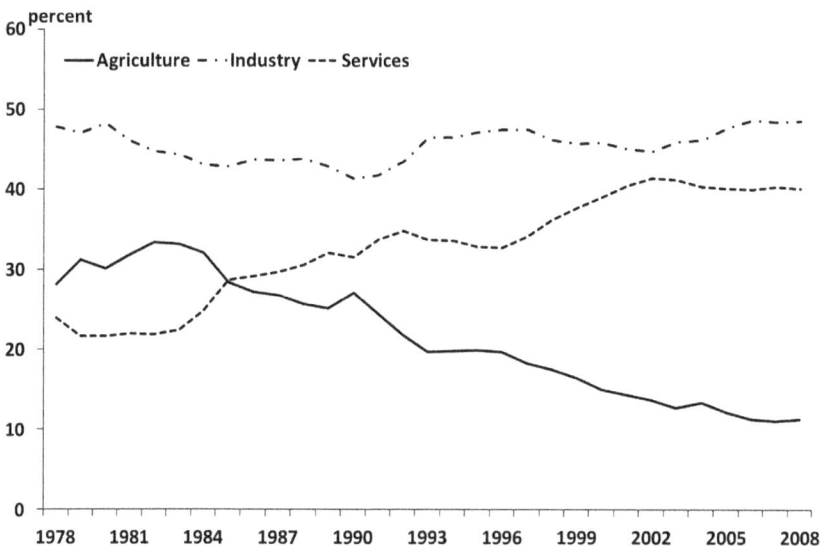

Source: Data from National Bureau of Statistics of China.

Structural imbalances similar to the ones found in China are arguably synonymous with the developmental state often found in East Asian countries. Strong state intervention combined with extensive planning and regulation in countries that are late to industrialise mean that it is the state itself that takes on different developmental functions and thus leads the industrialisation process (Amsden 1989; Johnson 1982; Wade 1990). China, perhaps more than any other country, portrays this development model and also shows how the success of state intervention during one phase might be followed by the state acting as an interest group and thus serving as an obstruction to ongoing adaptation. The empirical evidence found in Johansson and Wang (2011) and the fact that the developmental state most often is tied to a heavy reliance on the development of industry support the argument that less repressive financial policies would most likely help mitigate the disparities in China's economic structure. A rebalancing of the economic structure would in itself also have ramifications for a number of other areas of the Chinese economy, including its external balances, the labour market, and so on.

External Imbalances

China's large external imbalances have been a sensitive and heavily debated topic, especially since the beginning of the global financial crisis. While China has maintained what many have argued is a significantly undervalued currency during most of the past decade (Frankel 2006; Goldstein and Lardy 2006), the Chinese current account surplus has been persistent during this period. Figure 3.5 shows the current account and the trade balance during the past three decades. The trade balance widened dramatically from 2003 to 2007 from an already high level. It is only during the later stages of the global financial crisis that the trade surplus has decreased.

There are a number of plausible reasons for China's external imbalances. For example, the exchange rate has often been singled out as a main reason behind China's growing trade surplus. What has often been overlooked, however, is how repressive financial policies in general can affect a country's external balances. In a recent study, Johansson and Wang (2012a) use a panel of countries to analyse the relationship between financial repression and external balances. They suggested two hypotheses for how repressive financial policies could affect the current account. First, they build on the model developed in their earlier work (Johansson and Wang 2011) and argue that financial repression can cause external imbalances due to the imbalance in the basic economic structure. As in the case of China, if repressive financial policies are used to develop the industry sector at the expense of other sectors, the result is most likely a strong increase in exports, as manufacturing makes up a significant part of the industry sector. Second, financial repression can have an effect on external balances by way of hindering financial development. Financial development is associated with a lower level of the current account, since financially developed economies are less anxious about their international financial resilience. While the empirical results in Johansson and Wang (2012a) mainly support the first of these hypotheses, the second one is plausible, perhaps especially in the case of China. Recent research thus highlights fundamental structural features in the financial sector as being at least partly responsible for external imbalances. In the case of China, a heavily repressed financial sector is likely to have helped the country's external imbalance become even more severe during the past decade.

Figure 3.5 China's Current Account and Trade Balance, 1981–2010

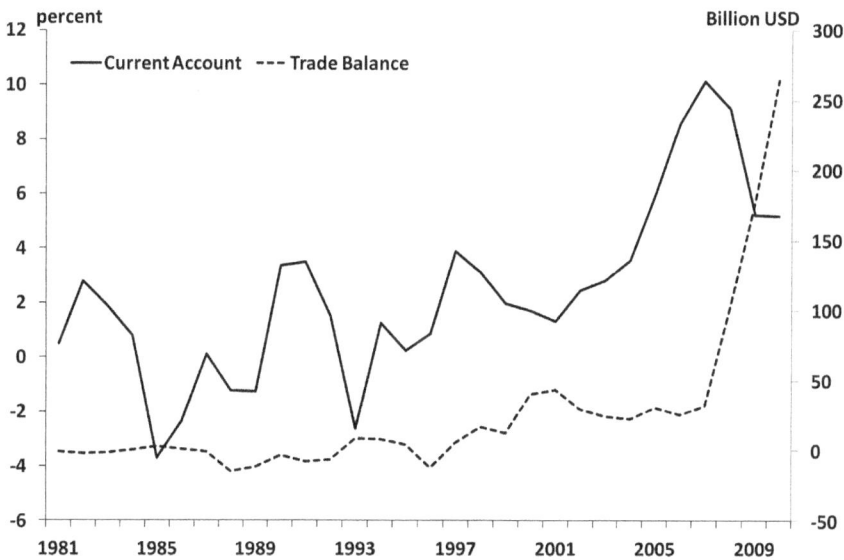

Note: The current account is on the left axis, the trade balance on the right.

Source: Data from National Bureau of Statistics of China.

Inequality

Rising inequality is one of the primary concerns of the Chinese Government. It fears that the growing divergence between rural and urban incomes and the general income inequality in the country could result in an increasing level of social instability. Figure 3.6 shows just how severe the level of inequality has become during the reform period. The Gini coefficient shows a steady increase during the whole period. Starting from a relatively modest level of 0.29 in 1978, it increased to close to 0.47 in 2005 (Fang and Yu 2012). The subject has become so sensitive that the Chinese Government will not even publish the

Gini coefficient and has not done so for the past decade.[6] While the National Bureau of Statistics argues that this is due to the problem of incomplete data, the Government has been criticised for trying to downplay the large wealth gap in the country (Fang and Yu 2012). Figure 3.6 also shows the disparity between rural and urban incomes in China. The urban–rural income ratio follows the general inequality as measured by the Gini coefficient closely, indicating that the growing divide between rural and urban households makes up a significant part of the overall income inequality in the country.

Figure 3.6 Gini Coefficient and Urban–Rural Income Ratio, 1978–2005

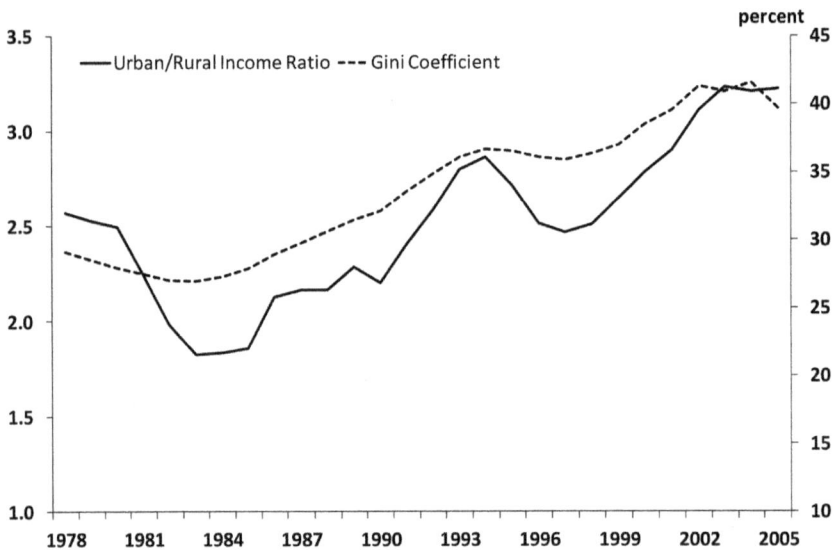

Note: The urban–rural income ratio is on the left axis, the Gini coefficient on the right.

Source: Data from National Bureau of Statistics of China.

Repressive financial policies can result in higher levels of income inequality. As Johansson and Wang (2012b) point out, repressed interest rates can lead to uneven returns to savings in countries with fragmented financial markets. One of the reasons for this is that affluent people might have better access to alternative investment instruments. For rural households in China, the number of alternatives for where to invest savings is limited and the most common form of savings is a typical bank account. For more affluent people, there are alternative investment opportunities, including a range of financial instruments and the investor housing market, which is unaffordable for ordinary Chinese. Furthermore, and as noted earlier, repressive financial policies can cause

---

6 The Gini coefficient measures inequality on a scale from zero to one, where zero reflects complete equality and one represents complete inequality. It has been argued that, when taking hidden income into account, China's Gini coefficient is most likely significantly higher than 0.5 (Wang and Woo 2011).

severe disruptions to the process of financial development. Demirguc-Kunt and Levine (2009) note that, with large financial market imperfections, investment opportunities become a function of dynastic assets. This is because a producer's wealth has a large effect on problems with moral hazard and adverse selection that put constraints on opportunities. Furthermore, financial development is linked to equality through other mechanisms. For instance, efficient credit markets allow for people with high ability to access quality schooling regardless of parental wealth, thus decreasing the potential for permanent, or intergenerational, inequality (Demirguc-Kunt and Levine 2009).

Given the potentially important effect that repressive financial policies can have on income inequality over time, such policies are working against what the Chinese Government is trying to achieve. Inequality is one of the imbalances emphasised in the Twelfth Five-Year Plan; however, policy discussions so far have not focused on the relationship between severe repressive financial policies and inequality. It is likely that the high level of financial repression in China, especially the excessive use of repressed interest rates, has added to the growing disparities in household income. Thus, if the Government were to ease up on such policies, it might prove productive in the battle against inequality.

Moving Forward with Financial Reforms

Financial liberalisation poses difficult challenges to any country. One of the fundamental lessons learned from failed liberalisation processes around the world is that sequencing is imperative. In the case of China, although capital account liberalisation is regarded as important and is even included in the Twelfth Five-Year Plan, a complete opening up of the capital account would preferably come after other financial reforms have taken place. The key role interest rate restrictions play in fuelling the banking system with cheap capital means that a sudden and comprehensive liberalisation of the capital account without taking the restrictive interest rate controls into account could generate a massive outflow of capital if Chinese households and companies were able to place their capital in investments in foreign markets and if expected returns abroad were to be much higher than those at home (net of foreign currency risk perceptions). Comparing interest rates in different countries, this would not constitute a significant problem at the moment as the Chinese interest rate is now significantly higher than interest rates in the United States and Europe. Nevertheless, the existing interest rate differences are a result of economic crises in both the United States and Europe and this could change as time passes. Similarly, if significant weaknesses are found in the domestic banking system, especially during a time of crisis, an open capital account would accelerate bank runs. Thus, supervision and regulatory practice in the banking system need to be in place before there is a complete reform of the capital account. Lardy and Douglass (2011) note that for capital account liberalisation to work well, there is also a need for sufficiently developed domestic capital markets, as they provide incentives for further commercialisation of domestic banks, enable absorption of large capital inflows and reduce the risk of currency mismatches. Lardy and Douglass also argue that there is a need for exchange rate flexibility, since a significantly under or overvalued currency would result in large capital inflows or outflows if the capital account is opened. A recent report by the People's Bank of China added macroeconomic stability and adequate foreign exchange reserves as important precursors for continued capital account reform (China Securities Journal 2012).

Besides interest rate liberalisation, continued efforts to strengthen the regulatory framework and supervision for both the banking sector and the securities markets are needed. The lack of independence for both the CBRC and the CSRC needs to be remedied so that both of these sectors will become more market driven.

Conclusions

Financial repression affects not only financial development and economic growth in general. It can also be the root cause of a number of different economic imbalances, some of which have been discussed in this chapter. Some of these economic imbalances have developed into difficult challenges for the Chinese Government. While the country's current account seems to have moved closer to a reasonable level of late, it is still too early to tell if this is temporary and due only to a significant fall in demand from its main trading partners due to the global financial crisis or if it is more permanent in nature. In addition to external imbalances, structural imbalances at home and a severe level of inequality constitute some of the primary difficulties that China's policymakers need to address. While financial repression is certainly not the only factor causing such imbalances in China, less repressive financial policies could help mitigate them. Financial liberalisation would decrease the heavy reliance on investment and heavy industrial development and free resources for the expansion of the service sector and consumption. Similarly, continued financial reforms would result in a significant increase in financial development, which would have multifarious benefits from higher returns to household savings and to better opportunities for individuals from less affluent households to access high-quality education. These potential changes are likely to help bring a stop to the negative trend of increasing inequality in China.

As noted in this chapter, recent research has brought the formerly disparate fields of financial repression and economic imbalances together. Additional research along these lines is important to fully understand the many ways in which repressive financial policies can affect an economy. Such research is also likely to help shed light on issues that have been overlooked in the debate on the positive and negative effects of financial liberalisation.

Looking at each of the dimensions of financial reform discussed in this chapter, it is clear that continued reforms are needed for China to develop a well-functioning financial system. It is also important, however, to identify a proper sequence for each of these reforms, as swift reforms in certain areas without taking related repressive policies into account could result in instability, which might discourage policymakers following through on the entire package, which would be a damaging outcome for both the Chinese and the global citizenry.

References

Abiad, A., Detragiache, E. and Tressel, T., 2008, *A new database of financial reforms*, IMF Working Paper WP/08/266, International Monetary Fund, Washington, DC.

Amsden, A., 1989, *Asia's Next Giant: South Korea and late industrialization*, Oxford University Press, New York.

Barboza, D., 2012, 'Wen calls China banks too powerful', *The New York Times*, 3 April, <http://www.nytimes.com/2012/04/04/business/global/chinas-big-banks-too-powerful-premier-says.html?_r=1>

China Securities Journal, 2012, 'The fundamental conditions for China to accelerate capital account opening are ripe', *China Securities Journal*, [Online; in Chinese], 24 February, <http://www.cs.com.cn/xwzx/07/201202/t20120223_3253890.html>

Chinn, M. D. and Ito, H., 2006, 'What matters for financial development? Capital controls, institutions, and interactions', *Journal of Development Economics*, vol. 81, pp. 163–92.

Demirguc-Kunt, A. and Levine, R., 2009, 'Finance and inequality: theory and evidence', *Annual Review of Financial Economics*, vol. 1, pp. 287–318.

Deng, Y., Morck, R., Wu, J. and Yeung, B., 2011, *Monetary and fiscal stimuli, ownership structure, and China's housing market*, NBER Working Paper Series No. 16871, National Bureau of Economic Research, Cambridge, Mass.

Fang, X. and Yu, L., 2012, 'Government refuses to release Gini coefficient', *Caixin Online*, 18 January, <http://english.caixin.com/2012-01-18/100349814.html>

Feng, X., Johansson, A. C. and Zhang, T., 2011, *Political participation and entrepreneurial initial public offerings in China*, China Economic Research Center Working Paper Series 2011-17, Stockholm School of Economics, Stockholm.

Frankel, J. A., 2006, 'On the yuan: the choice between adjustment under a fixed exchange rate and adjustment under a flexible rate', *CESifo Economic Studies*, vol. 52, pp. 246–75.

Goldstein, M. and Lardy, N., 2006, 'China's exchange rate dilemma', *American Economic Review, AEA Papers and Proceedings*, vol. 96, pp. 422–26.

Hellmann, T., Murdock, K. and Stiglitz, J., 1997, 'Financial restraint: toward a new paradigm', in M. Aoki, H.-K. Kim and M. Okuno-Fujuwara (eds), *The Role of Government in East Asian Economic Development: Comparative institutional analysis*, Clarendon Press, Oxford, UK.

Hellmann, T., Murdock, K. and Stiglitz, J., 2000, 'Liberalisation, moral hazard in banking and prudential regulation: are capital controls enough?', *American Economic Review*, vol. 90, pp. 147–65.

Hu, J., 2011, Full text of Chinese President Hu Jintao's speech at Opening Ceremony of Boao Forum, *Xinhua*, 15 April 2011, <http://news.xinhuanet.com/english2010/china/2011-04/15/c_13830786.htm>

Huang, Y. and Wang, B., 2010, 'Rebalancing China's economic structure', *East Asia Forum*, 3 September, <http://www.eastasiaforum.org/2010/09/03/rebalancing-chinas-economic-structure/>

Huang, Y. P. and Wang, X. 2011, 'Does financial repression inhibit or facilitate economic growth? A case study of Chinese reform experience', *Oxford Bulletin of Economics and Statistics*, vol. 73, pp. 833–55.

International Monetary Fund (IMF), 2011, *People's Republic of China: financial system stability assessment*, IMF Country Report No. 11/321, International Monetary Fund, Washington, DC.

Ito, H. and Chinn, M. D., 2010, Notes on the Chinn–Ito financial openness index: 2008 update, Unpublished ms.

Johansson, A. C. and Wang, X., 2011, *Financial repression and structural imbalances*, China Economic Research Center Working Paper 2011-19, Stockholm School of Economics, Stockholm.

Johansson, A. C. and Wang, X., 2012a, *Financial repression and external imbalances*, China Economic Research Center Working Paper 2012-20, Stockholm School of Economics, Stockholm.

Johansson, A. C. and Wang, X., 2012b, Financial repression and inequality, Unpublished ms, Stockholm School of Economics, Stockholm.

Johnson, C., 1982, *MITI and the Japanese Miracle*, Stanford University Press, Stanford, Calif.

King, R. G. and Levine, R., 1993, 'Finance, entrepreneurship, and growth: Theory and evidence', *Journal of Monetary Economics* 32, 513-542.

Lardy, N., 2008, *Financial repression in China*, Policy Brief PB08-8, Peterson Institute of International Economics, Washington, DC.

Lardy, N., 2012, *Sustaining China's Economic Growth After the Global Financial Crisis*, Peterson Institute for International Economics, Washington, DC.

Lardy, N. and Douglass, P., 2011, *Capital account liberalisation and the role of the renminbi*, Working Paper Series 11-6, Peterson Institute for International Economics, Washington, DC.

Levine, R., 2005. 'Finance and Growth: Theory, Mechanisms and Evidence', in Aghion, P. and Durlauf, S.N. (eds), *Handbook of Economic Growth*, Vol 1, Part A, Elsevier, 865-934.

Lu, S. F. and Yao, Y., 2009, 'The effectiveness of law, financial development, and economic growth in an economy of financial repression: evidence from China', *World Development*, vol. 37, pp. 763–77.

Lu, Y., Wang, Z. and Zheng, F., 2012, 'Can anyone save stock market supervision?', *Caixin Online*, 19 March, <http://english.caixin.com/2012-03-19/100369865_3.html>

McKinnon, R. I., 1973, *Money and Capital in Economic Development*, The Brookings Institution, Washington, DC.

Pagano, M., 1993, 'Financial markets and growth: an overview', *European Economic Review*, vol. 37, pp. 613–22.

Podpiera, R., 2006, *Progress in China's banking sector reform: has bank behavior changed?*, IMF Working Paper WP/06/71, International Monetary Fund, Washington, DC.

Roubini, N. and Sala-i-Martin, X., 1992, 'Financial repression and economic growth', *Journal of Development Economics*, vol. 39, pp. 5–30.

Shaw, A. S., 1973, *Financial Deepening in Economic Development*, Oxford University Press, New York.

Shih, V. C., 2008, *Factions and Finance in China: Elite conflict and inflation*, Cambridge University Press, New York.

Stiglitz, J. E., 1994, 'The role of the state in financial markets', in M. Bruno and B. Pleskovic (eds), *Proceedings of the World Bank Annual Conference on Development Economics, 1993: Supplement to the World Bank Economic Review and the World Bank Research Observer*, The World Bank, Washington, DC.

Stiglitz, J. E., 2000, 'Capital market liberalisation, economic growth and instability', *World Development*, vol. 28, pp. 1075–86.

Stiglitz, J. E. and Weiss, A., 1981, 'Credit rationing in markets with imperfect information', *American Economic Review*, vol. 71, pp. 393–410.

Wade, R., 1990, *Governing the Market: Economic theory and the role of government in East Asian industrialisation*, Princeton University Press, Princeton, NJ.

Walter, C. E. and Howie, F. J. T., 2011, *Red Capitalism*, John Wiley & Sons, Singapore.

Wang, X. and Woo, W. T., 2011, 'The size and distribution of hidden household income in China', *Asian Economic Papers*, vol. 10, pp. 1–26.

Wei, S.-J. and Wang, T., 1997, 'The Siamese twins: do state-owned banks favor state-owned enterprises in China?', *China Economic Review*, vol. 8, pp. 19–29.

World Bank, 2011, *China: Financial sector assessment*, The World Bank, Washington, DC.

World Bank, 2012, *China 2030: Building a modern, harmonious and creative high-income society*, The World Bank, Washington, DC.

Yao, Y., 2011, 'Weak global demand should be a wake-up call for China', *The Financial Times*, 20 October.

4. Narrowing China's Current Account Surplus:

The role of saving, investment and the renminbi

Guonan Ma, Robert McCauley and Lillie Lam[1]

Introduction

The widening of the Chinese current account surplus from the neighbourhood of 2 per cent of GDP about the turn of the century to as much as 10 per cent before the global financial crisis in 2008 led to calls for the renminbi (RMB) to be revalued. The rationale was that a stronger renminbi would make Chinese exports less competitive and imports cheaper for Chinese consumers. This rationale sees the external surplus as a function of relative prices so that exchange-rate appreciation can narrow the surplus to a desired level.[2]

Another, and in many ways richer, conception of China's external surplus is that it reflects a shortfall of the domestic absorption of output—whether consumption, investment or government spending—in relation to the economy's productive capacity. Viewed from this perspective, the Chinese economy in this century showed a rise in investment in relation to output, but an even larger rise in savings. The gap between investment's substantial rise and the stronger rise in savings widened the current account surplus. On this view, to understand the widening of China's current account requires an answer to the question: what drove savings up?

Our examination of China's savings rate emphasises the contribution of both corporate and government savings more than that of households. On this view, a popular account of the rise in Chinese savings—namely, higher household income insecurity—suffers from its silence on corporate and government savings, which rose more. Corporate savings rose in classical fashion as profits rose, and wages declined, in income. Government savings rose as the revenue dividend from higher growth was poured into public capital formation.

---

1   The views expressed in this chapter are not necessarily those of BIS. We would like to thank the participants of the SUERF Conference in Brussels in May 2011 and Stephen Cecchetti and Lu Feng for discussion.

2   Along these lines, Cline (2012) argues that the renminbi appreciation explains the 'lion's share' of the decline of the Chinese current account surplus of 7.4 per cent of GDP between 2007 and 2010, with help from higher oil prices and lower global interest rates. Moreover, he reports (p. 12) that 'the policy experiment in which the real effective level of the renminbi continues to rise at 3 per cent annually shows that the result would be [to] shift China into approximate current account balance by 2017'. Cline is right to single out returns on China's international assets as a determinant of the current account. He et al. (2012a) consider how these returns might be affected by increasing the proportion of China's external assets held in private Chinese hands.

When the global financial crisis hit, Chinese Government spending increased and agencies of sub-national governments borrowed from banks to boost infrastructure and other public investment. This response shrank the current account surplus substantially but only by raising investment to an unprecedented and unsustainable share of output. The scale and distribution of any credit losses from this investment boom remain a matter of keen debate.

Looking forward, demography and domestic policies are working together to narrow China's current account surplus, which indeed shrank in 2011 to below 3 per cent of China's GDP. As labour force growth slows, real wages are rising rapidly, making Chinese exports less competitive, allowing higher consumption and squeezing corporate profits and savings. For its part, the Government might shift its spending from building infrastructure to providing services.

In this scenario of a Chinese economy rebalancing towards consumption and government services, the exchange rate can continue to play a complementary role. If the renminbi continues to appreciate in real terms, it would help to shift production from exports to goods and services for home use. In fact, after policymakers broke the peg to the dollar in 2005, the renminbi traded so as to appreciate gradually against a broad basket of trading partner currencies in 2006–08. This experiment was interrupted by the global financial crisis, but appreciation resumed in some fashion from mid-2010.

However one interprets the underlying policy, the nominal renminbi had by the end of 2011 appreciated by 21 per cent against its trading partners' currencies since June 2005. China's relatively high inflation pushed up the real effective appreciation to 30 per cent over the same period. And this real appreciation approaches 50 per cent, if one focuses on unit labour costs rather than consumer prices. More likely than not, such a scale of broad real exchange rate appreciation is narrowing China's current account surpluses.

This chapter first reviews Chinese savings and investment behaviour, noting their more separate evolution over time. Then we review the management of the renminbi.

Saving–Investment Perspective

China has run one of the largest surpluses in the world in recent years. Its current account surplus widened from 5 per cent and 10 per cent of its own GDP between 2005 and 2007, before narrowing to less than 3 per cent by 2011. In terms of global GDP, it ranged between 0.3 per cent and 0.7 per cent. As a result, within one decade, China swung from net international debtor of 10 per cent of GDP to net international creditor of 30 per cent of GDP, despite per capita GDP still well below US$5000 (Ma and Zhou 2009). In order to examine the sources of China's current account surplus, we first focus on savings and investment, whose gap, by national income accounting identity, is the current account balance (Figure 4.1, top panel).

Figure 4.1 China's Gross National Saving and Gross Capital Formation as a Percentage of GDP

Saving–Investment Balance and Current Account[1]

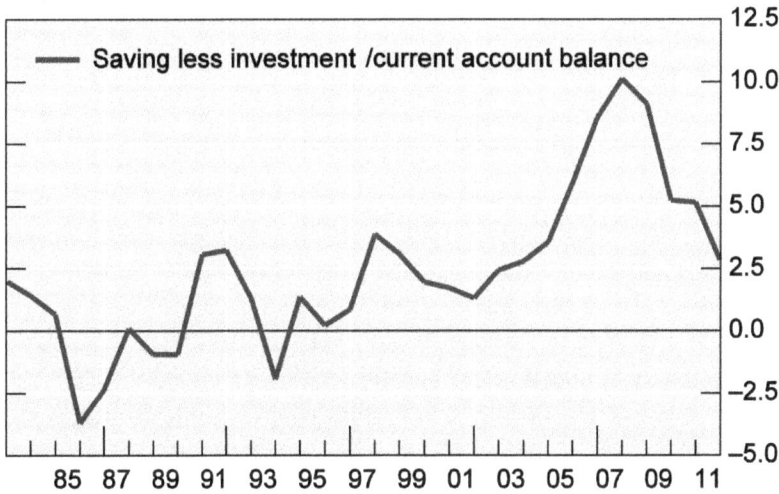

Gross National Saving and Capital Formation

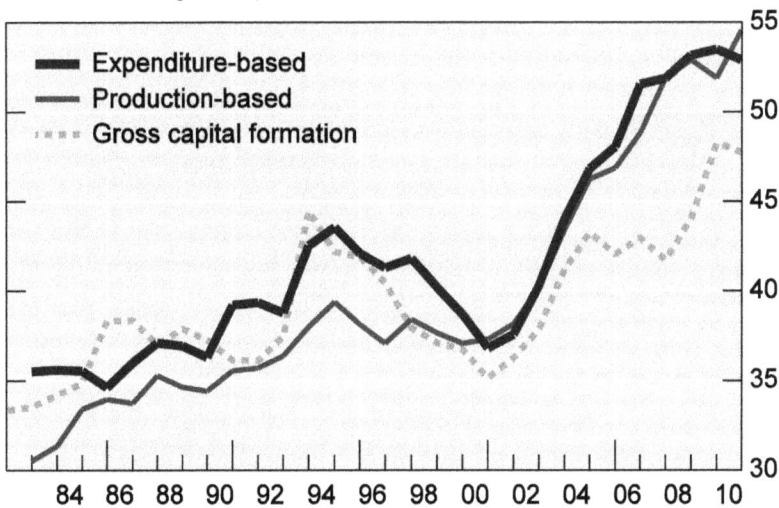

[1] Gross national saving is estimated using either expenditure-based GDP or production-based GDP. By definition, the current account balance equals expenditure-based gross national saving minus gross capital formation.

Sources: National Bureau of Statistics of China (NBS); authors' own estimates.

The Chinese economy both saves and invests a lot. In 2010, its gross national saving reached 53 per cent of GDP, and investment spending reached 48 per cent (Figure 4.1, bottom panel), leaving a current account surplus at 5 per cent of GDP. The contributions of such high saving and investment to global imbalances and financial crises have attracted much attention (ADB 2009; Bernanke 2005; Zhou 2009).

A high and rising saving rate implies a low and falling consumption share. Private consumption as a share of China's GDP declined from 50 per cent to 33 per cent between 1990 and 2010. Contrary to common perceptions, however, China's private consumption has grown at a strong pace of 8 per cent to 9 per cent per annum over the past 20 years; the penetration of colour televisions, refrigerators, washing machines and airconditioners has increased tenfold.

Yet, the overall Chinese economy grew even faster than consumer demand. GDP grew more than 10 per cent annually between 1990 and 2010, powered mainly by stronger investment demand. Gross capital formation increased at a breakneck speed of 15 per cent a year over these two decades, as its share in GDP rose from 36 per cent to a staggering 48 per cent by 2010. Remarkably, such rising investment has been more than fully financed by even faster rising saving since the early 2000s. China's gross national saving rose from less than 40 per cent of GDP in 1990 to 53 per cent in 2010. As noted, the current account surplus widened from 2 per cent of GDP in the early 2000s to 10 per cent in 2007, before narrowing to less than 3 per cent in 2011.

Thus, from the saving–investment perspective, not weak investment but extremely strong saving provides the key to understanding China's recent large current account surpluses. Here we first take a closer look at the dynamics of the Chinese saving rate before examining the trends in its investment rate and drawing their joint implication for its current account balance. Admittedly, saving and investment interact with each other and are jointly determined. Indeed, as we argue below, strong profitability raised corporate savings and in turn provided incentives for investment, while high investment boosted growth, thus lifting savings. Still, it is possible to discuss savings and investment separately because the Chinese economy has become more open in recent years, despite binding capital controls.

Figure 4.2 Feldstein–Horioka Time-Series Regression: Annual data for China

Year-on-Year Change as a Percentage of Lagged GDP[1]

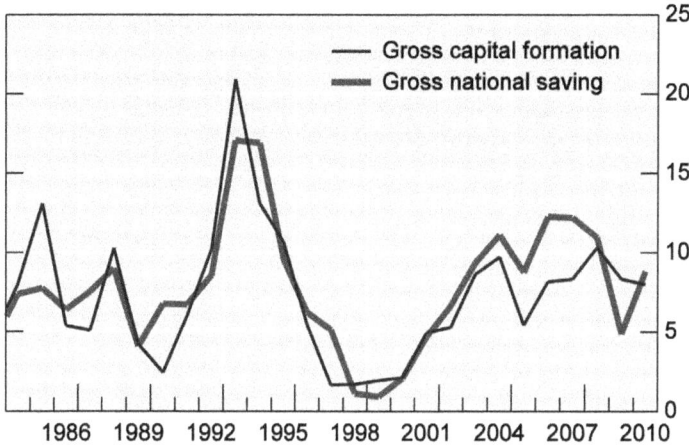

The Estimated Betas of Gross National Saving

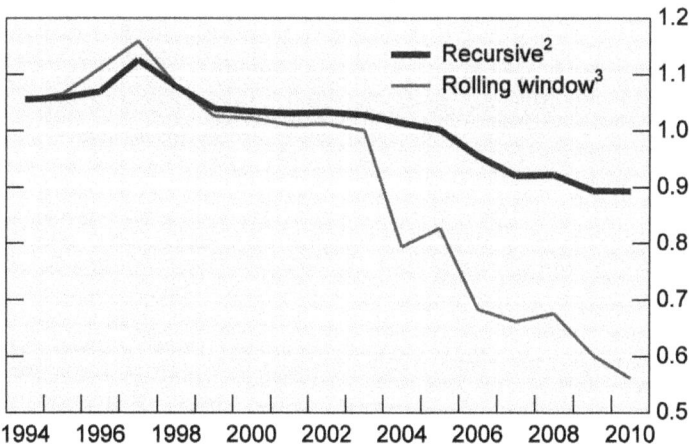

[1] $(\Delta I_t)/GDP_{t-1}$ and $(\Delta S_t)/GDP_{t-1}$, where I stands for gross capital formation and S is gross national saving.

[2] The regression equation is $(\Delta I_t)/GDP_{t-1} = \alpha + \beta\ (\Delta S_t)/GDP_{t-1}$. Recursive regressions, with 1984 as the starting year and the ending year corresponding with that indicated by the x-axis. Regressions of rolling 10-year windows, with ending year corresponding with the x-axis.

[3] The F-statistics, log likelihood ratio and Wald statistics all confirm a break point of 2001 in the data sample. The nulls that ß equals unity for the sub-sample of 1984–2001 and zero for the sub-sample of 2002–10 are both accepted.

Sources: CEIC; authors' own estimates.

In particular, a simple Feldstein–Horioka (1980) analysis shows that savings and investment no longer track each other as they used to (Figure 4.2, top panel). Whereas annual Chinese data indicate no significant difference from a one-to-one relationship between changes in investment and savings before 2000, subsequently a smaller change in investment is associated with a given change in saving. The beta in a regression of changes in investment as a ratio to lagged GDP on changes in savings as a ratio to lagged GDP run over progressively longer periods starting in 1984 dips towards 0.9. More tellingly, the beta estimated over a rolling 10-year window drops to 0.5 for the sample ending in 2010.[3] Given that the economy opened up with World Trade Organisation (WTO) accession in 2001, the Chow test rejects the identity of the estimated betas over the two sub-samples of 1984–2001 and 2002–10. A coefficient of 0.5 is close to the 0.58 that Blanchard and Giavazzi (2002) report for the Organisation for Economic Cooperation and Development (OECD) cross-section over 1975–2001, while it is above their estimates for the European Union in the 1990s. These regressions describe Chinese savings and investment that can to some extent be separately discussed.

China's Exceptionally High Saving Rate and Factors Behind It

China's aggregate saving rate has been exceptionally high relative to its own history, to the saving of its thrifty Asian peers or to any empirical model predictions. During the 2000s, China's aggregate marginal propensity to save exceeded 60 per cent. Relative to GDP, China has edged out Singapore to become the highest saver in the world. China emerges as a big outlier in cross-sectional or panel regressions, with its actual saving rate typically 10 to 15 percentage points higher than predictions (Ma and Wang 2010).

Both the dynamics and the composition of China's rising gross national saving defy simple interpretations. All three sectors in the Chinese economy—household, corporate and government—have been high savers. Yet, taken individually, none is an exceptional saver by comparison with its global counterparts. Instead, high saving by all three sectors makes China's aggregate saving rate exceptionally high. And contrary to conventional wisdom, the household sector accounted for less than one-sixth of the increase in China's gross national saving in the 1990s and 2000s. The corporate and government sectors made bigger contributions to the rising Chinese aggregate saving (Figure 4.3, top panel). In particular, the saving of the government sector almost tripled—from 4.4 per cent of GDP in 1992 to 11 per cent by 2008—as most of the robust gains in government revenues during this period were invested in physical infrastructure rather than used to boost social services. The share of China's government saving is also relatively high compared with other countries except Korea (Figure 4.3, bottom panel).

---

3 In statistical terms, a one-tailed test does not reject that the 2010 recursively estimated beta of 0.9 is equal to 1, while the betas estimated by the rolling 10-year regressions ending in each year 2007–10 are significantly smaller than unity at the 5 per cent level.

Figure 4.3 China's Gross National Saving, by Institutional Sector, as a Percentage of GDP

China's Gross National Saving[1]

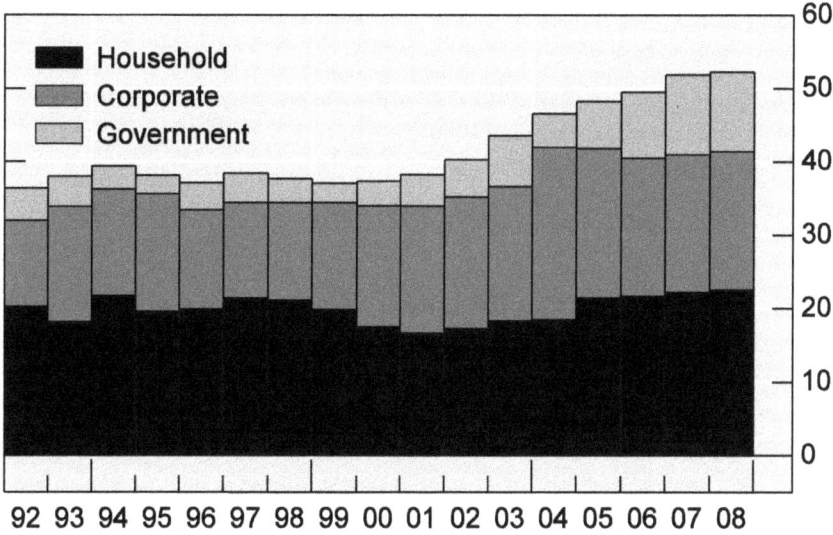

2005–07 Average, by Market

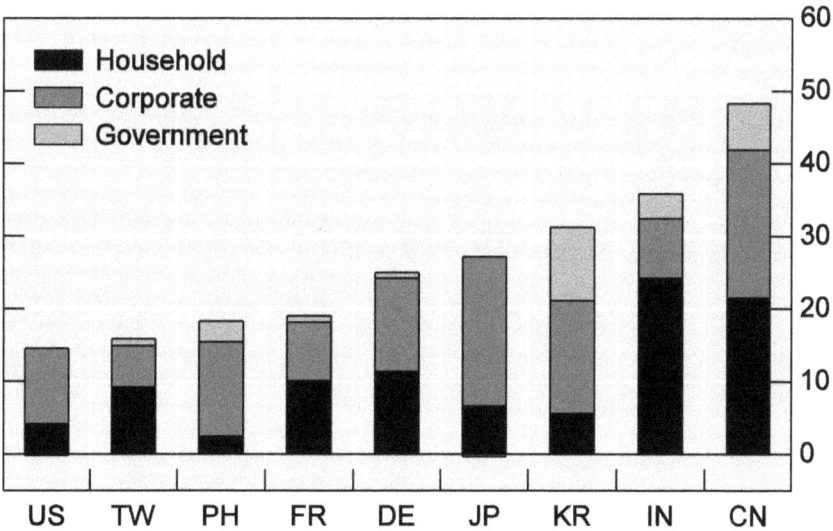

[1] Saving under flow-of-funds statistics.

Note: CN = China; DE = Germany; FR = France; IN = India; JP = Japan; KR = Korea; PH = Philippines; TW = Chinese Taipei; US = United States.

Sources: Asian Development Bank (ADB); CEIC; NBS; OECD; authors' own estimates.

The factors behind China's high and rising saving rate are multiple, leaving many puzzles to be resolved and suggesting that a cocktail of policies might be needed to rebalance the Chinese economy. At minimum, the principal causes for high Chinese saving in the 2000s include two sets of interacting forces (Ma and Wang 2010).

The first set consists of powerful structural forces in the domestic Chinese economy. As described by Lewis (1954), surplus rural labour allowed rapid industrialisation paced by capital-widening investment and provided ready migrants willing to work at the going wage. The potential was heightened by the commune system having kept millions of surplus peasants down on the farm for decades and a very compressed demographic transition, featuring a rapidly falling ratio of child dependants to working-age adults. This transfer started as the communes collapsed under Deng Xiaoping. A central result of such a large-scale transfer of labour at a relatively stable wage is a falling labour share of output and rising profit and savings rate. High returns to capital stimulated investment, driving faster growth, which further lifted the saving rate. China's WTO accession and the supportive global growth environment in the early 2000s also accommodated this profound transition.

The other set of factors encompasses institutional changes during the 1990s and 2000s. These include labour downsizing at state-owned companies, reform of the pension system and the introduction of private home ownership. First, employment at state-owned companies, which had provided much social welfare and security, almost halved during 1995–2005. This restructuring enhanced efficiency and profit in firms while presenting workers with increased job insecurity and expenditure uncertainty. These added to private saving by both the corporate and the household sectors. Second, pension reforms reduced pensions and increased contributions to government pension schemes, thereby lifting both private and public saving. Finally, the introduction of private home ownership in the 1990s boosted household planning for home purchase and increased land revenues to the Government in a high-growth environment, again pushing up both private and public saving.

In addition, other government policies might have played a role in lifting the Chinese saving rate. These include promoting officials who invest rather than provide social services, slow weaving of the new social safety net after the widespread layoffs by state-owned companies, retaining entry barriers to (and levying heavy taxes on) services and maintaining limits on credit access by small companies and households. Of these, the most important might be the promotion policy for officials. Since those presiding over rapid growth were rewarded, local government officials responded by investing additional public revenues to boost local GDP growth in the short term and their odds of their promotion. China's government consumption is 12 per cent of GDP—below the OECD average of 15 per cent.

Other commonly cited policies are somewhat less convincing accounts of the path of Chinese savings. It is sometimes suggested that high Chinese saving mostly arises from government subsidies, price distortions and the market power of state firms in telecommunications and energy. While such frictions can help explain inefficiency, they do not offer useful insights into why China's aggregate saving rate suddenly surged in the 2000s, after a period of significant economic liberalisation (Ma and Wang 2010).

Two examples help make the case. First, indigenous private firms have done much of the higher corporate saving. Their uncertain and restricted access to credit could account for their reliance on retained earnings to fund expansion. On this view, not subsidies and monopolistic state firms but rather limited credit access of private firms makes sense of higher corporate savings; however, limited access by small firms to external financing is felt to be a problem globally, and it is not clear whether the Chinese situation is worse than that of its emerging-market peers. Second, another frequently cited factor—the limited availability of consumer credit—could indeed force Chinese households to save more than otherwise. But in this century, household loans have expanded significantly relative to both the household income and the economy (see below), precisely at a time when both the gross national saving rate and the household saving rate rose markedly.

Structural Factors Influencing the Prospective Saving Rate

The medium-term outlook for China's saving rate matters not only for its future economic growth path but also for the rebalancing of the global economy. One key challenge for Chinese policymakers in the next decade, though, is to maintain robust internal demand while rebalancing the economy more towards consumption. Both domestic structural factors and policy measures could influence such a transition. Three structural factors stand out: state-enterprise restructuring, demographic change and continued urbanisation.

First, large-scale labour retrenchment is now behind us. Going forward, the scope for big, one-off cost savings and efficiency gains in the corporate sector is limited, as will be the associated income and expenditure uncertainties for Chinese households. What is more, new restructuring would cause less insecurity since the social safety net is nowadays provided by the Central Government. Less restructuring and insecurity will dampen private saving by both firms and households.

Second, China can hardly avoid a rapidly ageing population and slower growth of its labour force in this decade. Indeed, China's working-age population could stop growing in 2015 and thereafter shrink for 10 years or more. This could lead to a declining household saving rate and a slower pace of corporate investment spending, likely resulting in lower potential output growth unless productivity growth rises in an offsetting manner.

Third, while the migration from agriculture to the cities is likely to continue in the years ahead, there are signs that (and considerable academic debate about whether) China has reached the 'Lewis turning point' at which the modern economy has absorbed the surplus farmers (Garnaut 2010). When pressure on labour supplies in agriculture reaches this point, industrial wages rise to attract further migrants into industry. Then, wages can rise faster than productivity, raising labour's share of income and depressing corporate saving (while appreciating the renminbi in real terms), and personal consumption can displace investment. Recent reports of double-digit wage growth make this conjecture plausible.

Taken together, these medium-term structural forces suggest that China's aggregate saving rate over the coming years could plateau and then ease off noticeably from its current half of output. During this process, government policy can play a role in assisting the desired transition to a more balanced growth model, including: 1) further deregulation to reduce entry barriers in labour-intensive services to create more jobs and thereby to support the demand for labour and wage growth; 2) a stronger but sustainable social safety net; and 3) improved incentives for government provision of services (Ma and McCauley 2012).

China's High Investment Rate and Factors Behind It

We next turn to China's investment rate, highlighting its recent trends and reviewing its possible determinants. Over the past two decades, China's gross capital formation, like its savings, has been high and rising in relation to output. Between 1990 and 2010, its investment–GDP ratio rose from 36 per cent to 48 per cent—an exceptionally high level for a big economy (Figure 4.1, top panel). Much of the marked rise in the Chinese investment rate took place in the decade following China's 2001 WTO accession. It matches or exceeds peak investment rates reached during the high-growth phases of Korea and Singapore and on the eve of the Asian financial crisis by other Asian economies (Park and Shin 2009). Hence, the conventional wisdom is that China over invests.

Figure 4.4 China's Investment and Household Loans, as a Percentage of GDP

Gross Capital Formation, by Sector

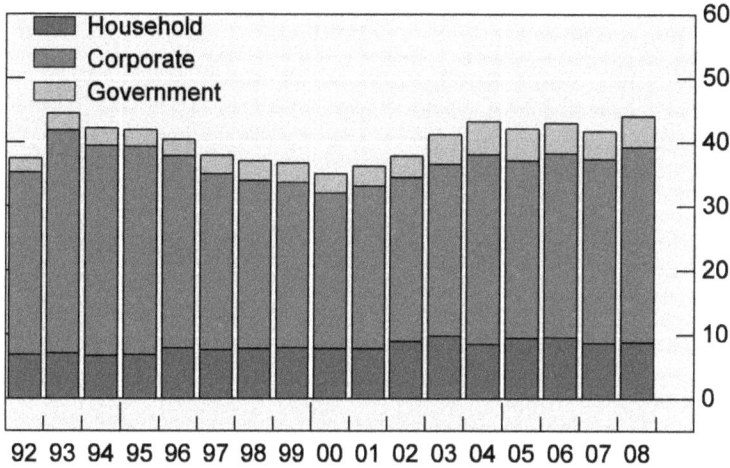

Real Estate Investment and Household Loans

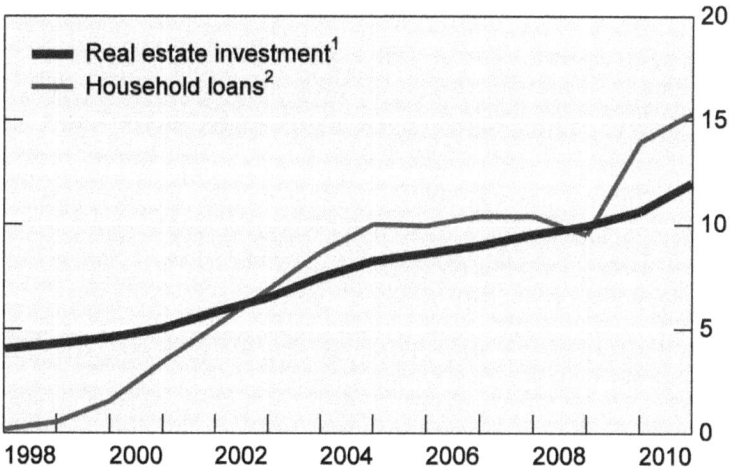

[1] Real estate investment includes land purchases and demolition expenses, which could exaggerate relative to gross capital formation.

[2] Household loans include mortgage loans, auto loans, credit card loans and others.

Source: CEIC.

As with Chinese saving, a breakdown of Chinese investment for the period 1992–2008 reveals that the three sectors all increased their investment, but not evenly. As of 2008, Chinese firms, households and government undertook 70 per cent, 20 per cent and 10 per cent, respectively, of the overall gross capital formation—similar to the OECD averages of 60 per cent, 25 per cent and 15 per cent. This raises a question about the assertion that housing and infrastructure investments in China have recently been excessive, especially in a decade when state-owned firms provided employees with fewer apartments. Over this period, all three sectors contributed to a rise in the aggregate investment rate (Figure 4.4, top panel). In particular, government investment relative to GDP more than doubled—from 2.2 per cent to 4.8 per cent. In contrast, firms and households each added less than 2 percentage points of GDP to investment. Finally, while government and household investment as a share of GDP rose steadily, corporate investment swung sharply, dropping by more than 3 per cent during 1992–99 and then surging by 5 per cent during 2000–08.

Policymakers, academics and market participants disagree over whether China has invested excessively (Knight and Ding 2010; Park and Shin 2009). In light of the domestic demand composition, the Chinese investment rate is often regarded as too high—a sign of the so-called 'internal imbalance'. But it remained lower than its even higher saving rate, giving rise to large current account surpluses in the mid-2000s—the so-called 'external imbalance'.

Documented high investment returns sit uneasily with claims of widespread over-investment. Anecdotal examples of wasteful investments include see-through apartments, traffic-free highways, idle stadiums and unused capacity in some industries. Yet most studies find high, typically double-digit, returns to capital in the past two decades (Bai et al. 2006; Knight and Ding 2010). High returns to investment are sometimes ascribed to low interest rates, yet subsidised corporate borrowers who invest more should earn lower returns. In any case, while administered interest rates held below equilibrium levels can boost investment, they should also lead to inefficiency, affording inefficient state firms preferred access to cheap credit. As a result, returns on capital could rise if the prevailing benchmark interest rates converge towards some higher equilibrium levels, thanks to improved allocative efficiency.

In our view, there are at least four proximate determinants of the sustained high Chinese investment rate over the past two decades. First is the high expected return to capital, as discussed below. Second is the reduced risk to investment (higher risk-adjusted returns), arising from more pro-business policy and increasing official recognition of private property. Third, managers even at state firms have increasingly faced financial rewards based on profit. Fourth, local government officials have faced promotion incentives to undertake investment projects, amid weak constraints on local government competition with the private sector in the marketplace (Ma and Wang 2010; Xu 2011).

Some of the factors contributing to high investment returns have already been identified as underpinning the high Chinese saving rate, though increased global integration has weakened the domestic saving and investment correlation. The initially large pool of surplus rural labour as well as the surge in the working-age share of the population restrained wage growth and lifted profits. Large-scale resource reallocation, both from the farm to manufacturing through labour migration and from state to non-state firms through tough corporate restructuring, improved allocative efficiency. High growth, high saving and high investment tended to reinforce each other, particularly from an initially low capital–labour ratio (Knight and Ding 2010). China's WTO accession in 2001 helped accommodate these structural transformations, allowing an expanding export sector to absorb surplus labour and to increase savings out of foreign sales to finance increased investment. Finally, private home ownership and more household credit led to rising real estate investment, accounting for as much as half of the rise in China's investment rate in the 2000s (Figure 4.4, bottom panel).

Structural Factors Influencing the Prospective Investment Rate

Going forward, these same forces could influence the prospects for the Chinese investment rate. On the one hand, three factors could lead to a somewhat slower pace of investment relative to that of the past two decades. First, one-off windfalls from both the Chinese corporate restructuring and WTO entry could fade, and the per capita capital stock has been rising—both pointing to falling returns to capital. Stimulus from international trade could fade if the global financial crisis has weakened medium-term global growth. Second, an expected decline in the Chinese saving rate could push up the costs of capital. But, as discussed earlier, higher interest rates can also enhance efficiency and returns to investment. Third, the recent property price booms could cool off considerably, resulting in a collapse in real estate investment. This possible headwind could be overstated if real estate's contribution to gross capital formation is exaggerated or if stimulus from public housing construction is overlooked.

On the other hand, high risk-adjusted expected returns to capital could continue. First, China's capital–labour stock ratio, though rising, is still only a small fraction of the OECD average (Qu 2012). Second, such infrastructure as railways, subways and highways all could have ample room to expand relative to China's population. Continued urbanisation and large-scale environmental projects could provide attractive investment opportunities for years to come, despite recent problems of bank lending to local government bodies. Third, ongoing technological progress, industrial upgrading and slower labour force growth could stimulate investment in labour-saving technology. Fourth, much-needed progress in the rule of law and contract enforcement could further reduce investment risks, while strengthened institutions might dampen cyclical volatility and enhance regulatory efficacy.

In sum, China's government and firms might continue investing strongly in infrastructure and manufacturing capacity for some years to come, to build up the physical capital stock (and corresponding pension assets) as the population ages, to invest in labour-saving processes in manufacturing, to expand cities and to meet environmental challenges. Thus, the Chinese investment rate seems unlikely to decline sharply anytime soon. In other words, any expected domestic rebalancing between investment and consumption should be modest and gradual over the next decade.

Outlook for China's Current Account

So far, we have discussed, separately, the determinants and prospects for China's saving and investment. We have suggested that they both could trend lower in the coming decade. To assess their impacts on the saving–investment (or current account) balance, however, we need to ascertain their interaction within a general equilibrium framework, which is beyond the scope of this chapter. Small variations in these two bigger variables can produce material changes in their balance.

How might China's domestic and external rebalancing play out in the coming decade? International experience offers mixed guidance. As emphasised by Kindleberger (1967) and seconded by Garnaut (2010), the Lewis turning point itself is likely to lead to a reduction of the current account surplus, as the rise in the wage share lowers savings. In China's case, Kuijs (2006) tabled a set of policy measures and reforms that could potentially lower both Chinese saving and investment as a share of GDP by 18 percentage points and 11.5 percentage points, respectively. These estimates imply a fall in the current account surplus of 6.5 per cent of GDP. Nevertheless, the Japanese experience in the 1980s cautions that domestic rebalancing does not necessarily bring about external rebalancing. In fact, the Japanese domestic rebalancing was accompanied by growing external imbalances—Japan's current account surpluses widened considerably during this transition phase (Fukumoto and Muto 2011).

As a baseline case, we envisage a more gradual scenario in which changing structural forces and sensible policy initiatives rebalance the Chinese economy. While growth remains respectable, the saving rate could fall more than the investment rate, further narrowing the current account surplus. The Chinese saving and investment rates could fall by 8 per cent and 4 per cent from the 2010 rates, respectively, to about 45 per cent and 44 per cent of GDP. The current account surplus could then narrow from 3 per cent of GDP in 2011 towards about 1 per cent over the coming decade. While this would require both private and public consumption spending to do more to drive economic growth, investment could remain a leading growth engine. One important variable helping to shape such a scenario is the Chinese exchange rate.

The Renminbi Exchange Rate Management

Besides the controversy over the fair value of the renminbi (Cheung et al. 2011), most observers see China's currency management since the unpegging from RMB8.28 per dollar in 2005 as stuck in the axis of renminbi per dollar (Figure 4.5, top panel). Their view is that the renminbi crawled upward against the dollar from mid-2005 to mid-2008 then held steady against it for two years, playing safe in the global financial crisis, and then resumed crawling upward against the dollar in June 2010 (Figure 4.5, bottom panel).

Figure 4.5 Bilateral Dollar Exchange Rate of the Renminbi (RMB per US$, daily)

Since 1994

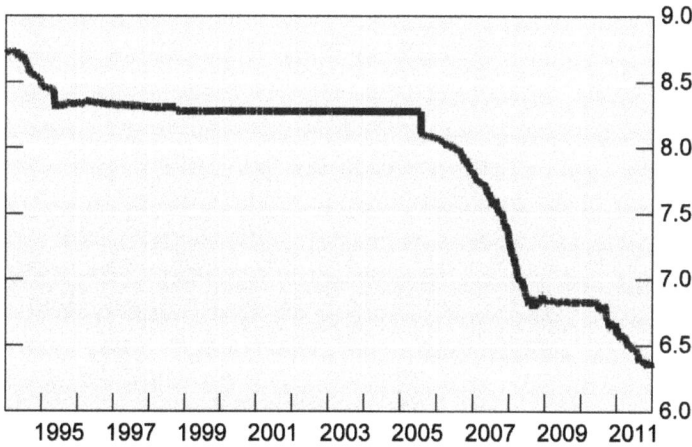

Since July 2005

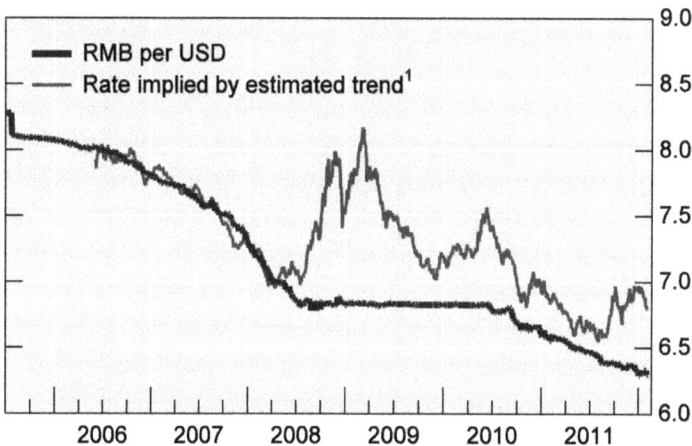

[1] Rate implied by the estimated linear trend of the RMB nominal effective exchange rate (NEER). The trend line is estimated over a two-year period of 1 June 2006 to 20 May 2008, regressing the RMB NEER against a constant and a trading-day trend.

Sources: BIS; authors' own estimates.

On this view, the years since mid-2005 have not well anticipated the renminbi playing a supporting role in the rebalancing of the Chinese economy. Such a supporting role would require that the renminbi gain value against the currencies of China's trading partners as a whole. Only accidentally can a gradual upward crawl against the dollar have this result.

We contend that this conventional view of the management of the renminbi is materially incomplete. Two developments in the renminbi's management over the seven years since 2005 have prepared for an exchange-rate contribution to the rebalancing of the Chinese economy. First, exchange-rate movements have shown a multi-currency orientation and, second, they have allowed a substantial real effective appreciation (Ma and McCauley 2011a, 2011b). Both a transition away from the focus on the dollar and a real appreciation are conducive to a rebalancing of the Chinese economy away from investment and exports to domestic consumption.

An extraordinary set of essays by a People's Bank of China deputy governor gives weight to both the nominal effective exchange rate (NEER) and the real effective exchange rate (REER). Hu (2010b) starts with the observation that '[t]heoretically, the best indicator to measure the international relative price of tradeables is [the] real effective exchange rate'. A lower price of tradeables (an appreciation of the real effective exchange rate) signals greater profit in production of services (whether haircuts or karaoke), than in production of goods for export, and so contributes to rebalancing the economy. She points out, however, two practical advantages of the NEER for policymaking: first, there is no need to agree on an appropriate and comparable price index; and second, the 'real time' availability of the NEER. Hu (2010c, 2010d) also refers to the power of renminbi appreciation to dampen imported inflation, pointing to the NEER as an important point of reference. Thus, both the NEER and the REER emerge as points of reference for Chinese currency policy.

We turn first to the renminbi movement against the basket of currencies of China's trading partners. Then we show how the real or price-adjusted renminbi has appreciated, considering a newly constructed index based on unit labour costs as well as the Bank for International Settlements (BIS) index based on consumer prices. By this new measure, the renminbi's competitiveness has eroded very substantially in this century.

Management of the Nominal Effective Exchange Rate

After the abandonment of the peg against the dollar in July 2005, for about a year the renminbi did in fact do little more than crawl upward against the dollar. As a result, the renminbi NEER tracked the dollar NEER.

Starting in late spring of 2006, however, there was a subtle shift. Observers were looking for a widening in the renminbi's daily moves against the US dollar but these remained very small by any standard. Despite continued tight management of daily fluctuations, however, over weeks and months, the renminbi NEER no longer shared the movements of the dollar NEER (Figure 4.6, top panel).

Figure 4.6 Nominal Effective Exchange Rate of the Renminbi (2005 = 100)[1]

RMB NEER and US Dollar NEER

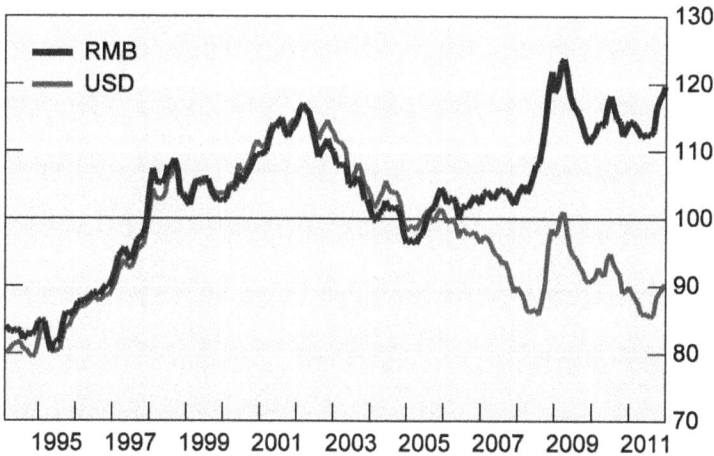

RMB NEER and its 2006–08 Trend[2, 3]

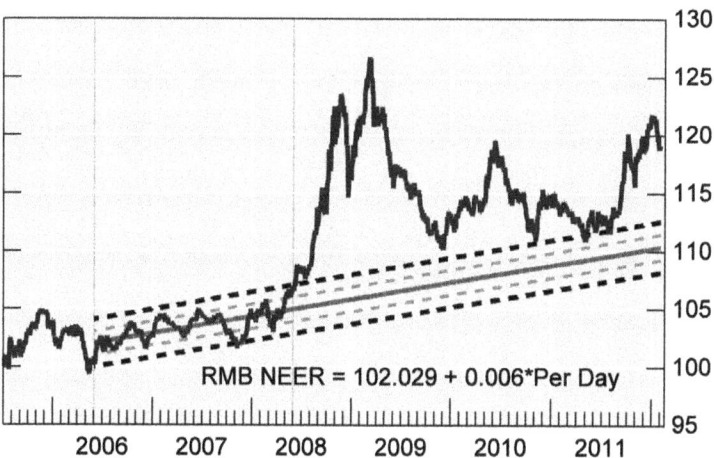

RMB NEER = 102.029 + 0.006*Per Day

[1] BIS effective exchange rate index based on 61 economies.

[2] The trend line is estimated over the two-year period 1 June 2006 to 30 May 2008, regressing the RMB NEER against a trading-day trend. The adjusted R-squared is 0.48, while both the constant term and the trend coefficient are statistically significant at 1 per cent.

[3] The thick dotted lines represent ±2 per cent of the trend line, while the thin dotted lines represent ±1 per cent of the trend line.

Sources: BIS; authors' own estimates.

Instead, the NEER of the renminbi showed steady upward movements. In short, what appeared to remain an upward crawl against the dollar slowly and imperceptibly turned into an upward crawl against China's trade-weighted currency basket as measured by the BIS NEER index (Figure 4.6, bottom panel). Daily movements suggested management against the dollar but weekly or monthly movements favoured a broader, multi-currency orientation.[4]

In mid-2008, the global financial crisis worsened, sending the dollar soaring as non-US banks scrambled to obtain dollars. The renminbi quietly reverted to a familiar and easily understood dollar peg (Hu 2010d). Considering that the US dollar rose sharply in value, a continuation of NEER stability would have required a sharp depreciation of the renminbi against the dollar—even if neighbours' currencies had not depreciated further in response to the renminbi movements (Figure 4.5, bottom panel). There is no telling how much more the offshore non-deliverable renminbi might have depreciated, and how much capital might have flowed out of China, had the renminbi not stabilised against the US dollar.

In June 2010, the renminbi resumed its movement against the dollar when the People's Bank of China (PBC) announced an end to the 'special measure' of pegging to the dollar, appreciating by almost 8 per cent by the end of 2011. Some observers detected a quickening of its appreciation vis-a-vis the dollar in August 2011 after the downgrade by Standard & Poor's of US Treasury obligations.

Looking at Figure 4.6 (bottom panel), the renminbi exchange rate policy since June 2010 is not clear. From mid-2010 to mid-2011, the NEER traded in a fairly narrow range against the currencies of China's trading partners, only to rise in late 2011. If the renminbi's NEER in 2006–08 described a basket, band and crawl (the so-called BBC of Williamson 2001) then the currency did not revert to it in 2010–11 (Figure 4.6, bottom panel).

Does this finding hold for the REER? After all, as noted, an appreciation of the REER provides incentives for production for domestic use rather than net exports. For China's role in the global rebalancing, the renminbi's REER, to which we now turn, is key.

---

4   Ma and McCauley (2011b) argue that the mid-2006 to mid-2008 data do not reject a hypothesis of a Singapore-style management with the NEER rising at 2 per cent per annum, mostly trading within 1 per cent of the centre and remaining within a ±2 per cent band (Figure 4.4, bottom panel, thin and thick dotted lines, respectively).

Management of the Real Effective Exchange Rate Based on Consumer Prices

A rising REER would complement a rebalancing of the Chinese economy to more domestic, consumption-led growth. The experience of gradual NEER appreciation described in the preceding section was at the same time an experience in slightly faster appreciation of the REER, as defined by consumer prices. The next section introduces our unit labour cost-based measure, which suggests a significantly faster appreciation.

The REER appreciation of the renminbi in the period mid-2006 to mid-2008 was more pronounced than its NEER appreciation (Figure 4.7, top panel). That is, higher inflation in those years in China than in her trading partners meant a steeper REER path than NEER path for the renminbi. In particular, using monthly data—inflation data are available only monthly in most economies—the rate of appreciation was 0.44 per cent per month or about 5 per cent per annum (Figure 4.7, bottom panel).

From mid-2005 to December 2011, the renminbi's REER appreciated by 30 per cent, while the nominal effective rate had appreciated by only 21 per cent. From June 2010 when the renminbi resumed fluctuations against the dollar, through December 2011, the NEER appreciated by some 3 per cent, while the REER appreciated by 6 per cent.

In contrast with the NEER, the REER in 2010–11 returned to the trend estimated in 2006–08. On this view, while the data for the earlier period could not distinguish between a NEER or a REER path for the renminbi, the data since mid-2010 weigh in for the REER path.

Looking forward, some observers have concluded that the policy of allowing substantial wage increases and rises in distorted administered prices (for energy, water, and so on) implies that future appreciation of the REER will be accomplished more through rises in the price level in China than through the nominal appreciation of the renminbi.

Figure 4.7 BIS Nominal and Real Effective Exchange Rates for the Renminbi (Index, 2005 = 100)[1]

Nominal Versus Real

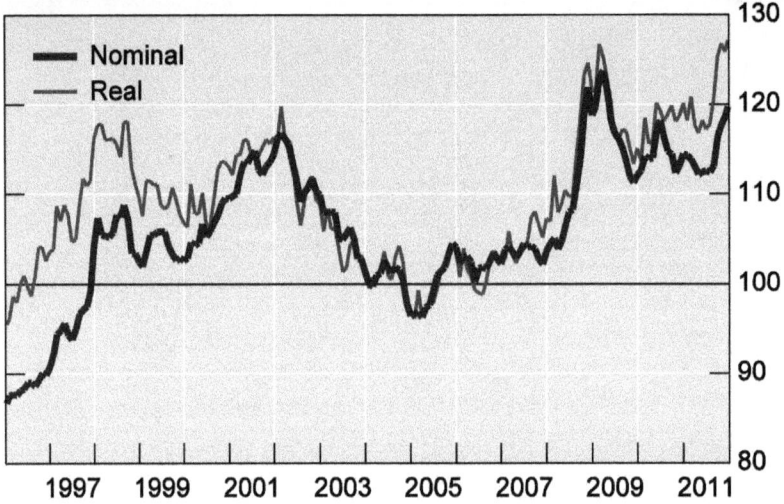

Real

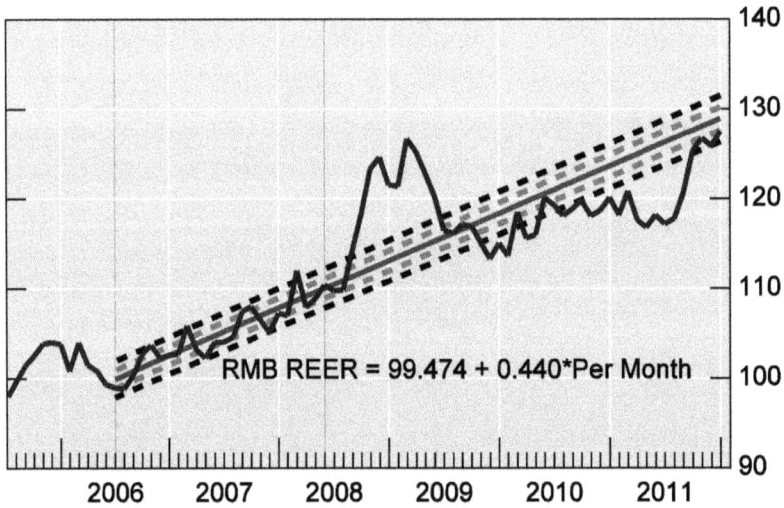

[1] BIS effective exchange rate index based on 61 economies. The trend line is estimated over the two-year period of 1 June 2006 to 30 May 2008, regressing the effective exchange rate against a trend. The thick dotted lines represent ±2 per cent of the trend line, while the thin dotted lines represent ±1 per cent of the trend line.

Sources: BIS; authors' own estimates.

The Renminbi's Real Exchange Rate Based on Unit Labour Costs

Reference to wage increases raises the question of how the renminbi's exchange rate looks to a manufacturer. For a manufacturer, the inflation that matters is not that in consumer prices, which are more relevant to a tourist. Instead, manufacturers would want to compare the evolution of unit labour costs—that is, wage inflation in relation to productivity increases. If wage gains just match productivity increases then unit labour costs are steady; if they exceed them, unit labour costs are rising.

Combined with an exchange rate, unit labour costs in two economies can answer how the cost of manufacturing goods in one economy is changing relative to the cost of manufacturing goods in another economy.[5] Is the exchange rate simply offsetting changes in relative unit labour costs, or amplifying them? Combined with the exchange rates of major manufacturing countries, unit labour costs can better answer the question of how the cost of manufacturing in one economy is changing relative to the cost of manufacturing in a weighted average of trading partner economies.

In any economy, measuring wages and productivity in manufacturing is challenging. It is all the more difficult in an economy like China's where structural change is rapid. We estimate China's unit labour cost by dividing total nominal wages paid in manufacturing by real GDP in manufacturing. For China's trading partners, we rely on the OECD data for OECD members as well as a few other economies (such as Brazil and India) and national data for some important Chinese trading partners: Hong Kong SAR, Malaysia, Singapore, Thailand and Chinese Taipei. The resulting coverage is 43 economies—fewer than the 61 economies for which the BIS effective exchange rates are calculated.[6]

---

5   A related question is how the internal exchange rate between traded and non-traded goods evolves. He et al. (2012b) find that prices in the non-tradable sectors have risen significantly faster than those in the tradable sectors, and China's internal real exchange rate has appreciated at a faster pace than the renminbi real effective exchange rate.

6   China's total wage bill series changed its coverage in 1998, so that the data before and after 1998 are not comparable (Lu 2007). We first bridged the 1998 break in the manufacturing wage series and then used percentage changes in the old series to pad the new series back to 1994 (see Figure 4.8 for more details). The 43 economies for which we have unit labour costs collectively account for 95 per cent of the 60 BIS trade weights for China. We increase each weight by about 5 per cent so that the 43 weights add up to 100 per cent. Our estimates are closely in line with the World Bank (2010) estimates that were later cited by the *Economist Magazine*.

Figure 4.8 The Renminbi's Real Exchange Rates Based on CPI and Unit Labour Costs (2005 = 100)

Effective Exchange Rates

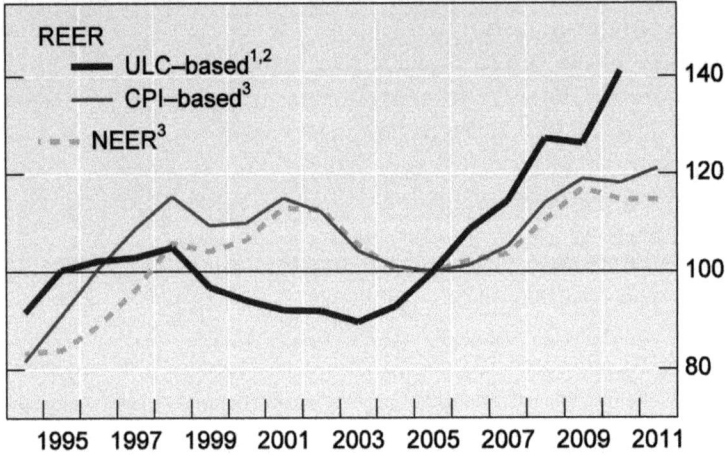

Bilateral Dollar Exchange Rates

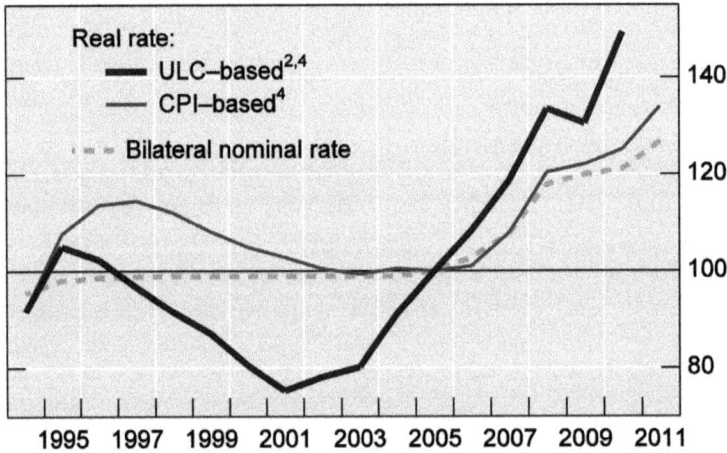

[1] The ULC–based REER basket covers 43 trading partners' currencies, with a combined trade weight of 95 per cent of the broad BIS basket for the renminbi. The 43 BIS trade weights are re-normalised for our ULC-based REER basket.

[2] Unit labour cost of the industry sector for the euro area and of manufacturing sector for others; China's unit labour cost is estimated using the ratio of the total nominal wage bill to the real GDP of the manufacturing sector. The coverage of the total wage bill was altered starting from 1998. The wage bill of 1997 is estimated by assuming the 1997–98 growth rate is the simple average of the 1996–97 growth rate and 1998–99 growth rate. The wage bill of 1993–96 is then estimated backwards using the growth rate of the original series.

[3] The CPI-based REER and NEER of the broad BIS basket consisting of 61 trading partners' currencies.

[4] Nominal bilateral rate adjusted for the relative unit labour cost or CPI.

Sources: BIS; CEIC; national data; OECD; authors' own estimates.

The resulting real effective exchange rate for the renminbi based on unit labour costs shows similarities in timing but differences in magnitude in comparison with its counterpart based on consumer prices (Figure 4.8, top panel). Both showed a local peak in 1998, when the Asian financial crisis resulted in sharp depreciation of the currencies of regional competitors like those of Korea and Thailand. Both subsequently showed the effect of deflation in China until the US dollar peaked in 2002. Both subsequently rose as wages and inflation rose faster in China than in its trading partners.

Quantitative differences are very striking. The earlier deflation of unit labour costs in China was much more severe than in consumer prices, as real output outran the wage bill from the late 1990s until 2002. The subsequent recovery of unit labour costs has likewise been much greater than that of consumer prices. As a result, the real renminbi based on unit labour costs showed much more pronounced movements than that based on consumer prices. With falling costs at home, China's manufacturers gained cost advantage against their aggregate of trading partners from the late 1990s until 2003. This steady improvement in China's competitiveness complements the shift from wages to profits in explaining the large subsequent widening of China's current account surplus.

By the same token, with the wage bill growing faster than real output in recent years, Chinese manufacturers have had to contend with an earlier and faster erosion of their cost advantage than is suggested by consumer prices. The real renminbi based on unit labour costs followed a steeper trajectory than that based on consumer prices. In particular, with the unpegging of the renminbi in 2005, the real renminbi strengthened during 2005–10 by 40 per cent or, on average, appreciated 7–8 per cent per annum—well above the 4–5 per cent of the rate of the measure based on consumer prices. It could have appreciated by as much as 50 per cent by the end of 2011.

Although a multilateral perspective best represents broad trends in China's manufacturing competitiveness, a glance at the real dollar/renminbi rate shows that the difference between a labour cost measure and a consumer price measure also holds in this narrower context. The bilateral real exchange rate against the US dollar based on unit labour costs has swung both ways even more sharply than that based on consumer prices (Figure 4.8, bottom panel). Not only has the renminbi appreciated more against the US dollar than against the currencies of China's trading partners overall, but also the rise in Chinese unit labour costs contrasts particularly sharply with the trend decline in US unit labour costs. Thus, over the past decade, US manufacturers have regained competitiveness against manufacturers in China more than their counterparts in most of China's trading partners.

How much real exchange rate appreciation would be required by the 2 per cent decline in net savings that we discussed above? Obstfeld and Rogoff (2007) analyse the implications of a hypothesised jump in US savings for the real exchange rate, given the need to maintain employment in the non-traded goods sector. Working through their argument for China, the challenge would be to keep a sudden decline in savings from leading to excess demand for non-traded goods and services, given the short-run capacity to produce them. One would have to take into account that the structure of the Chinese economy is different from that of the US economy, with a larger traded goods sector and a smaller non-traded goods and services sector.

As these authors acknowledge, however, if the adjustment takes place over the medium term, the problem changes. What price signals are sufficient to induce private investment in non-traded goods and services so that supply is sufficient given eventually lower savings and higher consumption? We do not have a rigorous answer to this question. Over five to 10 years, we conjecture that a continued real appreciation of something like 5 per cent per year might be sufficient. In any case, such a scale of the renminbi's real effective appreciation is most likely contributing to narrowing China's current account (Cline 2010).

Summary

This chapter has argued that China's current account surplus will likely trend lower from the 5–10 per cent of GDP seen in the mid-2000s towards 1 per cent in the coming decade, as saving declines more than investment and the renminbi continues its real appreciation. Factors that helped to account for the rise of Chinese savings over the past decade, such as one-off productivity gains and abundant supply of labour, point to their decline over the present decade. Investment is also likely to moderate but will remain robust on the back of large infrastructure projects and technical upgrading during China's still early catch-up phase. Thus, China's prospective saving–investment balance could well shrink on a trend basis. Policy might prove to cut in the same direction. The Government might deregulate services, strengthen the social safety net, bolster state-funded pensions and flush dividend income out of state-owned industry while shifting incentives for officials to deliver services rather than to pour concrete.

The exchange rate can play a supporting role in shifting to a more balanced growth model. Ongoing appreciation of the renminbi's real effective exchange rate provides signals of profit for investment in the non-traded goods sector. It has been under way in the past seven years, with a real effective appreciation of about 4–5 per cent per annum coming from a nominal effective appreciation against the currencies of China's trading partners of 2–3 per cent per annum, amplified by faster inflation in China than in its trading partners. Our new estimates based on unit labour costs rather than consumer prices suggest an even higher rate of 7–8 per cent per annum in real appreciation. There is no reason to believe that real appreciation cannot continue. Its balance between relative inflation of wages and prices, on the one hand, and nominal currency appreciation, on the other, remains to be seen.

Looking forward, a narrowed current account surplus and appreciated currency can eventually impart a greater sense of two-way risk in the trading of the renminbi. This sense would form a more propitious backdrop to further financial liberalisation and greater monetary autonomy as China makes the transition towards a more balanced economy.

Bibliography

Asian Development Bank (ADB), 2009, *Asian Development Outlook 2009: Rebalancing Asia's growth*, Asian Development Bank, Manila.

Bai, C., Hsieh, C. and Qian, Y., 2006, 'The return to capital in China', *Brookings Papers on Economic Activity*, vol. 2, pp. 61–88.

Bernanke, B., 2005, The global saving glut and the US current account deficit, Homer Jones Lecture, St Louis, 14 April.

Blanchard, O. and Giavazzi, F., 2002, 'Current account deficits in the euro area: the end of the Feldstein–Horioka puzzle?', *Brookings Papers on Economic Activity*, vol. 2, pp. 147–209.

Cheung, Y., Chinn, M. and Fujii, E., 2011, 'A note on the debate over renminbi undervaluation', in Y. Cheung and G. Ma (eds), *Asia and China in the Global Economy*, World Scientific Publishing, Singapore, pp. 155–87.

Cline, W., 2010, *Renminbi undervaluation, China's surplus, and the US trade deficit*, Policy Brief No. PB10-20, Peterson Institute of International Economics.

Cline, W., 2012, *Projecting China's current account surplus*, Policy Brief No. PB12-7, April, Peterson Institute of International Economics.

Feldstein, M. and Horioka, C., 1980, 'Domestic saving and international capital flows', *Economic Journal*, vol. 90, no. 358 (June), pp. 314–29.

Fukumoto, T. and Muto, I., 2011, *Rebalancing China's economic growth: some insights from Japan's experience*, Working Paper Series No. 11-E-5, July, Bank of Japan, Tokyo.

Garnaut, R., 2010, 'Macroeconomic implications of the turning point', *China Economic Journal*, vol. 3, no. 2, pp. 181–90.

He, D., Cheung, L., Zhang, W. and Wu, T., 2012a, *How would capital account liberalisation affect China's capital flows and the renminbi real exchange rates?*, Working Paper No. 09/2012, April, HKIMR.

He, D., Zhang, W., Han, G. and Wu, T., 2012b, *Productivity growth of the non-tradeable sectors in China*, Working Paper No. 08/2012, March, HKIMR.

Hu, X., 2010a, A managed floating exchange rate regime is an established policy, 15 July.

Hu, X., 2010b, Three characteristics of the managed floating exchange rate regime, 22 July.

Hu, X., 2010c, Exchange rate regime reform and monetary policy effectiveness, 26 July.

Hu, X., 2010d, Successful experiences of further reforming the RMB exchange rate regime, 27 August.

Kindleberger, C. P., 1967, *Europe's Postwar Growth: The role of labor supply*, Harvard University Press, Cambridge, Mass.

Knight, J. and Ding, S., 2010, 'Why does China invest so much?', *Asian Economic Papers*, vol. 9, no. 3, pp. 87–117.

Kuijs, L., 2006, *How will China's saving–investment balance evolve?*, World Bank Policy Research Working Paper No. 3958, The World Bank, Washington, DC.

Lewis, W., 1954, 'Economic development with unlimited supplies of labour', *The Manchester School*, vol. 22, no. 2, pp. 139–91.

Lu, F., 2007, *China's evolving manufacturing unit labour cost and its impact on the exchange rate*, Working Paper No. C2007003, China Centre for Economic Research.

Ma, G. and McCauley, R., 2011a, 'La gestion du renminbi depuis 2005', in *Finance Chinoise, Revue d'économie financière*, no. 102 (June), pp. 163–81.

Ma, G. and McCauley, R., 2011b, 'The evolving renminbi regime and implications for Asian currency stability', *Journal of the Japanese and International Economies*, no. 25, pp. 23–38.

Ma, G. and McCauley, R., 2012, 'China's saving and exchange rate in global rebalancing', *SUERF Studies*, vol. 2012, no. 1, pp. 123–40.

Ma, G. and Wang, Y., 2010, 'China's high saving rate: myth and reality', *International Economics*, no. 122 (December), pp. 5–40.

Ma, G. and Zhou, H., 2009, *China's evolving external wealth and rising creditor position*, Working Papers No. 286, July, Bank for International Settlements, Basel.

Obstfeld, M. and Rogoff, K., 2007, 'The unsustainable US current account position revisited', in R. Clarida (ed.), *G7 Current Account Imbalances*, Chicago, pp. 339–66.

Park, D. and Shin, K., 2009, *Saving, investment and current account surplus in developing Asia*, Economics Working Paper No. 158, Asian Development Bank, Manila.

People's Bank of China (PBC), 2008, *China's Monetary Policy Report*, May, People's Bank of China, Beijing.

People's Bank of China (PBC), 2010, Further reform of the RMB exchange rate regime and enhancing the RMB exchange rate flexibility, Policy announcement, 19 June 2010, People's Bank of China, Beijing, <http://www.pbc.gov.cn/english/detail.asp?col=6400&id=1488>

Qu, H., 2012, 'China macroeconomics: what overinvestment?', *HSBC Global Research*, February.

Williamson, J., 2001, 'The case for a basket, band and crawl (BBC) regime for East Asia', in Reserve Bank of Australia, *Future Directions for Monetary Policies in East Asia*, pp. 97–111.

World Bank, 2010, *China Quarterly Update*, June 2001, World Bank Office, Beijing, <http://www.worldbank.org/en/country/china/research/all?qterm=China+Quarterly+Update&lang_exact=English>

Xu, C., 2011, 'The fundamental institutions of China's reforms and development', *Journal of Economic Literature*, vol. 49, no. 4 (December), pp. 1076–151.

Zhou, X., 2009, On savings ratio, Speech at the High Level Conference hosted by Bank Negara Malaysia, Kuala Lumpur, 10 February, <http://www.bis.org/review/r090327b.pdf>

5. Has the 'Flying Geese' Phenomenon in Industrial Transformation Occurred in China?

Yue Qu, Fang Cai and Xiaobo Zhang

Introduction

In the past three decades, the Chinese economy has experienced phenomenal growth in large part thanks to rapid expansion in the labour-intensive manufacturing sector, mostly concentrated in the coastal areas. In 2009, China's per capita GDP reached $3774, qualifying it for status as a 'middle-income country'. Along with economic development, wages and other factor prices tend to increase over time. Consequently, labour-intensive industries will eventually lose their traditional comparative advantage, pushing enterprises to move to other regions or countries with lower costs. The existing literature focuses mainly on the patterns of industrial relocation across countries: as factor prices go up in a developed country, labour-intensive industries tend to move to other, less expensive places, while the developed country retains only those capital-intensive high–value-added industries. This pattern has been coined the 'flying geese model' in the literature (Kojima 2000; Okita 1985).

As China opened up to the world beginning in the late 1970s, its coastal regions enjoyed a geographic advantage compared with their interior counterparts because of their proximity to international markets. Chasing the abundant supply of cheap labour, massive foreign investment flew to the coastal regions. Coupled with favourable policy support from the Central Government, the coastal areas have witnessed a three-decade-plus manufacturing boom. Most of the manufacturing industries are clustered in the coastal areas (Long and Zhang 2011; Lu and Tao 2006). China has become a 'world factory' in just a few decades and achieved the level of industrialisation that took European countries more than a century to realise.

The booming manufacturing sector has generated ample employment opportunities, gradually exhausting the seemingly unlimited supply of labour. Since the early 2000s, there have been an increasing number of media reports of labour shortages, in particular in the coastal regions (Cai 2010; Zhang et al. 2011). Since 2004, the average wage has escalated by a double-digit percentage rate annually. Alongside the knowledge of demographic trends, there is consequently wide debate as to whether China has reached the Lewis turning point. Amidst rising labour costs, the spatial distribution of industrial activities has begun to change.

For a long time, China was a typical dual economy with a large supply of surplus labour in rural areas. As the industrial sector draws millions of workers from farms to factory floors, the number of excess labourers in the rural areas dwindles. Consequently, workers start to find themselves with more leverage when negotiating wages with employers. At this stage, the wage rate is likely to climb at a much faster pace than before. This is the so-called 'Lewis turning point'. After the turning point, the capital–labour ratio rises rapidly, imposing huge pressure on labour-intensive enterprises. In order to survive in the new paradigm of labour shortage, they have to make a choice: either introduce more capital-intensive technologies to replace labourers or relocate the business to a region with cheaper labour costs.

In the long run, China will have to upgrade its industries by introducing more capital-intensive techniques and producing more high-quality goods. In the short run, however, because of large regional variations in factor prices, there is a possibility for enterprises to move their operations to interior regions to take advantage of the cheaper labour and land. Early empirical studies (Fan 2004; Luo and Cao 2005) have shown that the historical relocation of business was actually from the interior to the coastal areas, which have become increasingly 'clustered'; however, these findings are now quite dated, covering the periods up to the late 1990s or the early 2000s. By comparing the regional difference in labour costs from 2000 to 2007, Cai et al. (2009) demonstrate that it is economically viable to move labour-intensive industries to the interior regions. Using provincial-level data, Ruan and Zhang (2010) further confirm that, in the textile sector, the pattern of 'flying geese' has occurred. Their finding is, however, based on only one sector and aggregated data at the provincial level. In this chapter, we expand the analysis by Ruan and Zhang (2010) to the firm level, while encompassing all the manufacturing industries. Our results show that since the mid-2000s, the share of manufacturing-sector assets located in inland regions has steadily increased, especially in labour-intensive industries.

Descriptive Statistics

Sample Representativeness

Our study is based on the above-scale manufacturing enterprise census data from 1998 to 2008, covering 31 provinces and 30 manufacturing industries classified according to SITC (Standard International Trade Classification) two-digit codes. All state-owned enterprises (regardless of size) and non-state enterprises with annual sales income exceeding RMB500 million are included in the sample. The number of businesses included in the sample ranges from about 100 000 in 1998 to about 300 000 in 2008. The dataset has some unique features. First, it is a census survey for large-scale enterprises rather than a sample survey. Second, the sample period encompasses the proposed Lewis turning point about 2004 as shown in Cai (2007) and Zhang et al. (2011). Of course, the dataset has a drawback in that it does not cover private enterprises with sales less than RMB500 million. To check for potential bias as a result of excluding these small firms, we compare the summary statistics drawn from our sample with those inferred from the China Economic Census in 2004 and 2008.

Table 5.1 presents the ratios of average assets, profit and employment calculated from our sample relative to those computed from the full economic census in 2004 and 2006 for major industries. Several features are apparent from the table. First, the difference is more salient for employment than for assets and profit. On average, our sample accounts for about two-thirds of total employment in 2004 compared with about 90 per cent of total assets and profit. Second, the gap in employment between the two data sources narrowed in 2008. The ratio of employment covered in our sample compared with the economic census increased to 73 per cent. Third, the difference in coverage varies greatly across industries. For example, the ratio is as low as 0.45 for the recycling industry in 2004, suggesting that the sector is dominated by small enterprises. In contrast, almost all the tobacco enterprises are in the above-scale category as shown by the greater ratios in assets, profit and employment, which are close to one. Overall, the sample has good coverage in terms of assets and profit, but has less thorough coverage of employment.

Table 5.1 Comparing the National Above-Scale Manufacturing Enterprise Survey with the Economic Census (2004, by industry)

Industry	Ratio						
	Assets		Profit		Employment		Main
	2004	2008	2004	2008	2004	2008	2004
Agriculture food products	0.8349	0.8608	0.7439	0.8380	0.6279	0.6964	0.8867
Food products	0.8433	0.8662	0.8779	0.8659	0.6523	0.7117	0.8836
Beverages	0.8664	0.8896	0.9042	0.8969	0.6577	0.6880	0.8957
Tobacco products	1.0046	0.9989	0.9897	0.9990	0.9846	0.9645	1.0062
Textiles	0.8717	0.8870	0.8577	0.8662	0.7441	0.8104	0.8921
Clothing	0.7913	0.8192	0.8932	0.8378	0.6586	0.7157	0.8558
Dressing and dyeing of furs	0.8268	0.8676	0.8481	0.8750	0.7332	0.8117	0.8854
Lumber	0.7118	0.7354	0.5469	0.6889	0.4559	0.5533	0.6926
Furniture	0.7194	0.7691	0.7092	0.6976	0.5637	0.6629	0.7738
Paper and paper products	0.8573	0.8961	0.8513	0.8610	0.6224	0.6959	0.8546

| Industry | Ratio | | | | | | Main |
| | Assets | | Profit | | Employment | | |
	2004	2008	2004	2008	2004	2008	2004
Publishing, printing	0.7261	0.7490	0.7964	0.7356	0.4818	0.5348	0.6959
Entertainment products	0.7958	0.8329	0.8562	0.7820	0.6987	0.7923	0.8553
Refined petroleum products	0.9693	0.9611	0.9709	1.0138	0.8416	0.9299	0.9877
Chemicals and chemical products	1.1044	0.9243	0.9347	0.9323	0.7132	0.7713	0.9270
Medical products	0.8999	0.9251	1.0404	0.9909	0.8355	0.9005	0.9717
Fibre products	0.9463	0.9536	0.9733	0.9504	0.8888	0.9292	0.9803
Rubber products	0.8812	0.9034	0.8772	0.8644	0.7100	0.7618	0.8881
Plastics products	0.7810	0.8114	0.7988	0.7923	0.5798	0.6593	0.8057
Non-metallic mineral products	0.8144	0.8211	0.6781	0.7449	0.4770	0.5346	0.7527
Basic metals	0.9706	0.9875	0.9834	0.9804	0.8873	0.9509	0.9811
Non-ferrous metals	0.9523		0.9764		0.8399		0.9614
Fabricated metal products	0.7677	0.7926	0.8235	0.7965	0.5866	0.6554	0.8176
General machinery and equipment	0.8348	0.8564	0.8500	0.8582	0.6322	0.6877	0.8318
Special machinery and equipment	0.8513	0.7768	0.9034	0.8491	0.6855	0.6281	0.8743
Transport equipment	0.9355	0.8804	0.9648	0.9180	0.7695	0.7652	0.9503
Electrical machinery and apparatus	0.8958	0.9186	0.9641	0.9492	0.7588	0.8447	0.9355
Computing machinery	0.9471	0.9106	1.0169	0.9381	0.8275	0.9230	0.9868
Precision and optical instruments	0.8526	0.8793	0.9795	0.9472	0.7087	0.7799	0.9150
Crafts	0.7534	0.6291	0.7127	0.6748	0.5987	0.5921	0.7778
Recycling	0.6722	0.7799	0.6492	0.7071	0.4539	0.6069	0.7796
All manufacturing	**0.8988**	**0.8477**	**0.9062**	**0.8411**	**0.6758**	**0.7275**	**0.9084**

Sources: National above-scale manufacturing enterprise data from National Bureau of Statistics of China: *The First Economic Census Bulletin* available from <http://www.stats.gov.cn/zgjjpc/cgfb/t20051206_402294807.htm>; *The Second Economic Census Bulletin* available from <http://www.stats.gov.cn/was40/reldetail.jsp?docid=402610156>

The Spatial Distribution of Manufacturing and Labour-Intensive Industries

Using the above-scale manufacturing enterprise dataset, we examine the distribution of manufacturing industries in assets, profits and output values during the period 1998–2008 in inland and coastal regions. We pay particular attention to labour-intensive industries. By definition, labour-intensive industries use more labour relative to capital input during the production process; however, there is no clear-cut definition of labour-intensive industries. The capital–labour ratio might differ between developed and developing countries. In this chapter, we select a group of industries that displays low capital–labour ratios in both China and the United States. Based on the above-scale manufacturing dataset, we sort the 30 manufacturing industries according to the value of the capital–labour ratio. The right column in Table 5.2 presents the 15 most labour-intensive industries according to this measure, while the left column exhibits 16 industries with low capital intensity in the United States, obtained from Ciccone and Rapaioannou (2009). There are 12 overlapping industries between the two columns. We categorise these 12 industries as labour-intensive industries: textiles, garments and footwear (18); leather products (19); wood processing (20); furniture (21); sporting goods (24); plastic products (30); fabricated metal products (34); general-purpose equipment (35); special equipment (36); instrumentation (39); communications equipment and computers (40); and electrical machinery and equipment (41).

Table 5.2 The Criteria for Labour-Intensive Industries (International/National)

| International criterion | | National criterion | |
Industry name	CAPINT	Industry name	Capital–labour ratio (RMB1000 per capita)
Footwear, except rubber or plastic	0.443	Dressing and dyeing of furs	31.28
Clothing, except footwear	0.481	Clothing	37.01
Professional and scientific equipment	0.654	Entertainment products	37.23
Leather products	0.663	Crafts	46.18
Tobacco	0.73	Furniture	61.16
Printing and publishing	0.785	Electrical machinery and apparatus	78.64
Furniture, except metal	0.789	Lumber	86.27
Chemicals, other	0.800	Fabricated metal products	91.35
Other manufactured products	0.878	Textiles	91.68
Machinery, electrical	0.924	Plastic products	94.33
Machinery, except electrical	1.017	Precision and optical instruments	94.36
Fabricated metal products	1.173	General machinery and equipment	110.24
Misc. petroleum and coal products	1.199	Recycling	110.51
Transport equipment	1.32	Special machinery and equipment	116.51
Food products	1.366	Computing machinery	116.56
Plastic products	1.416		

Notes: For the international criterion, see Ciccone and Rapaioannou (2009); the national criterion is based on the calculations using the above-scale manufacturing enterprise data for 2008.

Figure 5.1 plots the share of employment, assets and output values in the coastal regions spanning the period 1998–2008 for the manufacturing sector as a whole (the left panel) and for the labour-intensive industries only (right panel).[1] The figure reveals a few interesting features. First, the coastal region plays a dominant role in shaping China's manufacturing sector. It employed more than 55 per cent of workers, accumulated nearly two-thirds of assets and produced more than 70 per cent of output in 1998. By 2008, its shares of employment, asset and output values had all risen to more than 70 per cent. Second, despite the increasing importance of the coastal region in the manufacturing sector during the sample period, the speed of growth has slowed since 2004. In particular, the output share has decreased since then. Third, for the labour-intensive industries, the trend of firms flocking to the coast seems to have dwindled about the mid-2000s. Apart from output, the share of assets in the coastal region showed a declining trend from 2006 to 2008, suggesting a capital outflow from the coastal to interior regions. The share of employment has levelled off since 2004. Because our sample encompasses only the large firms, it might fail to capture the movement in employment from the coastal to interior regions, for vast numbers of small labour-intensive enterprises tend to be more responsive to rising labour costs on the coast.

Figure 5.1 The Share of Manufacturing and Labour-Intensive Industries in Coastal Areas

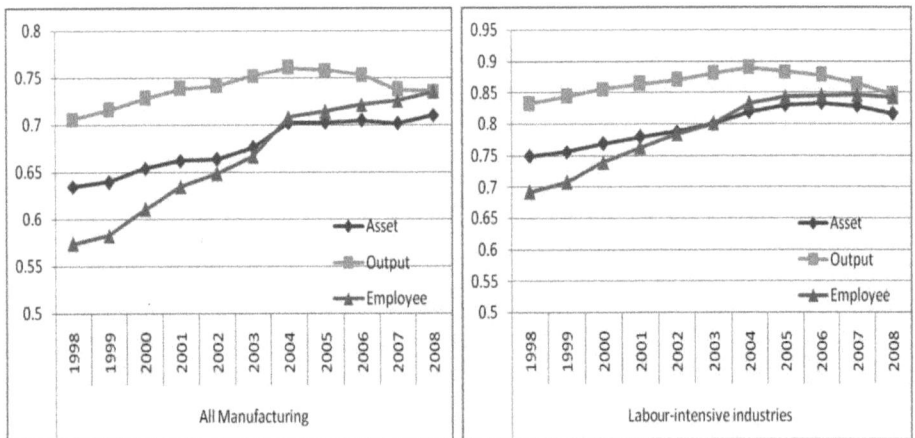

Source: Computed by authors based on the national above-scale manufacturing enterprises survey.

---

1   The eastern (or coastal) region includes Beijing, Tianjin, Hebei, Liaoning, Shanghai, Jiangsu, Zhejiang, Fujian, Shandong, Guangdong and Hainan; the interior (central and western) region comprises Shanxi, Jilin, Heilongjiang, Anhui, Jiangxi, Henan, Hubei, Hunan, Inner Mongolia, Guangxi, Chongqing, Sichuan, Guizhou, Yunnan, Tibet, Shaanxi, Gansu, Qinghai, Ningxia and Xinjiang.

Next, we further compare the return on assets (ROA) and per capita profit in the two regions over time. As shown in Figure 5.2, initially ROA in the coastal region exceeds that in the interior region. The gap is more evident for labour-intensive industries; however, over time, the regional difference disappears. By the end of the sample, the interior region even slightly outperforms the coastal region in ROA. Per capita profit shows a similar trend. Despite an initially unfavourable business environment, the interior region had become a more lucrative destination for business by 2008. Cai et al. (2009) also show that the total factor productivity in inland areas has increased faster than in coastal areas. The higher and rising returns to assets and profitability might be key factors behind the recent relocation of businesses to the interior regions.

Figure 5.2 Return on Assets and Profit Per Capita (By region)

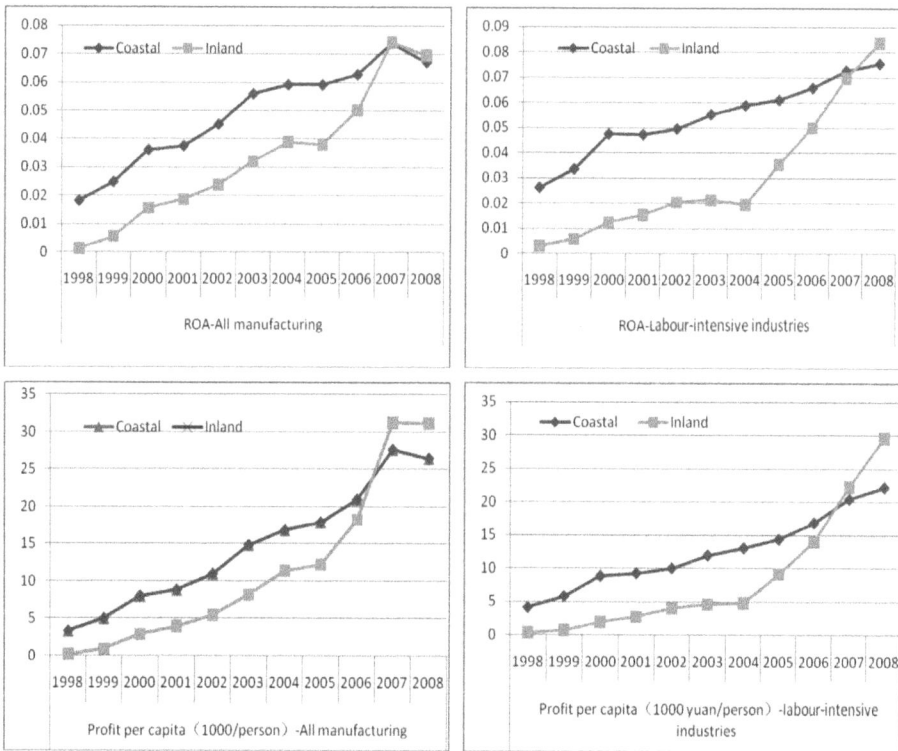

Note: ROA = return on assets.

Source: Computed by authors based on the national above-scale manufacturing enterprises survey.

Rising labour costs might be another driving force behind the migration. Figure 5.3 shows average labour costs in the two regions over the sample period. Overall, wages have steadily increased. The growth has accelerated since 2003. Moreover, labourers are more expensive in the coastal region than in the inland. In 2007, an average coastal worker earned RMB29 000, which was RMB5000 higher than his inland counterpart. In 1996, coastal workers in the labour-intensive industries earned less than the average of the entire manufacturing sector; however, by 2007, the wage difference across industries had disappeared within the coastal region, while it still exists in the inland regions. This suggests that there is still some room for the labour-intensive industries to move inland to take advantage of the relatively cheaper labour costs.

Figure 5.3 Labour Costs in Coastal and Inland Regions

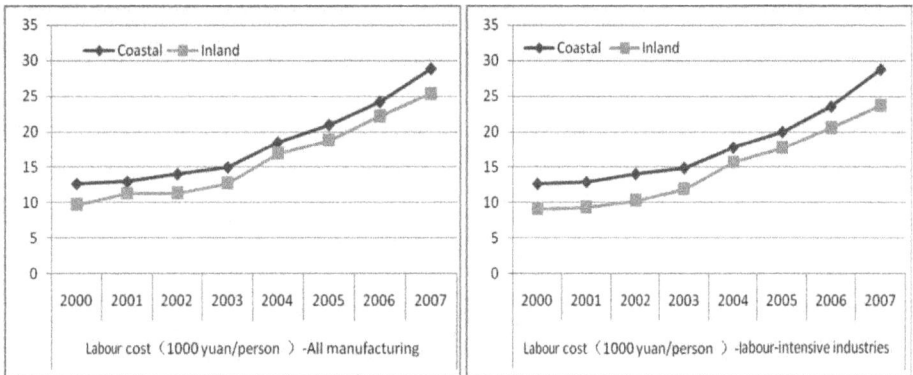

Labour cost (1000 yuan/person) -All manufacturing

Labour cost (1000 yuan/person) -labour-intensive industries

Source: Computed by authors based on the national above-scale manufacturing enterprises survey.

As more enterprises move into interior regions, they will hire a greater number of local workers, hence pushing up local wages. As a consequence, the regional variation in wage rates is likely to drop as businesses fly from high-wage coastal regions to low-wage inland regions. To check this, we compute a standard measure of inequality—the generalised entropy index (GE(0) index)—using wages at the firm level from the above-scale manufacturing dataset. The index dropped from 0.34 to 0.25 between 2000 and 2007,[2] suggesting wage convergence over time. To examine how much of the variation is due to coastal–inland difference, we further decomposed the overall GE(0) into two components: the mean difference between the coastal and inland regions and the intra-region variation.[3] The share between coastal and inland differences in total wage variation has declined from 0.058 to 0.029, indicating a narrowing wage gap between the inland and coastal regions. The trend in wage inequality seems to support the story that 'geese' have flocked to the inland regions.

---

2 The data for 1998, 1999 and 2008 do not include wage information. Consequently, the sample period used in the calculation of the inequality measure is 2000–07.

3 See Zhang and Kanbur (2001) for the application of the decomposition methodology.

Quantitative Analyses of Flying Geese

Having shown some descriptive evidence in support of the 'flying geese' pattern—industrial relocation to the inland regions since the mid-2000s—we next conduct a quantitative analysis to examine the relative importance of various factors behind the shifting spatial distribution of manufacturing activities. In the literature, the term 'flying geese' often refers to the movement of capital from a developed region to a less developed one. Following the convention, we present the results for assets only.[4] When firms select a location for investment, they often make agglomeration their top priority. As stated by Krugman (1991) and Marshall (1920), agglomeration offers several key advantages: proximity to the market, the easy flow of information and technology and labour pooling. Holding everything else constant, a region with a higher degree of agglomeration is likely to attract more business investment. So, the first variable of interest is a measure of agglomeration. We use the proximity measure at the county level computed by Long and Zhang (2011) based on firm-level data from China's Industrial Census of 1995 as a measure of agglomeration.

As more firms cluster in a place with high agglomeration, however, the space becomes congested and the demand for land rises. Because the conversion of land from agricultural to non-farm use is strictly controlled by the Government, the supply of land for industrial use can hardly keep pace with the rising demand. The combination of rising demand for and limited supply of land results in higher land prices. This makes it harder for many firms to expand their production in the increasingly congested coastal regions. If they want to expand their production base, they have to seek places endowed with cheaper land—mostly in inland regions. Unfortunately, land price information at the county level is not available. As a compromise, we use local population obtained from China's Population Census of 2000 as a proxy for land price.

The cost of living is generally higher in places with more expensive land. To attract workers, the coastal regions have to offer better wages. Labour-intensive industries are particularly sensitive to labour costs. As labour costs increase, these firms are more likely to move elsewhere to chase cheaper labourers (Duranton and Puga 2000; Puga and Venables 1996). Therefore, wage levels can be a major factor contributing to the relocation decisions of labour-intensive industries.

Although China has a unified tax code on paper, the effective tax rate differs greatly across regions (Zhang 2006). This is largely due to China's centralised political system and decentralised economic system. In China, the size of local government is largely proportional to the registered population; however, under

---

4   The results for output and employment are similar and available upon request.

fiscal decentralisation, local governments have had to raise most of the revenue to cover their operational costs and provide local public goods and services. Naturally, regions with a larger tax base can afford to collect less tax revenue from individual enterprises than their less fortunate counterparts. In view of this, we also include the effective tax rate, the ratio of taxes collected to gross industrial output, computed from *China Local Public Finance Yearbooks* in the regression analyses.

To test the relative importance of the above four factors to the spatial asset distribution over time, we run the following regressions year by year (Equation 5.1).

Equation 5.1

$$ln(K_i) = \beta_1 {}^*approx_i + \beta_2 {}^*ln(taxrate_i) + \beta_3 {}^*ln(wage_{i,-1}) + \beta_4 {}^*ln(popu_i) + \beta_5 {}^*dummy_{province} + \varepsilon_i$$

In Equation 5.1, i represents county; K is total assets aggregated at the county level; *approx* is a measure of local agglomeration; *taxrate* represents the effective tax rate; and $wage_{i,-1}$ refers to the average wage at the county level in the previous year. We use lagged wage data to primarily reduce the potential reserve causality. We also include a set of provincial fixed effects ($dummy_{province}$) in the regressions.

Because wage information is not available for 1998, 1999 and 2008, in the first set of regressions, we exclude the wage variable in the equation. Thus, the sample period ranges from 1998 to 2008. The upper part of Table 5.3 presents the estimations for the entire manufacturing sector, while the lower panel restricts the sample to labour-intensive industries.

The coefficient for the agglomeration variable is consistently positive and significant throughout the years, suggesting that a county with a higher degree of agglomeration attracts more business investment; however, the importance of agglomeration in the whole manufacturing sector peaked at 10.34 in 2001 and has declined since then (Figure 5.4, left-hand panel). Agglomeration commands a less important role in spurring asset accumulation for the labour-intensive industries than for the manufacturing sector as a whole. Interestingly, the significance of clustering in influencing spatial distribution of capital in the labour-intensive industries has declined more rapidly than the overall manufacturing industries as shown by the coefficient falling from 6.21 in 1998 to 3.32 in 2008.

Table 5.3 Industrial Assets Formation (Cross-section method)

All manufacturing

	1998	1999	2000	2001	2002	2003	2004	2005	2006	2007	2008
Approx.	8.88**	8.46**	9.80**	10.34**	9.73**	8.96**	9.32***	8.82**	8.99**	8.94**	9.16**
	(−1.66)	(−1.68)	(−1.61)	(−1.64)	(−1.6)	(−1.68)	(−1.43)	(−1.55)	(−1.43)	(−1.48)	(−1.51)
Population (ln)	1.25**	1.27***	1.28**	1.28**	1.21**	1.22**	1.15***	1.12**	1.08**	1.05**	1.04**
	(−0.06)	(−0.06)	(−0.06)	(−0.07)	(−0.07)	(−0.07)	(−0.06)	(−0.06)	(−0.06)	(−0.06)	(−0.06)
Taxrate (ln)	0.01	0.01	0.01	0.03	−0.03	−0.03	−0.03	−0.04	−0.06	−0.08*	−0.12**
	(−0.05)	(−0.05)	(−0.05)	(−0.05)	(−0.04)	(−0.04)	(−0.04)	(−0.04)	(−0.04)	(−0.04)	(−0.04)
r2_a	0.47	0.47	0.5	0.49	0.49	0.48	0.49	0.49	0.49	0.47	0.51
aic	5845	5902	5858	5913	6065	6121	6042	5979	5897	5850	5872
N	1660	1651	1682	1671	1706	1718	1728	1711	1702	1670	1716

Labour-intensive industries

	1998	1999	2000	2001	2002	2003	2004	2005	2006	2007	2008
Approx.	6.21**	6.10**	5.45**	5.21**	5.81**	2.86	3.93**	4.06**	4.86**	4.07**	3.32*
	(−1.93)	(−1.99)	(−1.98)	(−2.03)	(−1.9)	(−1.94)	(−1.92)	(−1.95)	(−1.84)	(−1.92)	(−1.85)
Population (ln)	1.14**	1.11**	1.16**	1.05**	1.00**	0.95**	1.05**	0.97**	0.93**	0.88**	0.92**
	(−0.08)	(−0.08)	(−0.08)	(−0.09)	(−0.09)	(−0.09)	(−0.09)	(−0.09)	(−0.09)	(−0.09)	(−0.08)
Taxrate (ln)	−0.05	−0.01	−0.03	−0.01	−0.04	−0.02	−0.01	−0.03	−0.06	−0.05	−0.09*
	(−0.06)	(−0.06)	(−0.06)	(−0.06)	(−0.05)	(−0.05)	(−0.05)	(−0.05)	(−0.06)	(−0.06)	(−0.05)
r2_a	0.38	0.4	0.41	0.39	0.4	0.38	0.39	0.41	0.42	0.42	0.45
aic	5824	5583	5690	5517	5572	5493	5626	5561	5409	5263	5481
N	1482	1434	1468	1418	1431	1409	1431	1434	1422	1386	1470

** represents significance level at 5 per cent

* represents significance level at 10 per cent

Note: The *t* values are in parentheses.

Source: Authors' own estimates.

The coefficient for the effective tax rate is generally insignificant for most of the years except for the last two (Figure 5.4, right-hand panel). The significant and negative coefficient in the last two years of the sample indicates that places with lower effective tax rates have become increasingly popular for business investment.

In the next set of regressions, we include the wage variable. Due to missing values for wage data in 1998 and 1999, the sample period is reduced to 2001–08. The estimated results are similar to those in Table 5.3 and are not reported here. Figure 5.5 plots only the coefficient for the wage variable from this new set of regressions. It is apparent from the figure that the coefficient first increased up to 2005 and has steadily declined since then. Prior to the 2000s, capital flocked to the coastal regions to take advantage of the agglomeration despite a higher labour cost. The rising coefficient for the wage variable in the first half of the 2000s suggests the positive agglomeration effect likely offset the rising labour cost; however, since 2005, counties' wage levels have become less correlated with local asset accumulation, suggesting that some firms have moved away from places with a higher degree of clustering—where workers often command higher wages—to lower-wage regions.

Figure 5.4 The Effect of Agglomeration and Tax Rate on Industrial Formation

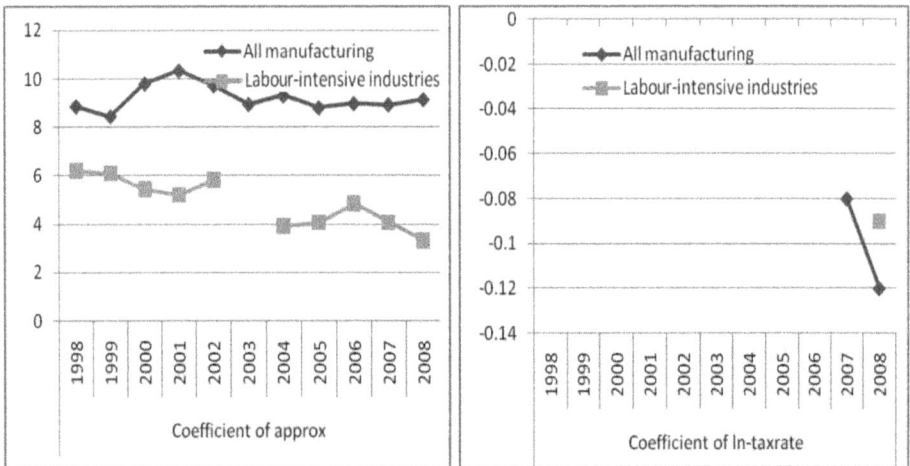

Note: The figure is depicted based on the estimated results included in Table 5.3.

Figure 5.5 The Effect of Labour Costs on Asset Formation

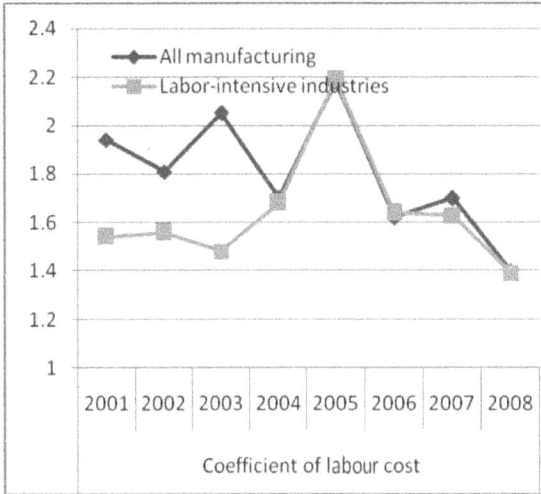

Note: The figure is depicted based on the estimated results included in Table 5.3.

The above regressions run year by year offer some suggestive evidence that capital first flowed from inland to coastal regions up to the mid-2000s and subsequently reversed this trend. This approach entails a drawback in that it is not statistically efficient to estimate the regressions year by year. In addition, it does not directly test whether the share of assets possessed by the coastal region has first gone up before coming down after controlling for the major determinants. To overcome the problems, we run further regressions on the pooled sample as follows (Equation 5.2).

Equation 5.2

$$
\begin{aligned}
Ln(K)_{it} = {} & \beta_1{}^*D + \beta_2{}^*T^*D + \beta_3{}^*T^2{}^*D \\
& + \beta_4{}^*approx_i + \beta_4{}^*T^*approx_i + \beta_6{}^*T^2{}^*approx_i \\
& + \beta_7{}^*ln(taxrate_i) + \beta_8{}^*T^*taxrate_i + \beta_9{}^*T^2{}^*taxrate_i \\
& + \beta_{10}{}^*wage_{it-1} + \beta_{11}{}^*T^*wage_{it-1} + \beta_{12}{}^*T^2{}^*wage_{it-1} \\
& + year\ effect + \varepsilon_{it}
\end{aligned}
$$

In Equation 5.2, i and t represent county and year, respectively; T is year-1998; D is a dummy variable for the coastal region; K is total assets aggregated at the county level; $approx$ is a measure of local agglomeration; $taxrate$ represents the effective tax rate; and $wage_{it-1}$ refers to the average wage at the county level in the previous year. Year fixed effects are also included. We interact the above variables with T and T^2 to capture the inverted-U shaped relationship between asset accumulation and several key determinant factors as identified in Figures 5.4 and 5.5.

Table 5.4 reports separate regression results for the entire sample, labour-intensive industries and other industries. For each sample, we present three specifications. The first regression (R1), excluding the wage variable, is based on the complete sample from 1998 to 2008. The third regression (R3) includes the wage variable. Due to missing values for the wage variable, the sample period is restricted to 2000–08. To check if any difference in the results between R1 and R3 is due to the additional wage variable or difference in the sample period, we repeat regression R1 on a smaller sample with reduced period 2000–08. The results for the coastal dummy variable and its interactions with T and T^2 are robust across all the specifications no matter which sample is used. Its interaction with the time variable is significant and positive across all nine regressions, while its interaction with T^2 is consistently statistically negative in all the specifications. This implies that after controlling for clustering, wage level and effective tax rate, the share of assets in the coastal region exhibits a clear trend: first rising and then declining. The results are consistent with the descriptive supporting evidence as shown in the previous section.

The relationship between local wages and asset accumulation also follows an inverted-U shape. The coefficient for the interaction term of wages with T is statistically positive, while the interaction terms with the squared term are negative and significant. This implies that, as time goes by, higher wages in the coastal region will eventually push capital away. The results hold no matter whether we use the whole sample, the restricted sample composed of only labour-intensive industries or the sample excluding the labour-intensive industries.

For the whole sample, the interaction term of the effective tax rate with the squared term of T is significantly negative. This suggests that, over time, effective tax rates become progressively more important in influencing asset accumulation in a location. When entrepreneurs select the destination of their investment, they have increasingly taken the 'friendliness' of the policy environment (lower taxes) into account; however, for labour-intensive industries, the results are not so robust. The coefficient for the interaction term of the effective tax rate with T^2 is significantly negative only in the first regression on the sample for the period 1998–2008. It loses significance when the sample period is cut to 2000–08.

Table 5.4 Industrial Asset Formation (Panel Regressions)

	All manufacturing			Labour-intensive industries			Others		
	Model 1	Model 2	Model 3	Model 1	Model 2	Model 3	Model 1	Model 2	Model 3
east	0.000	0.000	0.000	0.000	0.000	0.000	0.000	0.000	0.000
	(.)	(.)	(.)	(.)	(.)	(.)	(.)	(.)	(.)
T*east	0.043**	0.085**	0.078**	0.140**	0.284**	0.258**	0.029**	0.068**	0.060**
	(−0.011)	(−0.03)	(−0.029)	(−0.013)	(−0.036)	(−0.036)	(−0.011)	(−0.031)	(−0.03)
T²*east	−0.003**	−0.006**	−0.005**	−0.009**	−0.020**	−0.017**	−0.002**	−0.005**	−0.004*
	(−0.001)	(−0.002)	(−0.002)	(−0.001)	(−0.003)	(−0.003)	(−0.001)	(−0.002)	(−0.002)
approx	0.000	0.000	0.000	0.000	0.000	0.000	0.000	0.000	0.000
	(.)	(.)	(.)	(.)	(.)	(.)	(.)	(.)	(.)
T*approx	0.532**	0.236	0.241	−0.173	0.561	0.434	0.338*	0.464	0.324
	(−0.183)	(−0.481)	(−0.469)	(−0.246)	(−0.668)	(−0.662)	(−0.191)	(−0.508)	(−0.498)
T²*approx	−0.044**	−0.023	−0.019	−0.023	−0.075	−0.061	−0.012	−0.022	−0.007
	(−0.018)	(−0.037)	(−0.036)	(−0.024)	(−0.051)	(−0.05)	(−0.018)	(−0.039)	(−0.038)
Taxrate (ln)	−0.262	−0.415	−0.466	−1.023*	−1.393**	−1.634**	0.002	−0.032	−0.17
	(−0.482)	(−0.532)	(−0.532)	(−0.547)	(−0.61)	(−0.616)	(−0.495)	(−0.55)	(−0.552)
T*taxrate (ln)	−0.010**	0.007	0.005	0.003	0.001	−0.001	−0.007	0.003	0
	(−0.005)	(−0.012)	(−0.012)	(−0.006)	(−0.016)	(−0.016)	(−0.005)	(−0.013)	(−0.013)
T²*taxrate (ln)	−0.001*	−0.002**	−0.002**	−0.002**	−0.002	−0.002	−0.001**	−0.002*	−0.002
	(0)	(−0.001)	(−0.001)	(−0.001)	(−0.001)	(−0.001)	(−0.001)	(−0.001)	(−0.001)
Wage (ln)			0.190**			−0.076	(0)		0.235**
			(−0.092)			(−0.102)			(−0.092)
T*wage (ln)			0.059*			0.111**			0.053*
			(−0.03)			(−0.034)			(−0.03)
T²*wage (ln)			−0.006**			−0.010**			−0.006**
			(−0.002)			(−0.003)			(−0.002)
Year effects	Yes	Yes	Yes	Yes	Yes	Yes	Yes	Yes	Yes
r2_a	0.274	0.216	0.236	0.238	0.194	0.205	0.248	0.19	0.211
aic	44 980	29 991	28 489	41 467	27 775	26 464	46 014	31 002	29 640
N	24 131	17 648	17 495	19 733	14 227	13 892	23 988	17 567	17 410

** represents significance level at 5 per cent

* represents significance level at 10 per cent

Notes: The *t* values are in parentheses; Model 1 uses the sample 1998–2008; Model 2 and Model 3 use the sample 2001–08. Variables of *east* and *approx* are dropped in the function because of multi-collinearity with the year fixed effects.

Source: Authors' own estimates.

Conclusions

In the past several years, there have been more and more media reports on labour shortages, in particular in the coastal regions. Some have argued that China has passed the Lewis turning point (Cai 2008; Zhang et al. 2011). As labour costs keep rising, the labour-intensive manufacturing industries—most of which are located in coastal regions—will gradually lose their cost advantages in the international market. They have to either upgrade quality to move up the value chain or relocate their business to places with lower labour costs.

Based on the census-type survey for above-scale manufacturing enterprises from 1998 to 2008, this chapter shows that a transfer of capital from the coastal to the inland region has occurred since the mid-2000s—exactly corresponding with the timing of the Lewis turning point. As investment flocked inward, wage rates in the interior regions caught up with those on the coast. Consequently, the regional difference in wages narrowed over time. As China is a large country with huge regional differences, it could take some years for wages to equalise across regions. The geese won't stop flying inward until that date. After that, there are likely to be massive relocations of labour-intensive industries from China to other developing countries with cheaper labour, such as Bangladesh and Ethiopia; however, it is not clear when that day will come.

References

Cai, F., 2007, 'The Lewisian turning point of China's economic development', in *Reports on China's Population and Labour No. 8*, Social Sciences Academic Press, Beijing, pp. 147–69.

Cai, F., 2008, 'Chinese economy: how to break through the low middle income trap', *Journal of Graduate School of Chinese Academy of Social Sciences*, vol. 1, pp. 13–18.

Cai, F., 2010, 'Labour shortage (*mingong huang*): causes and policy implications', *The Opening Herald*, vol. 2, pp. 5–10.

Cai, F., Dewen, W. and Yue, Q., 2009, 'Flying geese within borders: how does China sustain its labour-intensive industries?', *Economic Research Journal*, vol. 9, pp. 4–14.

Ciccone, A. and Rapaioannou, E., 2009, 'Human capital, the structure of production and growth', *Review of Economics and Statistics*, vol. 91, no. 1, pp. 66–82.

Duranton, G. and Puga, D., 2000, 'Nursery cities: urban diversity, process innovation, and the life cycle of products', *American Economic Review*, vol. 91, no. 5, pp. 193–204.

Fan, J., 2004, 'Yangtze River Delta integration, regional specialization and the manufacturing transfer', *Management World*, no. 11, pp. 77–96

Kojima, K., 2000, 'The "flying geese" model of Asian economic development: origin, theoretical extensions, and regional policy implications', *Journal of Asian Economics*, vol. 11, pp. 375–401.

Krugman, P., 1991, 'Increasing returns and economic geography', *Journal of Political Economy*, vol. 99, no. 3, pp. 483–99.

Long, C. and Zhang, X., 2011, 'Cluster-based industrialization in China: financing and performance', *Journal of International Economics*, vol. 84, pp. 112–23.

Lu, J. and Tao, Z., 2006, 'Industrial agglomeration and co-agglomeration in China's manufacturing industries: with international comparison', *Economic Research Journal*, no. 3, pp. 103–14.

Luo, Y. and Cao, L., 2005, 'A positive research on fluctuation trend of China's manufacturing industrial agglomeration degree', *Economic Research Journal*, no. 8, pp. 106–27.

Marshall, A., 1920, *Principles of Economics*, Macmillan, London.

Okita, S., 1985, 'Special presentation: prospects of Pacific economies', in Korea Development Institute (ed.), *Pacific Cooperation: Issues and Opportunities, Report of the Fourth Pacific Economic Cooperation Conference, Seoul, Korea, April 29 – May 1*, pp. 18–29.

Puga, D. and Venables, A. J. 1996, *The spread of industry: spatial agglomeration in economic development*, Discussion Paper No. 279, Centre for Economic Performance.

Ruan, J. and Zhang, X., 2010, *Do geese migrate domestically? Evidence from the Chinese textile and apparel industry*, IFPRI Discussion Paper 01040.

Zhang, X., 2006. 'Fiscal Decentralization and political centralization in China: Implications for growth and regional inequality', *Journal of Comparative Economics'*, vol. 34, no. 4, pp. 713–26.

Zhang, X. and Kanbur, R., 2001, 'What difference do polarisation measures make?', *Journal of Development Studies*, vol. 37, no. 3, pp. 85–98.

Zhang, X., Jin, Y. and Shenglin, W., 2011, 'China has reached the Lewis turning point', *China Economic Review*, vol. 22, pp. 542–54.

6. China's Processing Trade:

A firm-level analysis[1]

Miaojie Yu[2] and Wei Tian[3]

Introduction

The processing trade, which has become hugely popular in China, involves domestic firms obtaining raw materials or intermediate inputs from abroad, processing them locally and exporting the value-added goods. Governments usually offer tariff reduction or tariff exemption to encourage the development of processing trade. The current chapter aims to provide a comprehensive review of various trends, characteristics and productivity levels of processing trade as opposed to ordinary trade in China.

We begin with an overview of processing trade, focusing on its size and main types. Thereafter, we analyse why processing trade has developed rapidly in China in the past three decades. China's open-door policy, particularly the establishment of special export zones, has played a significant role in the rapid growth of processing trade. We use transaction-level trade data (2000–06) from China to investigate various factors affecting processing trade. These include origin and destination countries, leading import and export commodities, transport modes, firm ownership, leading ports and their trade volume, and top cities and provinces where producers and consumers are located.

Our transaction-level trade dataset includes firm-level information. Each trade transaction is attributable to a particular firm. We investigate the number of products (that is, scope) imported and exported by firms, as well as their number of trading destinations. More importantly, because firm productivity is key to understanding trade performance (Melitz 2003), we investigate the productivity growth of firms by matching transaction-level trade data with firm-level production data, and using the Olley and Pakes (1996) semi-parametric approach for estimating firm productivity. Furthermore, in carefully scrutinising processing trade in China, the present chapter contributes

1 This chapter was prepared for the China Update (2012) conference organised by The Australian National University in Canberra in July 2012. We thank Dr Ligang Song for his invitation and helpful comments. Miaojie Yu thanks Yaqi Wang for her excellent research assistance. All errors are ours.
2 Corresponding author: China Center for Economic Research, National School of Development, Peking University, Beijing, 100871, China. Tel: (+86) 10-6275-3109; email: <mjyu@ccer.pku.edu.cn>
3 Department of Applied Economics, Guanghua School of Management, Peking University; email: <Wei.tian08@gmail.com>

to the literature by providing a novel and orderly way of matching two powerful datasets—transaction-level trade data and firm-level production data—given the complexity involved and restrictions in data format.

We find that processing firms mostly come from Korea, Hong Kong and Japan. The electrical machinery and transport equipment industry has the largest volume of processing imports. The majority of processing imports are shipped to China by sea and air. Shanghai, Shenzhen and Nanjing are the three busiest customs ports for processing imports, whereas Shenzhen, Pudong and Suzhou are the districts or areas with the highest volume of processing imports. The industry with the highest per-unit value of commodities is the aircraft and spacecraft industry. The top-five countries in terms of quality of goods shipped to China for processing are all in Europe: Norway, France, Finland, Germany and the Netherlands. With regard to importer ownership, foreign-owned enterprises are the major importers of processing goods. Approximately 20 per cent of all processing firms import a single variety, whereas approximately 50 per cent import less than 10 varieties. The number of imported varieties has also declined over the years, suggesting heightened specialisation, greater domestic intermediate input, or both. Moreover, we find that processing firms are considered less productive than ordinary firms.

The rest of the chapter is organised as follows. Section two discusses the policy setting that supports processing trade in China. Section three explores various characteristics of China's processing trade. Section four offers careful scrutiny of correlated data from firm-level production and transaction-level trade, followed by a precise measure of the total factor productivity of firms using a semi-parametric approach. Section five concludes.

Policy Setting to Promote Processing Trade

China's foreign trade has grown rapidly in the past three decades, alongside overall economic activity. From a low level of openness (the ratio of exports and imports over GDP) in the early 1980s, China increased its openness ratio to about 70 per cent by 2006; the country's exports accounted for 39 per cent of its GDP at this point, whereas imports accounted for 31 per cent of its gross domestic product (Figure 6.1). Although China's exports declined by 16 per cent in 2009 due to the global financial crisis, it still surpassed Germany in that year to become the world's largest exporter of goods. Today, China's foreign trade volume (that is, the sum of exports and imports) accounts for more than 10 per cent of the global trade volume.

Figure 6.1 China's Exports and Imports as a Percentage of GDP, 1978–2010

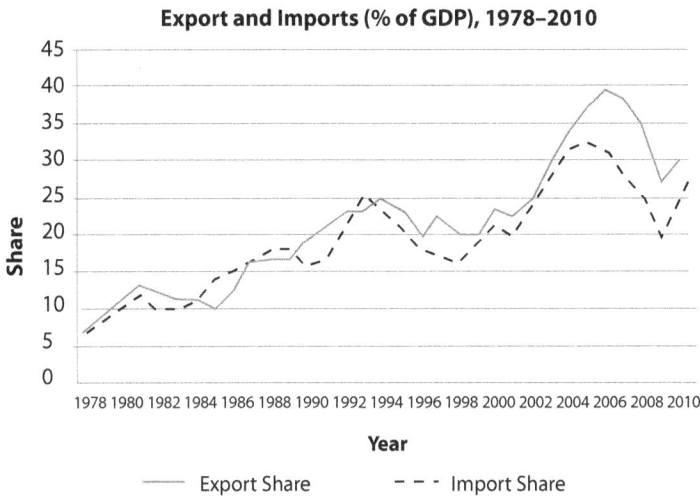

Source: NBS (2011a).

Processing trade now constitutes a very large proportion—usually one-half—of China's total trade. This trade began in China in the late 1970s. In the early 1980s, processing imports accounted for only a small proportion of total imports; however, China's processing imports dramatically increased in the early 1990s, and began to surpass ordinary imports in 1994 (Figure 6.2a). Processing trade peaked at 64 per cent of total trade in 1997 and then consolidated at about 50 per cent for a decade. Processing trade declined to about 37 per cent during the most recent financial crisis.

Figure 6.2a China's Processing Imports and Ordinary Imports, 1981–2010

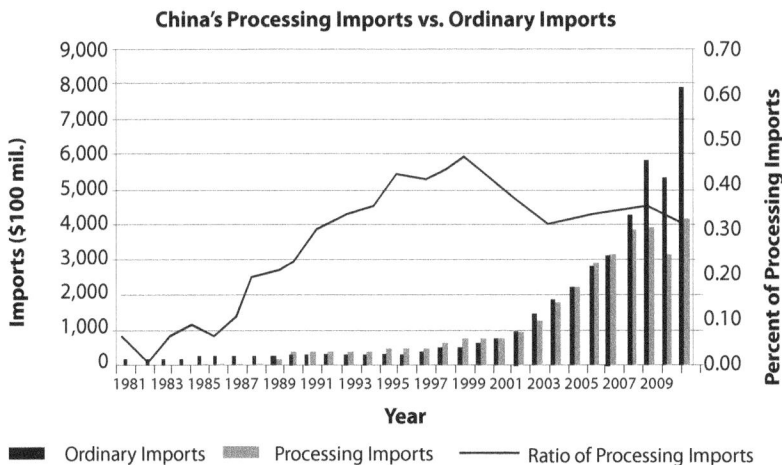

Source: NBS (2011a).

China's processing exports exhibit a similar evolution. After local assembly and processing, China exports the final value-added goods to the rest of the world. China's processing exports surpassed ordinary exports in 1998, a year after processing imports peaked in volume (Figure 6.2b). This suggests that processing and assembly usually take a considerable amount of time in China— on this evidence, more than one year but less than two. In the new century, China's processing exports have steadily accounted for more than half of its total exports. Even with the financial crisis in 2008, the proportion of China's processing exports remained higher than 50 per cent, whereas processing imports declined to about 35 per cent, indicating a gradual increase in value-adding activities associated with processing trade.

Figure 6.2b China's Processing Exports and Ordinary Exports, 1981–2010

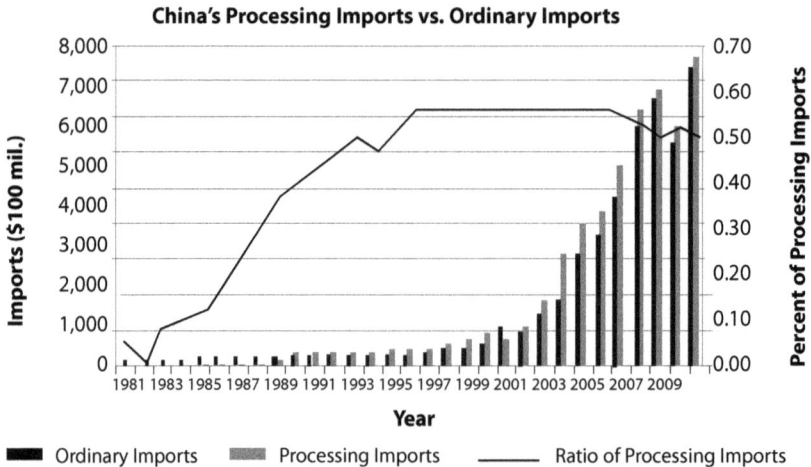

Source: NBS (2011a).

Classification by China's customs bureau shows 19 types of trade regimes: ordinary trade (code: 10), aid or donation from government or from international organisations (11), donations from Chinese overseas or Chinese with foreign citizenship (12), compensation (13), processing with assembly (14), processing using imported inputs (15), goods on consignment (16), border trade (19), contracting projects (20), equipment imported for processing and assembly (22), goods on lease (23), equipment investment by foreign-invested enterprises (25), outward processing (27), barter trade (30), duty-free commodities (31), customs warehousing trade (33), entrepot trade by bonded area (34), imported equipment by export processing zone (35), and others (39). Table 6.1 shows the percentage of trade value for each customs regime in 2010.

Table 6.1 Proportion of Customs Regime by Trade Value in 2010

Codes	Trade type by customs regime	Imports (%)	Exports (%)
10	Ordinary trade	55.096	45.673
11	International aid	0.002	0.019
12	Donation by overseas Chinese	0.013	0.000
13	Compensation trade	0.000	0.000
14	Process with assembling	7.117	7.118
15	Process with imported materials	22.783	39.802
16	Goods on consignment	0.000	0.000
19	Border trade	0.690	1.040
20	Equipment for processing trade	0.087	0.000
22	Goods for foreign-contracted project	0.000	0.800
23	Goods on lease	0.404	0.009
25	Equipment/materials investment by foreign-invested enterprise	1.168	0.000
27	Outward processing	0.009	0.012
30	Barter trade	0.000	0.000
31	Duty-free commodity	0.001	0.000
33	Warehousing trade	4.377	2.242
34	Entrepot trade by bonded area	7.826	2.313
35	Equipment imported into export processing zone	0.286	0.000
39	Other trade	0.141	0.972

Source: NBS (2011b).

Table 6.1 shows that processing imports accounted for approximately 45 per cent of total imports, whereas processing exports accounted for approximately 55 per cent of total exports in 2010. Processing imports are supposedly transformed into processing exports after local assembly and processing; however, some firms consider their imported intermediate inputs as 'processing imports' on arrival in the ports but sell their final value-added products in the domestic market.[4] Such behaviour reinforces the idea that the high share of processing exports is due to the addition of value involved in processing trade. Nevertheless, throughout this chapter, we rely on processing *imports* rather than on processing *exports* in measuring processing trade.

Besides ordinary trade, of the 18 other types of trade regime, processing with assembly and processing with intermediate inputs are the most important in China. As shown in Table 6.1, processing imports (exports) with assembly account for roughly 7.12 per cent of China's total imports (exports). In contrast,

---

4 Such imported intermediate inputs are not eligible for customs duty rebates.

processing imports with imported materials account for more than 22 per cent of total imports and 39.8 per cent of total exports. Processing with assembly was prevalent in the 1980s, and processing with imported inputs became popular after 1990.

There are two key differences between processing with assembly and processing with intermediate inputs. First, processing with assembly does not require firms to pay for the raw materials. Chinese firms, in fact, import embodied raw materials for free and then send the value-added products to the same firm in the country of origin. Chinese firms do not need to pay for intermediate costs but earn payment for their service (that is, assembly). In contrast, firms engaged in processing with imported materials are required to pay for the imported intermediate inputs. Firms import raw materials or intermediate inputs from abroad and then sell their valued-added products to the rest of the world. Here, the source and destination countries can be different.

Second, processing assembly is 100 per cent duty free. Meanwhile, firms engaged in processing using imported inputs must pay import duties for these inputs first. After exporting their processed or final goods, they may obtain a full duty rebate, indicating that firms engaged in processing using imported inputs face more credit constraints than pure assembly operations because they need to have sufficient cash flow to cover import duties (Feenstra et al. 2011). Table 6.1 clearly shows that processing with imported inputs currently exceeds processing with assembly and other types of processing trade in terms of trade volume. It is worthwhile exploring the rapid growth in China's processing trade over the past three decades.

The prevalence of processing trade in China can be directly attributed to the establishment of various free-trade zones—such as special economic zones (SEZs), economic and technological development zones (ETDZs), high-technology industrial development zones (HTIDZs) and export-processing zones (EPZs)—which underwent three phases. In the first phase, shortly before SEZs were established, several cities were allowed to contract with Hong Kong-based firms for processing with assembly. Small-scale trade was initially established.

In the spring of 1980, four coastal cities in Guangdong and Fujian provinces—namely, Shenzhen, Zhuhai and Shantou in Guangdong and Xiamen in Fujian—were selected as SEZs, mainly for their strong social connections with South-East Asia. People in Shantou and Xiamen, for instance, have enjoyed a long trading tradition and history with the region. Foreign firms found this social network favourable for investment in Mainland China. In SEZs, imports are completely duty free. Foreign investors likewise enjoy additional benefits, such as reduced income taxes. The Chinese Government grants foreign-invested enterprises (FIEs) located in the zones tax exemption in the first two years and tax reduction in the subsequent three years. In addition, firms located in SEZs enjoy greater administrative flexibility and easier access to foreign markets. These policies have proven to be highly effective. Shenzhen, formerly a small and poor village, is now one of two regional financial centres in China, with its own stock exchange.

In 1984, China's government allowed 14 eastern coastal cities to become 'open cities' in the sense that they would have similar privileges as those enjoyed by the four special economic zones. This marked the second phase of trade liberalisation. Shortly thereafter, China established two more SEZs: Pudong SEZ and Hainan Island Special Economic Zone. Furthermore, China designated the Pearl River Delta and the Yangtze River Delta as economic development areas, and opened four northern ports to trade with Mongolia, Russia and North Korea in 1991 (Figure 6.3).

Figure 6.3 China's Free-Trade Zones

◆ 1980.5 Special Economic Zone
▼ 1984 Coastal Port City
● 1984-85 National Economic Development Zone
▲ 1985-88 Economic Delta Zone
■ 1991 Northern Port
  1991 Free Trade Zone
● 1991 National New/High-Tech Development Zone

Source: Authors' own compilation from China's customs data (2010).

The third phase of China's trade liberalisation occurred in early 1992. China extended its open-door policy from the eastern coast to central and western China. Industrial cities in central and western China established various economic development zones and high-tech development zones. Table 6.2 shows that there were at least eight SEZs, 55 EPZs, 33 ETDZs, 49 HTIDZs and five bonded zones or export-oriented units (EOUs) by the end of 2010. Total processing imports in these free-trade zones accounted for more than 22 per cent of China's processing imports.

Table 6.2 Number of Special Economic Areas in China, up to 2010

Type of special economic area	Number	Proportion of processing imports
Special economic zones (SEZs)	8	3%
Export processing zones (EPZs)	55	11.2%
Economic and technological development zones (ETDZs)	33	12.8%
High-technology industrial development zones (HTIDZs)	49	4%
Bonded zones/export-oriented units (EOUs)	5	1%

Sources: Tian and Yu (forthcoming); and updated using China's customs data (2010).

Perhaps the most direct and relevant policy in promoting processing trade is the establishment of EPZs beginning in the year 2000. Barely a year before China's accession to the World Trade Organisation (WTO), China built EPZs in several eastern coastal cities. Only processing firms were allowed in the zones and were granted various privileges, such as freedom from duties and minimal administrative restrictions. By 2010, China had established 55 export processing zones. Table 6.3 ranks these EPZs and their proportion of imports over total country-wide processing imports. In 2010, all processing imports in the EPZs accounted for 11.5 per cent of China's total processing trade. Jiangsu has the largest number of EPZs, with 12 of the 55 export processing zones. Kunshan EPZ in Jiangsu Province is the largest among all EPZs, contributing 2.62 per cent of China's total processing imports.

Table 6.3 Ranking of Export Processing Zones by Processing Imports in 2010

Ranking	Name	Percentage	Ranking	Name	Percentage
1	Kunshan, JS	2.6213	29	Jinan, SD	0.0165
2	Songjiang, SH	1.8914	30	Nantong, JS	0.0157
3	Yantai, SD	1.3422	31	Yubei, CQ	0.0146
4	Xuzhou, JS	1.0562	32	Nanchang, JX	0.0144
5	Chengdu, SC	1.0019	33	Jiading, SH	0.0128
6	Wuxi, JS	0.6701	34	Shenyang, LN	0.0113
7	Ningbo, ZJ	0.5542	35	Changshu, JS	0.0109
8	Minhang, SH	0.4190	36	Jiaxing, ZJ	0.0099
9	Xi'an, SX	0.2945	37	Fuzhou, FJ	0.0097
10	Shenzhen, GD	0.1725	38	Zhuhai, GD	0.0081
11	Hanzhou, ZJ	0.1618	39	Zhenjiang, JS	0.0073
12	Fengxian, SH	0.1127	40	Wuhan, HB	0.0065
13	Weihai, SD	0.0971	41	Guangzhou, GD	0.0064
14	Nanjing, JS	0.0834	42	Shijiazhuang, HB	0.0062
15	Changzhou, JS	0.0538	43	Hohhot, IM	0.0057
16	Dalian, JN	0.0531	44	Tanggu, TJ	0.0057
17	Shunli, BJ	0.0437	45	Cixi, ZJ	0.0054
18	Xiamen, FJ	0.0411	46	Binzhou, HN	0.0048
19	Yanzhou, JS	0.0395	47	Lianyungang, JS	0.0040
20	Qingpu, SH	0.0374	48	Kunming, YN	0.0034
21	Beihai, GD	0.0349	49	Hunchun, JL	0.0031
22	Qingdao, SD	0.0339	50	Quanzhou, FJ	0.0028
23	Haiyin, JS	0.0303	51	Weifang, SD	0.0022
24	Zhengzhou, HN	0.0285	52	Mianyan, SC	0.0021
25	Wujiang, JS	0.0227	53	Qinhuangdiao, HB	0.0011
26	Wuhu, AH	0.0198	54	Ganzhou, JX	0.0004
27	Pudong, SH	0.0187	55	Urumqi, XJ	0.0002
28	Jiujiang, JX	0.0169			

Source: Authors' own compilation from China's customs data (2010).

Figure 6.4 presents a geographic distribution of EPZs in China. Processing imports are concentrated in three areas: Suzhou in Jiangsu Province and Shanghai and Yantai in Shandong Province. The cities of Xuzhou in Jiangsu Province, Chengdu in Sichuan Province, Wuxi in Jiangsu Province and Ningbo in Zhejiang Province yield processing imports that make up more than 1 per cent of country-wide processing imports. Most EPZs are located in eastern coastal cities, as expected. A notable and interesting finding is that all EPZs are located north of the Yangtze River. This suggests, to some degree, the Chinese Government's intention to promote processing trade in northern China.

Figure 6.4 Geographic Distribution and Proportion of Export Processing Zones in China, 2010

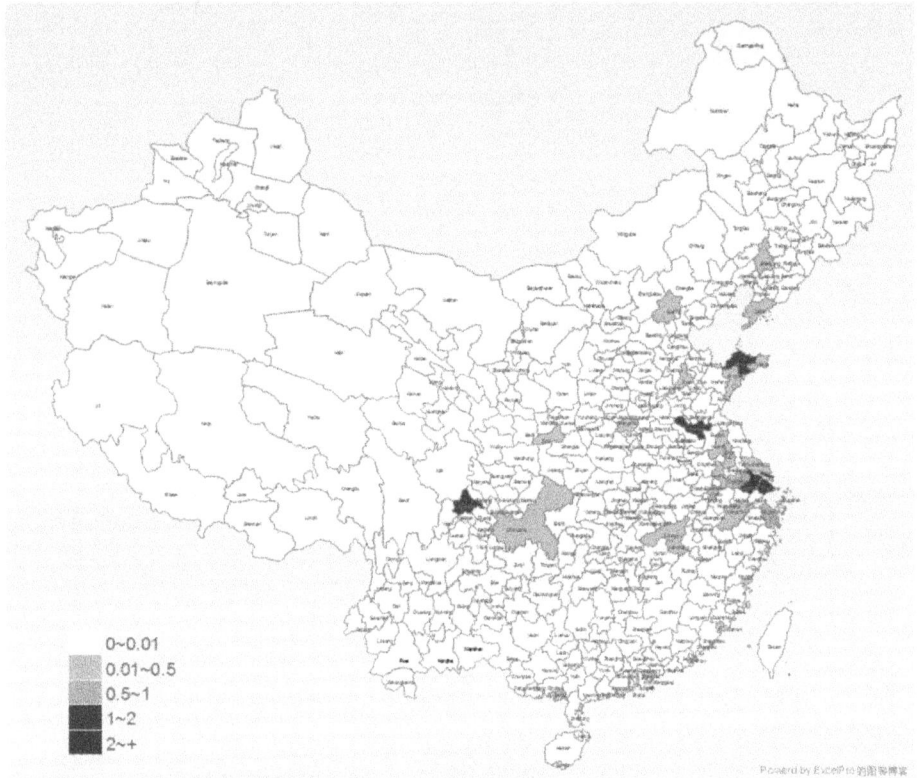

Note: Numbers shown in the figure represent the percentage of the export processing zone in total processing imports in China.

Source: Authors' own compilation from China's customs data (2010).

Aside from EPZs, other free-trade zones have contributed to the surge of processing trade in China. Although China has only eight SEZs, processing imports in these zones make up more than 3 per cent of the country's total processing trade, as illustrated in Table 6.4.

Table 6.4 Ranking of Special Economic Zones by Processing Imports in 2010

Ranking	Name	Percentage	Ranking	Name	Percentage
1	Shenzhen, GD	1.7464	5	Shantou, GD	0.0777
2	Zhuhai, GD	0.6235	6	Yunfu, GD	0.0538
3	Xiamen, FJ	0.5908	7	Other, HN	0.0152
4	Haikou, HN	0.1334	8	Sanya, HN	0.0029

Source: Authors' own compilation from China's customs data (2010).

Total processing imports from bonded areas are relatively small. There were five bonded areas in China in 2010: Tanggu, Pudong, Ningbo, Qingdao and Zhanjiagang. Only the bonded area of Tanggu, located in Tianjin Province, yielded a relatively large share of processing imports (0.81 per cent). Contributions from other bonded areas are relatively economically insignificant. By way of comparison, high-technology industrial development zones (HTIDZs) yield approximately 4 per cent of China's total processing imports. As shown in Table 6.5, there are 49 HTIDZs in China today, the largest of which is Suzhou HTIDZ in Jiangsu Province, which accounts for 1.38 per cent of China's total processing imports, as exhibited in Table 6.5.

Table 6.5 Ranking of High-Technology Industrial Development Zones by Processing Imports in 2010

Ranking	Name	Percentage	Ranking	Name	Percentage
1	Suzhou, JS	1.3834	26	Minhang, SH	0.0043
2	Wuxi, JS	1.0092	27	Fengtai, BJ	0.0037
3	Guangzhou, GD	1.0063	28	Xianyang, SX	0.003
4	Huizhou, GD	0.228	29	Mianyang, SC	0.0029
5	Wuhan, HB	0.2104	30	Changping, BJ	0.0028
6	Xuhui, SH	0.1231	31	Jilin, JL	0.0024
7	Shenzhen, GD	0.085	32	Anshan, LN	0.0015
8	Baoding, HB	0.0838	33	Zhongshan, GD	0.0015
9	Xiamen, FJ	0.0819	34	Guilin, GX	0.001
10	Weihai, SD	0.0551	35	Jiulongpo, CQ	0.001
11	Haidion, BJ	0.0534	36	Xiangfan, HB	0.001
12	Nankai, TJ	0.0495	37	Nanjing, JS	0.0009
13	Shenyang, LN	0.0344	38	Chaoyang, BJ	0.0008
14	Chengdu, SC	0.0321	39	Weifang, SD	0.0006
15	Nanchang, JX	0.0311	40	Changsha, HN	0.0003
16	Xi'an, SX	0.0301	41	Zhengzhou, HN	0.0002
17	Dalian, LN	0.021	42	Lanzhou, GS	0.0001
18	Kunming, YN	0.0207	43	Zhuzhou, HN	0.0000
19	Hefei, AH	0.0147	44	Urumqi, XJ	0.0000
20	Changzhou, JS	0.0138	45	Shijiazhuang, HB	0.0000
21	Nanjing, JS	0.012	46	Jinan, SD	0.0000
22	Hangzhou, ZJ	0.0109	47	Nanning, GX	0.0000
23	Zibo, SD	0.0052	48	Guiyang, GZ	0.0000
24	Zhuhai, GD	0.0052	49	Taiyuan, SX	0.0000
25	Changchun, JL	0.0045			

Source: Authors' own compilation from China's customs data (2010).

Economic and technological development zones (ETDZs) are the leading zones for processing imports. As shown in Table 6.6, Suzhou ETDZ in Jiangsu Province accounts for 4.83 per cent of China's total processing imports, which is significantly higher than that accounted for by the largest EPZ, Kunshan EPZ in Jiangsu. Combined processing imports from the 33 ETDZs (12.8 per cent) are higher than those from the 55 EPZs (11.5 per cent). One possible reason is that EPZs were established much later than ETDZs. This implies that the absorption of processing imports takes time to materialise. Jiangsu Province has outperformed other provinces in welcoming processing imports.

Table 6.6 Ranking of Economic and Technological Development Zones by Processing Imports in 2010

Ranking	Name	Percentage	Ranking	Name	Percentage
1	Suzhou, JS	4.8365	18	Shenyang, LN	0.034
2	Pudong, SH	2.1234	19	Taiyuan, SX	0.0277
3	Tanggu, TJ	1.4245	20	Hefei, AH	0.0277
4	Daxing, BJ	0.8821	21	Nanhui, SH	0.0258
5	Dalian, LN	0.8012	22	Lianyungang, JS	0.0252
6	Guangzhou, GD	0.7714	23	Wuhu, AH	0.0189
7	Yantai, SD	0.3768	24	Zhanjiang, GD	0.0117
8	Ningbo, ZJ	0.296	25	Changchun, JL	0.0047
9	Qingdao, SD	0.2247	26	Harbin, HLJ	0.0042
10	Other, HN	0.1621	27	Wenzhou, ZJ	0.0032
11	Fuzhou, FJ	0.1609	28	Nanan, CQ	0.001
12	Nantong, JS	0.1293	29	Chengdu, SC	0.0008
13	Hangzhou, ZJ	0.123	30	Xining, QH	0.0000
14	Wuhan, HB	0.0766	31	Yinchuan, NX	0.0000
15	Urumqi, XJ	0.0618	32	Shihezi, XJ	0.0000
16	Qinhuangdao, HB	0.0575	33	Changning, SH	0.0000
17	Minhang, SH	0.0469			

Source: Authors' own compilation from China's customs data (2010).

In brief, the rapid growth of China's processing trade is largely due to the establishment of various free-trade zones, such as SEZs, ETDZs, HTIDZs and EPZs, in the past three decades. ETDZs and EPZs lead in terms of promoting processing imports.

The Characteristics of Processing Trade

In this section, we discuss various characteristics of processing trade: the top 10 countries from which China imports processing intermediate inputs, the top 10 industries of processing imports, the percentage distribution of processing imports by transport mode, the percentage distribution of share of imports by ownership of firms, the scope of processing firms, and the quality of processing imports. Processing imports, ordinary imports and total imports are compared. To realise these comparisons, we rely on transaction-level trade data provided by China's customs bureau, which recorded about 3.3 million import transactions in 2010. The dataset includes information on the customs district, the location of the Chinese importer, customs regime, countries of departure/origin, location of Chinese consumers, transport modes, HS eight-digit codes, quantity and monthly values (measured in US dollars). This dataset does not, however, include firm-level information. Considering that firm-level analysis is critical to understanding China's processing trade from the micro-perspective, we resort to using transaction-level trade data (2000–06) from an earlier period, which include firm-level information.

The Origin of Processing Imports

Our initial inquiry rests on the origin of processing imports. We compile customs data for the year 2010 to determine the top 10 countries in terms of total imports, processing imports and ordinary imports. As shown in the last two columns of Table 6.7, China primarily imports from Japan, Korea and Taiwan Province. China also imports much from its entrepots, Hong Kong and Macao. Although the United States ranks only fifth in terms of total imports, it ranks next to Japan in terms of ordinary imports. In terms of processing imports, Korea ranks first, followed by Hong Kong, Japan and Taiwan Province. This suggests in part that China imports core intermediate inputs from Korea and Japan and then exports final value-added products to the United States and Europe.

Table 6.7 Ranking of Imports by Region by Customs Regime in 2010

Ranking	Country	Processing imports (%)	Country	Ordinary imports (%)	Country	Total imports (%)
1	Korea	14.97	Japan	11.77	Japan	12.80
2	China	14.43	United States	8.34	Korea	10.02
3	Japan	14.06	Germany	7.66	Taiwan	8.40
4	Taiwan	13.93	Australia	7.37	China	7.76
5	United States	6.17	Korea	5.95	United States	7.36
6	Malaysia	5.43	Brazil	4.58	Germany	5.40
7	Thailand	3.43	Taiwan	3.87	Australia	4.38
8	Germany	2.65	Saudi Arabia	3.41	Malaysia	3.66
9	Singapore	2.43	Angola	2.78	Brazil	2.77
10	Philippines	1.85	China	2.28	Thailand	2.41
Total		79.34		58.02		64.96

Notes: Here proportions denote the ratio of processing (ordinary or both) imports by country over China's total processing (ordinary or both) imports in 2010. 'China' here refers to imports from Hong Kong and Macao special administrative regions.

Source: Authors' own compilation from China's customs data (2010).

In terms of total import volume, the top 10 regions make up two-thirds of China's total imports and 80 per cent of China's processing imports. The remaining 20 per cent of processing imports are produced by 200 trading partners in the rest of the world. The next section discusses the kinds of products that China imports as intermediate inputs.

Top Products of Processing Imports

As shown in Table 6.8, the electrical machinery and transport equipment industry yields the largest volume of processing imports, accounting for approximately 40 per cent of China's total. Along with this industry, four other industries—machinery and mechanical appliances, optical and photographic instruments, mineral fuels and oils, and plastic—account for approximately 70 per cent of China's total processing imports. These five industries import a huge volume of intermediate inputs; however, it is still worthwhile investigating whether these industries adopt a large volume of domestic inputs.

Table 6.8 Ranking of Imports by Industry in 2010

Ranking	HS 2-Digit	Proportion of imports	HS 2-Digit	Proportion of imports
1	Electrical machinery and equipment	38.97	Electrical machinery and equipment	22.83
2	Machinery and mechanical appliances	13.99	Mineral fuels, mineral oils	13.71
3	Optical, photographic instruments	10.25	Machinery and mechanical appliances	12.51
4	Mineral fuels, mineral oils	5.98	Ores, slag and ash	7.90
5	Plastics and articles thereof	5.44	Optical, photographic instruments	6.54
6	Copper and articles thereof	3.10	Plastics and articles thereof	4.63
7	Organic chemicals	2.35	Vehicles other than railway	3.60
8	Iron and steel	1.74	Organic chemicals	3.50
9	Rubber and articles thereof	1.59	Copper and articles thereof	3.35
10	Aircraft, spacecraft and parts	1.10	Oil seeds, industrial plants	1.97

Notes: Here proportions denote the ratio of processing (or total) imports by HS two-digit industry over China's total processing (total) imports in 2010.

Source: Authors' own compilation from China's customs data (2010).

We calculate the ratio of *imported* intermediate inputs against total intermediate inputs for several industries. Industrial intermediate inputs combine both imported and domestic intermediate inputs. We utilise data on intermediate inputs maintained by China's customs bureau and China's input–output data for 2005 to calculate the ratio of imported intermediate inputs. As shown in Figure 6.5, the five aforementioned industries use a large amount of imported intermediate inputs (for example, the ratio for machinery is 30 per cent, whereas the ratio for non-metal minerals is 17 per cent).

Figure 6.5 Ratio of Imported Intermediate Inputs, 2006

Ratio of Imported Intermediate Input

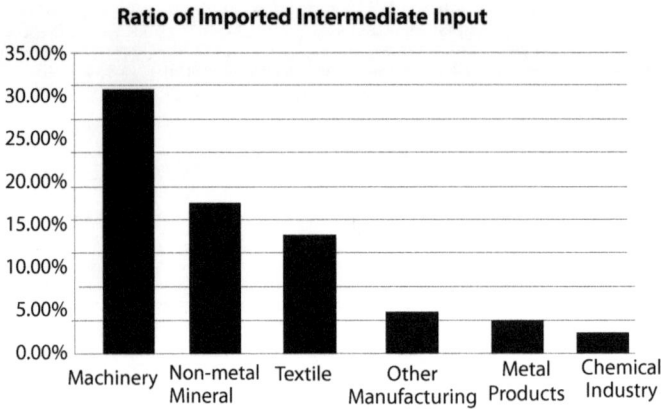

Source: Cited in Yu (2011a).

Transportation Modes

There is ample evidence showing electrical machinery and transport equipment commodities are the most dominant among processing imports in China. How these products reach China's ports is another interesting question. Do these imports arrive in China by sea, land or air? We classify these imports by transport mode used in 2010. Six types of transport mode are identified in this chapter: sea (or river if applicable), railway, truck, air, post and others. The last column of Table 6.9 shows that 62.52 per cent of processing imports (in terms of value) reached China by sea in 2010, suggesting sea shipment to be the prevailing mode of transportation. This observation is consistent with the fact that most of China's free-trade zones are located along its eastern Pacific coast. The second most common transport mode is air (19.63 per cent) and then by truck (15.72 per cent).

Table 6.9 Proportion of Imports by Transport Mode in 2010

Transport mode	Processing	Ordinary	Total
By sea	41.47	79.81	62.52
By railway	1.09	1.58	1.36
By truck	27.42	6.12	15.72
By air	29.56	11.47	19.63
By post	0.01	0.04	0.03
Other	0.45	0.99	0.75

Note: Here proportions denote the ratio of processing (ordinary or both) imports by transport mode over China's total processing (ordinary or both) imports in 2010.

Source: Authors' own compilation from China's customs data (2010).

The leading transport modes for all processing imports are the same as above. Sea shipment accounts for 41 per cent, whereas air shipment and truck shipment account for 29.56 per cent and 27.42 per cent, respectively. It is surprising to note that the percentage of air shipment is higher than that of truck shipment because, intuitively, there should be more commodities shipped by truck. The value of imports was used as a measurement, however, not the quantity of goods. The average per-unit price of commodities sent by air shipment is usually higher than that for commodities sent by truck.

The Most Important Ports

We switch our interest to customs ports in China with the largest volume of total imports, processing imports and ordinary imports. The top 10 ports in terms of the volume of processing imports in 2010 were Shanghai, Shenzhen, Nanjing, Qingdao, Huangpu in Guangzhou, Guangzhou, Tianjin, Gongbei in Shanghai, Dalian and Beijing (Table 6.10). Except for Beijing, these ports are seaports or river ports (for example, Nanjing) located on the eastern Pacific coast. The port of Shanghai is the largest port not only for processing imports but also for ordinary imports. Moreover, Shanghai's port is the largest port for total imports, followed by Shenzhen—a special economic zone located in Guangdong Province.

Table 6.10 The Top 10 Ports with Largest Volume of Imports, 2010

Ranking	Ports	Processing	Ports	Ordinary	Ports	Total imports
1	Shanghai	22.57	Shanghai	15.99	Shanghai	18.97
2	Shenzhen	17.77	Qingdao	10.46	Shenzhen	12.64
3	Nanjing	15.23	Tianjin	8.57	Nanjing	11.38
4	Qingdao	9.19	Shenzhen	8.42	Qingdao	9.15
5	Huangpu	7.57	Nanjing	8.23	Huangpu	6.46
6	Guangzhou	3.40	Ningbo	6.10	Tianjin	6.14
7	Tianjin	3.19	Dalian	4.62	Ningbo	4.42
8	Gongbei	3.02	Huangpu	4.23	Dalian	3.80
9	Dalian	2.80	Hangzhou	4.05	Guangzhou	3.69
10	Beijing	2.78	Guangzhou	3.92	Beijing	3.38

Source: Authors' own compilation from China's customs data (2010).

The top three ports with the largest share of processing imports are Shanghai, Shenzhen and Nanjing, comprising more than 55 per cent of China's total processing imports. This confirms that most processing imports are located in Shanghai, Guangdong and Jiangsu. In contrast, the top three ports with the most ordinary imports—namely, Shanghai, Qingdao and Tianjin—account for only 35 per cent of China's total ordinary imports. This suggests that China's processing imports are more concentrated than its ordinary imports.

The Most Strongly Demanded Locations

We next examine the destination of processing imports in China. Most processing goods are imported through Shanghai, Shenzhen and Nanjing, so a natural conjecture is that processing importers are concentrated in these areas. Processing firms would choose their closest port to reduce transport costs. To verify this conjecture, we determine the top 10 strongly demanded cities/districts using China's transaction-level trade data for 2010 (Table 6.11).

Table 6.11 The Top 10 Strongly Demanded Cities, 2010

Ranking	City	Processing	City	Ordinary	City	Total imports
1	Shenzhen, GD	7.40	Chaoyang, BJ	10.05	Chaoyang, BJ	6.41
2	Pudong, SH	6.11	Xicheng, BJ	5.71	Shenzhen, GD	3.58
3	Suzhou, JS	4.56	Haidian, BJ	3.06	Pudong, SH	3.27
4	Dongguan, GD	3.64	Chaoyang, BJ	2.87	Mentougou, BJ	3.22
5	Shenzhen, GD	2.38	Pudong, SH	1.76	Suzhou, JS	2.38
6	Chaoyang, BJ	1.98	Shenzhen, GD	1.47	Dongguan, GD	1.89
7	Songjiang, SH	1.74	Guangzhou, GD	1.13	Haidian, BJ	1.71
8	Dongguan, GD	1.74	Pudong, SH	1.06	Chanyang, BJ	1.58
9	Kunshan, JS	1.24	Shenzhen, GD	0.95	Pudong, BJ	1.33
10	Dongguan, GD	1.09	Pudong, SH	0.93	Shenzhen, GD	1.08

Note: Sometimes a city is displaced more than once since it could contain firms in different zones such as an EPZ, ETDZ or and HTIDZ.

Source: Authors' own compilation from China's customs data (2010).

Shenzhen, Pudong and Suzhou prove to be the top three districts with the most processing imports; however, they account for only 18 per cent of total processing imports. The leading destinations for processing imports are different from the leading destinations for ordinary imports (that is, Chaoyang, Xicheng and Haidian, which are all in Beijing). One possible explanation is that ordinary imports include more final consumption goods, whereas processing imports include mostly intermediate goods. Combining processing imports and ordinary imports, Chaoyang in Beijing replaces Shenzhen and Pudong as the top import destination in 2010, receiving 6.41 per cent of total imports in China.

Quality of Processing Imports

Another interesting issue is the quality of processing imports. China imports raw materials from many trading partners, so which countries ship products of the highest quality? Which goods have the highest quality? Answering these questions requires coming up with an appropriate measure of the quality of goods, which is a challenging task (Khandelwal 2010). A common gauge is the per-unit value of products (Hallak 2006), which is obtained by dividing a good's value by its quantity.

Figure 6.6 shows the top 10 countries that ship goods with the highest quality to China. Interestingly, nine of these 10 countries (regimes) are located in Europe. The top five countries are: Norway, France, Finland, Germany and the Netherlands. The United States ranks sixth. Meanwhile, the top five countries (regimes) with the highest quality of *ordinary* imports are Cayman Islands, Finland, Germany, Panama and Austria. Cayman Islands is capable of exporting high-quality products due to its 'tax-haven' privileges. Certain countries can export their products to Cayman Islands, which serves as an entrepot, for eventual shipment to China.

Figure 6.6 The Top 10 Countries with Highest Quality of Processing Goods Shipped to China

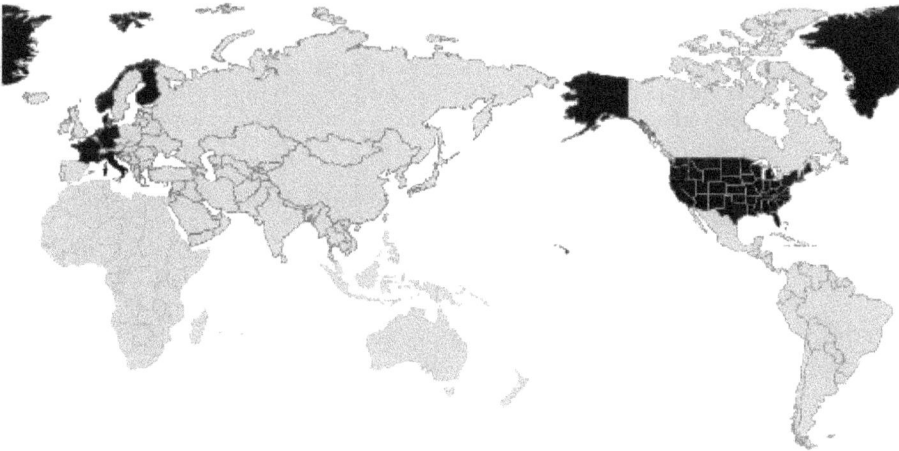

Note: The coloured areas denote the top 10 countries (regimes) with the highest product quality for processing goods shipped to China in 2010: Norway, France, Finland, Germany, the Netherlands, the United States, Austria, Switzerland, Italy and Denmark.

Source: Authors' own compilation from China's customs data (2010).

Table 6.12 lists industries that lead in terms of importing high-quality raw materials for processing. Imports for the aircraft and spacecraft industry have the largest per-unit value at approximately $2.39 million, followed by ships and boats, and machinery and mechanical appliances. The table likewise shows very high differences in the per-unit value of products imported by the top three importing industries.

Table 6.12 Top 10 Industries with Highest Quality of Processing Imports, 2010

Code	Descriptions of HS 2-digit codes	Unit value
88	Aircraft, spacecraft, and parts thereof	2 398 441
89	Ships, boats and floating structures	482 843
84	Nuclear reactors, boilers, machinery and mechanical appliances	42 994
90	Optical, photographic, medical or surgical instruments	17 576
87	Vehicles other than railway or tramway rolling stock	13 083
86	Railway or tramway locomotives, rolling stock and parts	3493
85	Electrical machinery and equipment and parts thereof	2890
30	Pharmaceutical products	1064
92	Musical instruments, parts and accessories	878
81	Other base metals, cement, articles thereof	727

Source: Authors' own compilation from China's customs data (2010).

Ownership of Processing Importing Firms

Thus far, we have gained some understanding of China's processing imports from the industrial perspective, specifically the origin countries, main products, transport mode, entry ports, consumption destinations and even quality of commodities. Now, we take a step forward to understand the micro-mechanism. In particular, we explore what types of firms frequently engage in processing trade. In terms of ownership, what types of firms account for the largest proportion of China's processing imports? We use China's customs transaction-level data for 2010 to answer this question.

Table 6.13 Proportion of Imports by Ownership of Firms in 2010

Firm type	Processing	Ordinary	Total
State-owned enterprise	12.24	41.23	28.16
Sino–foreign contractual joint venture	0.66	0.44	0.54
Sino–foreign equity joint venture	16.53	14.14	15.22
Foreign-invested enterprise	58.76	20.70	37.86
Collective enterprise	1.42	3.45	2.54
Private enterprise	10.17	20.00	15.57
Other, including foreign company's office in China	0.01	0.01	0.01

Note: Here proportions denote the ratio of processing (ordinary or both) imports by ownership of firms of China's total processing (ordinary or both) imports in 2010.

Source: Authors' own compilation from China's customs data (2010).

As shown in Table 6.13, more than half of processing imports are attributable to foreign-invested enterprises. Another 17 per cent of processing imports are attributable to Sino–foreign joint ventures (either contractual or equity joint ventures). State-owned and private enterprises account for only a relatively small proportion (12.2 per cent and 10.2 per cent, respectively). Meanwhile, state-owned enterprises (SOEs) are the most important type of firms involved in ordinary imports (third column of Table 6.13). Combining both processing and ordinary imports (last column of Table 6.10), foreign-invested enterprises are the most important type of importers (37.86 per cent), followed by state-owned enterprises (28.16 per cent).

The Scope of Activity Conducted by Import Processing Firms

How many varieties do processing firms import? Compared with ordinary importing firms, do processing firms import more varieties? Answering these questions requires a dataset containing firm-level information. China's 2010 customs dataset (the most recently released version) does not include such information. As a compromise, we have to rely on an older dataset. We therefore adopt China's transaction-level trade data for 2000–06, which include firm-level information, such as firm name, address, zip code and telephone numbers.

Figure 6.7 Four Types of Firms in China

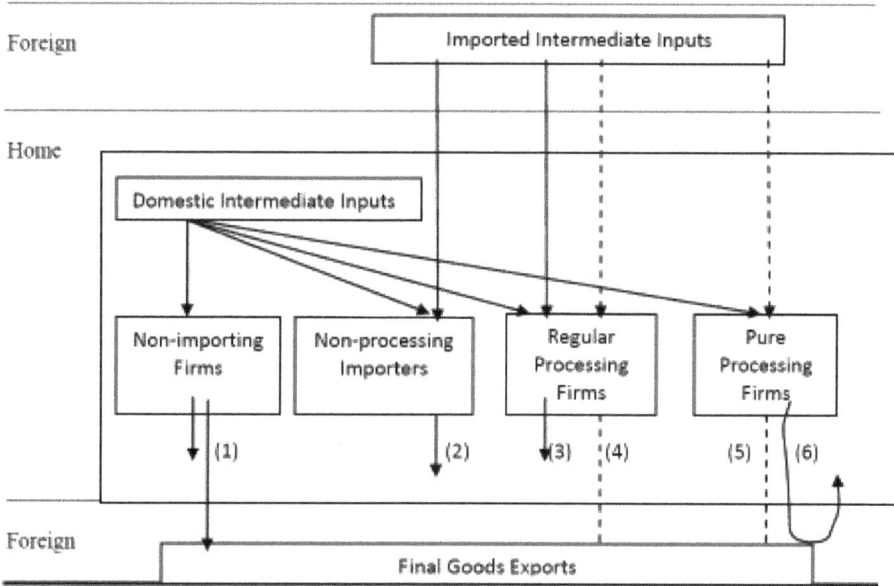

Note: Dotted lines represent firms' processing imports (exports) whereas solid lines denote firms' non-processing (that is, ordinary) imports (exports).

Sources: Cited from Yu (2011a).

Before investigating the importation scope of processing firms, we need to provide a formal definition of such firms. Yu (2011b) classified firms in China into four types, as shown in Figure 6.7: 1) non-importing firms that do not use any foreign intermediate inputs; 2) non-processing importing firms that use some foreign intermediate inputs but do not sell their final products abroad; 3) hybrid (or regular) processing firms that engage in both processing and ordinary imports; and 4) pure processing firms that only engage in processing imports and exports, and do not sell their products in the domestic market. In the present chapter, we define both hybrid and pure processing firms as processing importers. In other words, a firm engaging in some processing imports is labelled as a processing firm.

Table 6.14a The Scope of Importing Firms by Year, 2000–06

Scope	2000	2001	2002	2003	2004	2005	2006
1	19.04	18.9	19.76	20.32	21.65	22.66	23.6
2	10.27	10.14	10.55	10.77	11.43	11.97	12.19
3	6.67	7.15	7.23	7.34	7.66	7.93	8.1
4	5.26	5.39	5.42	5.76	5.64	5.78	5.96
5	4.38	4.41	4.5	4.62	4.63	4.65	4.62
6	3.61	3.87	3.9	3.79	3.8	3.69	3.76
7	3.29	3.26	3.34	3.34	3.2	3.17	3.2
8	2.98	2.89	2.89	2.81	2.79	2.7	2.73
9	2.44	2.66	2.54	2.53	2.49	2.38	2.34
10	2.33	2.35	2.36	2.26	2.12	2.13	2.11
11–50	31.21	30.68	28.23	28.24	26.71	25.74	24.51
51–100	5.05	4.23	4.9	4.97	4.78	4.43	4.34
101–1000	3.24	3.1	2.94	2.99	2.86	2.58	2.34
> 1000	0.23	0.97	1.34	0.26	0.24	0.19	0.2
Maximum	3497	3404	3321	3211	3070	3023	2839

Source: Authors' own calculation from China's customs data (2000–06).

Table 6.14a reports the scope of processing trade by year. In 2000–06, about 20 per cent of firms imported only a single variety, and about 10 per cent imported two varieties. In 2000, about 45 per cent imported less than five varieties, whereas about 50 per cent imported less than 10 varieties. Another 31 per cent imported more than 10 but less than 50 varieties. The other 3.24 per cent imported more than 50 but less than 1000 varieties. Only 0.23 per cent of the firms imported more than 1000 varieties, with 3497 the highest number of varieties imported.

Table 6.14a also shows the dynamic pattern for each cohort. In the same period, the proportion of firms importing less than five varieties increased from 45 per cent to 54 per cent. Similarly, the proportion of firms importing less than 10 varieties increased from 60 per cent to 68 per cent. In contrast, the proportion of firms importing more than 10 varieties but less than 50 varieties declined from 31.2 per cent to 24.5 per cent. The highest number of varieties imported also declined, to 2839 in 2006.

Table 6.14b The Scope of Processing Importing Firms by Year, 2000–06

Scope	2000	2001	2002	2003	2004	2005	2006
1	20.6	20.34	21.6	22.37	23.41	24.4	25.42
2	10.69	10.56	11.09	11.45	11.71	11.97	12.32
3	6.82	7.21	7.39	7.66	7.7	7.98	8.07
4	5.42	5.7	5.55	5.78	5.77	5.86	6.07
5	4.53	4.57	4.67	4.83	4.72	4.69	4.69
6	3.69	4.06	3.9	3.95	3.87	3.88	3.81
7	3.38	3.32	3.47	3.35	3.46	3.25	3.33
8	2.9	2.95	2.86	2.99	2.98	2.79	2.75
9	2.63	2.72	2.68	2.5	2.54	2.5	2.45
10	2.32	2.44	2.44	2.34	2.29	2.21	2.16
11–50	31.04	30.62	29.37	27.93	26.73	25.96	24.51
51–100	3.96	3.73	3.45	3.36	3.37	3.09	3.1
101–1000	1.83	1.58	1.34	1.3	1.3	1.27	1.18
> 1000	0.19	0.2	0.19	0.19	0.15	0.15	0.14
Maximum	3489	3397	3319	3199	3070	3023	2836

Source: Authors' own calculation from China's customs data (2000–06).

Processing and non-processing firms share a similar importation scope pattern; however, more processing firms import a single variety than non-processing firms. In 2006, the proportion of single-variety processing importers (25.4 per cent) was higher than that of single-variety non-processing importers (23.6 per cent). In the same year, the proportion of processing firms (4.42 per cent) importing more than 50 varieties was lower than that of non-processing firms (6.88 per cent), as shown in Tables 6.14a and 6.14b.

Figure 6.8 The Maximum Scope for Importing Firms and Processing Importing Firms

Scope: Total Importers vs Processing Importers

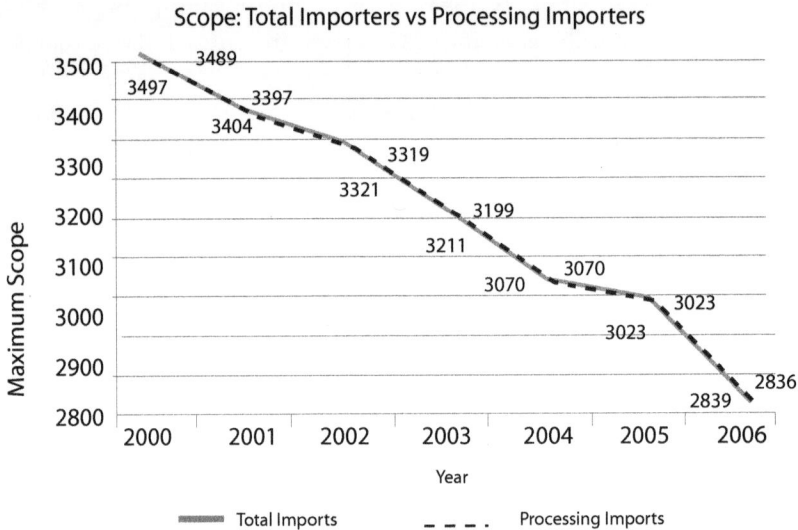

Source: Authors' own compilation from China's customs data (2000–06).

Figure 6.8 shows that the number of varieties that firms import has declined over time. Such a pattern is true for both processing and ordinary importers. For most years in the sample, processing firms have imported fewer varieties than ordinary firms. A lower variety of imports could reflect increased specialisation or it could reflect an increased sourcing of domestically produced intermediate goods, or both.

Thus far, we have understood that processing firms mostly come from Korea, Hong Kong and Japan. The industry with the largest processing imports is electrical machinery and transport equipment. Most of the processing imports are shipped to China by sea and air. The top three busiest customs ports for processing imports are Shanghai, Shenzhen and Nanjing, whereas the three districts/areas that have the most processing imports are Shenzhen, Pudong and Suzhou. The industry with the highest per-unit value of commodities is the aircraft and spacecraft industry. The five countries with the highest quality of goods shipped to China for processing are all located in Europe: Norway, France, Finland, Germany and the Netherlands. In terms of types of importer ownership, foreign-invested enterprises are the top importers of processing goods. About 20 per cent of processing firms import only a single variety, and about 50 per cent import less than 10 varieties. Furthermore, the number of imported varieties declines over time. An important question, however, is still unanswered: do processing firms have higher (or lower) productivity than non-processing firms? We now seek to answer this question.

Matching Transaction-Level Trade Data and Firm-Level Production Data

To explore the productivity performance of processing firms, we need data on processing firms' output level and labour input. If productivity is measured as total factor productivity, we also need data on capital and intermediate inputs. Transaction-level trade data offer rich information but do not contain information on production factors, such as output and input factors. Hence, we have to appeal to firm-level production data and use a merged dataset. Below, we begin by describing the two datasets, and we present a detailed technique for their merging. Thereafter, we discuss the performance of the matched dataset. Indeed, the two datasets are widely accepted in the study of China's foreign trade and firm heterogeneity. Yet, as far as we know, beyond our own work there is not yet on offer a detailed and reliable means of matching these two datasets. Thus, our chapter aims to fill a research gap on the heterogeneity of Chinese firms.

Transaction-Level Trade Dataset

Extremely disaggregated transaction-level monthly trade data for 2000–06 are obtained from China's General Administration of Customs. Each transaction is described at the HS eight-digit level. The number of monthly observations increased from about 78 000 in January 2000 to more than 230 000 in December 2006. As shown in column one of Table 6.15, the annual number of observations was more than 10 million in 2000 and 16 million in 2006, ending with a huge number of observations (118 333 831 in total) for seven years. Column two of Table 6.15 shows that 286 819 firms engaged in international trade during this period.

For each transaction, the dataset compiles three types of information: 1) five variables on basic trade information, including value (measured in current US dollars), trade status (export or import), quantity, trade unit and value per unit (value divided by quantity); 2) six variables on trade mode and pattern, including country of destination for exports, country of origin for imports, routing (whether the product is shipped through an intermediate country/regime), customs regime (processing trade or ordinary trade), trade mode (by sea, truck, air or post) and customs port (where the product departs or arrives); and 3) seven variables on firm information associated with each transaction, including firm name, identification number set by customs, Chinese city where the firm is located, telephone number, zip code, name of the manager/CEO and ownership type of firm (foreign affiliate, private or state-owned).

Firm-Level Production Dataset

The sample used in this chapter comes from a rich firm-level panel dataset covering about 230 000 manufacturing firms per year for the period 2000–06. The number of firms doubled from 162 885 in 2000 to 301 961 in 2006. The data, including full information on three accounting items—that is, balance, loss and benefit, and cash flow—are collected through an annual survey of manufacturing enterprises and maintained by China's National Bureau of Statistics (NBS). On average, the annual entire value of industrial production covered by this dataset accounts for about 95 per cent of China's total annual industrial production. Aggregated data on the industrial sector in the *China Statistical Yearbook* from the NBS are compiled from this dataset. The dataset includes more than 100 financial variables listed in the balance sheets of all firms covered. Briefly, two types of manufacturing firms are covered: all SOEs and all non-SOEs with annual sales more than RMB5 million. The number of firms increased from more than 160 000 in 2000 to 301 000 in 2006. As shown in column three of Table 6.15, the number of firms included in the dataset at any time in 2000–06 is 615 951 in total.

The raw production dataset is, however, still quite noisy given that many unqualified firms are included, largely due to misreporting by some firms. For example, information on some family-based firms, which usually have no formal accounting system in place, is based on a unit of RMB1, whereas the official requirement is a unit of RMB1000. Following Cai and Liu (2009) and Feenstra et al. (2011), we delete observations according to generally accepted accounting principles if any of the following are true: 1) liquid assets are higher than total assets; 2) total fixed assets are larger than total assets; 3) the net value of fixed assets is larger than total assets; 4) the firm's identification number is missing; or 5) an invalid established time exists (for example, the opening month is later than December or earlier than January). Accordingly, the total number of firms covered in the dataset is reduced to 438 165, and about one-third of firms are dropped from the sample after this filtering process. As shown in column four of Table 6.15, the filter ratio is even higher in the initial years: about one-half of firms in 2000 are dropped.

Matching Method

Although the two available datasets have rich information on production and trade, matching them is challenging. Both datasets contain firm identification numbers; however, the coding systems in these datasets are completely different. For example, the length of firm identifications in the transaction-level dataset is 10 digits, whereas that in the firm-level dataset is only nine digits. China's customs administration has a coding system that is completely different from that adopted by the National Bureau of Statistics.

We go through two stages to match transaction-level trade data with firm-level production data. In the first stage, we match the two datasets by firm name and year. If a firm has the exact same Chinese name in both datasets in a particular year, it should be the same firm. The year variable is necessary as an auxiliary identification variable because some firms could have different names across years and newcomers could possibly take their original names. Using the raw production dataset, we come up with 83 679 matching firms; this number is further reduced to 69 623 with the more accurate filtered production dataset.

In the second stage, we use another matching technique as a supplement. Here, we rely on two other common variables to identify firms: zip code and the last seven digits of a firm's phone number. The rationale is that firms should have different and unique phone numbers within a postal district. Although this method seems straightforward, subtle technical and practical difficulties still exist. For example, the production-level trade dataset includes both area codes and a hyphen in phone numbers, whereas the firm-level production dataset does not. Therefore, we use the last seven digits of the phone number to serve as the proxy for firm identification for two reasons. First, in 2000–06, some large Chinese cities added one more digit at the start of their seven-digit phone numbers. Therefore, sticking to the last seven digits of the number will not confuse firm identification. Second, in the original dataset, phone numbers are defined as a string of characters with the phone zip code; however, it is inappropriate to de-string such characters to numerals because a hyphen is used to connect the zip code and phone number. Using the last seven-digit sub-string neatly solves this problem.

A firm might not include its name information in either the trade or the production dataset. Similarly, a firm could lose its phone and/or zip code information. To be sure that our matched dataset can cover as many common firms as possible, we then include observations in the matched dataset if a firm occurs in *either* the name-adopted matched dataset *or* the phone-and-post-adopted matched dataset. The number of matched firms increases to 90 558 when the raw production dataset is used, as shown in column seven of Table 6.15. Our matching performance is comparable with (or even better than) that of other similar studies. For example, Ge et al. (2011) used the same datasets and similar matching techniques, but ended up with 86 336 matching firms. Meanwhile, if we match the more rigorously filtered production dataset with the firm-level dataset, we end up with 76 823 firms in total, as shown in the last column of Table 6.15.

Table 6.15 Matched Statistics: Number of firms

Year Number	Trade data		Production data		Matched data			
	Transactions	Firms	Raw Firms	Filtered Firms	w/raw Firms	w/filtered Firms	w/raw Firms	w/filtered Firms
	(1)	(2)	(3)	(4)	(5)	(6)	(7)	(8)
2000	10 586 696	80 232	162 883	83 628	18 580	12 842	21 665	15 748
2001	12 667 685	87 404	169 031	100 100	21 583	15 645	25 282	19 091
2002	14 032 675	95 579	181 557	110 530	24 696	18 140	29 144	22 291
2003	18 069 404	113 147	196 222	129 508	28 898	21 837	34 386	26 930
2004	21 402 355	134 895	277 004	199 927	44 338	35 007	50 798	40 711
2005	24 889 639	136 604	271 835	198 302	44 387	34 958	50 426	40 387
2006	16 685 377	197 806	301 960	224 854	53 748	42 833	59 133	47 591
All years	118 333 831	286 819	615 951	438 165	83 679	69 623	90 558	76 823

Notes: Column (1) reports the number of observations of HS eight-digit monthly transaction-level trade data from China's General Administration of Customs by year. Column (2) reports the number of firms covered in the transaction-level trade data by year. Column (3) reports the number of firms covered in the firm-level production dataset compiled by China's NBS without any filter or cleaning. In contrast, Column (4) presents the number of firms covered in the firm-level production dataset with careful filtering according to the requirement of GAAP. Accordingly, Column (5) reports the number of matched firms using identical company names in both the trade dataset and the raw production dataset. In contrast, Column (6) reports the number of matched firms using identical company names in both the trade dataset and the filtered production dataset. Finally, Column (7) reports the number of matched firms using identical company names and identical zip code and phone numbers in both the trade dataset and the raw production dataset. In contrast, Column (8) reports the number of matched firms using identical company names and identical zip code and phone numbers in both the trade dataset and the filtered production dataset.

Source: Authors' own compilation from China's customs data (2010) and firm-level prdocution dataset.

How does our matched dataset perform? Table 6.16 compares several key firm-level variables between the matched dataset and the full-sample production dataset. The matched sample clearly has higher means for sales, exports, number of employees, log of capital–labour ratio and even the log of labour productivity compared with the full sample, suggesting that the merged sample is skewed towards large firms. By construction, the full-sample firm-level production dataset contains only large firms (that is, with annual sales larger than $770 000), and our matched dataset contains about 70 per cent of total exports. Thus, our matched dataset is sufficiently representative of large Chinese exporting firms.

Table 6.16 Comparison of the Merged Dataset and the Full-Sample Production Dataset

	Mean	Min.	Max.	Mean	Min.	Max.
Sales	156 348	5000	1.57e+08	85 065	5000	1.57e+08
Exports	51 751	0	1.52e+08	16 544	0	1.52e+08
Number of employees	479	10	157 213	274	10	165 878
Log of capital–labour ratio	3.62	−5.71	9.87	3.53	−6.22	11.14
Log of labour productivity	3.86	−7.75	10.78	3.84	−8.96	10.79

Note: Variables = matched dataset full-sample production dataset.

Source: Cited from Qiu and Yu (2012).

Productivity for Processing Firms

With a matched trade and firm-level production dataset, we are now ready to explore the productivity of processing firms. Labour productivity is a simple and straightforward measure of productivity; however, labour productivity cannot measure the contribution of input factors other than labour. As such, total factor productivity (TFP) is a better measure because it captures contributions from all input factors.

The TFP literature usually suggests using the Cobb-Douglass production function to introduce technology improvement (Equation 6.1).

Equation 6.1

$$Y_{it} = \pi_{it} M_{it}^{\beta_m} K_{it}^{\beta_k} L_{it}^{\beta_l},$$

In Equation 6.1 Y_{it}, M_{it}, K_{it}, L_{it} is firm i's output, materials, capital and labour at year t, respectively. To measure a firm's TFP, π_{it}, one needs to estimate Equation 6.1 by taking a log function first (Equation 6.2).

Equation 6.2

$$\ln Y_{it} = \beta_0 + \beta_m \ln M_{it} + \beta_k \ln K_{it} + \beta_l \ln L_{it} + \epsilon_{it},$$

Traditionally, TFP is measured by the estimated Solow residual between the true data on output and its fitted value, $\ln \hat{Y}_{it}$. That is Equation 6.3.

Equation 6.3

$$TFP_{it} = \ln Y_{it} - \ln \hat{Y}_{it}.$$

This approach, however, suffers from two problems: simultaneity bias and selection bias. As first suggested by Marschak and Andrews (1944), at least some parts of TFP changes could be observed by firms early enough for them to change their input decisions and maximise profit. Thus, TFP could have reverse endogeneity in its input factors. The lack of such a consideration would make the maximised choice of firms biased. In addition, the dynamic behaviour of firms also introduces selection bias. With international competition, firms with low productivity would die and exit the market, whereas those with high productivity would remain (Melitz 2003). In a panel dataset, the firms observed are those that have already survived. Meanwhile, firms with low productivity, which collapsed and exited the market, are excluded from the dataset. This means that the firms included in the regression are not randomly selected, resulting in estimation bias.

Econometricians have strived to address the empirical challenge of measuring TFP but were unsuccessful until the pioneering work of Olley and Pakes (1996). In the beginning, researchers used two-way (firm-specific and year-specific) fixed-effects estimations to mitigate simultaneity bias. Although the fixed-effect approach controls for several unobserved productivity shocks, it does not offer much help in dealing with reverse endogeneity and thus remains unsatisfactory. Similarly, to mitigate selection bias, one might estimate a balanced panel by dropping observations that have disappeared during the investigation. The problem is that a substantial part of the information contained in the dataset is wasted, and the dynamic behaviour of firms is completely unknown.

Fortunately, the Olley–Pakes methodology contributes significantly in addressing the challenge of TFP measurement. Assuming that the expectation of the future realisation of the unobserved productivity shock, v_{it}, relies on its contemporaneous value, firm i's investment is modelled as an increasing function of both unobserved productivity and log capital, $k_{it} \equiv \ln K_{it}$. Following previous studies, such as van Biesebroeck (2005) and Amiti and Konings (2007), we revise the Olley–Pakes approach by adding the export decisions of firms as an extra argument in the investment function because most export decisions are determined in the previous period (Tybout 2003) (Equation 6.4).

Equation 6.4

$$I_{it} = \tilde{I}(\ln K_{it}, \upsilon_{it}, EF_{it}, IF_{it}),$$

In Equation 6.4, $EF_{it}(IF_{it})$ is a dummy variable measuring whether firm i exports (imports) at year t. Therefore, the inverse function of investment is

Equation 6.5

$$\upsilon_{it} = \tilde{I}^{-1}(\ln K_{it}, I_{it}, EF_{it}, IF_{it}).$$

Unobserved productivity also depends on log capital and firm i's export decisions.[5] Accordingly, Equation 6.2 can now be written as Equation 6.6.

Equation 6.6

$$\ln Y_{it} = \beta_0 + \beta_m \ln M_{it} + \beta_l \ln L_{it} + g(\ln K_{it}, I_{it}, EF_{it}, IF_{it}) + \varepsilon_{it}$$

In Equation 6.6, $g(\ln K_{it}, I_{it}, EF_{it})$ is defined as $\beta_k \ln K_{it} + \tilde{I}^{-1}(\ln K_{it}, I_{it}, EF_{it})$. Following Olley and Pakes (1996) and Amiti and Konings (2007), fourth-order polynomials are used in log-capital, log-investment, export dummy and import dummy to approximate $g(\cdot)$.[6] In addition, our firm dataset covers the period 2000–06, so we include a WTO dummy (that is, one for a year after 2001 and zero for before) to characterise the function $g(\cdot)$ as follows (Equation 6.7).

Equation 6.7

$$g(k_{it}, I_{it}, EF_{it}, IF_{it}, WTO_t) = (1 + WTO_t + EF_{it} + IF_{it}) \sum_{h=0}^{4} \sum_{q=0}^{4} \delta_{hq} k_{it}^h I_{it}^q.$$

After finding the estimated coefficients $\hat{\beta}_m$ and $\hat{\beta}_l$, we calculate the residual, R_{it}, which is defined as $R_{it} \equiv \ln Y_{it} - \hat{\beta}_m \ln M_{it} - \hat{\beta}_l \ln L_{it}$.

The next step is to obtain an unbiased estimated coefficient of β_k. Amiti and Konings (2007) suggested estimating the probability of a survival indicator on a high-order polynomial in log-capital and log-investment to correct selection bias as mentioned above. We can then accurately estimate the following specification (Equation 6.8).

---

5   Olley and Pakes (1996) showed that the investment demand function is monotonically increasing in the productivity shock υ_{ik}, by making some mild assumptions about the production technology of firms.
6   Using higher-order polynomials to approximate $g()$ does not change the estimation results.

Equation 6.8

$$R_{it} = \beta_k \ln K_{it} + \tilde{I}^{-1}(g_{i,t-1} - \beta_k \ln K_{i,t-1}, \hat{pr}_{i,t-1}) + \varepsilon_{it},$$

In Equation 6.8, $\hat{pr}_i$ is the fitted value of the probability of firm i's exit in the next year. The specific 'true' functional form of the inverse function $\tilde{I}^{-1}(\cdot)$ is unknown, making it appropriate to use fourth-order polynomials in $g_{i,t-1}$ and $\ln K_{i,t-1}$ as approximation. In addition, Equation 6.8 requires the estimated coefficients of the log-capital in the first and second terms to be identical. Therefore, nonlinear least squares seem to be the most desirable econometric technique (Arnold 2005; Pavcnik 2002). Finally, the Olley–Pakes type of TFP for each firm i in industry j is obtained once the estimated coefficient $\hat{\beta}_k$ is obtained (Equation 6.9).

Equation 6.9

$$TFP_{ijt}^{OP} = \ln Y_{it} - \hat{\beta}_m \ln M_{it} - \hat{\beta}_k \ln K_{it} - \hat{\beta}_l \ln L_{it}.$$

As discussed above, the revised Olley–Pakes approach assumes that capital responds to an unobserved productivity shock with a Markov process, whereas other input factors do so without any dynamic effects; however, labour could be correlated with unobserved productivity shocks as well (Ackerberg et al. 2006). This consideration might fit with China's case very closely, given that China is a country with abundant labour. When facing unobserved productivity shocks, firms might prefer adjusting their labour rather than their capital to reoptimise their production behaviour. We then use the Blundell and Bond (1998) system GMM approach to capture the dynamic effects of other input factors. Assuming that the unobserved productivity shock depends on firm i's previous period realisations, the system GMM approach models TFP to be affected by all types of firm i's inputs in both current and past realisations.[7] In particular, this model has a dynamic representation as follows (Equation 6.10).

Equation 6.10

$$\ln y_{it} = \gamma_1 \ln L_{it} + \gamma_2 \ln L_{i,t-1} + \gamma_3 \ln K_{it} + \gamma_4 \ln K_{i,t-1} + \gamma_5 \ln M_{it}$$
$$+ \gamma_6 \ln M_{i,t-1} + \gamma_7 \ln y_{i,t-1} + \varsigma_i + \zeta_t + \omega_{it},$$

---

7   Note that the first-difference GMM introduced by Arellano and Bond (1991) also allows a firm's output to depend on its past realisation. Such an approach would, however, lose instruments for the factor inputs because the lag of output and factor inputs is correlated with past error shocks and the autoregressive error term. In contrast, by assuming that the first difference of instrumented variables is uncorrelated with the fixed effects, the system GMM approach can introduce more instruments and thereby dramatically improve efficiency.

In Equation 6.10, ς_i is firm i's fixed effect and ς_t is the year-specific fixed effect. The idiosyncratic term ω_{it} is serially uncorrelated if no measurement error exists.[8] We can obtain consistent estimates of the coefficients in (12) using a system GMM approach. The idea is that labour and material inputs are not taken as exogenously given. Instead, they are allowed to change over time as capital grows. Although the system GMM approach still faces a technical challenge to control for selection bias when a firm exits, using this approach to estimate a firm's TFP as a robustness check is still worthwhile.

Table 6.17 summarises the estimates of the Olley–Pakes input elasticity of Chinese firms at the HS two-digit level. We first cluster the 97 HS two-digit industries into 15 categories and calculate their estimated probability and input elasticity. The estimated survival probability of a firm in the next year varies from 0.977 to 0.996, with a mean of 0.994, suggesting that firm exits are less severe in the sample and in the given period.[9]

Table 6.17 presents differences in the estimated coefficients for labour, materials and capital using both the Olley–Pakes methodology and the system GMM approach. The last row of Table 6.17 suggests that, on average, the Olley–Pakes approach yields a higher elasticity of capital $(\alpha_k^{OP} = .117, \alpha_k^{GMM} = .001)$, whereas the system GMM approach yields a higher elasticity of labour $(\alpha_l^{OP} = .052, \alpha_l^{GMM} = .240)$. Summarising all the estimated elasticity, the implied scale elasticity is 0.989 using the Olley–Pakes approach,[10] which is close to the constant returns-to-scale elasticity.[11] Turning to the comparison between the OLS and the Olley–Pakes approaches, the estimates suggest that the usual OLS approach has a downward bias $(TFP^{OLS} = .958; TFP^{OP} = 1.188)$ largely because of the lack of control for simultaneity bias and selection bias.

Finally, for a cross-country comparison of the Olley–Pakes estimates, the estimation results suggest that intermediate inputs are more important for Chinese firms than for American firms (Keller and Yeaple 2009) or for Indonesian firms (Amiti and Konings 2007). The elasticity of capital input is, however, less important for Chinese firms than for American or Indonesian firms. This implies that processing trade does play a significant role in China's productivity growth.

---

8   As discussed by Blundell and Bond (1998), even if there is a transient measurement error in some of the series (that is, $\omega_{it} \sim MA(1)$), the system GMM approach can still reach consistent estimates of the coefficients in Equation 6.6.

9   Note that here, firm exit means a firm either stops trading and exits the market or has an annual sales figure lower than the 'large-scale' amount (RMB5 million in sales per year) and dropped from the dataset. Owing to dataset restrictions, we cannot distinguish the difference between the two.

10 This is calculated as .052 + .820 + .117 = .989 using the Olley–Pakes approach.

11 Note that here we use the industrial deflator as a proxy of a firm's price. Indeed, it is even possible that Chinese firms exhibit the increasing returns-to-scale property in the new century when the actual prices of firms are used to calculate 'physical' productivity. This is a possible future research topic provided that relevant data are available.

Table 6.17 Estimates of Olley–Pakes Input Elasticity of Chinese Firms

HS 2-digit	Labour		Materials		Capital	
	OP	GMM	OP	GMM	OP	GMM
Animal products (01–05)	.056**	.053	.888**	.970**	.048**	−.022
	(3.32)	(.87)	(55.36)	(17.71)	(1.80)	(−.43)
Vegetable products (06–15)	.007	.031**	.891**	.571**	.052**	.019
	(.49)	(8.55)	(68.05)	(9.82)	(5.49)	(.46)
Foodstuffs (16–24)	.036**	−.020	.874**	.595**	.044	.027
	(2.23)	(−.25)	(68.48)	(10.73)	(1.07)	(.46)
Mineral products (25–27)	.035*	.241**	.872**	.671**	.099**	.089
	(1.70)	(3.78)	(51.00)	(15.51)	(2.69)	(1.57)
Chemicals and allied industries (28–38)	.014**	.127**	.831**	.488**	.103**	.071
	(1.98)	(1.95)	(121.70)	(10.99)	(7.79)	(1.48)
Plastics/rubber (39–40)	.064**	.321**	.796**	.298**	.103**	−.003
	(8.49)	(6.98)	(107.17)	(4.54)	(5.59)	(−.08)
Raw hides, skins, leather and furs (41–43)	.102**	.125*	.810**	.738**	.090**	.043
	(7.76)	(1.85)	(65.53)	(11.55)	(3.36)	(.66)
Wood products (44–49)	.039**	.041	.855**	.266**	.012	.118**
	(4.29)	(.46)	(97.11)	(6.83)	(.47)	(2.99)
Textiles (50–63)	.085**	.157**	.810**	.653**	.066**	.043*
	(19.50)	(4.81)	(192.59)	(22.96)	(10.38)	(1.95)
Footwear/headgear (64–67)	.072**	.138	.864**	.703**	.033**	.108**
	(5.93)	(1.62)	(73.17)	(10.77)	(5.43)	(2.38)
Stone/glass (68–71)	.104**	.233**	.785**	.448**	.103**	.063
	(9.14)	(3.56)	(67.02)	(11.58)	(8.19)	(1.16)
Metals (72–83)	.045**	.191**	.832**	.400**	.109**	.084**
	(6.30)	(4.22)	(131.73)	(11.67)	(16.23)	(2.72)
Machinery/electrical (84–85)	.065**	.056	.825**	.548**	.150**	.175**
	(13.36)	(1.15)	(206.22)	(13.43)	(10.83)	(4.97)
Transportation (86–89)	.042**	.147*	.883**	.426**	.043**	.068
	(2.80)	(1.70)	(69.58)	(8.81)	(3.47)	(1.08)
Miscellaneous (90–98)	.083**	.195**	.796**	.276**	.098**	.007
	(10.32)	(3.58)	(110.01)	(8.15)	(10.70)	(.22)
All industries	.052**	.240**	.820**	.486**	.117**	.001
	(30.75)	(17.05)	(493.33)	(44.54)	(27.08)	(.11)

* indicates significance at 5 per cent level

** indicates significance at 1 per cent level

Note: Numbers in parentheses are robust t-values.

Source: Authors' own estimation.

Our final interest is in comparing the productivity of processing firms and non-processing firms. As discussed in Figure 6.7, three types of firms that engage in both processing and non-processing activities are important: non-processing firms (that is, ordinary firms), pure processing firms and hybrid firms. Figure 6.9 shows the dynamic evolution of the productivity of these three firm types. The productivity of all these firms has increased over time in the new century. Processing firms have the lowest productivity and ordinary firms have the highest productivity, with the productivity of hybrid firms in between. This strongly suggests that processing firms, compared with non-processing firms, have lower productivity.

Figure 6.9 Chinese Firms' Log of Total Factor Productivity, 2000–06

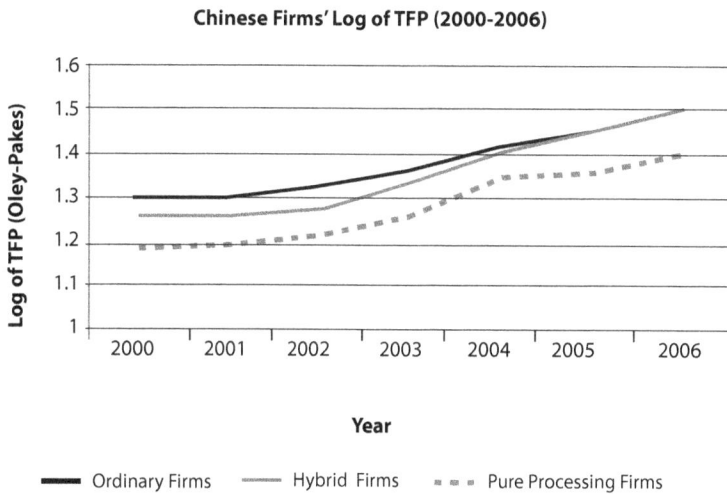

Chinese Firms' Log of TFP (2000-2006)

— Ordinary Firms   — Hybrid Firms   ▪ ▪ ▪ Pure Processing Firms

Source: Authors' calculation and estimates from China's firm-level production data and transaction-level trade data.

Conclusions

This chapter aimed to provide an overview of China's processing trade using highly disaggregated data (firm-level data and transaction-level data) from the new century. We started by highlighting that processing trade plays a fundamental role in China's foreign trade, and then explored why processing trade has developed rapidly in the past three decades. China's free-trade policy has dramatically fostered processing trade. Various free-trade zones, such as export processing zones and economic and technological development zones, have served as important instruments boosting processing trade.

With such a background in hand, we then explored various characteristics of processing imports. We investigated China's processing imports from the industrial perspective, including the origin countries, main products, transport mode, entry ports, consumption destinations and even the quality of the commodities. We provided very detailed firm-level evidence for the scope of processing trade.

Similarly, to gain a rich understanding of processing trade, we carefully measured and calculated total factor productivity using the semi-parametric Olley–Pakes and GMM approaches. Our estimates show that the productivity of all firms has increased in the new century; however, processing firms usually have lower productivity levels than non-processing firms.

Last but not least, we also contribute to the literature by providing a careful and very precise method of matching firm-level production data with transaction-level trade data. The match is not perfect due to data format restrictions, but the resulting matched dataset is still sufficiently representative of China's trading firms.

References

Ackerberg, D., Caves, K. and Frazer, G., 2006, Structural identification of production functions, Mimeo., University of California, Los Angeles.

Amiti, M. and Konings, J., 2007, 'Trade liberalization, intermediate inputs, and productivity: evidence from Indonesia', *American Economic Review*, vol. 93, pp. 1611–38.

Arellano, M. and Bond, S., 1991, 'Some tests of specification for panel data: Monte Carlo evidence and an application to employment equations', *Review of Economic Studies*, vol. 58, pp. 277–97.

Arnold, J. M., 2005, Productivity estimation at the plant level: a practical guide, Mimeo., Bocconi University, Milan.

Blundell, R. and Bond, S., 1998, 'Initial conditions and moment restrictions in dynamic panel data models', *Journal of Econometrics*, vol. 87, pp. 11–143.

Cai, H. and Liu, Q., 2009, 'Does competition encourage unethical behavior? The case of corporate profit hiding in China', *Economic Journal*, vol. 119, pp. 764–95.

Feenstra, R., Li, Z. and Yu, M., 2011, Export and credit constraints under private information: theory and empirical investigation from China, Mimeo., University of California, Davis.

Ge, Y., Lai, H. and Zhu, S., 2011, Intermediates import and gains from trade liberalization, Mimeo., University of International Business and Economics, China.

Hallak, J. C., 2006, 'Product quality and the direction of trade', *Journal of International Economics*, vol. 68, pp. 238–65.

Keller, W. and Yeaple, S. R., 2009, 'Multinational enterprises, international trade, and productivity growth: firm-level evidence from the United States', *Review of Economics and Statistics*, vol. 91, no. 4, pp. 821–31.

Khandelwal, A., 2010, 'The long and short (of) quality ladders', *Review of Economic Studies*, vol. 77, no. 4, pp. 1450–76.

Marschak, J. and Andrews, W., 1944, 'Random simultaneous equations and the theory of production', *Econometrica*, vol. 12, no. 4, pp. 143–205.

Melitz, M., 2003, 'The impact of trade on intra-industry reallocations and aggregate industry productivity', *Econometrica*, vol. 71, no. 6, pp. 1695–725.

National Bureau of Statistics of China (NBS), 2011a, *China Statistical Yearbook*, China Statistics Press, Beijing.

National Bureau of Statistics of China (NBS), 2011b, *China Trade and External Economic Statistical Yearbook*, China Statistics Press, Beijing.

Olley, S. and Pakes, A., 1996, 'The dynamics of productivity in the telecommunications equipment industry', *Econometrica*, vol. 64, no. 6, pp. 1263–97.

Pavcnik, N., 2002, 'Trade liberalization, exit, and productivity improvements: evidence from Chilean plants', *Review of Economic Studies*, vol. 69, no. 1, pp. 245–76.

Qiu, D. L. and Yu, M., 2012, Exporter scope, productivity, and trade liberalization: theory and evidence from China, Mimeo., Peking University, Beijing.

Tian, W. and Yu, M., forthcoming, 'A trade tale of two countries: China and India', *Journal of China and Global Economics*.

Tybout, J., 2003, 'Plant and firm-level evidence on "new" trade theories', in J. Harrigan and K. Choi (eds), *Handbook of International Trade*, Blackwell, New York, pp. 388–415.

van Biesebroeck, J., 2005, 'Exporting raises productivity in sub-Saharan African manufacturing firms', *Journal of International Economics*, vol. 67, no. 2, pp. 373–91.

Yu, M., 2011a, 'Moving up the value chain in manufacturing for China', in H. Yiping and J. Zhuang (eds), *Can China Avoid the Middle-Income Trap?*, Asian Development Bank Institute, Tokyo.

Yu, M., 2011b, Processing exports, firms' productivity and tariff reductions: evidence from Chinese products, Mimeo., Peking University, Beijing.

7. Upgrading China's Economy through Outward Foreign Direct Investment

Bijun Wang[1]

Introduction

A key concern regarding China's economy, among others, is the quality of growth. The surprisingly rapid economic growth over the past 30 years in China has resulted from reliance upon extensive growth, which has been at the expense of the environment and resources. The situation has worsened in the twenty-first century. The industrial sector—the largest contributor to the country's economic growth—has experienced an obvious heavy industrialisation process since the middle to late 1990s. Within the industrial sector, manufacturing is still at the low end of the international value chain since a majority of profits flow to foreign multinationals for their provision of technology, design and other services (Wang and Wang 2011).

On the other hand, beyond mainly investing foreign reserves in low-yield foreign government bonds, China has taken the world by surprise by exporting large amounts of capital, which is increasingly in the form of outward foreign direct investment (ODI). The country's ODI flows rose sharply from US$2.85 billion in 2003 to US$68.8 billion in 2010—a twentyfold increase within eight years!

This raises important questions. Could ODI be a contributing factor in improving China's growth quality or, more specifically, upgrading the country's economy by moving it up the value chain? If the answer is yes, by what mechanism? Does the motivation for undertaking ODI have a bearing on growth? Are there any necessary preconditions to ensure a positive outcome? Do Chinese firms undertaking ODI meet those conditions? This chapter attempts to answer these questions by analysing statistics drawn from comprehensive firm-level investment information between 2003 and the first half of 2011.

There are three main findings. First, the key reasons underpinning Chinese pursuit of ODI, especially for the country's manufacturers, are the acquisition of resources (resource-seeking ODI) and the strategic purchase of assets (strategic

1   This chapter is partly supported by the Key Research Base of Humanities and Social Sciences, the Ministry of Education of the People's Republic of China (project number 11JJD790027).

assets-seeking ODI), such as advanced technology, established brand names and developed distribution channels. Efficiency-seeking ODI—taking advantage of lower production costs in other less developed countries—is currently not a main attraction for Chinese investors. Second, we also find that firm capability is a significant determinant for Chinese strategic assets-seeking ODI, but not a crucial factor for resource-seeking ODI. For the latter, competition plays a key role, pushing Chinese manufacturers abroad. Finally, Chinese firms in industries with either overcapacity or backward capacity are more likely to pursue resource-seeking ODI and less likely to conduct strategic assets-seeking ODI.

The implications for upgrading the country's economy are profound. Resource-seeking ODI is likely to help Chinese firms become more efficient by overcoming resource bottlenecks. But without proper institutional reforms, such as a more liberalised market for production factors, this kind of investment could result in a heavier use of resources, greater externalities in the form of carbon emissions and other pollution and a deteriorating economic structure.

In contrast, we argue that the outlook for upgrading the Chinese economy through strategic assets-seeking ODI is more favourable. For one thing, firms undertaking strategic assets-seeking ODI tend to possess a certain degree of technological capability, which facilitates their assimilation of the acquired strategic assets. For another, those firms are more likely to be in industries with lower competition and higher profit margins. As a result, they not only have capital available to purchase strategic assets, but also their profit margins are a good buffer against possible losses in the short term, which allows those strategic assets to play a role in the long run. But we also acknowledge that these two favourable conditions might not guarantee success. Weak corporate governance, a lack of transparency and experience, as well as differing cultures at the national and corporate levels, all present challenges ahead. There is still a long way for Chinese firms to go to become real international players and for China's economy to upgrade and transform.

The remainder of this chapter examines the key industrial characteristics of the Chinese economy, and the possible ODI mechanism that could upgrade the country's domestic industries, with reference to the Japanese experience, and explores the current literature on reverse knowledge spillovers. Subsequently, the basic pattern of Chinese ODI is presented, followed by an identification of Chinese motivations for ODI, as well as an independent assessment and a probit regression test. After that, an empirical analysis of the impact of firm capability and industrial competition is conducted. Finally, we discuss the implications of using Chinese ODI to upgrade the country's economy before some concluding remarks are drawn.

What Are China's Industrial Characteristics?

There has been an exceptionally large secondary industry in China. Its share of the country's GDP averaged 46.5 per cent between 2000 and 2010. In 2008, secondary industry constituted 47.5 per cent of China's GDP, compared with 21.4 per cent in the United States, 28 per cent in Japan and the world average of 27 per cent. This large secondary industry underpins China as the world's biggest manufacturer and largest exporter of global consumable products.

In addition to a large secondary industry, there has been an obvious heavy industrialisation process occurring in China since the middle to late 1990s. Heavy industry's share in above-scale total industrial output value rose sharply from 57.1 per cent in 1998 to 71.4 per cent in 2010 (Figure 7.1). The development of heavy industry is typical when a large economy enters later periods of industrialisation. Yet, unsustainably, China has approached this development with a focus on extensive growth, which in turn has increased resource constraints and environmental pressures.

Figure 7.1 Different Components in Above-Scale Total Industrial Output Value, 1998–2010 (per cent)

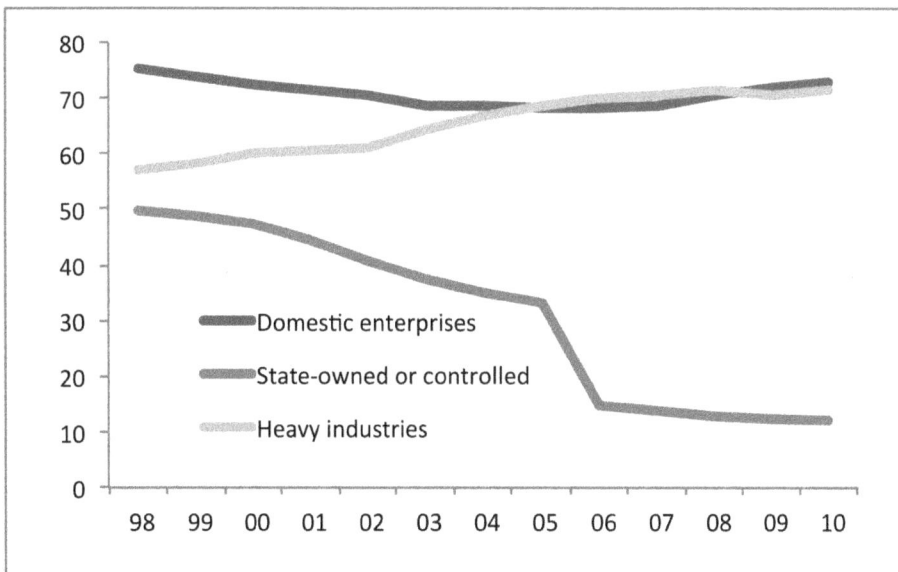

Source: NBS (various years).

In terms of ownership structure, China's domestic enterprises have produced an increasing share of the country's total industrial output, while the production weight of domestic state-owned or controlled enterprises (SOEs) is shrinking (Figure 7.1). Domestic enterprises' share in the country's total industrial output, although decreasing from 75.3 per cent in 1998 to 68.6 per cent in

2004, has picked up since 2005 and reached 72.8 per cent in 2010. But the contribution of SOEs to industrial output dropped to 12.2 per cent in 2010 from 49.6 per cent in 1998. Nevertheless, the privileged position held by SOEs allows them to devour an outsized share of the country's resources, such as bank loans and direct financing, and enjoy the unreasonably high profits that the monopolised industries like tobacco, oil and natural gas provide. Alternatively, non-SOEs compete intensely for limited resources and are subject to increasingly unfavourable domestic macro-conditions such as rising costs of labour and raw materials, as well as a slowing of external demand.

Structurally, extensive governmental economic intervention, in association with distorted factor markets, has led to serious structural problems, such as excessive investment, overcapacity, redundant construction and backward production capacity in segments of China's industrial sector. Steel, cement and other traditional industries with overcapacity problems, subsidised by their parent governments, are still expanding. Some emerging industries such as wind-power equipment and polycrystalline silicon, encouraged by the Government's industry development policy, also fell into the hole of excess investment and repeated construction. Some 15–25 per cent of total capacity in 18 industries—iron, steel, coke, iron alloy, calcium carbide, electrolysed aluminium, copper smelting, lead smelting, zinc smelting, cement, glass, papermaking, alcohol, monosodium glutamate (MSG) production, citric acid, hide processing, printing and dyeing, and chemical fibre manufacturing—is inefficient backward production capacity that is seriously detrimental to the environment.

The structure of China's industrial sector—the most important part of the Chinese economy—needs profound adjustment. Overcapacity needs to be absorbed, backward production needs to be eliminated and, above all, industrial upgrading must occur. Completing the marketisation of key energy and resource prices, the strict implementation of environmental supervision mechanisms and liberalising the country's financial system are all important steps that need to occur. Another important method of achieving this goal could be through ODI.

How Does ODI Affect Domestic Industrial Upgrading?

Mechanism

Industrial upgrading, from a value chain perspective, can be defined as the process by which economic actors—nations, firms and workers—move from low-value to relatively high-value activities in global production networks (Gereffi 2005). Industrial upgrading usually appears in four forms: 1) process upgrading—the improvement of production quality by introducing more efficient production methods and advanced technologies; 2) product upgrading—moving to the production of more sophisticated and higher value-added products or services; 3) functional upgrading—undertaking new functions with higher incomes or abandoning old functions with lower incomes; and 4) inter-sectoral upgrading—moving horizontally into new sectors (Gereffi 1999).

In a market economy, industrial upgrading is a natural, albeit not guaranteed, process and is pushed forward by market competition, technological advancement and economic development. Globalisation has tremendously hastened this process, with freer information and capital flow, as well as better resource allocation on a global scale.

Marginal industry expansion theory suggests that ODI could facilitate industrial upgrading in the home country (Kojima 1978). In this context, a marginal industry is one consisting of home manufacturers that are losing comparative advantage because of rising labour costs, appreciating local currencies and increasing environmental pressures. When ODI starts from marginal industries, resources are freed up for better usage. Some non–sector-specific resources (for example, finance) are transferable to the expanding sectors and contribute to their development. Other sector-specific resources can be transferred to, and utilised in, other countries with favourable factor conditions, which would otherwise be wasted at home (Ozawa 1979).

Marginal industry expansion theory mainly explains the industrial upgrade effect of efficiency-seeking ODI, which is usually located in developing host countries and secures access to cheaper input factors, especially labour. In addition to the desire for lower production costs in less developed countries, other incentives for pursuing ODI could positively affect industrial upgrading in a country, although the channel and magnitude can vary.

Market-seeking ODI is often pursued to defensively maintain a market position or offensively strengthen market share. In theory, if an investing firm's financial performance is elevated, they will have more resources to undertake research and development (R&D) and upgrade their production processes and products.

Natural-resource-seeking ODI removes the resource bottleneck faced by enterprises in growth and development. Detrimentally, however, there is also less pressure to develop resource-conserving and environmentally friendly technologies, which in turn undermines any industrial upgrading in the home country.

In the case of strategic assets-seeking ODI, the acquisition of technology or brand names is conducive to enhancing the firm's competitive edge by introducing more efficient production, transitioning the firm towards the production of higher value-added goods or services, and undertaking new functions with higher income. All of these are important aspects of industrial upgrading. In addition to technology and brand names, another crucial component of strategic assets-seeking ODI is improved access to distribution channels. The investing firms benefit from higher sales and, consequently, increased profits. On this front, as with market-seeking ODI, firms have greater financial resources to upgrade their production capacity and products.

There are, however, necessary preconditions that must be met before strategic assets-seeking ODI confers benefits. Investing firms should be capable of managing and assimilating the additional strategic assets. Otherwise, the enormous upfront expenses required to purchase the assets will not be justified by the eventual return.

Japanese Experience

Japan is an ardent practitioner of marginal industry expansion theory. In early postwar Japan, labour-intensive light industries occupied the majority of Japan's manufacturing sector, accounting for 74.7 per cent of the manufacturing output and 43.5 per cent of the country's total exports in 1955. But in the 1960s, especially after 1963, with rising wage levels, those industries gradually lost their competitive advantages at home and, thus, Japanese firms moved to Singapore, Taiwan, South Korea and other Asian countries with lower labour costs.

In the 1970s, following the demise of labour-intensive light industries, heavy industries led the second wave of Japanese ODI. The development of heavy industries, and the associated massive investment, intensive energy consumption and severe pollution, increasingly proved unsustainable in a country with limited land and resources like Japan. Japan's economy was pressured into restructuring away from heavy industries towards a knowledge and technology-intensive structure. To survive, Japanese chemical, steel and other heavy industrial firms were forced to shift abroad.

Japanese ODI has helped Japanese firms maintain and grow foreign market shares and assisted with the restructuring of the country's economy away from older industries (Blomström et al. 2000; Cantwell and Tolentino 1990; Hiley 1999). Some newly industrialised countries, such as Hong Kong, Taiwan and Korea, have also successfully transformed from being exporters of raw materials to high-tech products through ODI activities and achieved industrial upgrading along the way (Lipsey 2002).

Reverse Knowledge Spillovers

ODI could channel international knowledge diffusion, not only from investing firms to host countries but also vice versa in certain circumstances.

First, the investment destination matters. Generally, firms investing in a host country with a relatively high level of technology are more likely to receive technology spillovers and enjoy productivity gains. For example, Potterie and Lichtenberg (2001) found that ODI transferred technology only in one direction: the country's productivity increased if it invested in R&D-intensive foreign countries but not if foreign R&D-intensive countries invested in it. They also found that this effect was higher for large countries than it was for small ones. Hijzen et al. (2006), using French firm-level data, argued that ODI in developed countries increased an investing firms' productivity, while ODI in developing economies had no productivity effects. Similar findings were also found in Italian multinational enterprises (MNEs) (Falzoni and Grasseni 2005).

There is also evidence of reverse knowledge spillover in emerging market (EM) ODI. For instance, Chen et al. (forthcoming), drawing on data from 493 EM MNEs between 2000 and 2008 from 20 different EMs and 43 different industries, found evidence that EM MNEs that have subsidiaries in host-developed markets exhibited stronger technological capabilities at home.

Second, the investment motivation matters. Firms undertaking international knowledge-sourcing ODI are found to enjoy substantially, and significantly, higher productivity growth. For example, Pradhan and Singh (2008) found that technology-sourcing ODI by Indian automotive firms had a strong and positive effect on the firms' R&D intensity, particularly if such investments were located in developed countries. While Branstetter (2006) found evidence that ODI increased the flow of knowledge spillovers both from and to Japanese firms investing in the United States, such knowledge spillovers received by the investing Japanese firms tended to be strongest via R&D and product development facilities.

Finally, the capabilities of the investing firm matter. The realisation of reverse knowledge transfer depends on the investing firm's productivity, absorptive capacity[2] and technology transfer skills. Only when these factors are present are investing firms capable enough to absorb and transfer spillovers, allowing the entire company, rather than just foreign subsidiaries, to benefit from the external knowledge (Smeets and Bosker 2011).

---

2 Defined as the firm's ability to recognise the value of new, external information, to assimilate it and apply it to commercial ends (Cohen and Levinthal 1990).

Where is Chinese ODI Going?

What are the main destinations of Chinese ODI? What are the key sectors attracting Chinese investors? These are critical questions for analysing the upgrading effects of ODI. But these questions are difficult to answer, especially if one relies only on figures from China's official reports released annually by the Ministry of Commerce of the People's Republic of China (MOFCOM). According to the official data, from 2003 to 2009, 78.26 per cent of the country's ODI flow went to Hong Kong, the Cayman Islands and the British Virgin Islands. The largest category of investment during the same period, accounting for 32.26 per cent, was commercial services. Interpretation of these figures could be misleading since MOFCOM's data report only the first destination of ODI, which in many cases is a transit intermediary. For instance, some of the reported Chinese ODI in Hong Kong returns to the Mainland, or uses Hong Kong as a platform for making further investments in other countries such as Australia or Europe. As a result, reliance upon MOFCOM data does not greatly assist in the analysis of Chinese ODI.

To fill this gap, we construct datasets with detailed investment information at the project level. First, we use the approved ODI project information from the National Development and Reform Commission (NDRC). Then, we scrutinise these data according to the following rules.

We retain the data where

1. the investment amount is reported or can be found
2. the investment content is reported or can be found
3. Chinese investors control more than 10 per cent of the total share in the project.

We discard the data if

1. the buyer and seller are both Chinese firms
2. round-tripping ODI—the final destination of ODI is the home country—is apparent
3. the investment is to set up a trade centre, industrial, scientific or technological parks, or an economic zone.

Table 7.1 Top Destinations of Chinese ODI Between 2003 and the First Half of 2010

Number of projects			Investment amount (US$billion)		
Australia	43	14.68%	Australia	12.16	12.23%
Hong Kong	21	7.17%	South Africa	7.63	7.68%
United States	21	7.17%	Hong Kong	6.97	7.01%
Germany	20	6.83%	Canada	6.00	6.03%
Canada	18	6.14%	Russia	5.99	6.03%
Russia	13	4.44%	Singapore	5.95	5.98%
Vietnam	10	3.41%	Kazakhstan	5.83	5.86%
Laos	9	3.07%	United States	5.67	5.70%
Singapore	8	2.73%	Norway	4.50	4.53%
Cambodia	7	2.39%	Afghanistan	4	4.02%
Indonesia	7	2.39%	Laos	2.44	2.45%
Developed	176	60.07%	Developed	52.44	52.75%
Developing	117	39.93%	Developing	46.98	47.25%

Source: Author's calculation based on the constructed datasets.

After the application of the above parameters, 293 investment projects totalling US$99.43 billion were made by 216 Chinese firms from 2003 to the first half of 2011. Table 7.1 describes the top destinations and the distribution of Chinese ODI between developed and developing economies.

As shown, Australia is the biggest recipient of Chinese investment. Australia's resources are its major attraction. More than 80 per cent of Chinese investment in Australia is in the mining sector, nearly half of this goes to iron ore and the rest goes to coal, zinc, aluminium, copper, uranium, and so on. Real estate, finance and manufacturing constitute 10 per cent of China's investment portfolios, while agriculture and infrastructure have been gaining importance in recent years. Similarly, a large amount of Chinese ODI pours into Canada, Russia and South Africa for their resources—specifically, oil and oil-sands in Canada, oil and forest resources in Russia and gold and platinum in South Africa.

Hong Kong is the second-largest destination of Chinese ODI in terms of the number of projects and third-largest in value of total investment (Table 7.1). Unlike Chinese ODI in resource-rich economies, Chinese investments in Hong Kong centre on services, such as finance, shipping, telecommunications and electronic information.

Other top destinations include the United States, Germany, Vietnam, Laos and Cambodia. The United States and Germany attract Chinese manufacturers for a variety of reasons: their advanced technology, prestigious brand names and large domestic markets. The Association of South-East Asian Nations (ASEAN) members presumably offer mainly low production costs. Yet overall, developed economies have attracted more Chinese ODI and account for 60.07 per cent of the number of projects and 52.75 per cent in dollar terms.

About 80 per cent of Chinese ODI is focused on industry, including mining, manufacturing and electricity, gas and water.[3] Within the industrial sector, mining is the largest recipient of Chinese ODI in dollar terms while manufacturing is the largest recipient in terms of the number of investments (Table 7.2).

Of the 94 investments in the mining sector, seven are coal projects; 18 target oil and natural gas; 29 are in ferrous metals; and 39 are for nonferrous metals. The majority of sectors that attract Chinese manufacturing ODI are quite capital intensive. Automobiles, general-purpose and special-purpose equipment, electrical machinery, nonferrous metals and ferrous metal smelting and processing, communication equipment and chemical manufacturing account for 86.2 per cent of Chinese ODI in manufacturing.

Table 7.2 Sector Distribution of Chinese ODI

	Number of projects		Investment amount (US$billion)	
Agriculture	12	4.10%	0.37	0.38%
Industry	231	78.84%	83.34	83.82%
Mining	94	32.08%	52.10	52.40%
Manufacturing	124	42.32%	23.07	23.20%
Automobile industry	16	9.37%	4.78	17.94%
General-purpose equipment manufacturing	15	8.78%	0.26	0.97%
Special-purpose equipment manufacturing	15	8.78%	2.65	9.96%
Electrical machinery manufacturing	11	6.44%	0.45	1.68%
Nonferrous metal smelting and processing	9	5.27%	1.11	4.17%
Communication equipment, computer, other electronic equipment	9	5.27%	3.10	11.64%
Chemicals manufacturing	8	4.68%	5.96	22.37%
Ferrous metal smelting and processing (steel and iron)	7	4.10%	1.47	5.53%
Electricity, gas and water	13	4.44%	8.18	8.22%
Other	50	17.06%	15.71	15.80%
Total	293	100%	99.43	100%

Source: Author's calculation based on the constructed datasets.

---

3   As defined using the National Bureau of Statistics of China (NBS) definitions.

The distribution by sector of Chinese ODI is in line with the country's own industrial features, as discussed earlier in this chapter. The heavy industrialisation process requires more resources and energy input. For the past decade, China has been relying on imports to meet its increased demands for commodities. But the commodities boom has increased prices beyond the point where Chinese producers can maintain their profit margins. The combination of the country's stockpiles of foreign exchange reserves and an appreciating currency ensured the country's enterprises looked outwards, taking major stakes in overseas mining projects and acting as both shareholders and customers. Meanwhile, rapid development of the heavy industries at home also pushed those capital-intensive enterprises abroad.

Chinese ODI Motivations

Firms engaging in ODI are generally driven by one, or a combination, of the following four motivations: market-seeking ODI, natural-resource-seeking (henceforth resource-seeking) ODI, technology and other strategic-asset-seeking ODI (henceforth strategic assets-seeking), and efficiency-seeking ODI (Buckley et al. 2007; Cross and Voss 2008; Dunning 1992, 1993). Our identification of the core causes of Chinese ODI occurs over three stages. First, the author and an outside researcher separately made an independent assessment of the primary and secondary reasons for each investment based on accessible project data and definitions outlined in the existing literature. Second, the two assessments are collated. Third, a probit model is used to empirically test the determinants of Chinese ODI by different motivations and support our assessment.

Determinants

Market-Seeking ODI

Market-seeking ODI occurs when the investing firm expands horizontally into markets to secure or defend a market position established through arm's-length relationships or to develop a new, previously unserved market (Buckley et al. 2007). Market-seeking ODI can be used defensively if a foreign country imposes or threatens to impose barriers to imports, or if a firm wishes to better serve its established customers and strengthen their loyalty by setting up a foreign affiliate close to its local customers. It can also be a positive strategy to explore new markets.

Market-seeking ODI responds to variables that measure market opportunities such as host-market size, income and growth momentum. To account for this, we incorporate three variables: the gross domestic product (GDP) of the host country, *GDP*; GDP per capita, *GDPP*; and GDP growth rate, *GDPG*. These three variables are from the World Bank's database, *World Development Indicators* (*WDI*). GDP and GDPP are converted to logarithms for the estimation.

Given other conditions, market-seeking ODI should positively respond to the host country's *GDP* and *GDPG*. As for *GDPP*, the signs are unclear. A higher GDP per capita suggests a higher purchasing power. But there is also evidence that developing countries usually invest heavily in other developing countries (UNCTAD 2006). One of the reasons for this is that products made by developing firms are more likely to suit the tastes and needs of consumers in countries with a similar level of economic development.

Resource-Seeking ODI

Resource-seeking ODI is directed to exploit local factor endowments such as oil, gas, minerals, timber and other natural resources. The abundance of natural resources in the host country is the key determinant of this type of ODI. We adopt two measures: orefuelsh—the share of ores and fuel in the host country's total exports; and imrawsh—the host country's share in China's total imports of raw materials.[4] These two variables are calculated based on the merchandise trade matrix from the UN Conference on Trade and Development (UNCTAD) database. It can be expected that resource-seeking ODI should be positively related to orefuelsh and imrawsh.

Strategic Assets-Seeking ODI

Strategic assets-seeking ODI includes technology-seeking ODI and other strategic assets-seeking ODI. Technology-seeking ODI is directed to destinations that either already possess advanced technologies or are in the process of developing them (perhaps through technology clusters). Investing firms seeking this type of ODI tap the knowledge pool either directly, by cooperating with local companies, or indirectly, through spillover and demonstration effects. The remainder of the category—other strategic assets-seeking ODI—is normally aimed at acquiring brand names and obtaining improved access to distribution channels and tacit assets, with a view to helping the acquirer fulfil certain long-term strategic objectives.

---

4 Raw materials are calculated as: China's total imports of goods minus the total imports of manufactured goods.

We use the revealed comparative advantage (RCA) index in high-tech exports, *RCA_hi*, as a proxy for the abundance of strategic assets in the host economies. Balassa (1965) originally proposed the RCA index. He argued that the comparative advantage of a country's industry could be revealed by the ratio of the share of an individual sector's exports in total exports to that share for the world. An index value less than 1 implies relative disadvantage, whereas a value greater than 1 indicates relative advantage.

We follow Balassa's definition (Equation 7.1).

Equation 7.1

$$RCA_{c,i,t} = \frac{\dfrac{EX_{c,i,t}}{\sum_c EX_{c,i,t}}}{\dfrac{\sum_i EX_{c,i,t}}{\sum_i \sum_c EX_{c,i,t}}}$$

In Equation 7.1, $EX_{c,i,t}$ denotes the exports of industry i of country c in year t. $RCA_{c,i,t}$ denotes the revealed comparative advantage of industry i of country c in year t.

In this study, we calculate *RCA_hi* using the trade matrix from the UNCTAD database. In addition to *RCA_hi*, to some extent, rich countries with high GDP per capita, *GDPP*, also possess more strategic assets, mainly technology and brand names. So, we expect a significantly positive response of strategic assets-seeking ODI to both *RCA_hi* and *GDPP*.

Efficiency-Seeking ODI

Efficiency-seeking ODI is undertaken to generate economies of scale and scope and/or to secure access to cheaper input factors, especially labour, by dispersing design and production facilities globally. In doing so, firms take advantage of factor endowment differences between locations to improve efficiency levels.

Efficiency-seeking ODI is normally quite sensitive to cost factors. Thus, we introduce three variables: 1) GDP deflator, *inflation*, is an inflation indicator; 2) the change of nominal exchange rate against the US dollar relative to the previous year, *exchanf*, measures the exchange rate fluctuation; and 3) *GDPP* represents the labour cost. The data source for *inflation* and *GDPP* is the World Bank's *World Development Indicators*, and the calculation for *exchanf* is based on the UNCTAD database. It can be expected that efficiency-seeking ODI should be negatively related to *inflation*, *exchanf* and *GDPP*.

Results

Table 7.3 lists the distribution of the assessed primary motivation of Chinese ODI projects in the aggregate. As seen, overall, the largest attraction is to seek natural resources; 41 per cent of projects are in overseas resources and account for 51 per cent of total investments in dollar terms. Market-seeking ODI comes second while strategic assets-seeking ODI is the third-largest group.

If we focus only on manufacturing firms, their primary motivation is slightly different. The key driver turns to strategic assets-seeking ODI, which represents 35 per cent of projects and absorbs 46 per cent of all investments. This demonstrates that Chinese producers, who have been struggling in low value-added activities, are trying to seek strategic assets—advanced technology, established brand names and distribution channels—to increase their profit margins and climb the value chain. But still, natural resource-seeking ODI, or securing the supply of raw materials, is an important objective for Chinese manufacturers going abroad. This is especially true for Chinese steel companies, who rush into Australia and take equity in iron ore projects so as to secure the future supply of iron ore and hedge against the possibility of unfavourable price movements.

Table 7.3 Primary Motivation Distribution of Chinese ODI

	By number		By value	
	Number	Total share	Value (US$billion)	Total share
Overall				
Market-seeking	87	30%	28.2	28%
Resource-seeking	121	41%	51.0	51%
Strategic assets-seeking	78	27%	20.0	20%
Efficiency seeking	7	2%	0.2	0%
Manufacturing				
Market-seeking	49	27%	6.9	22%
Resource-seeking	61	34%	9.9	32%
Strategic assets-seeking	63	35%	14.2	46%
Efficiency seeking	7	4%	0.2	1%

Source: Author's own compilation and calculation based on the constructed datasets.

Notably, taking advantage of lower production costs in other less developed countries is not a main driver of Chinese ODI. Only seven projects out of the 293 investments are primarily to increase efficiency. This is possibly because there are large inland areas in China. Despite rising labour costs in recent years, Chinese producers prefer moving their factories inward to less prosperous inland areas (see Chapter 5 of this volume) rather than operating across borders, which could entail huge uncertainties. The other possible reason involves data qualifications. Our sample covers mainly large investment projects based on reported information. It is harder to track the numerous small investments that might be undertaken by efficiency-seeking investing enterprises.

Our assessment of Chinese ODI motivations is supported by the empirical tests (Table 7.4). Indeed, market-seeking ODI is significantly affected by market variables *GDP*, *GDPP* and *GDPG*. As expected, *GDP* and *GDPG* have a positive effect but *GDPP* is negatively linked to a destination's market attraction. Also as predicted, strategic assets-seeking ODI has a significantly positive reaction to *GDPP* and *RCA_hi*, and resource-seeking ODI is also significantly positively related to *orefuelsh* and *imrawsh*; but the result for efficiency-seeking ODI is unsatisfactory. Although *inflation* has a significantly negative impact as predicted, the coefficient of *exchanf*, although still negative, is not significant. This is probably due to the limited size of observations for efficiency-seeking ODI (Table 7.3), which makes estimation difficult.

Table 7.4 Results of the Identification of Chinese ODI Motivations

Dependent variable	Market- seeking (1; otherwise 0)	Strategic assets- seeking (1; otherwise 0)	Resource- seeking (1; otherwise 0)	Efficiency seeking (1; otherwise 0)
lnGDP	0.245***	0.103	−0.383***	0.169
	−3.12	(−0.82)	(−3.54)	(−0.64)
lnGDPP	−0.335***	1***	0.128	−0.251
	(−3.05)	−2.62	(−0.89)	(−0.81)
GDPG	0.081**	−0.049	−0.152***	0.259*
	−2.45	(−1.16)	(−2.75)	−1.84
RCA_hi	−0.101	0.895**	−0.424	−1.882
	(−0.35)	−2.04	(−1.1)	(−1.35)
orefuelsh	−0.425	−2.333**	1.451***	−0.603
	(−0.91)	(−2.29)	−2.63	(−0.62)
imrawsh	−7.851*	−7.965	20.998***	−8.851
	(−1.67)	(−1.4)	−3.74	(−0.23)
inflation	0	−0.109*	0.084***	−0.093*
	(−0.02)	(−1.73)	−2.76	(−1.71)
exchanf	3.172**	−0.179	−0.72	−1.468
	−2.07	(−0.1)	(−0.4)	(−0.25)
Industry dummy	Yes	Yes	Yes	Yes
Year dummy	Yes	Yes	Yes	Yes
Observations	289	289	289	289
Pseudo R-squared	0.3138	0.5196	0.6302	0.4901

*** indicates the coefficient is significant at the 1 per cent level

** indicates the coefficient is significant at the 5 per cent level

* indicates the coefficient is significant at the 10 per cent level

Note: Value of z statistics in parentheses.

Source: Author's own estimation.

The Impact of Firm Capability and Industrial Competition

The dominant explanation for the emergence of trans-border production by national firms asserts that firms going abroad must possess a bundle of intangible assets, which yield a rent to the firm capable of meeting the cost of 'foreignness' and offer an edge over local and third-country competitors in particular markets (Caves 1971; Hymer 1960; Kindleberger 1969).

Firms engaged in asset-augmenting ODI are motivated to venture into international markets to acquire strategic assets such as brand names, technology, distribution networks, R&D facilities and managerial competencies. Nevertheless, these firms still have to possess some resources or capabilities to assimilate and manage the acquired strategic assets and apply them to commercial ends.

Do Chinese firms possess the capabilities needed to invest overseas? Without doubt, they have ample funds and can leverage a huge domestic market. But these advantages are not firm specific or ownership specific. At the enterprise level, they are still painfully weak in areas of technology, management capability and brand names when compared with the global giants.

Compared with the primary and service sectors, the manufacturing sector indeed has a comparative advantage in terms of performance in export markets and development in the domestic economy (Huang and Wang 2011). But the advantages of Chinese manufacturers have focused on products such as simple bulk goods like steel, coal and cement, and the assembly of the various components of televisions, washing machines, refrigerators, airconditioners, microwaves and motorbikes that require minimal technological investment from the final assembler (Wang and Wang 2011).

Nevertheless, after 60 years of development, China has established a mature manufacturing system. It maintains high standards, if not necessarily while using up-to-date technology, in certain industries like mechanical manufacturing, metal smelting, household appliances and textiles (Li 2007). The mature technology in these industries is well matched to the requirements of China and other less developed economies.

In addition to firm capability, the degree of industrial competition is an important factor that determines a firm's internationalisation strategies and performance (Boter and Holmquist 1996). Intense competition in a home market can drive subordinate firms to undertake ODI so as not to be squeezed by dominant domestic incumbents (Dawar and Frost 1999; Mascarenhas 1986). A relatively low level of competition at home might not provide enough incentives to venture abroad, especially to developed economies (Yamakawa et al. 2008); however, the impact of industrial competition can vary on different motivations of ODI.

This section dissects the impact of firm capability and industrial competition on three reasons for Chinese ODI: market-seeking ODI, resource-seeking ODI and strategic assets-seeking ODI.

Variables

Firm Capability

Firm capability is difficult to measure since it is inherently unobservable. Here, we construct three dummy variables to measure whether a firm is provided with a labour-intensive capability, *labourcapa*; a capital-intensive capability, *capitalcapa*; and a technological-intensive capability, *techcapa*. To construct these variables, we first label the firm a 'market leader' if it is one of the top-500 enterprises in China, in the Chinese Manufacturing Industry 500 or Chinese Service 500, ranked by the China Enterprise Confederation (CEC). Then, if a 'market leader' invests in labour-intensive industries, it is said to possess a labour-intensive capability, and its *labourcapa* equals 1; if not, it equals zero. We use the same approach for *capitalcapa* and *techcapa*.

Industrial Competition

Industrial competition is proxied by profit margins at the sectoral level. The higher the profit margins, the lower the industrial competitive pressure should be. We incorporate two profit margin measures at the sectoral level: the profit ratio of sales, *profit_sale*, and the profit ratio of costs, *profit_cost*.

We also control five other sectoral variables: *Growth*, the year-on-year growth rate of total output value; *Significance*, the share of each sectoral total output value in total industrial output value; *State* power, the share of state capital in total paid-in capital; *Exports share*, the share of exports in total sales; and *Intensity*, total assets per worker. All of these sectoral-level variables are first-lagged to ease endogeneity issues and are calculated from various years of the *China Industry Economy Statistical Yearbook*.

We are also interested in the behaviour of firms from industries with large overcapacity or backward technology. Thus, we include a dummy variable, *overbackcapacity*, which equals 1 if the investing firm is from an industry with excess or backward capacity, as specified by the Ministry of Industry and Information Technology of the People's Republic of China. If not, it equals zero.

Findings

From the results of the probit regression analysis reported in Table 7.5, there are four main findings.

Table 7.5 Results of Probit Regression Analysis[5] for Manufacturing ODI

Dependent variable	Market seeking (1; otherwise 0)		Strategic assets seeking (1; otherwise 0)		Resource seeking (1; otherwise 0)	
labourcapa	0.266	0.233	−0.296	−0.248	−0.678	−1.034
	(0.59)	(0.51)	(0.58)	(0.47)	(1.16)	(1.61)
capitalcapa	−0.076	−0.06	0.533*	0.49*	−0.323	−0.303
	(0.28)	(0.23)	(1.93)	(1.75)	(1.03)	(0.95)
techcapa	−1.074**	−1.022*	1.307***	1.174**	−0.712	−0.584
	(2.08)	(1.96)	(2.89)	(2.55)	(1.01)	(0.81)
profit_sale	0.876	1.223	16.345***	15.176***	−17.114**	−14.623*
	(0.26)	(0.37)	(3.20)	(3.18)	(2.20)	(1.85)
State power	0.866	1.003	−3.913**	−4.982**	1.5	1.486
	(0.48)	(0.55)	(1.96)	(2.29)	(0.6)	(0.59)
Exports share	5.081**	5.941**	−3.854	−7.016**	−55.309***	−53.403***
	(2.15)	(2.21)	(1.52)	(2.25)	(2.91)	(2.93)
overbackca-pacity		0.218		−0.696**		0.724*
		(0.69)		(1.93)		(1.77)
Growth	0.824	0.833	-0.502	−0.475	0.307	0.191
	(1.03)	(1.04)	(0.53)	(0.49)	(0.29)	(0.17)
Significance	−5.201	−8.282	17.177**	28.785***	20.805	12.853
	(0.77)	(1.02)	(2.37)	(2.97)	(1.5)	(0.9)
Intensity	−0.002	−0.003	−0.031**	−0.025	−0.01	−0.013
	(0.19)	(0.27)	(2.01)	(1.54)	(0.61)	(0.8)
Year	Yes	Yes	Yes	Yes	Yes	Yes
Pseudo R-squared	0.0584	0.0608	0.2539	0.2714	0.3541	0.3689
Observations	170	170	170	170	170	170

* indicates the coefficient is significant at the 10 per cent level

** indicates the coefficient is significant at the 5 per cent level

*** indicates the coefficient is significant at the 1 per cent level

Note: Absolute value of z statistics in parentheses.

Source: Author's own estimation.

First, firm capability is a significant determinant for Chinese strategic assets-seeking ODI, but not a crucial factor for market-seeking or resource-

---

5 The result using *profit_cost* is similar. So, for simplicity, we do not report it.

seeking ODI. The results indicate the coefficient for *techcapa* and *capitalcapa* is significantly positive for strategic assets-seeking ODI but insignificant (or significantly negative) for market-seeking and resource-seeking ODI. This means that the greater the investing firm's technology-intensive capability or capital-intensive capability the more likely it is that the firm will conduct strategic assets-seeking ODI.

Second, competition increases the likelihood of Chinese manufacturers seeking natural resources overseas, while it has no significant impact on manufacturers seeking a larger market overseas. In contrast, lower competition encourages Chinese firms to undertake strategic assets-seeking ODI. This is evidenced by the *profit_sale* coefficient, the proxy for industrial competition, which is significantly positively linked with the probability of strategic assets-seeking ODI, negatively linked with resource-seeking ODI, while insignificant for market-seeking ODI.

Third, although firms pursuing strategic assets-seeking ODI might face less competition currently, the potential for future competitive pressure cannot be ignored. The coefficient of *State power* is significantly negatively associated with the choice for strategic assets-seeking ODI; the lower the state power, the more likely a firm is to undertake strategic assets-seeking ODI. Usually, in sectors with lower state power, entry barriers, at least administratively, are also lower. Firms in these sectors, although presently enjoying relatively high profit margins, will likely face severe potential competition in the future. Thus, they have incentives to go overseas and acquire strategic assets to maintain their competitive edge at home.

Finally, firms from industries with excess or backward capacity are more likely to enter into resource-seeking ODI, less likely to conduct strategic assets-seeking ODI and are indifferent to market-seeking ODI. As shown in Table 7.5, the coefficient of the dummy variable *overbackcapacity* is significantly positive for resource-seeking ODI, significantly negative for strategic assets-seeking ODI and insignificant for market-seeking ODI.

Implications for Upgrading China's Economy

Japanese ODI has greatly facilitated the restructuring of the country's economy by moving abroad labour-intensive, resource-consuming and environmentally detrimental activities between the 1960s and 1980s. What remain at home are operations with a greater technological content and higher added value. As a result, despite losing nearly two decades after the burst of the Japanese asset price bubble, the Japanese economy is still competitive, its environmental situation has improved considerably, it is a very efficient consumer of resources and Japanese goods are still respected for their exceptionally high quality.

Any upgrade of China's economy through ODI, if possible, will, however, be quite different from Japan's experience. The desire to seek lower production costs overseas is not a major motivation for Chinese firms. Also, rising labour costs, the appreciating renminbi and increasingly severe environmental policies do not—at least currently—push Chinese enterprises to shift labour and energy-intensive, low value-added businesses abroad on a large scale. Instead, factories are moving within China to the western and central regions where production costs are lower than in the coastal areas. Other Chinese firms wish to grow their global footprint by pursuing overseas resources with the intention of locking in, or even lowering, the costs of raw materials.

As confirmed by the above results, domestic competition has played a crucial role in forcing Chinese manufacturers to invest abroad to secure their resource supply. While it removes the resource bottleneck, increases a firm's profit margin and thus equips them with greater resources to undertake innovation and move up the value chain, it also steers firms away from resource competition and potentially towards competition for ideas, management and technologies.

But resource-seeking ODI is a double-edged sword. Investment in the resource sector is risky and requires a large amount of funds, while directing money elsewhere could have a more positive impact on upgrading a firm's products and processes.

Chinese firms are known for their ability to draw on a great deal of money. But, even for the country's state-owned enterprises (SOEs), commercial pressures are mounting rapidly. After all, they still must pay millions of dollars in interest every year and undergo the economic performance evaluation required by the State-Owned Assets Supervision and Administration Commission (SASAC). Notably, the 2011 dismissal of Sinosteel's CEO by SASAC was partly because of the large losses of the company's Australian investment, Midwest Mining Corp.

Moreover, inadequate supporting infrastructure, extensive local bureaucracy (especially in relation to the environment and indigenous landowners) and high labour costs (especially for unskilled workers) all increase the risks for Chinese investment in overseas resources and these conditions are especially apparent in developed economies like Australia and Canada. Similarly, resource exploration in developing countries must contend with unstable social and political situations, as well as possible expropriation hazards that all add greater uncertainty to resource-seeking Chinese ODI.

Setting aside the risks mentioned above, resource-seeking ODI might discourage Chinese firms from developing resource-conserving and environmentally friendly technologies, while promoting heavier energy use and carbon production.

The above is readily apparent for firms from industries with overcapacity or backward technology. Our probit regression analysis suggests that those firms are more likely to enter resource-seeking ODI, less likely to conduct strategic assets-seeking ODI and are indifferent to market-seeking ODI. This means that a significant number of firms from industries in this category neither digest excess production capacity through market-seeking ODI nor reduce backward production capacity or optimise incremental control structures through strategic assets-seeking ODI. Instead, they prefer resource-seeking ODI. This could result in more blind investment and low-level expansion, intensifying China's structural imbalances. Admittedly, factor market distortions, such as cheap capital and energy, could play a key role, but ODI only adds another dimension to this problem.

The more promising method for upgrading China's economy is through strategic assets-seeking ODI. It is apparent that strategic assets-seeking ODI has become the most important driver of Chinese overseas manufacturing investments (Table 7.3). Chinese firms have been heavily reliant on importing core components and technologies. Their Foreign Technology Dependence Ratio is more than 50 per cent, while developed economies do not exceed 30 per cent and the United States and Japan are about 5 per cent (Lu and Zhang 2007). Chinese firms also lack global brand names. According to the '100 World Best Brands in 2009', eight of the top 10 were US companies, and no Chinese company made the list.

Acquiring strategic assets through ODI helps elevate the competitiveness of Chinese firms by promoting their movement up the value chain, and in turn upgrading the Chinese economy. But such a favourable outcome is by no means preordained. At least two conditions have to be satisfied. The first requirement is that investing firms should possess a certain degree of capability—namely, an absorptive ability—the technology transfer skills to manage the acquired strategic assets, absorb spillovers and also transfer them back to the parent country. The second requirement is that investing firms should be patient enough or tolerant commercially to bear short-term losses while the advantages of the strategic assets come to fruition.

Our empirical results indicate that Chinese strategic assets-seeking ODI firms have partially met the above requirements. Their technological capabilities have facilitated their assimilation of acquired strategic assets. As shown in

Table 7.5, the higher the investing firm's technology-intensive capability or capital-intensive capability, the more likely it will be to conduct strategic assets-seeking ODI.

Chinese firms are also willing to absorb short-term losses and allow strategic assets to realise their value in the long run. Unlike resource-seeking ODI firms, which are significantly in industries with severe competition and low profit margins, strategic assets-seeking ODI firms are more likely to be from industries with lower current competition and higher profit margins—albeit in many instances where there is the potential for competitive pressure to increase. Under these circumstances, and in the current absence of competition, firms have the funds to buy strategic assets, but also could use their profits to buffer against near-term losses without concern for being squeezed out of the industry.

Conclusions

China, with its need to accelerate structural readjustment and improve the quality and efficiency of economic growth, is at a critical juncture. In the country's Twelfth Five-Year Plan, covering 2011 to 2015, the key message was that the mode of economic development must be transformed. The core competitiveness of the manufacturing industries must be improved and resource conservation, as well as a concern for the environment, should be high on the agenda.

In this chapter, we argued that ODI could play a role in upgrading the country's economy. The statistical evidence suggests Chinese firms are motivated to invest overseas predominantly to acquire resources and strategic assets. It is also apparent that firms seeking resources overseas are often pushed abroad by domestic competition, while those investing in overseas strategic assets are already exhibiting a certain degree of technological capability.

The impact of resource-seeking ODI on upgrading China's economy is mixed. On the one hand, the resource bottleneck faced by enterprises in development might be eased, which allows investing firms to pay more attention to other aspects of competition such as product and process innovation. On the other hand, their incentive to develop resource-conserving and environmentally friendly technologies is also weakened. This could result in a wasteful use of resources and be detrimental to growth quality.

The impact of strategic assets-seeking ODI on upgrading China's economy is, however, more positive. Technology and brand acquisition are conducive to enhancing a firm's competitive edge, while improved access to distribution channels is helpful to boost sales, increase profits and provide financial resources for the upgrading of a firm's production and products. One question remains, however: whether Chinese firms are able to best utilise strategic assets. Our analysis suggests that they are indeed equipped with certain technological capabilities that will assist with the assimilation of acquired assets. Also, firms pursuing strategic assets-seeking ODI are from industries with lower competition and higher profit margins. As a result, sufficient room (time, in the main) is available for the strategic assets to take effect.

Nevertheless, Chinese ODI faces other challenges ahead. Cultures at the national and corporate levels need to be reconciled and both must learn to engage with foreign regulators, unions and local communities, which remain unfamiliar territory. Firms also need to improve corporate governance and management skills to consolidate, absorb and operate foreign assets. While these challenges are also often present when conducting business abroad, that these challenges exist reflects the institutional background at home and, therefore, highlights problems with China's economy as well.

Chinese ODI is still small in size but its growing global importance is striking. It not only has the ability to upgrade China's economy if properly managed but might also facilitate deeper reforms of SOEs, improve corporate governance, strengthen the notion of corporate social responsibility and, eventually, create a better and more orderly economic and business environment in China.

References

Balassa, B., 1965, 'Trade liberalization and revealed comparative advantage', *Manchester School of Economic and Social Studies*, vol. 33, no. 2, pp. 99–117.

Blomström, M, Konan, D., and Lipsey, R., 2000, 'FDI in the Restructuring of the Japanese Economy', *NBER working paper,* No 7693, May.

Boter, H. and Holmquist, C., 1996, 'Industry characteristics and internationalization process in small firms', *Journal of Business Venturing*, vol. 11, pp. 471–87.

Branstetter, L., 2006, 'Is foreign direct investment a channel of knowledge spillovers: evidence from Japan's FDI in the US', *Journal of International Economics*, vol. 68, pp. 325–44.

Buckley, P. J., Clegg, L. J., Cross, A. R., Liu, X., Voss, H. and Zheng, P., 2007, 'The determinants of Chinese outward foreign direct investment', *Journal of International Business Studies*, vol. 38, no. 4, pp. 499–518.

Cantwell, J. and Tolentino, P., 1990, 'Technological accumulation and third world multinationals', Discussion Papers in International Investment and Managements, No. 139 (Reading: University of Reading), mimeo.

Caves, R. E., 1971, 'International corporations: the industrial economics of foreign investment', *Economica*, vol. 38, no. 149, pp. 1–27.

Chen, V. Z., Li, J. and Shapiro, D. M., forthcoming, 'Emerging-market multinational enterprises in developed markets: exploring reverse spillover effects on parent firms', *European Management Journal, Special Issue: Emerging Multinationals*.

Cohen, W. M. and Levinthal, D. A., 1990, 'Absorptive capacity: a new perspective on learning and innovation', *Administrative Science Quarterly*, vol. 35, no. 1, pp. 128–52.

Cross, A. R. and Voss, H., 2008, Chinese direct investment in the United Kingdom: an assessment of motivations and competitiveness, Paper presented at Corporate Strategies in the New Asia, University of Bremen, Germany, 1–2 February.

Dawar, N. and Frost, T., 1999, 'Competing with giants', *Harvard Business Review*, vol. 77, no. 2, pp. 119–30.

Dunning, J. H., 1992, *Multinational Enterprises and the Global Economy*, Addison-Wesley, New York.

Dunning, J. H., 1993, *Globalisation of Business*, Routledge, London and New York.

Falzoni, A. and Grasseni, M., 2005, *Home country effects of investing abroad: evidence from quantile regressions*, KITeS Working Papers 170, Bocconi University, Milano.

Gereffi, G., 1999, 'International trade and industrial upgrading in the apparel commodity chain', *Journal of International Economics*, vol. 48, pp. 37–70.

Gereffi, G., 2005, 'The global economy: organization, governance, and development', in N. J. Smelser and R. Swedberg (eds), *The Handbook of Economic Sociology*, [Second edition], Princeton University Press and Russell Sage Foundation, Princeton, NJ, pp. 160–82.

Hiley M., 1999, 'The Dynamics of Changing Comparative Advantage in the Asia-Pacific Region', *Journal of the Asia Pacific Economy*, Vol. 4, No. 3, pp.446–67.

Hijzen, A., Jean, S. and Mayer, T., 2006, The effects at home of initiating production abroad: evidence from matched French firms, Ms, CEPII, Paris.

Huang, Y. and Wang, B., 2011, 'Chinese outward direct investment: is there a China model?', *China & World Economy*, vol. 19, no. 4, pp. 1–21.

Hymer, S., 1960, The international operations of national firms: a study of direct foreign investment, PhD thesis, MIT, Cambridge, Mass.

Kindleberger, C. P., 1969, *American Business Abroad: Six lectures on direct investment*, Yale University Press, New Haven, Conn.

Kojima, K., 1978, *Direct Foreign Investment: A Japanese model of multination business operations*, Groom Helm, London.

Li, G., 2007, *Chinese Firms' Overseas Direct Investment Analysis Report*, China Economics Publishing House, Beijing.

Lipsey, R. E., 2002, *Home and host country effects of FDI*, Working Paper Series, National Bureau of Economic Research, Cambridge, Mass.

Lu, J. and Zhang, Z., 2007, *Enterprises' own intellectual property rights and going global strategy*, Chinese Firms' Overseas Direct Investment Analysis Report, China Economics Publishing House, Beijing.

Mascarenhas, B., 1986, 'International strategies of non-dominant firms', *Journal of International Business Studies*, vol. 17, pp. 1–25.

National Bureau of Statistics of China (NBS), various years, *China Statistical Yearbook*, National Bureau of Statistics, China Statistics Press, Beijing.

Ozawa, T., 1979, 'International investment and industrial structure: new theoretical implications from the Japanese experience', *Oxford Economic Papers*, [NS], vol. 31, no. 1, pp. 72–92.

Pradhan, J. P. and Singh, N., 2008, *Outward FDI and knowledge flows: a study of the Indian automotive sector*, MPRA Paper No. 12332, Munich.

Potterie, B. V. P. D. L. and Lichtenberg, F., 2001, 'Does foreign direct investment transfer technology across borders?', *Review of Economics & Statistics*, vol. 83, no. 3, pp. 490–7.

Smeets, R. and Bosker, E. M., 2011, 'Leaders, laggards and technology seeking strategies', *Journal of Economic Behavior & Organization*, vol. 80, no. 3 (December), pp. 481–97.

United Nations Conference on Trade and Development (UNCTAD), 2006, *World Investment Report 2006: FDI from developing and transition economies— Implications for development*, United Nations Conference on Trade and Development, New York and Geneva.

Wang, B. and Wang, H., 2011, 'Chinese manufacturing firms' overseas direct investment: patterns, motivations and challenges', in J. Golley and L. Song (eds), *Rising China: Global challenges and opportunities*, ANU E Press, Canberra, pp. 99–119.

Yamakawa, Y., Peng, M. W. and Deeds, D., 2008, 'What drives new ventures to internationalise from emerging to developed economies?', *Entrepreneurship Theory and Practice*, vol. 32, no. 1, pp. 59–82.

8. Intra-Provincial Inequality in China:

An analysis of county-level data

Tsun Se Cheong and Yanrui Wu

Introduction

Many studies have been carried out to investigate China's regional inequality, which has increased considerably since the initiation of economic reforms. Most of the studies in the literature, however, are based on provincial-level data while intra-provincial inequality has not been examined thoroughly (Cheong 2012). In particular, the patterns and trends of inequality between the county-level units (CUs, including counties and county-level cities) within the provinces are virtually unknown. In order to get a full grasp of the pattern and dynamic trend of the inequality between the county-level units, the data have to be continuous and must have a long time span. Even though some researchers employ county-level data in their studies, many of these studies are still plagued by the problem of either limited coverage or a short time span. In-depth studies of intra-provincial regional inequalities are mainly confined to the provinces in China's eastern zone with the rest of the country being ignored. The objective of this chapter is to estimate and decompose regional inequality using county-level data from the provinces in both the inland and the coastal regions for an extended period.

The county-level data used in this study can provide an opportunity to examine the pattern and evolution of regional inequality in greater detail. Specifically, this study decomposes overall inequality into the intra-provincial and inter-provincial components and hence makes it possible to identify the role of each province. Further decomposition of intra-provincial inequality can provide important insights into the effect on regional inequality of subregions within each province. The empirical exercise is carried out through a three-tier decomposition process so as to examine the contributions of the components in different spatial levels. The chapter begins with a literature review. Section three discusses the method of decomposition, while section four describes the data. Section five analyses the empirical findings and section six concludes and outlines some policy suggestions.

Literature Review

One of the major analytical tools used in the analysis of regional inequality is the decomposition method. This study is based on the decomposition of inequality by subgroups, which are defined as different spatial groupings in the literature. The common spatial groupings used in the literature are the provinces, the economic zones (eastern, central, western and north-eastern) as well as the inland and coastal regions. The focus of this study is on regional inequality measured by gross regional product (GRP) per capita at the county level. Therefore, this literature review is mainly confined to the studies that use regional output in their calculations. The studies are grouped according to the different spatial levels used in the decomposition.

Provincial-Level Decomposition

Tsui (1993) analysed inter-CU inequality using gross value of industrial and agricultural output (GVIAO) per capita in 1982. He decomposes overall inequality into two components: the inter-provincial and the intra-provincial components. Lee (2000) considered data for 1994 and compared his findings with those of Tsui. Lee found that the contribution of inter-provincial inequality to overall inequality increased between 1982 and 1994, while the contribution of intra-provincial inequality decreased. Herrmann-Pillath et al. (2002) also examined the contributions of inter-provincial and intra-provincial inequalities to overall inequality, but their study was based on GRP per capita amongst the prefectures. They found that the contribution of the inter-provincial inequality component to overall inter-prefectural inequality increased during 1993–98, whereas the contribution of the intra-provincial inequality component to overall inter-prefectural inequality decreased. Li and Xu (2008) also investigated regional inequality using prefectural-level GRP per capita and showed that the contribution of the intra-provincial component declined from 61.6 per cent in 1997 to 59.4 per cent in 2005, while the contribution of the inter-provincial component increased from 38.4 per cent to 40.6 per cent during the period considered. Their results provide further empirical evidence supporting the findings of both Lee (2000) and Herrmann-Pillath et al. (2002). Although overall inequality measures in the aforementioned studies are calculated using data compiled at different spatial levels, the conclusions are very similar. These studies all show that the contribution of inter-provincial inequality to overall regional inequality increased while the share of intra-provincial inequality declined.

Zonal-Level Decomposition

The decomposition of inequality into inter-zonal and intra-zonal components is very common in the studies of inequality for China. Bhalla et al. (2003), Yao and

Zhang (2001) and Yao et al. (2005) all conducted research on the contributions of the inter-zonal inequality and intra-zonal inequality components to overall inequality using provincial-level GRP per capita data. They all come to the same conclusion that the contribution of the inter-zonal inequality component increased, while that of the intra-zonal inequality component decreased. Yao and Zhang (2001) found that the contribution of the inter-zonal component was about 80 per cent in 1997. Cai et al. (2002) studied inter-provincial inequality using GRP per capita during 1978–98 and they considered three economic zones. They showed that in 1978 the eastern zone's contribution to overall inequality was more than 60 per cent; however, the contribution of the inter-zonal component increased significantly in the following 20 years and was about 60 per cent in 1998. The contribution of the eastern zone component declined dramatically over this period. Therefore, they argued that there was evidence of club convergence within the eastern zone. They also argued that the contributions of the central and western zone components remained very small during that period. Bhalla et al. (2003), who used provincial-level data in their study, showed that the eastern zone contributed the most to overall provincial inequality. Li and Xu (2008) decomposed inter-provincial inequality into contributions of four different zones using GRP per capita data during 1978–2005. They observed that the eastern zone component contributed about 20 per cent of overall inequality in 2005, while the sum of the contributions of the central, western and north-eastern zones was only 10 per cent. Moreover, they also showed that the contribution of the inter-zonal component rose from 40 per cent in 1978 to about 70 per cent in 2005. Therefore, they concluded that inter-provincial inequality was mainly caused by the disparity between the four economic zones. Gries and Redlin (2009) decomposed inequality in provincial GRP per capita during 1978–2004. They showed that the eastern zone component contributed to most of the overall inter-provincial inequality back in 1978; however, the contribution of this component decreased sharply after 1978. In contrast, the contribution of the inter-zonal component increased dramatically and became the largest contributor to overall inequality in 2004. Villaverde et al. (2010) found that the contribution of the inter-zonal component increased considerably, from below 20 per cent in 1978 to about 50 per cent in 2007, while the contribution of the intra-zonal component declined from 80 per cent to about 50 per cent during the same period. Liu (2006) investigated rural regional inequality using the data for agricultural output (AO), rural non-agricultural output (RNAO) and gross value of rural social product (GVRSP). Liu's findings supported the existing consensus that the contributions of the inter-zonal components to overall inequality during the period 1980–2002 increased while the contributions of the intra-zonal components decreased.

Inland and Coastal-Level Decomposition

It is well known that a large disparity exists between the inland and the coastal regions in China. Hao and Wei (2010), Jian et al. (1996), Tsui (2007) and Ying (1999) are representative works establishing this notion using provincial GRP per capita data. In these studies it is found that inequality between the inland and coastal regions increased while that within the inland and coastal regions decreased over time. Another study, by Fujita and Hu (2001), used regional GRP rather than GRP per capita in their calculation. They also reached the same conclusion: that there was an increase in inequality between the inland and coastal regions. Hao and Wei (2010) considered GRP per worker and showed that inequality between the inland and coastal regions increased sharply during 1978–2004. They repeated their exercises by excluding the municipalities, and their findings remained the same.

Decomposition Based on Other Spatial Groupings

Some researchers presented their own definitions in constructing spatial subgroups for decomposition exercises. Herrmann-Pillath et al. (2002) divided the provinces in China into seven 'macro-regions'. Similarly, Huang et al. (2003) divided the provinces into seven 'areas'. Herrmann-Pillath et al. (2002) examined inter-prefectural inequality using GRP per capita and found that the contribution of the inter-regional inequality component to overall inter-prefectural inequality decreased during 1993–98. Huang et al. (2003) explored inter-provincial inequality during 1991–2001 and found that the contribution of inter-area inequality to overall inter-provincial inequality increased, while the contribution of intra-area inequality to overall inequality decreased. Huang et al. (2003) thus concluded that inter-area inequality is the major driving force underlying the increase in overall inter-provincial inequality. On the surface, it appears that Herrmann-Pillath et al. (2002) and Huang et al. (2003) reached different conclusions; however, their results cannot be compared directly. First, the time span is not the same. Second, the results of Herrmann-Pillath et al. (2002) are based on prefectural-level data, whereas those of Huang et al. (2003) are based on provincial-level data. Third, Herrmann-Pillath et al. (2002) used GRP per capita data in their analysis, whereas Huang et al. (2003) used provincial GRP data unscaled by population. In addition, their methods of categorisation of the provinces into seven groups are not identical.

The aforementioned studies show that progress in raising living standards across China has been very uneven amongst the regions. Moreover, it is now well established that spatial groupings play a major role in inequality and thus it is necessary to study inequality with due respect to spatial factors.

Methodology

Overall inequality can be decomposed into several components and the contribution of each component can be computed accordingly. This is an excellent tool for determining the relative importance of each component, which is valuable in determining the priority of government policies. The most common approaches used in the literature are the decompositions by subgroups (Shorrocks 1980, 1984) and income sources (Yao 1997, 1999). Decomposition by subgroups can be applied to household survey or regional data (for example, see Cai et al. 2002; Cheng 1996b; Gries and Redlin 2009; Huang et al. 2003; Kanbur and Zhang 1999, 2005; Lee 2000; Li and Xu 2008; Lin et al. 2008; Liu 2010; Sicular et al. 2007; Tsui 1993; Wan 2007; Yang 1999; Yao and Liu 1998; Ying 1999), while decomposition by income sources is mostly used with household survey data to determine the significance of each income component (for instance, Cheng 1996a; Fang and Rizzo 2011; Gustafsson and Li 2001; Khan and Riskin 1998; Khan et al. 1993; Liu and Sicular 2009; Rozelle 1994; Zhou 2009). Theil-T and Theil-L indices are often employed in the decomposition by subgroups (Cowell 2000; Shorrocks 1980; Theil 1967, 1972), while the Gini coefficient is popularly used in the decomposition by income sources (for instance, Cheng 1996a; Yao 1997, 1999).

Decomposition of Inequality by Subgroups

The decomposition of inequality by subgroups is used to determine the contributions of the subgroups to overall inequality (Theil 1967, 1972). First, overall inequality is calculated using all the entities. Second, the entities are then divided into two or more subgroups. These subgroups can be defined by spatial relationship, quantifiable data or qualitative information. Overall inequality for all the entities is then decomposed into the weighted sum of the inequality within these subgroups (the intra-subgroup component) and the inequality between these subgroups (the inter-subgroup component).[1] Theil-T and Theil-L indices are often used in the decomposition of inequality by subgroups because both indices can be decomposed completely into the inter-subgroup and intra-subgroup components (Bourguignon 1979; Shorrocks 1980, 1984). The Gini coefficient, however, does not have this property (Yao 1999); therefore, the Gini coefficient has seldom been used in this kind of exercise (Bourguignon 1979).

The decomposition process can be carried out in successive tiers, so that the relationship between the various components can be investigated. There are five spatial levels in our decomposition: the county (level one), the provincial

---

1 For a detailed discussion, refer to Bourguignon (1979) and Shorrocks (1980, 1984).

(level two), the zonal (level three), the inland and coastal (level four), and the national (level five). Let $I_i^{j,k}$ be the inequality index for the kth region at level j. The subscript i and superscript j represent different spatial levels, where j is always higher than i by one spatial level. The measurement of inequality is based on population and GRP data compiled at level I, which is represented by subscript i and represents inequality as measured amongst the level-i units. Superscript j represents the level of the spatial grouping that is used in the measurement of inequality. Every spatial grouping in level j is made up of the level-i units. Generally, there are several spatial groupings in each level (except level five, which is the national level, so it has only one entity), and the kth region is one of the many spatial groupings at spatial level j. For example, the inter-CU inequality within the ath province can be represented by $I_1^{2,a}$. The subscript 1 (county-level) shows that the inequality measurement is based on the county-level units, while the superscript 2 (provincial level) shows that the county-level units are grouped into province, and the inequality measurement refers to the inequality amongst the county-level units within a province. The a behind the comma in the superscript refers to the ath province. Similarly, zonal level is level three and thus, the inter-provincial inequality within the bth economic zone can be represented by $I_2^{3,b}$. It should be noted that the overall inequality of the whole nation based on county-level data is represented by I_1^5. There is no region notation after the number 5 in the superscript, because superscript 5 represents the whole nation and it is the only spatial grouping at the national level.

The inequality of the inter-subgroup component measured at any level i can be decomposed into the sum of the intra-subgroup component and inter-subgroup component measured at a higher spatial level, j. Overall inter-CU inequality for China (I_1^5) can be decomposed into the intra-provincial component and the inter-provincial component (I_2^5). The intra-provincial component is equal to the weighted sum of the inter-CU inequalities within all the provinces in the dataset. The inter-CU inequality within the ath province is represented by $I_1^{2,a}$ (Equation 8.1).

Equation 8.1

$$I_1^5 = \sum_{a=1}^{22} W_a \, I_1^{2,a} + I_2^5$$

In Equation 8.1, $a = 1$ to 22 since there are 22 provinces in this study and W_a is the weight for the ath province. The weights for the Theil-L and Theil-T decompositions are population and income based, respectively (Gustafsson and Li 2002). Specifically, the weight for the ath province is n_a/N for the Theil-L decomposition and Y_a/Y for the Theil-T decomposition where n_a and Y_a represent the population and GRP in the ath province, while N and Y denote the total population and GRP of all the regions.

Similarly, the inter-provincial inequality (I_2^5) can then be decomposed into the sum of the intra-zonal component and the inter-zonal component (I_3^5). The intra-zonal component is equal to the weighted sum of the inter-provincial inequalities within all the zones. The inter-provincial inequality within the bth zone is represented by $I_2^{3,b}$ (Equation 8.2).

Equation 8.2

$$I_2^5 = \Sigma_{b=1}^4 W_b \, I_2^{3,b} + I_3^5$$

In Equation 8.2, $b = 1$ to 4 since there are four economic zones; W_b is the weight for the bth zone.

In the third tier of decomposition, inter-zonal inequality (I_3^5) can be further decomposed into the sum of the component of the inequalities within the inland and coastal regions, and the component of the inequality between the inland and coastal regions (I_4^5). The component of the inequalities within the inland and coastal regions is equal to the weighted sum of the inter-zonal inequalities within the inland and coastal regions. The inter-zonal inequality within the cth region is represented by $I_3^{4,c}$ (Equation 8.3).

Equation 8.3

$$I_3^5 = \Sigma_{c=1}^2 W_c \, I_3^{4,c} + I_4^5$$

In Equation 8.3, $c = 1, 2$, since there are two regions—namely, the inland and the coastal regions—and W_c is the weight for the cth region.

Substitute Equation 8.3 into Equation 8.2 to obtain Equation 8.4.

Equation 8.4

$$I_2^5 = \Sigma_{b=1}^4 W_b \, I_2^{3,b} + \Sigma_{c=1}^2 W_c \, I_3^{4,c} + I_4^5$$

Thus, Equation 8.1 becomes Equation 8.5.

Equation 8.5

$$I_1^5 = \Sigma_{a=1}^{22} W_a \, I_1^{2,a} + \Sigma_{b=1}^4 W_b \, I_2^{3,b} + \Sigma_{c=1}^2 W_c \, I_3^{4,c} + I_4^5$$

The contribution of the various spatial components to overall inequality in China can be derived from Equation 8.5. The percentage contribution of each component can then be found by dividing the value of each individual component by overall inequality. Overall inequality can be decomposed into the spatial components at four levels. This form of decomposition is the vertical decomposition, which can be applied across different administrative levels.

All components in Equation 8.5, except I_4^5, are the weighted sums of inequality measured at a lower level. These intra-subgroup components can be further decomposed into their constituents within each level. The value of each constituent unit is the inequality of that entity times its weight. For example, the weighted sum of the inter-CU inequalities within all the provinces, which is made up of the contributions of 22 provinces, can be decomposed into the contribution of each province. This can identify major contributors to overall inequality for each spatial grouping. Similarly, the intra-provincial regional inequality (that is, the inter-CU inequality within each province) can be further decomposed into three components within each province: the components of the inter-county inequality, the intercity inequality and the inequality between city and county subgroups. The information can reveal the disparity between the cities and counties within each province. Accordingly, intra-provincial development policy can be formulated for each province.

Data

Regional inequality can be investigated using different indicators. Duncan and Tian (1999) noted that it is important to distinguish between studies using livelihood and output indicators, as they can lead to different results. Many inequality studies are based on expenditure, consumption, wages, total earnings and household income data. These indicators are good measures for the livelihood and economic wellbeing of people. On the other hand, output per capita is deemed to be a good measure of economic development for a region. Because the focus of this study is on regional inequality in economic development, regional output per capita is used in this study. Gross regional product (GRP) per capita is selected as the indicator of economic development in this research because it is the most frequently used indicator of output and is more comprehensive than other measures such as the gross value of industrial and agricultural output (GVIAO) and national income (NI).

The present study is based on a dataset of real GRP per capita for the counties and county-level cities in China. There are three kinds of county-level units: the counties, the county-level cities and the city districts (or simply 'districts') in the prefectural-level cities and municipalities. The data for the city districts, however, are unavailable for some provinces in the earlier years of the study period. Moreover, in some cases, only an aggregated value of the city districts, rather than the data for each individual district, is available. Therefore, this study is based on the data for the counties and county-level cities only. Many studies that examine inequality amongst the county-level units do not include city districts but are based on the data for the county-level cities and counties only.[2] In this study, the four municipalities—Beijing, Tianjin, Shanghai and Chongqing—are not included because most of the administrative regions in the municipalities are districts.

The data are largely compiled from the *Provincial Statistical Yearbook* (NBS 1998–2008a) of each province; however, where the data are unavailable, the data from the *China Statistical Yearbook for Regional Economy* (NBS 2004–08) and the *Provincial Yearbook* (NBS 1998–2008b) for each province are used. Some cities and counties are dropped from the dataset because of incomplete information in the sources. All the county-level GRP data are adjusted for inflation and expressed in 1997 constant prices. Since the deflator for each individual county-level unit is not available, the provincial deflator is used for all the counties and county-level cities within a province. To ensure consistency of data, the database has been thoroughly checked for changing administrative status/boundaries and so on.[3] Aggregation has been used in some instances, following Fan (1995), where boundaries have changed over time. The shortcoming of aggregation is the possible underestimation of inequality in the aggregated county-level units, although according to the web site of administrative divisions in China, there were few changes in administrative divisions during the period covered.

The county-level units are divided into spatial groupings at four levels: national, inland and coastal, economic zonal, and provincial. In this study, the coastal region and the eastern zone are identical, whereas the inland region is defined to comprise all the provinces in the central, western and north-eastern zones. The definition of the inland and coastal regions used in this study is slightly different from the official definition. As the data for some provinces are not available in some years, the county-level units within these provinces cannot be included in the measurement of inequality conducted at the national, inland and coastal, and economic zonal levels. Eventually, only the county-level units in 22 provinces are included in these three levels of analyses, and these provinces are grouped as follows.

- Eastern zone: Hebei, Jiangsu, Zhejiang, Fujian, Guangdong and Hainan. The municipalities of Beijing, Tianjin and Shanghai are excluded from this study. The province of Shandong is not included because of unavailability of data.

- Central zone: Anhui, Jiangxi, Henan and Hunan. The provinces of Shanxi and Hubei are not included because of unavailability of data.

---

2 Examples include Brajer et al. (2010); Gustafsson and Li (2002); Lee (2000); Jones et al. (2003); Li and Xu (2008); Rozelle (1994); Song et al. (2000); Veeck and Pannell (1989); Wei and Kim (2002); Wu and Zhu (2011); Yu et al. (2007); Zhou and Zou (2010).

3 Detailed descriptions are available in Cheong and Wu (2012).

- Western zone: Inner Mongolia, Guangxi, Sichuan, Guizhou, Yunnan, Gansu, Qinghai, Ningxia and Xinjiang. The municipality of Chongqing is excluded from this study. The provinces of Shaanxi and Tibet are not included because of unavailability of data.

- North-eastern zone: Liaoning, Jilin and Heilongjiang.

The categorisation of the zones is based on the *2006 China Statistical Yearbook* (NBS 2006). The final dataset used in the study comprises 1485 counties and county-level cities covering the period 1997–2007. Population data are compiled from the *Provincial Statistical Yearbook* (NBS 1998–2008a), *Provincial Yearbook* (NBS 1998–2008b) and *China Statistical Yearbook for Regional Economy* (NBS 2004–2008). It is well known that the provincial population data in China are based on the household registration system (*hukou*) population, and the number of temporary migrants is not taken into consideration. This could distort the final results and cannot be resolved given the resources available.[4]

Wan (2008) suggests that China's regional inequality can be divided into two dimensions: the east–central–west divide and rural–urban inequality. The latter contributes to more than 70 per cent of overall inequality. The data for rural and urban areas within the county-level units are not available, therefore, it is impossible to study inequality between the rural and urban areas at the county level. Lee (2000) and Tsui (1993) treated the county-level cities as urban areas and the counties as rural areas in their analysis. They decompose overall inter-CU inequality into the contributions of the 'intra-rural', 'intra-urban' and 'rural-urban' components. The same approach will be used in this chapter. To avoid confusion, the components are renamed as inter-county inequality, intercity inequality and inequality between city and county subgroups.

Results and Discussion

The dataset used in this research comprises data for the counties and county-level cities. The terms 'county-level city' and 'city' are used interchangeably hereinafter. The term 'inter-county-level-unit inequality' or simply 'inter-CU inequality' refers to the inequality amongst all the counties and county-level cities within a region. The term 'intra-provincial regional inequality' or simply

---

4   The data of the actual population in 2000 for each county-level unit are available in the *County Data of 2000 Census* (*2000 ren kou pu cha fen xian zi liao*) (NBS 2003). As the census data for 2010 are not yet available, for the time being, it is impossible to adjust the population data by interpolation because the only data available are for 2000. Further adjustment can be made when the data become available. Another concern is the quality of output data in China. Researchers have raised doubts about the reliability and accuracy of China's GDP statistics (Chow 1986; Holz 2006; Rawski 2001; Wu 1997). The official source is, however, still the only channel for statistics used in this type of exercise. Thus, caution should be exercised in interpreting the results here.

'intra-provincial inequality' refers to the inequality amongst the county-level units within a province (that is, the inter-CU inequality within each province). This section has two parts: the results based on decomposition of overall inequality into different spatial components are presented first. Then, intra-provincial inequality is further decomposed into three components: inter-county inequality, intercity inequality and inequality between city and county subgroups.

Decomposition of Inequality into Spatial Components

Table 8.1 shows the three-tier decomposition of inequality. The first tier is the decomposition of overall inter-CU inequality into the intra-provincial component (that is, the weighted sum of the inter-CU inequalities within all the provinces) and the inter-provincial component as shown in Equation 8.1. The contribution of each component is expressed as a percentage of the overall inter-CU inequality. The second tier is the decomposition of inter-provincial inequality into the intra-zonal component (that is, the weighted sum of the inter-provincial inequalities within all the zones) and the inter-zonal component as shown in Equation 8.2. The contribution at this level is expressed as a fraction of inter-provincial inequality. The third tier is the decomposition of the inter-zonal inequality into the component of inter-zonal inequality within the inland and coastal regions (that is, the weighted sum of the inter-zonal inequalities within the inland and coastal regions) and the component of the inequality between the inland and coastal regions as shown in Equation 8.3. The contributions of the components are expressed as a percentage of the inter-zonal inequality.

The first-tier decomposition in Table 8.1 shows that the contributions of inter-CU inequality within all the provinces and inter-provincial inequality to overall inter-CU inequality remain relatively constant during the period 1997–2007. It is interesting to note that the contribution of inter-provincial inequality (Theil-T is used in this calculation) decreased slightly between 1997 and 2007, but it increased slightly when Theil-L is used. The difference is, however, very small. In contrast, the contribution of inter-provincial inequalities within all the zones to overall inter-provincial inequality increased substantially according to either Theil-T or Theil-L measure, as shown in the second-tier decomposition in Table 8.1. In 1997, the contributions were about 26 per cent and 28 per cent according to Theil-T and Theil-L measures, respectively. These contributions increased enormously to reach about 48 per cent in both cases in 2007, while the contribution of the inter-zonal inequality decreased significantly. Finally, the third-tier decomposition results illustrate that the changes in the contributions of the components are relatively small. The contribution of inter-zonal inequality within the inland and coastal regions dropped about 4 per cent, whereas the contribution of inequality between the inland and coastal regions increased slightly during 1997–2007. The contribution of inequality between the inland and coastal regions to overall inter-zonal inequality reached about 90 per cent in 2007.

Table 8.2 shows the overall result of the decomposition into different spatial components using Equation 8.5. The contribution of each component is expressed as a percentage of overall inter-CU inequality. Although there are some minor differences in the percentage contribution derived from the two indices, the magnitude and trend are similar. The component of inter-CU inequality within all the provinces contributed the most to overall inter-CU inequality and was about 60 per cent in 2007. The contributions of inter-provincial inequality within all the zones and inequality between the inland and coastal regions were very close in 2007, being 19 per cent and 18 per cent according to the Theil-T measure. The component of inter-zonal inequalities within the inland and coastal regions contributed about 2 per cent of overall inequality in 2007.

Table 8.3 shows the changes in the contributions of the spatial components to overall inter-CU inequality. It can be observed that the contribution of inter-CU inequality within all the provinces to overall inter-CU inequality remained fairly constant over time. The contribution of inter-provincial inequality within all the zones increased, while the contributions of inequality between the inland and coastal regions and inter-zonal inequality within the inland and coastal regions were found to decrease. According to the Theil-T method, the percentage increase in the contribution of inter-provincial inequality within all the zones was about 8.6 per cent during 1997–2007 while inter-zonal inequality within the inland and coastal regions declined 2.2 per cent and inequality between the inland and coastal regions declined 7.7 per cent. This finding highlights the importance of monitoring the increase in inequality amongst the provinces within the economic zones.

Table 8.1 Three-Tier Decomposition of Inter-CU Inequality into Spatial Components

		1997	1998	1999	2000	2001	2002	2003	2004	2005	2006	2007
First tier	Theil-T	Inter-CU inequality within all the provinces (%)	59.49	57.84	57.04	57.58	57.53	56.79	56.77	57.28	59.75	60.56	60.74
		Inter-provincial inequality (%)	40.51	42.16	42.96	42.42	42.47	43.21	43.23	42.72	40.25	39.44	39.26
	Theil-L	Inter-CU inequality within all the provinces (%)	57.19	55.55	54.93	55.70	55.71	54.67	54.14	54.08	55.98	56.56	56.46
		Inter-provincial inequality (%)	42.81	44.45	45.07	44.30	44.29	45.33	45.86	45.92	44.02	43.44	43.54
Second tier	Theil-T	Inter-provincial inequality within all the zones (%)	26.19	22.98	22.75	25.80	26.61	28.27	29.67	33.02	42.70	45.71	48.90
		Inter-zonal inequality (%)	73.81	77.02	77.25	74.20	73.39	71.73	70.33	66.98	57.30	54.29	51.10
	Theil-L	Inter-provincial inequality within all the zones (%)	28.28	24.38	23.44	26.27	26.92	28.06	29.11	32.94	41.85	44.95	48.26
		Inter-zonal inequality (%)	71.72	75.62	76.56	73.73	73.08	71.94	70.89	67.06	58.15	55.05	51.74
Third tier	Theil-T	Inter-zonal inequality within the inland and coastal regions (%)	14.07	14.94	14.91	12.63	12.02	11.98	10.89	10.70	10.71	9.10	10.03
		Inequality between the inland and coastal regions (%)	85.93	85.06	85.09	87.37	87.98	88.02	89.11	89.30	89.29	90.90	89.97
	Theil-L	Inter-zonal inequality within the inland and coastal regions (%)	17.34	18.49	18.40	15.66	14.97	14.93	13.72	13.51	13.49	11.60	12.56
		Inequality between the inland and coastal regions (%)	82.66	81.51	81.60	84.34	85.03	85.07	86.28	86.49	86.51	88.40	87.44

Notes: The coastal region is treated the same as the eastern zone. The inland region includes the central, western and north-eastern zones.

Source: Authors' own calculation.

Table 8.2 Decomposition of Inter-CU Inequality into Spatial Components

		1997	1998	1999	2000	2001	2002	2003	2004	2005	2006	2007
Theil-T	Inequality between the inland and coastal regions (%)	25.70	27.62	28.24	27.50	27.42	27.28	27.09	25.55	20.59	19.46	18.05
	Inter-zonal inequality within the inland and coastal regions (%)	4.21	4.85	4.95	3.98	3.75	3.71	3.31	3.06	2.47	1.95	2.01
	Inter-provincial inequality within all the zones (%)	10.61	9.69	9.77	10.94	11.30	12.21	12.82	14.11	17.19	18.03	19.20
	Inter-CU inequality within all the provinces (%)	59.49	57.84	57.04	57.58	57.53	56.79	56.77	57.28	59.75	60.56	60.74
Theil-L	Inequality between the inland and coastal regions (%)	25.38	27.40	28.16	27.55	27.52	27.74	28.05	26.63	22.14	21.14	19.70
	Inter-zonal inequality within the inland and coastal regions (%)	5.32	6.22	6.35	5.12	4.85	4.87	4.46	4.16	3.45	2.77	2.83
	Inter-provincial inequality within all the zones (%)	12.10	10.84	10.57	11.64	11.92	12.72	13.35	15.13	18.43	19.53	21.01
	Inter-CU inequality within all the provinces (%)	57.19	55.55	54.93	55.70	55.71	54.67	54.14	54.08	55.98	56.56	56.46

Notes: The coastal region is treated the same as the eastern zone. The inland region includes the central, western and north-eastern zones.

Source: Authors' own calculation.

Table 8.3 Changes in the Contributions of the Spatial Components to Inter-CU Inequality (per cent)

		1997	2007	Differences
Theil-T	Inequality between the inland and coastal regions	25.70	18.05	−7.65
	Inter-zonal inequality within the inland and coastal regions	4.21	2.01	−2.19
	Inter-provincial inequality within all the zones	10.61	19.20	8.59
	Inter-CU inequality within all the provinces	59.49	60.74	1.25
Theil-L	Inequality between the inland and coastal regions	25.38	19.70	−5.68
	Inter-zonal inequality within the inland and coastal regions	5.32	2.83	−2.50
	Inter-provincial inequality within all the zones	12.10	21.01	8.91
	Inter-CU inequality within all the provinces	57.19	56.46	−0.73

Notes: The coastal region is treated the same as the eastern zone. The inland region includes the central, western and north-eastern zones.

Source: Authors' own calculation.

Decomposition techniques can also be applied to analyse the *changes* in inequality itself. This extends the conventional decomposition of inequality. The decomposition of changes in inequality can provide detailed information about the contributions of the changes in different components to the change in overall inequality. The conventional approach shows the significance of the component to the absolute level of inequality. The results of the decomposition of the changes in overall inter-CU inequality over the period 1997–2007 are shown in Table 8.4. The increase in inter-CU inequality within all the provinces contributed substantially to the change in overall inequality during the period considered (63 per cent and 55 per cent according to Theil-T and Theil-L measures respectively), followed by the increase in inter-provincial inequality within all the zones (35 per cent and 43 per cent according to Theil-T and Theil-L). A comparison of Table 8.4 with Table 8.3 shows that inequality between the inland and coastal regions registered a decrease in its contribution to overall inequality in Table 8.3, whereas Table 8.4 shows that 4 per cent (given Theil-T) of an increase in overall inequality can be explained by the increase in inequality between the inland and coastal regions. This information is quite revealing. It suggests that inequality between the inland and coastal regions increased in the study period, but the increase was not as dramatic as those of other components and hence led to a decline in its total contribution. Therefore, this component should not be overlooked just because it had a decline in total contribution.

All the county-level units in a province can be further divided into city and county subgroups, and an additional tier of decomposition can be performed to investigate the contribution of the city and county subgroups to intra-provincial regional inequality. The latter can be further decomposed into three intra-provincial components: inter-county inequality, intercity inequality and inequality between the city and county subgroups in each province.[5] The results are shown in Table 8.5. It is observed that inter-county inequality within all the provinces has the largest contribution to overall inequality—namely, 23 per cent and 31 per cent in 2007 according to the Theil-T and Theil-L measures respectively. The changes in the contributions of these components are shown in Table 8.6. It is shown that the changes of the three intra-provincial components were very small and remained fairly constant over the whole period.

Table 8.4 Decomposition of the Changes in Inter-CU Inequality, 1997–2007

Changes in	Contribution to inter-CU inequality change		Contribution to inter-CU inequality change (%)	
	Theil-T	Theil-L	Theil-T	Theil-L
Inequality between the inland and coastal regions	0.005	0.004	4.072	5.447
Inter-zonal inequality within the inland and coastal regions	−0.002	−0.003	−1.999	−3.426
Inter-provincial inequality within all the zones	0.039	0.034	34.892	43.338
Inter-CU inequality within all the provinces	0.070	0.042	63.035	54.641

Notes: The coastal region is treated the same as the eastern zone. The inland region includes the central, western and north-eastern zones.

Source: Authors' own calculation.

Table 8.7 shows the contributions of the changes in different spatial components (first three rows in the table) and the three intra-provincial components (last three rows in the table) to the change in overall inequality. It is shown that the contributions of the changes in the three intra-provincial components (inter-county, intercity and between city and county subgroups) were respectively 25 per cent, 26 per cent and 12 per cent according to the Theil-T technique (or 33 per cent, 13 per cent and 9 per cent if Theil-L indices are used). It is worth noting that in Table 8.6 the contribution of inequality between city and county subgroups within all the provinces exhibited a declining trend while the increase in this component still contributed to 12 per cent (as measured by Theil-T) of the increase in overall inequality. Similarly, though in Table 8.6 the changes in the contributions of the other two intra-provincial inequality components remained constant, the increases in these two components contributed to more than 50 per cent (as measured by Theil-T) of the change in overall inequality during the period 1997–2007. Therefore, these inequality components should not be overlooked and efforts should also be made to mitigate these intra-provincial inequalities.

5 The decomposition of inequality into city and county subgroups cannot be conducted for Ningxia because there is only one county-level city in Ningxia, and there has also been a boundary change in this city that makes the data incomparable. This city is thus removed from the dataset.

Table 8.5 Decomposition of Inter-CU Inequality into Spatial Components and the Three Intra-Provincial Components

		1997	1998	1999	2000	2001	2002	2003	2004	2005	2006	2007
	Inequality between the inland and coastal regions (%)	25.70	27.62	28.24	27.50	27.42	27.28	27.09	25.55	20.59	19.46	18.05
	Inter-zonal inequality within the inland and coastal regions (%)	4.21	4.85	4.95	3.98	3.75	3.71	3.31	3.06	2.47	1.95	2.01
	Inter-provincial inequality within all the zones (%)	10.61	9.69	9.77	10.94	11.30	12.21	12.82	14.11	17.19	18.03	19.20
Theil-T	Inter-county inequality within all the provinces (%)	22.23	21.64	21.92	22.07	22.24	21.19	20.47	20.83	22.25	22.66	23.31
	Intercity inequality within all the provinces (%)	20.85	20.79	20.19	20.69	20.47	20.88	21.39	21.41	22.26	22.75	22.62
	Inequality between city and county subgroups within all the provinces (%)	16.41	15.41	14.93	14.82	14.83	14.72	14.92	15.04	15.24	15.15	14.81
	Inequality between the inland and coastal regions (%)	25.38	27.40	28.16	27.55	27.52	27.74	28.05	26.63	22.14	21.14	19.70
	Inter-zonal inequality within the inland and coastal regions (%)	5.32	6.22	6.35	5.12	4.85	4.87	4.46	4.16	3.45	2.77	2.83
	Inter-provincial inequality within all the zones (%)	12.10	10.84	10.57	11.64	11.92	12.72	13.35	15.13	18.43	19.53	21.01
Theil-L	Inter-county inequality within all the provinces (%)	29.66	28.87	29.12	29.44	29.81	28.80	28.22	28.32	29.92	30.38	30.57
	Intercity inequality within all the provinces (%)	12.61	12.71	12.33	12.91	12.49	12.51	12.39	12.24	12.49	12.74	12.72
	Inequality between city and county subgroups within all the provinces (%)	14.93	13.96	13.49	13.35	13.41	13.36	13.52	13.52	13.56	13.43	13.17

Notes: The coastal region is treated the same as the eastern zone. The inland region includes the central, western and north-eastern zones.

Source: Authors' own calculation.

Table 8.6 Changes in the Contributions of Inequality Components (per cent)

		1997	2007	Differences
Theil-T	Inequality between the inland and coastal regions	25.70	18.05	−7.65
	Inter-zonal inequality within the inland and coastal regions	4.21	2.01	−2.19
	Inter-provincial inequality within all the zones	10.61	19.20	8.59
	Inter-county inequality within all the provinces	22.23	23.31	1.08
	Intercity inequality within all the provinces	20.85	22.62	1.78
	Inequality between city and county subgroups within all the provinces	16.41	14.81	−1.60
Theil-L	Inequality between the inland and coastal regions	25.38	19.70	−5.68
	Inter-zonal inequality within the inland and coastal regions	5.32	2.83	−2.50
	Inter-provincial inequality within all the zones	12.10	21.01	8.91
	Inter-county inequality within all the provinces	29.66	30.57	0.92
	Intercity inequality within all the provinces	12.61	12.72	0.11
	Inequality between city and county subgroups within all the provinces	14.93	13.17	−1.75

Notes: The coastal region is treated the same as the eastern zone. The inland region includes the central, western and north-eastern zones.

Source: Authors' own calculation.

Table 8.7 Decomposition of the Change in Inter-CU Inequality, 1997–2007

Changes in each component	Contribution to overall changes		Contribution to overall changes (%)	
	Theil-T	Theil-L	Theil-T	Theil-L
Inequality between the inland and coastal regions	0.005	0.004	4.072	5.447
Inter-zonal inequality within the inland and coastal regions	−0.002	−0.003	−1.999	−3.426
Inter-provincial inequality within all the zones	0.039	0.034	34.892	43.338
Inter-county inequality within all the provinces	0.028	0.025	25.277	32.876
Inter-city inequality within all the provinces	0.029	0.010	25.875	12.985
Inequality between city and county subgroups within all the provinces	0.013	0.007	11.882	8.780

Notes: The coastal region is treated the same as the eastern zone. The inland region includes the central, western and north-eastern zones.

Source: Authors' own calculation.

Further Decomposition Analyses

Further analysis can be performed to gain more insights into inequality in each province. Decomposition can be conducted horizontally amongst the provinces so as to identify the contributions of individual provinces.

The results are shown in Tables 8.8 and 8.9 (corresponding to the Theil-T and Theil-L methods). As the two sets of results are similar, our discussions are based on the Theil-T results in Table 8.8. The values in column CU in Table 8.8 represent percentage contributions of individual provinces to overall inequality and they sum to one hundred. Individual provinces' contributions are then decomposed into three components reported in columns Co, Ci and Co-Ci in Table 8.8. According to this table, in 2007 Jiangsu made the largest contribution to overall inequality. This finding is in agreement with the results of Sakamoto and Fan (2010), who showed that Jiangsu contributed considerably to the income disparity within the Yangtze River Delta and that its contribution was growing. Other large contributors in 2007 were, in turn, Hebei, Henan, Inner Mongolia and Zhejiang. Together, these top-five contributors have a share of about 63 per cent. These provinces are situated close to each other. That could imply that spatial factors play major roles in inequality in China. Table 8.8 also shows that inter-county inequality in Hebei, Henan and Inner Mongolia dominates each province's contribution while intercity inequality in Jiangsu is the most important contributing factor. Intercity inequality within Fujian, Guangdong, Hebei, Zhejiang, Henan and Xinjiang also contributed greatly to overall inequality. Most of these provinces belong to the eastern zone. It shows that the great disparity amongst the cities in the eastern zone further reinforced overall inequality. The inequality between city and county subgroups in Fujian, Hebei, Jiangsu, Zhejiang, Henan and Xinjiang contributed significantly to overall inequality. Four of these provinces also belong to the eastern zone.

Table 8.10 shows the changes in the contributions of the three intra-provincial components of the provinces to overall inequality during 1997–2007. It is observed that inter-CU inequality in Jiangsu had the largest increase in its contribution (using the Theil-T technique), which is largely attributed to the increase in the intercity inequality component. The contribution of inter-county inequality did not, however, change significantly though that of inequality between city and county subgroups increased moderately. It is also observed that inter-CU inequality in Inner Mongolia had the second-largest increase in its contribution (according to Theil-T). This change was mainly caused by the increase in the contribution of the inter-county inequality component. The results using the Theil-L method, however, show that inter-CU inequality in Hebei had the largest increase in its contribution, which was mainly due to the increase in the contribution of the inter-county inequality component. Table 8.10 also shows that inter-CU inequality in Guangdong had the largest decrease in its contribution (3.46 per cent according to Theil-T), which was mainly due to the decline in the contribution of the intercity inequality component (2.04 per cent) and a modest decline in the inter-county inequality component (0.96 per cent). According to the Theil-L method, inter-CU inequality in Sichuan had the largest decrease in its contribution (3.05 per cent).

Table 8.8 Decomposition of Inter-CU Inequality within the Provinces in 1997 and 2007 (Theil-T)

			1997				2007			
			CU	Co	Ci	Co-Ci	CU	Co	Ci	Co-Ci
Coastal	Eastern	Fujian	6.76	1.23	2.78	2.75	4.13	0.64	1.86	1.63
		Guangdong	6.47	2.28	3.72	0.47	3.01	1.32	1.68	0.00
		Hainan	0.27	0.09	0.05	0.13	0.12	0.05	0.04	0.02
		Hebei	7.33	3.57	1.39	2.37	10.46	4.98	2.96	2.52
		Jiangsu	23.31	1.21	14.40	7.70	30.09	1.39	18.96	9.74
		Zhejiang	6.62	2.98	1.86	1.78	5.32	2.39	1.78	1.15
Inland	Central	Anhui	2.58	1.54	0.36	0.68	1.20	0.88	0.18	0.14
		Henan	8.94	3.21	1.99	3.75	9.43	4.19	2.05	3.18
		Hunan	2.74	2.24	0.38	0.13	3.29	2.46	0.54	0.29
		Jiangxi	1.14	0.90	0.18	0.05	1.94	1.33	0.44	0.16
	Western	Gansu	2.02	1.55	0.08	0.39	1.92	1.32	0.14	0.46
		Guangxi	2.47	1.98	0.47	0.02	1.32	1.19	0.12	0.00
		Guizhou	1.28	0.72	0.08	0.48	1.28	0.64	0.14	0.49
		Inner Mongolia	2.04	1.33	0.42	0.28	7.66	6.79	0.85	0.02
		Qinghai	0.49	0.25	0.03	0.22	0.81	0.21	0.06	0.55
		Sichuan	7.51	4.26	1.15	2.09	4.42	2.82	0.71	0.89
		Xinjiang	4.99	2.38	1.78	0.83	4.69	2.02	1.63	1.04
		Yunnan	5.13	2.45	1.08	1.59	2.72	1.62	0.43	0.67
	North-eastern	Heilongjiang	1.75	0.92	0.48	0.35	2.31	0.84	0.86	0.61
		Jilin	0.82	0.30	0.38	0.14	1.05	0.40	0.61	0.03
		Liaoning	5.16	1.76	2.00	1.40	2.70	0.75	1.18	0.77

Notes: The coastal region is treated the same as the eastern zone. The inland region includes the central, western and north-eastern zones. CU = inter-CU inequality; Co = inter-county inequality; Ci = intercity inequality; Co-Ci = inequality between city and county subgroups.

Source: Authors' own calculation.

Table 8.9 Decomposition of Inter-CU Inequality within the Provinces in 1997 and 2007 (Theil-L)

			1997				2007			
			CU	Co	Ci	Co-Ci	CU	Co	Ci	Co-Ci
Coastal	Eastern	Fujian	3.76	0.99	1.11	1.65	3.10	0.74	1.01	1.35
		Guangdong	6.05	2.57	3.04	0.44	4.42	2.04	2.37	0.01
		Hainan	0.31	0.12	0.04	0.14	0.19	0.09	0.06	0.04
		Hebei	6.20	3.47	0.86	1.87	9.44	5.37	1.87	2.20
		Jiangsu	13.78	1.46	6.83	5.49	15.25	1.66	7.21	6.38
		Zhejiang	3.94	2.09	0.91	0.95	3.13	1.65	0.86	0.62
Inland	Central	Anhui	2.95	2.01	0.22	0.72	2.64	2.08	0.27	0.29
		Henan	10.45	4.57	1.58	4.30	10.52	5.57	1.53	3.42
		Hunan	3.60	3.02	0.42	0.17	5.36	4.13	0.74	0.49
		Jiangxi	1.86	1.52	0.25	0.09	3.44	2.59	0.57	0.28
	Western	Gansu	5.07	4.24	0.08	0.75	4.50	3.55	0.11	0.83
		Guangxi	3.45	2.84	0.58	0.03	2.57	2.34	0.22	0.01
		Guizhou	3.36	2.06	0.13	1.16	3.59	2.04	0.27	1.29
		Inner Mongolia	2.53	1.83	0.37	0.33	5.17	4.65	0.50	0.02
		Qinghai	0.75	0.46	0.02	0.27	0.96	0.39	0.02	0.55
		Sichuan	10.36	6.35	1.23	2.79	7.31	4.96	0.86	1.49
		Xinjiang	4.70	2.72	1.14	0.84	5.14	2.91	1.05	1.18
		Yunnan	8.61	5.19	1.04	2.38	5.67	3.94	0.52	1.21
	North-eastern	Heilongjiang	1.93	1.18	0.40	0.35	3.63	1.77	0.94	0.92
		Jilin	0.92	0.38	0.38	0.16	1.04	0.42	0.58	0.04
		Liaoning	4.84	2.19	1.42	1.22	2.66	0.97	0.97	0.71

Notes: The coastal region is treated the same as the eastern zone. The inland region includes the central, western and north-eastern zones. CU = inter-CU inequality; Co = inter-county inequality; Ci = intercity inequality; Co-Ci = inequality between city and county subgroups.

Source: Authors' own calculation.

Table 8.11 presents the results of the decomposition of the change in overall inter-CU inequality into the changes in the three components of intra-provincial inequality for each province. According to the estimates using Theil-T, the increase in inter-CU inequality in Jiangsu contributed to 26.35 per cent of the change in overall inequality in China. The increase in intercity inequality accounted for 16.91 per cent, while the increase in inequality between the city and county subgroups accounted for 8.37 per cent. It implies that more than one-quarter of the increase in inter-CU inequality in China over the study period could be due to the increase in intra-provincial inequality in Jiangsu. Furthermore, it is observed that the increases in inter-CU inequalities in Hebei and Inner Mongolia also contributed significantly to overall inequality. These three provinces combined contributed to about 47 per cent of the increase in overall inequality according to the Theil-T estimates. It means that if the levels of inter-CU inequality in these provinces had remained unchanged during the entire study period then the overall increase in inequality in China would have been reduced by nearly one-half.

The relative importance of the three intra-provincial inequality components in every province can also be estimated. In Table 8.12 the contributions of inter-county inequality, intercity inequality and inequality between city and county subgroups in every province are expressed as a percentage of the sum of these three components. For example, inter-county inequality in Hainan contributed to 34.58 per cent of the intra-provincial inequality of Hainan in 1997 while this figure increased to 43.88 per cent in 2007 according to the Theil-T estimates. The contribution of intercity inequality increased from 18.61 per cent to 35.63 per cent while that of inequality between city and county subgroups decreased from 46.81 per cent to 20.49 per cent during the same period. The contribution of the intercity component increased substantially in this period. This could have important policy implications for local government as well as the Central Government.

Table 8.12 provides additional information about the characteristics of the provinces in each zone. According to the Theil-T measurement, inter-county inequality in 2007 contributed to more than 50 per cent of the intra-provincial regional inequality in Anhui, Hunan, Jiangxi, Gansu, Guangxi, Guizhou, Inner Mongolia, Sichuan and Yunnan. These provinces are all in the central and western zones. The intercity component contributed to more than 50 per cent of intra-provincial regional inequality in Guangdong, Jiangsu and Jilin. Both Guangdong and Jiangsu are in the eastern zone. Inequality between city and county subgroups contributed to about 67 per cent of intra-provincial regional inequality in Qinghai, which is in the western zone.

Table 8.10 Changes in the Contributions of Intra-Provincial Components During 1997–2007 (per cent)

			Theil-T change				Theil-L change			
			CU	Co	Ci	Co-Ci	CU	Co	Ci	Co-Ci
Coastal	Eastern	Fujian	-2.63	-0.59	-0.92	-1.12	-0.66	-0.25	-0.10	-0.30
		Guangdong	-3.46	-0.96	-2.04	-0.47	-1.63	-0.53	-0.67	-0.43
		Hainan	-0.15	-0.04	-0.01	-0.11	-0.12	-0.03	0.02	-0.10
		Hebei	3.13	1.41	1.57	0.15	3.24	1.90	1.01	0.33
		Jiangsu	6.78	0.18	4.56	2.04	1.47	0.20	0.38	0.89
		Zhejiang	-1.30	-0.59	-0.08	-0.63	-0.81	-0.44	-0.05	-0.33
	Central	Anhui	-1.38	-0.66	-0.18	-0.54	-0.31	0.07	0.05	-0.43
		Henan	0.49	0.98	0.06	-0.57	0.07	1.00	-0.05	-0.88
		Hunan	0.55	0.22	0.16	0.16	1.76	1.11	0.32	0.32
		Jiangxi	0.80	0.43	0.26	0.11	1.58	1.07	0.32	0.19
Inland	Western	Gansu	-0.10	-0.23	0.06	0.07	-0.57	-0.69	0.03	0.08
		Guangxi	-1.15	-0.79	-0.35	-0.02	-0.88	-0.50	-0.36	-0.02
		Guizhou	0.00	-0.08	0.06	0.01	0.23	-0.02	0.14	0.13
		Inner Mongolia	5.62	5.46	0.43	-0.26	2.64	2.82	0.13	-0.31
		Qinghai	0.32	-0.04	0.03	0.33	0.21	-0.07	0.00	0.28
		Sichuan	-3.09	-1.44	-0.44	-1.20	-3.05	-1.39	-0.37	-1.30
		Xinjiang	-0.30	-0.36	-0.15	0.21	0.44	0.19	-0.09	0.34
		Yunnan	-2.41	-0.83	-0.65	-0.92	-2.94	-1.25	-0.52	-1.17
	North-eastern	Heilongjiang	0.56	-0.08	0.38	0.26	1.70	0.59	0.54	0.57
		Jilin	0.23	0.10	0.23	-0.11	0.12	0.04	0.20	-0.12
		Liaoning	-2.46	-1.01	-0.82	-0.63	-2.18	-1.22	-0.45	-0.51

Notes: The coastal region is treated the same as the eastern zone. The inland region includes the central, western and north-eastern zones. CU = inter-CU inequality; Co = inter-county inequality; Ci = intercity inequality; Co-Ci = inequality between city and county subgroups.

Source: Authors' own calculation.

Table 8.11 Decomposition of Changes in Inter-CU Inequality, 1997–2007, into Changes in Three Intra-Provincial Components

		Change in component	Theil-T				Theil-L			
			CU	Co	Ci	Co-Ci	CU	Co	Ci	Co-Ci
Coastal	Eastern	Fujian	-0.25	-0.23	0.18	-0.19	0.75	0.06	0.40	0.30
		Guangdong	-1.87	-0.21	-1.15	-0.50	0.08	0.36	0.34	-0.62
		Hainan	-0.08	-0.01	0.02	-0.09	-0.05	0.01	0.06	-0.12
		Hebei	10.00	4.68	3.56	1.76	9.80	5.67	2.47	1.67
		Jiangsu	26.35	1.08	16.91	8.37	10.45	1.19	4.49	4.77
		Zhejiang	1.94	0.86	1.04	0.04	0.54	0.27	0.40	-0.12
	Central	Anhui	-0.73	-0.16	-0.08	-0.50	1.00	1.25	0.22	-0.47
		Henan	6.47	3.72	1.36	1.39	5.85	4.48	0.75	0.61
		Hunan	2.67	1.79	0.51	0.36	5.44	3.84	0.87	0.73
		Jiangxi	2.09	1.31	0.57	0.22	4.15	2.95	0.78	0.43
Inland	Western	Gansu	1.11	0.59	0.16	0.36	1.63	0.95	0.11	0.57
		Guangxi	-0.41	-0.10	-0.30	-0.02	0.14	0.56	-0.39	-0.02
		Guizhou	0.80	0.32	0.15	0.32	2.30	1.07	0.33	0.89
		Inner Mongolia	10.94	10.22	0.99	-0.27	6.60	6.59	0.46	-0.44
		Qinghai	0.86	0.08	0.07	0.71	0.82	0.11	0.02	0.69
		Sichuan	-0.57	0.21	-0.03	-0.75	-0.38	0.73	-0.06	-1.04
		Xinjiang	2.64	0.87	0.88	0.89	3.44	1.86	0.45	1.13
		Yunnan	-0.90	0.12	-0.44	-0.58	-1.11	0.37	-0.46	-1.02
	North-eastern	Heilongjiang	2.06	0.44	0.95	0.67	4.41	1.81	1.27	1.33
		Jilin	0.91	0.35	0.65	-0.09	0.74	0.29	0.61	-0.15
		Liaoning	-0.97	-0.62	-0.15	-0.20	-1.68	-1.21	-0.12	-0.35

Notes: The coastal region is treated the same as the eastern zone. The inland region includes the central, western and north-eastern zones. CU = inter-CU inequality; Co = inter-county inequality; Ci = intercity inequality; Co-Ci = inequality between city and county subgroups.

Source: Authors' own calculation.

Table 8.12 Decomposition of Intra-Provincial Inequality in 1997 and 2007

| | | | Theil-T | | | | | | Theil-L | | | | | |
| | | | 1997 | | | 2007 | | | 1997 | | | 2007 | | |
Region	Zone		Co	Ci	Co-Ci	Co	Ci	Co-Ci	Co	Ci	Co-Ci	Co	Ci	Co-Ci
Coastal	Eastern	Fujian	18.21	41.07	40.72	15.54	45.04	39.42	26.30	29.66	44.03	24.00	32.48	43.52
		Guangdong	35.32	57.47	7.21	43.93	55.96	0.11	42.52	50.23	7.25	46.23	53.65	0.11
		Hainan	34.58	18.61	46.81	43.88	35.63	20.49	39.37	14.63	46.00	47.07	32.35	20.59
		Hebei	48.68	18.99	32.33	47.64	28.25	24.11	56.03	13.86	30.11	56.96	19.78	23.26
		Jiangsu	5.20	61.79	33.02	4.63	62.99	32.37	10.59	49.56	39.85	10.87	47.27	41.86
		Zhejiang	45.07	28.06	26.87	44.90	33.54	21.56	52.98	23.01	24.02	52.66	27.41	19.93
	Central	Anhui	59.74	13.86	26.40	73.34	15.11	11.55	68.08	7.43	24.49	78.92	10.21	10.87
		Henan	35.86	22.24	41.90	44.47	21.78	33.75	43.72	15.13	41.15	52.96	14.51	32.54
		Hunan	81.50	13.86	4.63	74.72	16.39	8.89	83.83	11.59	4.59	77.07	13.81	9.12
		Jiangxi	79.55	15.79	4.66	68.81	22.95	8.24	81.99	13.37	4.64	75.28	16.66	8.06
Inland	Western	Gansu	77.01	3.87	19.12	68.85	7.47	23.68	83.59	1.54	14.87	78.94	2.51	18.56
		Guangxi	80.06	19.05	0.88	90.35	9.36	0.29	82.31	16.89	0.80	90.97	8.73	0.30
		Guizhou	56.34	6.31	37.35	50.57	11.08	38.36	61.46	3.98	34.56	56.67	7.38	35.95
		Inner Mongolia	65.43	20.73	13.84	88.68	11.04	0.29	72.36	14.52	13.12	90.03	9.63	0.33
		Qinghai	50.25	5.57	44.18	25.20	7.39	67.41	61.55	2.15	36.30	40.53	2.26	57.21
		Sichuan	56.78	15.31	27.90	63.73	16.10	20.17	61.26	11.84	26.90	67.86	11.70	20.44
		Xinjiang	47.76	35.59	16.65	42.98	34.83	22.19	57.83	24.26	17.91	56.57	20.47	22.96
		Yunnan	47.80	21.17	31.03	59.64	15.74	24.62	60.24	12.07	27.69	69.47	9.14	21.40
	North-eastern	Heilongjiang	52.47	27.51	20.02	36.23	37.25	26.52	61.15	20.91	17.94	48.70	25.80	25.50
		Jilin	37.17	45.79	17.04	38.05	58.70	3.25	41.28	41.34	17.38	40.30	56.04	3.67
		Liaoning	34.09	38.78	27.13	27.80	43.71	28.49	45.25	29.43	25.31	36.65	36.60	26.75

Notes: The coastal region is treated the same as the eastern zone. The inland region includes the central, western and north-eastern zones. Co = inter-county inequality; Ci = intercity inequality; Co-Ci = inequality between city and county subgroups.

Source: Authors' own calculation.

Conclusions

Important information can be obtained from the decomposition of inequality based on county-level data. In this chapter, we found that intra-provincial regional inequality (that is, inequality amongst the county-level units within the provinces) contributed about 60 per cent of China's overall inequality in 2007, whereas the increase in intra-provincial regional inequality contributed to about 63 per cent of the overall increase in regional inequality during 1997–2007. Thus, intra-provincial regional inequality is the crux of the problem of regional inequality in China. It was also found that the contribution of inter-provincial inequality within all the zones increased significantly while the contributions of other components remained relatively constant or even tended to decline during the period considered. Therefore, more specific government policies should be implemented in order to reduce intra-provincial regional inequality.

The results of our decomposition analysis imply that inequality alleviation might need a local rather than a national approach in the first instance. For example, the results of the Theil-T decomposition of the changes in inequality show that immediate actions are needed at least in three provinces: Jiangsu, Inner Mongolia and Hebei. These three provinces together contributed to about 47 per cent of the increase in overall inequality in China during 1997–2007.

It is shown that the evolution of regional inequality in each province has its own characteristics and patterns. Thus, it is necessary for the provincial governments to formulate province-specific policies for the county-level units. For instance, the provinces in the central and western zones should focus more on inter-county inequality, while the provinces in the eastern zone should concentrate on both inter-county and intercity inequalities. The provinces in the north-eastern zone should focus on intercity inequality. The provinces of Fujian, Jiangsu, Henan, Guizhou and Qinghai should pay special attention to inequality between city and county subgroups.

Bibliography

Bhalla, A. S., Yao, S. and Zhang, Z., 2003, 'Causes of inequalities in China, 1952 to 1999', *Journal of International Development*, vol. 15, pp. 939–55.

Bourguignon, F., 1979, 'Decomposable income inequality measures', *Econometrica*, vol. 47, pp. 901–20.

Brajer, V., Mead, R. and Xiao, F., 2010, 'Adjusting Chinese income inequality for environmental equity', *Environment and Development Economics*, vol. 15, pp. 341–62.

Cai, F., Wang, D. and Du, Y., 2002, 'Regional disparity and economic growth in China: the impact of labor market distortions', *China Economic Review*, vol. 13, pp. 197–212.

Chen, Y. P., Liu, M. and Zhang, Q., 2010, 'Development of financial intermediation and the dynamics of urban–rural disparity in China, 1978–1998', *Regional Studies*, vol. 44, pp. 1171–87.

Cheng, Y. S., 1996a, 'A decomposition analysis of income inequality of Chinese rural households', *China Economic Review*, vol. 7, pp. 155–67.

Cheng, Y. S., 1996b, 'Peasant income in China: the impact of rural reforms and structural changes', *China Report*, vol. 32, pp. 43–57.

Cheong, T. S., 2012, Trends, determinants and consequences of regional inequality in China: new evidence, Doctoral dissertation, Business School, University of Western Australia, Perth.

Cheong, T. S. and Wu, Y., 2012, *Intra-provincial inequality in China: an analysis of county-level data*, Economics Discussion Papers, Business School, University of Western Australia, Perth.

Chow, G. C., 1986, 'Chinese statistics', *The American Statistician*, vol. 40, pp. 191–6.

Cowell, F. A., 2000, 'Measurement of inequality', in A. B. Atkinson and F. Bourguignon (eds), *Handbook of Income Distribution*, Elsevier, Oxford, UK.

Duncan, R. and Tian, X., 1999, 'China's inter-provincial disparities: an explanation', *Communist and Post-Communist Studies*, vol. 32, pp. 211–24.

Fan, C. C., 1995, 'Of belts and ladders: state policy and uneven regional development in post-Mao China', *Annals of the Association of American Geographers*, vol. 85, pp. 421–49.

Fang, H. and Rizzo, J. A., 2011, 'Income inequality dynamics in rural China from 1991 to 2006: the role of alternative income sources', *Applied Economics Letters*, vol. 18, pp. 1307–10.

Fujita, M. and Hu, D., 2001, 'Regional disparity in China 1985–1994: the effects of globalization and economic liberalization', *The Annals of Regional Science*, vol. 35, pp. 3–37.

Goh, C.-C., Luo, X. and Zhu, N., 2009, 'Income growth, inequality and poverty reduction: a case study of eight provinces in China', *China Economic Review*, vol. 20, pp. 485–96.

Gries, T. and Redlin, M., 2009, 'China's provincial disparities and the determinants of provincial inequality', *Journal of Chinese Economics and Business*, vol. 7, pp. 259–81.

Gustafsson, B. and Li, S., 2001, 'The effects of transition on the distribution of income in China: a study decomposing the Gini coefficient for 1988 and 1995', *Economics of Transition*, vol. 9, pp. 593–617.

Gustafsson, B. and Li, S., 2002, 'Income inequality within and across counties in rural China 1988 and 1995', *Journal of Development Economics*, vol. 69, pp. 179–204.

Hao, R. and Wei, Z., 2010, 'Fundamental causes of inland–coastal income inequality in post-reform China', *The Annals of Regional Science*, vol. 45, pp. 181–206.

Herrmann-Pillath, C., Kirchert, D. and Pan, J., 2002, 'Disparities in Chinese economic development: approaches on different levels of aggregation', *Economic Systems*, vol. 26, pp. 31–54.

Hertel, T. and Zhai, F., 2006, 'Labor market distortions, rural–urban inequality and the opening of China's economy', *Economic Modelling*, vol. 23, pp. 76–109.

Holz, C. A., 2006, 'Why China's new GDP data matters', *Far Eastern Economic Review*, vol. 169, pp. 54–7.

Huang, J.-T., Kuo, C.-C. and Kao, A.-P., 2003, 'The inequality of regional economic development in China between 1991 and 2001', *Journal of Chinese Economic and Business Studies*, vol. 1, pp. 273–85.

Jian, T., Sachs, J. D. and Warner, A. M., 1996, 'Trends in regional inequality in China', *China Economic Review*, vol. 7, pp. 1–21.

Jones, D. C., Owen, A. L. and Li, C., 2003, 'Growth and regional inequality in China during the reform era', *China Economic Review*, vol. 14, pp. 186–200.

Kanbur, R. and Zhang, X., 1999, 'Which regional inequality? The evolution of rural–urban and inland–coastal inequality in China from 1983 to 1995', *Journal of Comparative Economics*, vol. 27, pp. 686–701.

Kanbur, R. and Zhang, X., 2005, 'Fifty years of regional inequality in China: a journey through central planning, reform, and openness', *Review of Development Economics*, vol. 9, pp. 87–106.

Khan, A. R. and Riskin, C., 1998, 'Income and inequality in China: composition, distribution and growth of household income, 1988 to 1995', *The China Quarterly*, vol. 154, pp. 221–53.

Khan, A. R., Griffin, K., Riskin, C. and Zhao, R., 1993, 'Sources of income inequality in post-reform China', *China Economic Review*, vol. 4, pp. 19–35.

Lee, J., 2000, 'Changes in the source of China's regional inequality', *China Economic Review*, vol. 11, pp. 232–45.

Li, S. and Xu, Z., 2008, *The trend of regional income disparity in the People's Republic of China*, ADBI Discussion Paper 85, Asian Development Bank Institute, Tokyo.

Lin, T., Zhuang, J., Yarcia, D. and Lin, F., 2008, 'Income inequality in the People's Republic of China and its decomposition: 1990–2004', *Asian Development Review*, vol. 25, pp. 119–36.

Liu, H., 2006, 'Changing regional rural inequality in China 1980–2002', *Area*, vol. 38, pp. 377–89.

Liu, X., 2010, 'Decomposition of China's income inequality, 1995–2006', *Chinese Economy*, vol. 43, pp. 49–72.

Liu, X. and Sicular, T., 2009, 'Nonagricultural employment determinants and income inequality decomposition', *Chinese Economy*, vol. 42, pp. 29–43.

Lu, D., 2002, 'Rural–urban income disparity: impact of growth, allocative efficiency, and local growth welfare', *China Economic Review*, vol. 13, pp. 419–29.

Lu, M. and Chen, Z., 2006, 'Urbanization, urban-biased policies, and urban–rural inequality in China, 1987–2001', *The Chinese Economy*, vol. 39, pp. 42–63.

Lu, M. and Wang, E., 2002, 'Forging ahead and falling behind: changing regional inequalities in post-reform China', *Growth and Change*, vol. 33, pp. 42–71.

National Bureau of Statistics of China (NBS), 1998–2008a, *Provincial Statistical Yearbook*, China Statistics Press, Beijing.

National Bureau of Statistics of China (NBS), 1998–2008b, *Provincial Yearbook*, China Statistics Press, Beijing.

National Bureau of Statistics of China (NBS), 2003, *County Data of 2000 Census*, China Statistics Press, Beijing.

National Bureau of Statistics of China (NBS), 2004–08, *China Statistical Yearbook for Regional Economy*, China Statistics Press, Beijing.

National Bureau of Statistics of China (NBS), 2006, *China Statistical Yearbook*, China Statistics Press, Beijing.

Rawski, T. G., 2001, 'What is happening to China's GDP statistics?', *China Economic Review*, vol. 12, pp. 347–54.

Rozelle, S., 1994, 'Rural industrialization and increasing inequality: emerging patterns in China's reforming economy', *Journal of Comparative Economics*, vol. 19, pp. 362–91.

Sakamoto, H. and Fan, J., 2010, 'Distribution dynamics and convergence among 75 cities and counties in Yangtze River Delta in China: 1990–2005', *Review of Urban and Regional Development Studies*, vol. 22, pp. 39–54.

Shen, L., 2009, 'The urban–rural disparity: a demand side analysis', *Journal of Developing Areas*, vol. 43, pp. 87–107.

Shorrocks, A. F., 1980, 'The class of additively decomposable inequality measures', *Econometrica*, vol. 3, pp. 613–25.

Shorrocks, A. F., 1984, 'Inequality decomposition by population subgroups', *Econometrica*, vol. 52, pp. 1369–85.

Sicular, T., Yue, X., Gustafsson, B. and Li, S., 2007, 'The urban–rural income gap and inequality in China', *Review of Income and Wealth*, vol. 53, pp. 93–126.

Song, S., Chu, G. S.-F. and Cao, R., 2000, 'Intercity regional disparity in China', *China Economic Review*, vol. 11, pp. 246–61.

Sutherland, D. and Yao, S., 2011, 'Income inequality in China over 30 years of reforms', *Cambridge Journal of Regions, Economy and Society*, vol. 4, pp. 91–105.

Theil, H., 1967, *Economics and Information Theory*, North-Holland, Amsterdam.

Theil, H., 1972, *Statistical Decomposition Analysis*, North-Holland, Amsterdam.

Tsui, K.-Y., 1993, 'Decomposition of China's regional inequalities', *Journal of Comparative Economics*, vol. 17, pp. 600–27.

Tsui, K.-Y., 2007, 'Forces shaping China's interprovincial inequality', *Review of Income and Wealth*, vol. 53, pp. 60–92.

Veeck, G. and Pannell, C. W., 1989, 'Rural economic restructuring and farm household income in Jiangsu, People's Republic of China', *Annals of the Association of American Geographers*, vol. 79, pp. 275–92.

Villaverde, J., Maza, A. and Ramasamy, B., 2010, 'Provincial disparities in post-reform China', *China and World Economy*, vol. 18, pp. 73–95.

Wan, G., 2007, 'Understanding regional poverty and inequality trends in China: methodological issues and empirical findings', *Review of Income and Wealth*, vol. 53, pp. 25–34.

Wan, G., 2008, *Poverty reduction in China: is high growth enough?*, Policy Brief, United Nations University, Helsinki.

Wei, Y. D. and Kim, S., 2002, 'Widening inter-county inequality in Jiangsu Province, China, 1950–95', *The Journal of Development Studies*, vol. 38, pp. 142–64.

Whalley, J. and Yue, X., 2009, 'Rural income volatility and inequality in China', *CESifo Economic Studies*, vol. 55, pp. 648–68.

Wu, H. X., 1997, *Measuring China's GDP*, Briefing Paper Series No. 8, East Asia Analytical Unit, Canberra.

Wu, X. and Perloff, J. M., 2005, 'China's income distribution, 1985–2001', *Review of Economics and Statistics*, vol. 87, pp. 763–75.

Wu, Y. and Zhu, J., 2011, 'Corruption, anti-corruption, and inter-county income disparity in China', *The Social Science Journal*.

Yang, D. T., 1999, 'Urban-biased policies and rising income inequality in China', *The American Economic Review*, vol. 89, pp. 306–10.

Yao, S., 1997, 'Decomposition of Gini coefficients by income factors: a new approach and application', *Applied Economics Letters*, vol. 1997, pp. 27–31.

Yao, S., 1999, 'On the decomposition of Gini coefficients by population class and income source: a spreadsheet approach and application', *Applied Economics*, vol. 31, pp. 1249–64.

Yao, S. and Liu, J., 1998, 'Economic reforms and regional segmentation in rural China', *Regional Studies*, vol. 32, pp. 735–46.

Yao, S. and Zhang, Z., 2001, 'On regional inequality and diverging clubs: a case study of contemporary China', *Journal of Comparative Economics*, vol. 29, pp. 466–84.

Yao, S., Zhang, Z. and Feng, G., 2005, 'Rural–urban and regional inequality in output, income and consumption in China under economic reforms', *Journal of Economic Studies*, vol. 32, pp. 4–24.

Ying, L. G., 1999, 'China's changing regional disparities during the reform period', *Economic Geography*, vol. 75, pp. 59–70.

Yu, L., Luo, R. and Zhang, L., 2007, 'Decomposing income inequality and policy implications in rural China', *China & World Economy*, vol. 15, pp. 44–58.

Zhou, H. and Zou, W., 2010, 'Income distribution dynamics of urban residents: the case of China (1995–2004)', *Frontiers of Economics in China*, vol. 5, pp. 114–34.

Zhou, Y., 2009, 'The factors that impact income inequality of rural residents in China: decomposing the Gini coefficient from income components', *Frontiers of Economics in China*, vol. 4, pp. 617–32.

9. Mapping Modes of Rural Labour Migration in China

Sylvie Démurger

Introduction

China's rapid economic development and government policy changes towards higher inter-regional labour mobility have encouraged a massive rural–urban labour force exodus since the mid-1980s. The National Bureau of Statistics of China estimated the total number of rural migrants working in cities in 2011 at about 158 million.[1] Compared with developed countries, where similar population movements occurred in the nineteenth and twentieth centuries, in China, the much larger scale and pace of population movements confront the Chinese authorities with extremely challenging policy issues that call for a better understanding of the motives of and constraints to labour mobility.

Rural-to-urban migration has become a norm for rural households in China. In 2007, about one-half of rural households had at least one member working outside the home village. As part of their diversification strategy, rural households use migration as one of their main sources of income, with remittances accounting for about 21 per cent of total rural income and 43 per cent of migrant-sending households' total income in 2007 (Démurger and Li 2012). Multiple sources of incentives can motivate households and individuals to migrate. The economic literature on the determinants of migration usually highlights two sets of factors: the 'pull' and the 'push' factors (Barrett et al. 2001). Since Todaro (1969), the expected urban–rural income gap is considered the most important pull factor for the migration decision. On the other hand, push factors typically include *ex-ante* risk management, *ex-post* risk coping or response to a surplus of rural labour driven by land constraints and population pressure.

From a theoretical perspective, the seminal works of Oded Stark (for example, Stark 1991) and the 'new economics of labour migration' (NELM) literature have revitalised interest in the motives for and the consequences of migration in developing countries. The general framework proposed by the NELM departs from the neoclassical approach to migration in two ways (Taylor 1999). First, it considers the household, rather than the individual, as the most

---

1 Source: <http://www.stats.gov.cn/tjfx/fxbg/t20120427_402801903.htm> This number refers to the rural labour force that has migrated for work out of their township of residential registration for at least six months in the year of investigation.

appropriate decision-making unit. By integrating migration decisions into a household strategy, individual income maximisation is no longer the only motive for migration and income risk minimisation can be specifically considered. Second, it accounts for the imperfection of markets other than the labour market in explaining migration behaviour.

The existing empirical research on the motivations for labour migration in China has documented that both the rural labour surplus and the rural–urban income gap are major driving forces of migration decisions (Zhao 1999, 2005; Zhu 2002). Using a village survey conducted in 1996, Rozelle et al. (1999) also showed that the poorest households were often not capable of participating in migrant labour markets. In addition, both land size and land-tenure insecurity reduce migration (Mullan et al. 2011). At the individual level, age, gender and marital status have been consistently found to play a significant role in migration decisions (Hare 1999; Zhao 1999), whereas evidence for the role of education is mixed. Finally, drawing on a sample of 824 households surveyed in six provinces in 1999, Zhao (2003) pointed out the role of migrant networks in labour migration, in particular through practical assistance provided in the process of migration. Chen et al. (2010) confirmed the role of social interactions in job-related migration based on data from the 2006 China agricultural census. They found evidence of the effect being mostly driven by co-villagers helping each other to reduce moving costs and find job opportunities at the destination.

Using household-level data from the Rural Household Survey of the National Bureau of Statistics of China for 2007, this chapter updates the existing empirical literature on the determinants of migration by differentiating various modes of migration and by extending the analysis of the role of family and community networks. Following the NELM, we use the household as the unit of analysis. Our focus is on understanding several aspects of the migration decision and migration size by analysing the determinants of migration, migration destination and migration duration. In particular, we aim to map out different types of migration across space (namely, short-distance versus long-distance migration) and time (short-term versus long-term migration). Drawing on various estimations, we argue that the various types of migration are driven by different factors. Moreover, in addition to household characteristics, assets and geographic attributes, we account for the specific impact of family and community networks.

The following research questions are successively examined: 1) what determines the participation of Chinese rural households in migration; 2) what determines their destination choice and the time spent in migration; 3) what determines the size of migration? We explore these issues by estimating bi-variate probit and Poisson models that include a number of relevant characteristics of the family and community situation and background on household-level data for 2007.

The chapter is structured as follows. Section two presents the methodological framework used for the empirical analysis of the determinants of migration. The data are briefly discussed in section three and the econometric results are presented in the next two sections. Section four is devoted to a discussion of the determinants of household migration decision, by destination and duration. Section five extends the analysis to the size of migration, measured through the number of household members sent to migration and section six concludes.

Methodological Framework

We examine the household-level migration decision using multi-variate analysis. We proceed in two steps and successively examine the decision to migrate (including the choice of destination and the duration of migration) and the size of migration.

The framework for estimating the determinants of the migration decision is as follows. The household decision to engage in migration is postulated to reflect its underlying (unobserved) utility (Equation 9.1).

Equation 9.1

$$y_i^* = Z_i \beta + \varepsilon_i$$

In Equation 9.1, ε_i is assumed to be independent of Z_i and to have a standard normal distribution (probit model). The actual decision to send a migrant is given by the following (Equation 9.2).

Equation 9.2

$$y_i = \begin{cases} 1 & if \quad y_i^* > 0 \\ 0 & otherwise \end{cases}$$

In the model above, Z is a vector of household demographics and assets and of village attributes that are supposedly influencing migration decision, destination and duration. Drawing on the theoretical literature on the determinants of the migration decision, it includes the following variables.

First, household demographics and assets are captured by the household size, the share of male adults, the number of elderly dependants, the number of children below the age of sixteen, the age and education level of the household head[2] and the household land size per capita. In the vein of the push and pull factors detailed above, most household-level variables refer to the coping capacity of households facing risks or to their risk exposure. Typically, household size and composition together with the household's land assets account for potential diminishing labour returns in the presence of land constraints.

Beyond specific household characteristics, migration networks can also be important drivers of the migration decision, as they can serve as cost-reducing devices. A body of theoretical and empirical literature has highlighted the role of information networks in lowering the cost of migration through information on employment opportunities at the destination, better access to employment at the destination and as a source of help to settle down at the destination (Görlich and Trebesch 2008; Haug 2008; Taylor 1986; Winters et al. 2001). In their study of the role of migrant networks in Mexico, Winters et al. (2001) further distinguish the differentiated role of family and community networks, the former being identified as 'strong ties' networks while the latter are defined as 'weak ties' networks. They find that both family and community networks lower the cost of migration and that they are substitutes—once migration is well established in a community, family networks become less important. Moreover, once migration networks are established, they are also more important than household characteristics in explaining migration patterns. To investigate the role of migration networks, we follow Winters et al. (2001) and define two different indicators: 1) a community-level network—the village population share of migrants in 2005; and 2) a family-level network—whether the household has more than one member with a migration experience. This second variable includes both ongoing migrants and returning migrants, and thus measures the accumulated experience of migration at the household level.

Finally, we account for location attributes by including dummies for villages located in a central or a western province. We also employ village-level information on access to an asphalt road to account for proximity to market.

Besides migration decision, we also explore the determinants of destination and duration probability. For that, we employ a recursive model to account for unobservable characteristics such as motivation or risk aversion that might simultaneously determine the migration decision and the destination/duration decision. If unobservable heterogeneity has a direct influence on both decisions (to migrate as well as how far or how long to migrate) then the migration

---

2   As argued by Mullan et al. (2011), education can be used as a proxy for off-farm wages that should ideally be introduced as determinants of the migration decision, but are not available.

destination/duration variable will be correlated with the error term ε_i, which will make it effectively endogenous in the selected sample. As suggested by Greene (2008), this unobservable heterogeneity can be captured by using a recursive bi-variate probit model, which estimates the migration duration/destination choice together with migration decision. The system of equations is identified by nonlinearities even if the vectors of observables overlap completely.

Finally, to examine the determinants of the level of migration, we use a Poisson model of the number of migrants in a household, classified by destination and duration. A model similar to the above migration decision model is estimated with key independent variables including household demographics and assets, migration networks and community characteristics.

Data and Stylised Facts

We use data from the Rural Household Survey carried out by the National Bureau of Statistics (NBS) under the Rural–Urban Migration in China (RUMiC) project[3] in 2008. The survey covers 8000 rural households in nine provinces: Hebei, Jiangsu, Zhejiang, Anhui, Henan, Hubei, Guangdong, Chongqing and Sichuan.

We identify migrants as household members who work outside their home village and have been living away for at least six months. This rather broad definition includes individuals who work off the farm in the neighbourhood of their home village (for example, county seat), which will allow us to differentiate migrants according to their distance from their home village. With this definition, 48 per cent of the 8000 surveyed households had at least one migrant member in 2007 and migrant-sending households had on average 1.7 migrant members. The survey provides additional information on migration destination and duration that is also useful here.

Concerning destination, the records include the location of employment for working household members, which allows us to categorise migrants through the distance of their working destination from their home village as follows: working in the local county seat/working in a city or another county within the province/working in a city or a county outside the province. In 2007, 19 per cent of the sending households had at least one migrant member working in the local county seat, 30 per cent had at least one migrant member working outside the county within the province and 44 per cent had at least one migrant member working outside the province. As far as the level of migration

---

3 For details about the whole project and the survey design and implementation, see Meng et al. (2010). See also <http://cbe.anu.edu.au/schools/eco/rumici/> for a map of the surveyed provinces and for survey questionnaires.

is concerned, Table 9.1 shows that migrant-sending households have on average 0.70 members working in the local county seat, 0.46 members working within the province and 0.26 members working in another province. By comparison with the shares of sending households by destination, these figures indicate that the number of migrants is inversely proportional to the share of sending households by distance. Hence, while sending households actively participate in 'long-distance' migration (with a share of 44 per cent), they send few members far away. In contrast, sending households marginally contribute to 'short-distance' migration (with a share of 19 per cent), but households involved in 'local' migration send more members locally.

Concerning duration, we separate 'short-run' migrants, whose maximum migration duration in 2007 was less than seven years, and 'long-run migrants' otherwise.[4] The overwhelming proportion of migrant-sending households (60 per cent) have at least one migrant member working outside the village for less than seven years, but summary statistics also indicate that 44 per cent have at least one migrant member outside the village for more than seven years. Numbers indicating the size of migration by duration confirm the higher incidence of short-run migration: migrant-sending households send on average 0.89 members for less than seven years and 0.61 members for seven years or more.

To sum up, the above statistics highlight some key stylised facts about migration. They confirm the high incidence of rural migration in China as well as its temporary, or at least short-run, nature. Interestingly, they also point to migration patterns involving both long-distance and short-distance movements.

---

4   One should note that the design of the question does not allow us to distinguish different individual sojourns that could have been interrupted by a temporary return. As a consequence, the duration calculated here is a maximum for each individual.

Table 9.1 Summary Statistics of Sending and Non-Sending Households

	Total	Non-sending households	Sending households	Mean test
Percentage of total number of households	100	51.9	48.1	
Number of migrants per household	0.81	0	1.68	
Percentage of migrant-sending households *with at least* one migrant member:				
— working in the local county seat			18.9	
— working within the province			29.6	
— working outside the province			43.8	
— for less than seven years			60.4	
— for seven years or more			44.7	
Number of migrants per household:				
— working in the local county seat	0.34	0	0.70	
— working within the province	0.22	0	0.46	
— working outside the province	0.13	0	0.26	
— for less than seven years	0.43	0	0.89	
— for seven years or more	0.30	0	0.61	
Household characteristics and assets				
Household size	3.974	3.553	4.428	***
Percentage of adult males	0.514	0.507	0.521	***
Number of elderly dependants	0.176	0.198	0.154	***
Number of children below 16 years	0.666	0.639	0.695	***
Age of household head	50.33	50.32	50.33	NS
Years of education of household head	7.190	7.184	7.197	NS
Per capita household land	1.354	1.456	1.244	***
Networks				
Village share of migrants in 2005	0.167	0.142	0.194	***
Family migration network	0.303	0.0855	0.537	***
Locational characteristics				
Asphalt road in the village	0.751	0.761	0.740	**
Central province	0.362	0.331	0.397	***
Western province	0.200	0.171	0.231	***
Sample size	8000	4152	3848	

NS = not significant

˙ significant at 10 per cent

˙˙ significant at 5 per cent

˙˙˙ significant at 1 per cent

Notes: Family network is a dummy variable for households with more than one member with a migration experience. Some averages/percentages are calculated over a smaller number of observations because of missing values. We only report the total number of observations for reference. The mean test column indicates the significance level of mean differences between migrant-sending households and non–migrant-sending households.

Source: RUMiC Rural Household Survey 2007.

Table 9.1 also contains baseline characteristics of migrant sending and non-sending households for the key variables used in the empirical analysis. There is a clear gap in household characteristics between the two groups, as indicated by mean tests significant for almost all variables. Sending households are significantly larger and have a higher share of adult males: the average migrant-sending household size is 4.4 persons (against 3.5 for non-sending households), with 52 per cent of adult males. In terms of age composition, they have fewer elderly members (0.15 on average, against 0.2 for non-sending households), but more children below the age of sixteen (0.7 on average, against 0.64 for non-sending households). With regard to household assets, an interesting feature is that the average land endowment per person is significantly lower for sending households, who have an average of 1.24 *mu* (or 0.08 hectares) per capita, compared with 1.46 *mu* (or 0.10 ha) per capita for non-sending households. This significant difference could reflect both land shortages and labour surplus in migrant-sending households—a dimension that will be further explored in section four. In contrast, summary statistics on household human capital show no significant difference between sending and non-sending households: the average age of the household head is slightly above fifty years and the education level of the household head is about 7.2 years of schooling. That is two years below the nine-year compulsory education system.

As for migration networks, the data show that 53.7 per cent of migrant-sending households have a family migration experience, whereas the share is only 8.6 per cent for non-sending households. At the village level, sending households also have a significantly larger village network than non-sending households. Finally, geographic characteristics also exhibit significant differences between migrant sending and non-sending households. Not surprisingly, the incidence of migrant-sending households is significantly higher in both central and western provinces, which are emigration provinces compared with coastal provinces. Interestingly, access to an asphalt road is significantly higher for non-sending households than for sending households.

The Migration Decision

Table 9.2 presents marginal effects (at mean values) from the estimation of a simple probit model for whether households have any migrant member (column one) and of recursive bi-variate probit models for the choice of destination and duration (columns two to six) that allow for selection on unobservable characteristics.[5]

---

5 Because of space constraints, columns two to six report only the destination/duration equation of the recursive bi-variate probit model. The full model includes the migration decision equation. Since this equation is estimated separately as a first step (column one) and since the estimates are stable across specifications, we do not report the migration decision estimate for the recursive bi-variate probit models.

Table 9.2 Probit and Recursive Bi-Variate Probit Estimates of Migration Decision

	Migration	Destination			Duration	
		Another province	City	Local	Less than 7 years	7 years and above
Household characteristics and assets						
Household size	0.133*** (0.000)	0.0388*** (0.00491)	0.0374*** (0.00440)	0.0129*** (0.00402)	0.0994*** (0.00648)	0.0137 (.)
Percentage of adult males	0.246*** (0.000)	0.0871*** (0.0280)	0.106*** (0.0263)	0.00546 (0.0211)	0.115*** (0.0408)	0.140*** (0.0325)
Number of elderly dependants	-0.115*** (0.000)	-0.0388*** (0.00981)	-0.0403*** (0.00828)	-0.0165** (0.00722)	-0.113*** (0.0135)	-0.00234 (0.00957)
Number of children below 16	-0.115*** (0.000)	-0.0439*** (0.00695)	-0.0366*** (0.00610)	-0.0264*** (0.00557)	-0.170** (0.00986)	0.0460 (.)
Age of household head	-0.00253*** (0.001)	-0.00106** (0.000512)	-0.000001 (0.000467)	-0.000931*** (0.000390)	-0.00461** (0.000644)	0.00143 (.)
Years of education of household head	0.00472* (0.081)	-0.00467*** (0.00166)	0.00379** (0.00157)	0.00395*** (0.00120)	0.00260 (0.00219)	0.000354 (0.00195)
Per capita household land	-0.0166*** (0.009)	-0.00533 (0.00411)	0.0000313 (0.00290)	-0.0201*** (0.00518)	0.00411 (0.00385)	-0.0225*** (0.00548)
Networks						
Village share of migrants in 2005	0.720*** (0.000)	0.359*** (0.0666)	0.194*** (0.0519)	-0.0683 (0.0457)	0.258*** (0.0664)	0.508*** (0.0663)
Family migration network	0.433*** (0.000)	0.220*** (0.0151)	0.164*** (0.0141)	0.0392*** (0.0106)	0.346*** (0.0151)	0.307*** (0.0149)
Locational characteristics						
Asphalt road in the village	0.0150 (0.541)	-0.0329** (0.0153)	0.0247*** (0.0124)	0.0400*** (0.0114)	0.00132 (0.0175)	0.00781 (0.0159)
Central province	0.0676*** (0.003)	0.311*** (0.0214)	-0.129*** (0.0111)	-0.0392*** (0.0104)	0.101*** (0.0172)	-0.00479 (0.0161)
Western province	0.130*** (0.000)	0.237*** (0.0307)	-0.0423*** (0.0127)	0.00986 (0.0162)	0.0646*** (0.0231)	0.0706*** (0.0222)
Sample size	7900	7900	7900	7900	7900	7900
Log pseudolikelihood	-4109.5	-6211.7	-6180.0	-5801.2	-6376.3	-6449.5

* significant at 10 per cent
** significant at 5 per cent
*** significant at 1 per cent

Notes: See Table 11.1. A probit model is estimated for migration decision (column 1) and recursive bi-variate probit models are estimated for migration destination and migration duration (columns 2–6). Marginal effects are reported in the table. They measure the change in the probability of sending migrant (total and by destination and duration) from a unit change in the explanatory variable. Robust standard errors are adjusted for clustering by villages (790 villages).

Source: Author's own estimation based on RUMiC Rural Household Survey 2007.

On the migration decision model (column one), we observe that the likelihood of sending a migrant increases with household size and male labour force, whereas it decreases with the number of elderly dependants and the number of children below the age of sixteen. This is consistent with the empirical literature showing that migration is associated with larger households and larger male labour force—both factors that reduce the opportunity cost for the family to send a migrant to cities.[6] In contrast, a higher dependency ratio of the household (through both elderly and children) significantly reduces family labour availability for migration. Moreover, we find that older households have a lower probability of participating in migration: older household heads might be more reluctant to send family members to cities most probably because of a higher risk aversion with old age. Among other reasons, the lack of access to healthcare services outside the home province could also influence the reluctance of older household heads. As a measure of the demand for farm labour, the per capita size of land is, unsurprisingly, found to have a negative and significant impact on the probability of a household to send migrants. In the specific case of China, it could also reflect the need for households to keep farming their land if they want to protect their land-use rights[7] (Mullan et al. 2011). Once the labour force size is controlled, only families with smaller landholdings can afford to send household members to migrate.

The importance of both family and village network effects in the household migration decision is also highlighted in column one. Having more than one member with migration experience strongly increases the household's probability of sending a migrant—the probability is increased by 43.3 per cent compared with households with no migration experience. Likewise, a 1 per cent increase in the village share of migrants increases the household's migration probability by 72 per cent. Hence, both family and community networks seem to facilitate migration and their marginal effect is important. In contrast, after controlling for location in emigration provinces, the ease of access to markets, as proxied by the asphalt-road dummy, is not found to significantly influence migration decisions. For households living in villages with easier access to the market, migration might not be the most attractive option since there could be other, local opportunities to diversify.

Columns two to four show estimates for a specific destination: another province, any city in the same province or the local county seat. A comparison of the three estimations reveals interesting differences as well as similarities. Household size has a significant and positive effect on all migration destinations.

---

6   See, for example, Dercon and Krishnan (1996) on Ethiopia and Tanzania; Winters et al. (2001) on Mexico; or Zhao (2003) on China.

7   Mullan et al. (2011) show that migration is associated with an increased risk of land expropriation because land-tenure arrangements in rural China involve administrative redistribution of some household lands to maintain egalitarian landholdings.

Interestingly, the marginal effect is three times larger for long-distance migration compared with local migration. Likewise, the adult gender composition of the household significantly (and positively) influences the probability to send a migrant to a city in another county or another province, whereas the estimated impact is non-significant on local labour mobility. In contrast, the presence of old and young dependants significantly lowers the probability of sending migrants to any destination, and, again, the marginal impact seems stronger for long-distance migration (as opposed to the local county seat). Hence, family demographics are important in shaping general migration as well as migration destination, with seemingly larger impacts for long-distance migration. As long-distance migration means that the migrant cannot easily return if needed, these results are fully consistent and stress the key importance of household demographics in shaping long-distance migration.

Interestingly, household human capital and assets play a differentiated role depending on the destination. First, available per capita land lowers the probability of short-distance migration, but we do not find any significant impact on long-distance migration decisions. Second, a higher educational level of the household head correlates positively with medium or short-distance migration, but correlates negatively with long-distance migration. This finding conforms to the ambiguous role of education in off-farm labour force participation in rural China found in the literature. In particular, there is evidence that better-educated individuals tend to choose local off-farm work over migration (Zhao 2003).

Migration networks also play a prominent and differential role across long-distance and short-distance migration. Both community and family networks are at play in long-distance migration, whereas only the family network is found to significantly influence short-distance migration. This result is consistent with the intuition that networks are a means to reduce migration costs. As long-distance migration usually involves higher costs and higher risks, migration networks at both the village and the family levels are unsurprisingly important drivers for such migration decisions.

Finally, we find interesting differences in the role played by locational characteristics of the sending community. Better access to markets lowers the probability of sending migrants to another province, while it increases the probability of sending migrants to the local county seat. In remote places, the only available means to diversify income-generating activities is to send migrants to cities, possibly far away, whereas in better-connected villages, sending migrants a short distance can be sufficient. Putting that another way, in better-connected villages, there are more local opportunities for off-farm jobs. This is confirmed by the significantly higher incidence of long-distance migrants in central and western provinces and a significantly lower incidence of medium and short-distance migrants in central provinces (and to a lesser extent in western provinces).

The last two columns of Table 9.2 show recursive bi-variate probit estimation results by migration duration (below or above seven years). Here again, the determinants of the duration of migration differ substantially between short-term and long-term migration. As far as household characteristics and assets are concerned, we still find a positive and significant impact of household size and gender composition in facilitating migration decisions, for both short-term and long-term migration. Interestingly, the marginal effect of the household size is larger for short-term migration, whereas the marginal effect of the share of male adults is slightly larger for long-term migration. This could illustrate the fact that the male labour force is an important input for agricultural work. In this context, having enough male members to farm the land on a stable basis might be a prerequisite for sending migrants to cities for more than seven years. Long-term migration decisions also depend more strongly on household landholdings: larger land size significantly reduces the probability of a household sending a migrant member for seven years or more, whereas it does not significantly influence the decision to send a migrant for a short period. Again, this finding can be interpreted in terms of land-tenure insecurity. As households might be concerned about potential administrative land reallocation, their incentive to send migrants for a long time could be lowered by the fear of losing their land.

Turning to the effect of migration networks, we find that both family migration experience and village migrant networks strongly increase the probability of a household sending a migrant for either a short or a long period. As an example, the probability of sending a migrant for less than seven years is increased by 30 per cent compared with households with no migration experience. Interestingly, the marginal effect of community networks is twice as strong for long-term migration.

The Level of Migration

To complement the above analysis on migration decisions, Table 9.3 presents the determinants of the number of migrating household members—again by destination and duration. Generally speaking, the factors that affect the number of migrating household members are similar to those that affect the household decision to send a migrant. Household characteristics and assets are found to be important drivers of the size of migration in a similar way as for the decision to migrate, and all our results regarding destination and duration choices hold with the number of migrant members.

Table 9.3 Poisson Estimates of the Number of Migrant Members

	Total	Destination			Duration	
		Another province	City	Local	Less than 7 years	7 years and above
Household characteristics and assets						
Household size	0.173*** (0.00679)	0.0436*** (0.00345)	0.0406*** (0.00337)	0.0232*** (0.00507)	0.0885*** (0.00469)	0.0256*** (0.00394)
Percentage of adult males	0.191*** (0.0417)	0.0686*** (0.0211)	0.0621*** (0.0239)	-0.0231 (0.0306)	0.0488 (0.0302)	0.110*** (0.0289)
Number of elderly dependants	-0.134*** (0.0157)	-0.0353*** (0.00827)	-0.0314*** (0.00759)	-0.0206* (0.0107)	-0.105*** (0.0123)	0.000653 (0.00784)
Number of children below 16	-0.161*** (0.00934)	-0.0386*** (0.00481)	-0.0427*** (0.00472)	-0.0315*** (0.00781)	-0.147*** (0.00799)	0.0210*** (0.00722)
Age of household head	-0.00218*** (0.000755)	-0.000626* (0.000368)	0.000448 (0.000354)	-0.000953* (0.000514)	-0.00338*** (0.000525)	0.00173*** (0.000456)
Years of education of household head	0.00182 (0.00226)	-0.00385*** (0.00112)	0.00278** (0.00123)	0.00423*** (0.00150)	0.00194 (0.00173)	-0.000721 (0.00149)
Per capita household land	-0.0261*** (0.00775)	-0.00337 (0.00369)	-0.00132 (0.00326)	-0.0244*** (0.00734)	0.00463 (0.00304)	-0.0216*** (0.00522)
Networks						
Village share of migrants in 2005	0.517*** (0.0743)	0.202*** (0.0465)	0.133*** (0.0377)	-0.0647 (0.0593)	0.127*** (0.0454)	0.335*** (0.0453)
Family migration network	0.911*** (0.0293)	0.309*** (0.0235)	0.257*** (0.0203)	0.0626*** (0.0158)	0.557*** (0.0236)	0.414*** (0.0212)
Locational characteristics						
Asphalt road in the village	0.0147 (0.0198)	-0.0263* (0.0108)	0.0201 (0.0124)	0.0501*** (0.0153)	-0.00463 (0.0144)	0.00406 (0.0119)
Central province	0.0611*** (0.0200)	0.366*** (0.0300)	-0.135*** (0.0104)	-0.0623*** (0.0133)	0.0695*** (0.0136)	0.00216 (0.0127)
Western province	0.111*** (0.0288)	0.319*** (0.0458)	-0.0455*** (0.00995)	0.0102 (0.0207)	0.0428** (0.0203)	0.0612*** (0.0173)
Sample size	7900	7900	7900	7900	7900	7900
Log pseudolikelihood	-7490.9	-4432.9	-3665.3	-3049.3	-5337.9	-4422.1

* significant at 10 per cent

** significant at 5 per cent

*** significant at 1 per cent

Notes: See Table 9.1. Marginal effects are reported. Robust standard errors are adjusted for clustering by villages (790 villages).

Source: Author's own estimation based on RUMiC Rural Household Survey 2007.

Besides expected similarities, one result deserves a specific comment. Indeed, we find an ambiguous effect of children on the size of migration: the number of children in the household is negatively correlated with the number of short-term migrants, but it is positively (and significantly) correlated with the number of long-term migrants in the household. Though the marginal effect is rather small, the positive correlation with long-term migration probably reflects the trade-off that Chinese rural households face. The institutional constraints imposed on rural households make the migration of a whole family very difficult, if not impossible. Indeed, land-tenure arrangements induce rural households to keep some members in the countryside to protect their land-use rights (Mullan et al. 2011), and the household registration system (*hukou*) induces them to leave their children behind so that they can receive free primary and secondary education (Démurger and Xu 2011). Confronted with these strong institutional constraints, rural households with children might have higher incentives to send more family members to migrate for a longer period in order to cover the cost of the future education of their children. On the other hand, the presence of more children could lower the motivation to send household members in the short run because of the potentially high psychological costs of separation.

Overall, the impact of migration networks is confirmed for the level of migration. The migration history of a household not only influences its propensity to send a migrant, it also increases the number of members sent to migrate. Likewise, if a village is sending a large share of migrants, families in this village are more likely to send more migrants than families living in villages with a smaller migration network. As for the migration decision, migration networks are found to be more important for long-distance rather than short-distance migration—the number of migrants sent to cities or to another province is positively related to both the family and the community networks. In contrast, it is the family rather than the community network that counts for determining the number of members sent to migrate locally, and the family network's marginal effect is fairly small compared with the estimates for long-distance migration.

Finally, locational characteristics are found to influence the number of household members that migrate in a way similar to their impact on the likelihood to participate in migration. Rural households living in central or western provinces are more likely to send more migrants than households living in coastal provinces. As for destination and duration, they are also more likely to send more members farther from their home village, but for a shorter period compared with households in coastal provinces.

Conclusion

This chapter aimed to unravel the main factors driving rural households in their decision to send family members to migrate. Migration was fairly widespread among households in rural China in 2007: about half of the sample households had at least one member working outside the village and, for the sending households, the average number of migrant members was close to 1.7. We examined both the decision and the level of migration and highlighted a number of differences across destination choices as well as duration choices. Our key results can be summarised according to two main lines. First, differentiating migration decisions by distance and by duration emphasises different modes of rural labour migration in China. Interestingly, household demographics and composition are found to be particularly constraining for long-distance as well as long-term migration. On the other hand, short-distance migration is negatively correlated to per capita household land—an additional mu of land per capita reducing the probability of sending a member to the local county seat by 2 percentage points.[8] Household human capital, proxied by the number of years of education of the household head, reveals contrasting effects on migration that corroborate Zhao's (1999) findings for the mid-1990s that educated farmers prefer local non-farm work to migration. In our household-level estimates, education reduces long-distance migration whereas it increases short or medium-distance migration. Second, regarding migration networks, our results indicate that family and community networks do not play the same roles in facilitating migration, and in this sense they can be thought of as complementary means of reducing costs for migrant candidates. While family migration networks uniformly influence migration, migration duration, migration destination and migration size, community networks appear to be less important for short-distance migration, which is relatively low cost and low risk, but very important for long-distance migration, which carries high levels of risk.

From a regional development perspective, our findings on the various modes of labour migration have a number of interesting implications. In her study of rural migrants at the end of the 1990s, Zhao (2003:510) concluded that 'with migrant networks, migration becomes a self-sustaining and self-enforcing process'. What our findings show is that this process has indeed been reinforcing over time and that it also shapes the extent of migration. With migrant networks, long-distance migration is facilitated, which contributes to the inter-provincial redistribution of the population. Moreover, in inter-provincial flows, the effect of migrant networks goes beyond the family circle and community networks are found to play an active role. In addition to the self-enforcing process of migration through networks, our finding that better access to local markets

---

8   Since the observed probability of short-distance migration is 18.9 per cent (Table 9.1), this effect is rather large.

reduces migration also highlights another potentially important spatial issue. China is now experiencing a rapid rural labour exodus—a phenomenon that occurred in developed countries in the nineteenth and twentieth centuries—which could lead to the desertion of remote rural areas. Our finding that people living in remote areas are more likely to migrate further away from their home village than those living close to markets stresses the potential for such desertion. Hence, another key challenge for the Central Government in coming years might be to find an efficient means of keeping remote areas alive and preventing a further agglomeration of people in a limited number of urban metropolises.

References

Barrett, C., Reardon, T. and Webb, P., 2001, 'Nonfarm income diversification and household livelihood strategies in rural Africa: concepts, issues, and policy implications', *Food Policy*, vol. 26, no. 4, pp. 315–31.

Chen, Y., Jin, G. Z. and Yue, Y., 2010, *Peer migration in China*, NBER Working Paper No. 15671, National Bureau of Economic Research, Cambridge, Mass.

Démurger, S. and Li, S., 2012, *Migration, remittances and rural employment patterns: evidence from China*, GATE Working Paper, Lyon University, St Etienne.

Démurger, S. and Xu, H., 2011, *Left-behind children and return decisions of rural migrants in China*, GATE Working Paper No. 1122, Lyon University, St Etienne.

Dercon, S. and Krishnan, P., 1996, 'Income portfolios in rural Ethiopia and Tanzania: choices and constraints', *Journal of Development Studies*, vol. 32, no. 6, pp. 850–75.

Görlich, D. and Trebesch, C., 2008, 'Seasonal migration and networks—evidence on Moldova's labour exodus', *Review of World Economics*, vol. 144, no. 1, pp. 107–33.

Greene, W. H., 2008, *Econometric Analysis*, [Sixth edition], Prentice Hall, Upper Saddle River, NJ.

Hare, D., 1999, '"Push" versus "pull" factors in migration outflows and returns: determinants of migration status and spell duration among China's rural population', *Journal of Development Studies*, vol. 35, no. 3, pp. 45–72.

Haug, S., 2008, 'Migration networks and migration decision-making', *Journal of Ethnic and Migration Studies*, vol. 34, no. 4, pp. 585–605.

Meng, X., Manning, C., Li, S. and Effendi, T., 2010, *The Great Migration: Rural–urban migration in China and Indonesia*, Edward Elgar, Cheltenham, UK.

Mullan, K., Grosjean, P. and Kontoleon, A., 2011, 'Land tenure arrangements and rural–urban migration in China', *World Development*, vol. 39, no. 1, pp. 123–33.

Rozelle, S., Guo, L., Shen, M., Hughart, A. and Giles, J., 1999, 'Leaving China's farms: survey results of new paths and remaining hurdles to rural migration', *The China Quarterly*, vol. 158, pp. 367–93.

Stark, O., 1991, *The Migration of Labour*, Blackwell, Cambridge, UK.

Taylor, J. E., 1986, 'Differential migration, networks information and risk', in O. Stark (ed.), *Migration, Human Capital and Development*, JAI Press, Greenwich, Conn.

Taylor, J. E., 1999, 'The new economics of labour migration and the role of remittances in the migration process', *International Migration*, vol. 37, no. 1, pp. 63–88.

Todaro, M., 1969, 'A model of labor migration and urban unemployment in less developed countries', *American Economic Review*, vol. 59, no. 1, pp. 138–48.

Winters, P., de Janvry, A. and Sadoulet, E., 2001, 'Family and community networks in Mexico–US migration', *Journal of Human Resources*, vol. 36, no. 1, pp. 159–84.

Zhao, Y., 1999, 'Labor migration and earnings differences: the case of rural China', *Economic Development and Cultural Change*, vol. 47, no. 4, pp. 767–82.

Zhao, Y., 2003, 'The role of migrant networks in labor migration: the case of China', *Contemporary Economic Policy*, vol. 21, no. 4, pp. 500–11.

Zhao, Z., 2005, 'Migration, labor market flexibility, and wage determination in China: a review', *The Developing Economies*, vol. 43, no. 2, pp. 285–312.

Zhu, N., 2002, 'The impacts of income gaps on migration decisions in China', *China Economic Review*, vol. 13, pp. 213–30.

10. Climbing the Intergenerational Ladder of Education in Urban, Migrant and Rural China

Jane Golley and Sherry Tao Kong

Introduction

During the six decades of the People's Republic, China has made great achievements in raising national average standards of educational quality and attainment. These achievements have, however, been distributed unevenly across the country. According to one recent study, by the late 2000s, while more than 90 per cent of primary school students in rural China went on to junior high, less than 20 per cent made it through to high school, with a mere 1.3 per cent entering tertiary-level education. As a result, children born in Beijing, Shanghai or Tianjin were 35 times more likely to attend college than children born in rural areas.[1] While labour market reforms have raised the returns to education across China,[2] the incompleteness of these reforms—in particular, ongoing constraints to permanent rural-to-urban migration[3] and segmentation in urban labour markets[4]—means that the incentives for pursuing higher educational outcomes in pursuit of higher wage returns are uneven across urban, rural and migrant populations. The combination of uneven development in education and urban-biased labour market reforms has undoubtedly contributed to the gap between urban and rural incomes in China, which is not only large but rising over time (Sicular et al. 2005).

For a country that claims to be intent on reducing rural–urban income inequality, as a core element of its quest for a more harmonious and balanced society, understanding the link between each individual's educational opportunities, achievements and returns is critical. This link in turn hinges on intergenerational dynamics, in which the educational achievements and earning

---

1 See *Barriers for the rural poor on the road to college: new evidence from REAP*, REAP Brief No. 107, Stanford University, Stanford, Calif., <http://iis-db.stanford.edu/pubs/22773/REAP_brief_107_EN_web.pdf>
2 See De Brauw and Giles (2006); Liu et al. (2010); Yang (2005); Zhang et al. (2002, 2004, 2005).
3 See Cai and Wang (2010); Golley and Meng (2011); Knight et al. (2010); Kong et al. (2010); Lee and Meng (2009); Zhao (1999).
4 See Appleton et al. (2004); Chen et al. (2007); Démurger et al. (2007, 2009); Meng and Zhang (2001).

capacities of one generation—themselves the result of a complex interaction of ability and opportunity—impact on those of the next generation in complex ways.

Most of the literature relating to intergenerational patterns of educational attainment in China has been confined to one or other of the rural or urban populations, and much of it has focused on the impact of the Cultural Revolution (1966–76) on different members of society at the time, or on subsequent generations.[5] For urban China, there is some debate over whether the policies of the Cultural Revolution even succeeded in making educational attainment more egalitarian with respect to social origins at the time, let alone in the future, with Meng and Gregory (2002) reaching the somewhat unexpected conclusion that the largest negative impacts of the Cultural Revolution were in fact on children with parents of lower educational achievement and lower occupational status. There is, however, little dispute over the claim that urban educational inequality has increased in China since 1978, favouring 'the most advantaged groups in the population: the children of high-rank cadres and professionals, residents of large cities, and men more than women' (Zhou et al. 1998:217).

Sato and Li's (2008) analysis of the impact of family origin on educational attainment in rural China essentially echoes those of Meng and Gregory (2002) and Zhou et al. (1998), by showing that class-based discrimination during the Cultural Revolution did not last long enough to have a permanent effect on educational attainment across generations; instead, those higher up the social strata have continued to 'out-educate' those below them. A recent string of papers indicates that shortcomings in China's rural education system from early childhood onwards seriously impinge on the educational opportunities for rural and migrant children, which in turn impacts on their ultimate levels of educational attainment (Luo et al. 2011; Teng 2005; Wang et al. 2010). These papers emphasise the low incomes of poor rural households relative to rising educational costs and the poor quality of rural education as the major impediments to upward mobility of the poorest members of Chinese society.

These findings combine to depict a possible future of rising intra-rural, rural–urban and intra-urban inequalities in educational opportunities and outcomes, in which a positive and possibly strengthening relationship between the educational achievements of parents and their children will be a prominent feature.

---

5   During the Cultural Revolution, the Chinese Government implemented a range of policies to promote the educational opportunities and outcomes of children from peasant and worker families at the expense of those from higher status backgrounds. Notable measures included the closure of most schools in urban China for six years beginning in 1966, with senior high schools reopening in 1972; the 'sending down' of urban youths to live and work in rural villages; and various forms of discrimination against landlords and rich peasants in rural areas, and intelligentsia and cadre families in urban areas. For details of these policies, see Deng and Treiman (1997); and Meng and Gregory (2002).

This chapter investigates intergenerational patterns of educational attainment over time and space in China. Drawing on the Rural–Urban Migration in China and Indonesia (RUMiCI) Survey for 2008, which provides unique access to data on the educational attainments of up to three generations of people within the same household across China's rural, urban and migrant populations, we find that intergenerational 'mobility', as reflected by low regression and correlation coefficients between a child's and parents' education levels, is higher in rural and migrant populations than in urban ones. A closer look at the sources of this correlation reveals, however, that the low values observed in rural and migrant China stem from the fact that the majority of these children complete only junior high, with some children in the youngest cohorts actually moving down the educational ladder relative to their parents. In contrast, for urban children, the only way is up. This combination of results has clear and undesirable implications for China's rural–urban divide.

Should College-Educated Parents Have College-Educated Children?

There are many reasons to expect a positive relationship between the education levels of parents and those of their children, as measured by the regression coefficient in a bi-variate regression of a child's years of schooling on parents' years of schooling, or by the simple correlation coefficient between these two variables.[6] The strength of this correlation—often referred to as 'persistence'— depends not only on the degree of inheritability, but will also be greater if, for example, more educated parents invest more time (in a productive way) in supporting their children's educational achievements (Black and Devereux 2010). Credit constraints and the higher average income of parents with higher levels of education provide two other reasons for the positive relationship between parent and child education, although these income advantages could be offset by government investment in education that is progressive to parental income (Solon 2004).

The fundamental question of interest is whether the persistence in educational achievements across generations reflects genuine differences in genetic ability, or if they are instead the result of uneven *opportunities* for the pursuit of higher educational outcomes, or uneven *returns* to pursuing those higher outcomes. This question is critical as it determines the extent to which educational policies might be able to reduce part of the intergenerational transmission of inequality. Measures of intergenerational persistence—or its converse, mobility—provide

---

6   See the seminal work of Becker and Tomes (1979, 1986); and Solon (1999, 2004); and also Black and
    Devereux (2010) for an excellent survey.

the first critical step in seeking to establish any kind of causal effect. It is this measurement, and how it has differed across China's rural, migrant and urban populations during the People's Republic of China (PRC) era, that is the focus of this chapter.

The positive relationship between the socioeconomic status of parents and their children is hardly unique to China, but has instead been observed almost universally across societies, and using a variety of measures of social status, of which education is just one. Hertz et al. (2007) provide estimates of 50-year trends in the intergenerational persistence of educational attainment for 42 nations, including (rural) China. Dividing a cross-sectional survey for each country into 10 age cohorts of people aged twenty to sixty-nine, they show that the regression coefficient of a child's education on parents' education has fallen substantially over time, while there is no such trend for the correlation coefficient, which fell in about as many countries as it rose. Checchi et al. (2008) show a reduction in the correlation coefficient between the levels of schooling of fathers and children over time in Italy. Despite this overall decline, however, their decomposition of the correlation coefficient (explained further below) reveals a rise in persistence at the upper end of the education tail, evidenced by the large and non-decreasing proportion of the correlation that is explained by college-educated children and fathers with either college or high school degrees.

Following Hertz et al. (2007), we begin with a simple bi-variate regression (Equation 10.1).

Equation 10.1

$$y_i^j = \alpha + \beta y_i^k + \varepsilon_i$$

In Equation 10.1, y is the number of years of schooling; $j = c, s, d$ for child, son or daughter; $k = p, f, m$ for parent, father or mother; and subscript $_i$ refers to the birth cohort of the child. The regression coefficient β is our first measure of the degree of intergenerational transmission of educational attainment, with low values suggesting low persistence, or high mobility. Another measure of interest is the intergenerational correlation coefficient, ρ, which is bounded between −1 and 1,[7] and which is related to β as follows (Equation 10.2).

---

7   While the expectation is that the intergenerational correlation coefficient will be positive (that is, lying between 0 and 1), it is theoretically possible for it to be negative—that is, the case in which policy measures were strong enough to eliminate any non-observable links between children and parents' educational outcomes, although in practice this outcome is extremely unlikely.

Equation 10.2

$$\beta = \frac{\sigma_i^{\,j}}{\sigma_i^{\,k}}\rho$$

The main difference between β and ρ is that the former provides a relative measure, while the latter is absolute, abstracting away from possible changes in the dispersion of education within each cohort (Checci et al. 2008). That is, β could fall over time because the variance of education in the child's generation is lower than that in the parents' generation (for example, following the introduction of compulsory primary school education), or because the correlation itself has fallen (for example, because of policies to promote mobility). For both β and ρ, higher values indicate that a child's level of schooling is more strongly related to his/her parents' level. As Hertz et al. (2007) show, these two coefficients can move in opposite directions, and for this reason Black and Devereux (2010) recommend reporting both, which we do below.

Our data come from the RUMiCI Survey for 2008, which covers three groups of Chinese households: 5000 urban migrant households who worked in 15 designated cities (Urban Migrant Survey, UMS); 5000 urban local incumbent households in the same cities (Urban Household Survey, UHS); and 8000 rural households with and without migrant members from the nine provinces where the 15 cities are located (Rural Household Survey, RHS). The nine provinces or metropolitan areas are Shanghai, Guangdong, Jiangsu, Zhejiang, Anhui, Hubei, Sichuan, Chongqing and Henan. The first four of these are the largest migrant destinations; the remaining five are the largest migration sending areas. The RUMiCI survey of migrant workers in urban cities, to the best of our knowledge, is the only random sample of migrant workers for China so far.[8]

Each of the households in the UHS, UMS and RHS provides information at the individual level for up to three generations of members: the household head and his/her spouse (generation two), their parents (generation one) and their children (generation three). For generations two and three, we have years of schooling, while generation one provides only the completed level of education, which we convert into years of schooling. We use this set of information to construct a dataset that comprises 10 five-year birth cohorts of 'children', from 1941–45 through to 1986–90, with total sample sizes of 11 831, 6247 and 25 126 in the urban, migrant and rural surveys respectively. All of the tables and figures presented below are based on results calculated by the authors using these survey data, unless otherwise noted.

---

8   The detailed sampling procedure can be found at <http://rumici.anu.edu.au>

Results: Take one

Table 10.1 presents some preliminary statistics for the urban, migrant and rural surveys, which include the percentage of people in each (child) cohort to obtain no education, primary school, junior high, high school and college education, along with the average years of schooling for each cohort and their parents.[9] The table confirms the general trend of rising educational attainments across the country, with the percentage of people receiving only primary education or less plummeting from 15 per cent to 2 per cent, 50 per cent to 4 per cent and 65 per cent to 8 per cent between the first and ninth cohorts in the urban, rural and migrant surveys respectively. These trends are reflected in the average number of years of schooling, which rises over time for each population subgroup with the exception of a slight drop between the 1941–45 and 1946–50 (that is, first and second) cohorts in the urban and migrant surveys, which presumably relates to the disruption caused by the Cultural Revolution,[10] and a slight fall between the 1961–65 and 1966–70 (that is, the fifth and sixth) cohorts in the migrant survey, which is likely to be connected to the changing opportunities for migration from 1978 onwards.[11]

As expected, education levels are highest in the urban survey, at 14.1 years on average for the ninth cohort, compared with 10.2 years for rural China and 10.4 years for migrants. The significant drop to 12.4 years for the tenth urban cohort is driven by the fact that 22 per cent of this cohort had in fact not yet finished their tertiary education at the time of the survey, and so could not be counted as having completed college. This issue is less important for the migrant and rural surveys given their lower levels of education, with 7 per cent of the same cohort in the RHS and just 1.7 per cent of the migrant survey. For this reason, the results for this final urban cohort are excluded in what follows, while those for the other two surveys are presented as a reasonable approximation.

---

9 In cases where only the father's or the mother's level is provided, we use this level alone in order to maximise the number of observations.

10 According to Meng and Gregory (2002), the Cultural Revolution (1966–77) had the greatest impact on educational attainment for those whose high school education was interrupted—that is, those in the latter half of the 1946–50 cohort and the first half of the 1951–55 cohort.

11 In particular, Zhao (1999) shows that between 1979 and 1988 there were strong incentives for rural residents to obtain high school education as the primary means of obtaining urban *hukou*, while de Brauw and Giles (2006) show that the increased ability to migrate and the consequent dramatic rise in migration volumes during the 1990s created disincentives for increases in educational attainment among rural youth. This combination of findings is consistent with a *fall* in educational attainment between these two cohorts, who fell into the prime migration age in the mid to late 1980s and early 1990s respectively. In the UMS 2008, migration rates peak at age twenty-four for men and age twenty-one for women, with rates of 60 and 64 per cent respectively. Rates decline with age, in part due to the institutional barriers to migration, as explained in Golley and Meng (2011).

Table 10.1 Preliminary Statistics for the Urban, Migrant and Rural Surveys, 2008

		Highest degree (percentage of child cohort)					Average years of school	Average years of school (parents)	No. obs
		None	Primary	Junior high	High school	College			
Birth cohort	Urban survey								
No.	Years								
1	1941–45	2	13	32	31	22	10.8	3.5	454
2	1946–50	2	14	40	28	16	10.3	4.1	749
3	1951–55	1	9	43	32	15	10.6	4.7	1236
4	1956–60	1	4	24	53	17	11.5	5.5	1425
5	1961–65	0	2	23	45	30	12.3	6.6	1705
6	1966–70	1	4	24	34	37	12.3	8.0	1685
7	1971–75	1	2	16	33	48	31.1	8.7	1602
8	1976–80	0	1	9	30	60	13.8	9.1	1272
9	1981–85	1	1	5	26	67	14.1	10.3	1021
10	1986–90	2	0	11	54	32	12.4	10.4	231
Migrant survey									
1	1941–45	0	50	50	0	0	7.5	3.0	2
2	1946–50	22	44	22	11	0	6.0	1.0	18
3	1951–55	13	35	39	13	0	7.2	1.8	46
4	1956–60	8	23	56	12	1	8.1	2.7	145
5	1961–65	5	19	53	22	2	8.8	2.8	352
6	1966–70	3	25	58	13	1	8.4	3.9	743
7	1971–75	2	20	59	16	3	8.9	4.3	889
8	1976–80	1	9	57	27	7	9.9	5.3	996
9	1981–85	0	4	56	30	10	10.4	6.9	1439
10	1986–90	0	3	53	39	5	10.4	7.5	1616
Rural survey									
1	1941–45	16	49	30	5	0	6.3	2.4	764
2	1946–50	14	53	27	6	0	6.4	2.6	1589
3	1951–55	12	47	31	9	1	6.8	2.8	2464
4	1956–60	7	33	39	19	1	8.0	3.1	2140
5	1961–65	3	25	52	18	2	8.6	3.7	3125
6	1966–70	2	26	57	12	2	8.6	4.6	3462
7	1971–75	1	19	60	15	5	9.1	5.7	3018
8	1976–80	1	12	59	21	8	9.8	6.4	2676
9	1981–85	0	8	58	20	13	10.2	7.4	2923
10	1986–90	0	8	60	25	7	9.9	7.9	2584

Source: Authors' calculations based on RUMiCI Survey 2008.

The most striking differences are at the higher end of the education spectrum. In the ninth cohort, 93 per cent of urban children attained either high school or college degrees, compared with 40 per cent of migrants and 43 per cent of rural children. As expected, the greatest divergence is at the college level, with urban children in this cohort more than six and five times more likely to attend college than their migrant and rural counterparts. Another point worth noting is that a higher proportion of rural children in the three youngest cohorts attains college degrees than their migrant counterparts, and yet a higher proportion is also more likely to complete only primary education. Migrants, on the other hand, are more likely to have high school degrees—a point that is true across all cohorts apart from the fourth one. While there are clear differences in the educational attainments of China's migrant and rural populations, these are dwarfed by the urban–non-urban divide.

Table 10.2 turns to the results of the child–parent regression and correlation coefficients based on Equations 10.1 and 10.2 for $i = 1, \ldots, 10, j = c$ and $k = p$. There are five key points.

The first point regards the standard deviations of years of education for children and parents, and the ratio of the two. While these differ across the three samples and over time, the ratio of the child's to parents' standard deviations, σ^c/σ^p, varies only slightly over the cohort range in each survey, and these variations are not enough to create any substantive differences in the trends for the regression or correlation coefficients; as seen in Figure 10.1, these are rising or falling simultaneously within each survey. It is also worth noting that for every cohort, the standard deviations of children and parents are both higher in the urban than the rural populations, but their ratio is lower. Thus, it is not the case that a high ratio of standard deviations is the driving force for the relatively high regression coefficients in the urban sample; something other than dispersion is going on.

Table 10.2 Regression and Correlation Coefficients for Child–Parents

Birth cohort		β	ρ	σ^χ	σ^π	σ^χ/σ^π
Urban						
1	1941–45	0.20	0.22	3.5	3.9	0.89
2	1946–50	0.23	0.30	3.2	4.2	0.76
3	1951–55	0.16	0.23	2.8	4.2	0.67
4	1956–60	0.20	0.30	2.8	4.3	0.65
5	1961–65	0.17	0.26	2.7	4.2	0.64
6	1966–70	0.23	0.31	3.1	4.1	0.75
7	1971–75	0.23	0.30	3.0	3.9	0.75
8	1976–80	0.22	0.28	2.6	3.4	0.77
9	1981–85	0.30	0.31	2.5	2.6	0.97
10	1986–90	0.27	0.24	2.7	2.4	1.15
Migrant						
1	1941–45	..	..	..	..	..
2	1946–50	..	..	..	..	..
3	1951–55	..	..	..	..	..
4	1956–60	0.09	0.10	3.0	3.2	0.93
5	1961–65	0.12	0.24	2.8	3.2	0.09
6	1966–70	0.13	0.17	2.4	3.3	0.72
7	1971–75	0.17	0.23	2.5	3.3	0.76
8	1976–80	0.19	0.26	2.4	3.3	0.72
9	1981–85	0.17	0.23	2.3	3.1	0.73
10	1986–90	0.15	0.21	2.0	2.7	0.74
Rural						
1	1941–45	0.20	0.18	3.2	3.0	1.10
2	1946–50	0.13	0.12	3.1	2.9	1.05
3	1951–55	0.13	0.12	3.2	3.0	1.07
4	1956–60	0.13	0.13	3.1	3.0	1.04
5	1961–65	0.17	0.19	2.7	3.0	0.87
6	1966–70	0.19	0.23	2.4	2.9	0.83
7	1971–75	0.21	0.23	2.4	2.6	0.91
8	1976–80	0.21	0.21	2.5	2.5	1.01
9	1981–85	0.24	0.23	2.7	2.5	1.07
10	1986–90	0.24	0.24	2.3	2.3	0.99

.. = not available

Source: Authors' own calculation based on RUMiCI survey (2008).

Figure 10.1a Regression Coefficients by Cohort Across Surveys

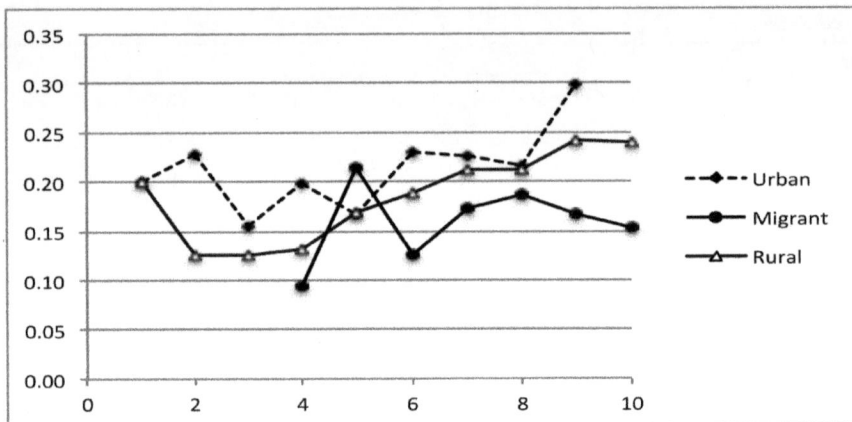

Figure 10.1b Correlations by Cohort Across Surveys

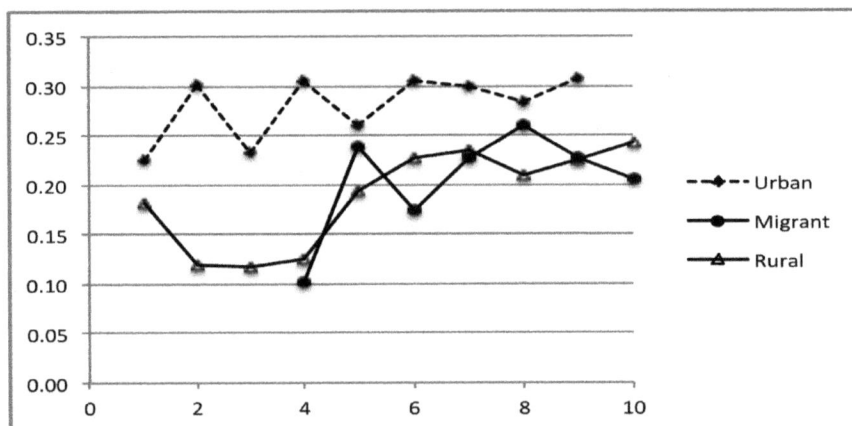

Figure 10.1c Children's Standard Deviations by Cohort Across Surveys

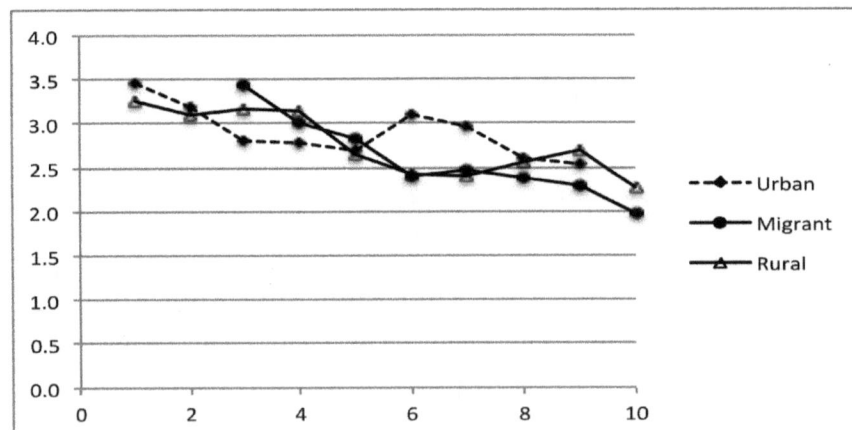

The second point to make is that the regression coefficients and correlations are low in all three samples and lowest in the rural survey. The average regression coefficients and correlations across all cohorts are 0.21 and 0.28 for the urban survey, 0.16 and 0.20 for the migrant survey and 0.18 and 0.19 for the rural survey. In contrast, Hertz et al. (2007) find average regression coefficients and correlations taken across all cohorts for each of 42 countries ranging from 0.88 and 0.66 in Peru to 0.20 in Kyrgyzstan and 0.10 in (rural) Ethiopia, with rural China having the second-lowest values of both at 0.34 and 0.20 respectively.

Third, for all three surveys, both the regression coefficients and the correlations display a general trend of rising persistence over time, albeit with fluctuations. This contrasts with the key finding of Hertz et al. (2007) that the regression coefficient had fallen substantially for most countries over half a century, including for rural China. Our finding is not, however, inconsistent with Hertz et al.'s finding for rural China, as the period they cover is 1928–73, and much of the fall in their regression coefficient happens between 1928 and 1943 (see Hertz et al. 2007:Appendix 1).

Fourth, the relationship between child and parent education is clearly different across the three populations—in both levels and trends. If it were simply the case that rural China was behind urban China in levels, but along the same path of educational development, we would expect these trends to be in the same direction over time. Instead, these results suggest that the determinants of the child–parent educational relationship differ across China's rural, migrant and urban populations in more substantial ways than pure developmental differences would suggest.

The final point is that there are striking differences in the intergenerational patterns of different gender combinations of child–parent pairs, as illustrated in Figure 10.2 for the regression coefficients through to the ninth cohort in each survey. In particular, across all subgroups, the daughter–parent coefficient is the highest in virtually all age cohorts, driven mainly by the daughter–father relationship, while the son–mother relationship is the weakest. In all comparisons, the educational attainments of daughters are more, and often much more, highly associated with the parent–father–mother than that of sons. In other words, the socioeconomic status of women as reflected in their educational achievements is more tightly bound to their family's social status than that of men.[12]

---

12 This is consistent with the findings of Gong et al. (2010), who find coefficients on years of schooling for urban China of 0.26 for father–son, 0.22 for mother–son, 0.37 for father–daughter and 0.38 for mother–daughter, using the Urban Household Education and Employment Survey 2004 for people aged sixteen to seventy-four.

Figure 10.2a Urban Regression Coefficients for Different Gender Pairs

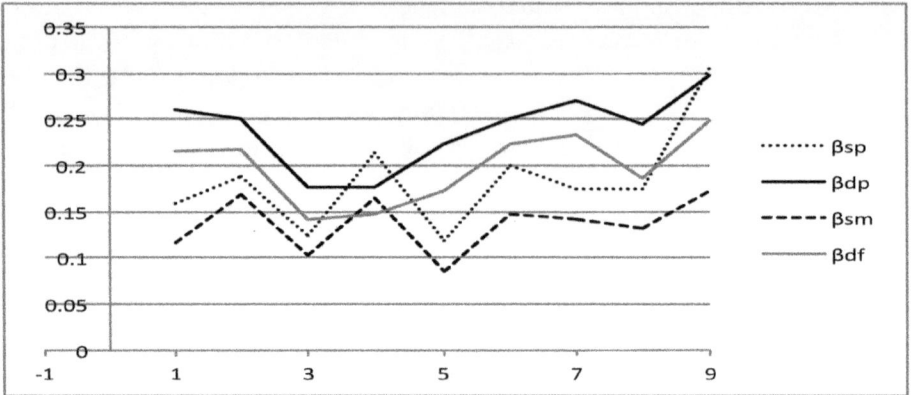

Figure 10.2b Migrant Regression Coefficients for Different Gender Pairs

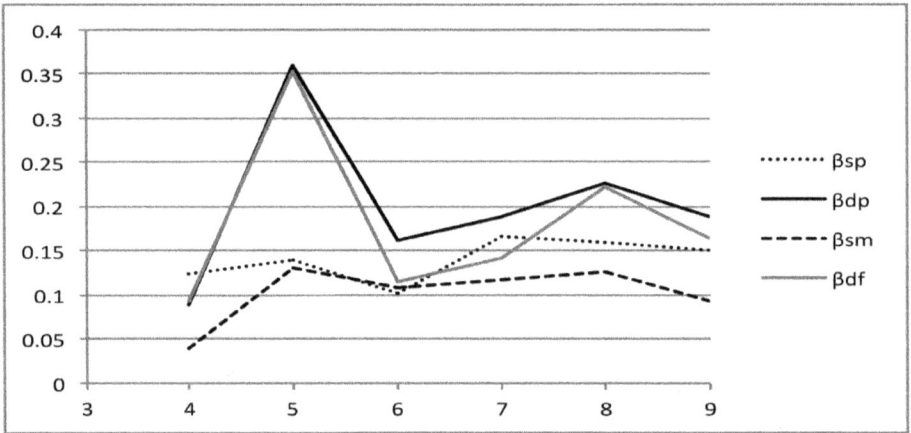

Figure 10.2c Rural Regression Coefficients for Different Gender Pairs

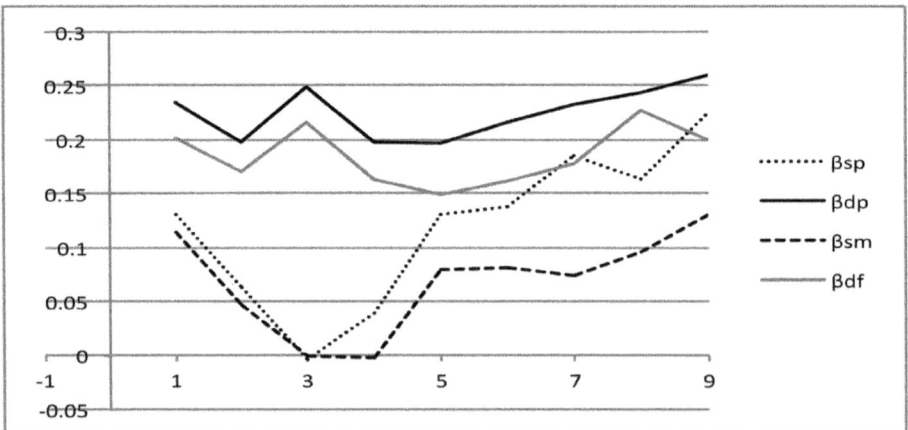

'Persistence' and 'Mobility': A closer look at ρ

Given the rise in average educational levels nationwide, not only the levels but also the sources of persistence within the educational distribution are likely to change over time. To examine these changes, following Checci et al. (2008), we decompose the correlation coefficient as follows (Equation 10.3).

Equation 10.3

$$\rho = \sigma^{cf}/_{\sigma^{cf}} = \frac{\sum_{c,p} \tilde{1}(y^c - \mu^c)(y^f - \mu^f \tilde{1}) \Pr\left(y^c \backslash y^f\right) \Pr(y^f)}{\sigma^c \sigma^f}$$

In Equation 10.3, μ denotes the mean and the set of possible values for education is set at {0, 6, 9, 12, 16}, corresponding with no education (NE), primary school (PS), junior high school (JH), high school (HS) and college (C), and σ^{cf} is the covariance between the child's and father's levels of educational attainment, y^c and y^f. This implies that the correlation coefficient depends on the combined deviations of the child's and the father's education from the mean, the conditional probability of a child achieving a certain education level given the father's level of education and the probability of the father achieving that level of education.[13]

As long as both generations of a given child–father pair (for example, college-educated children and college-educated father) achieve levels of education above (or below) the mean for their own cohort, this child–father pair will contribute positively to ρ, while if one is above (below) and the other below (above) the pair will make a negative contribution. Checci et al. (2008) use this approach in their Italian study to show that about one-third of the correlation coefficient in older cohorts results from the correlation between the most uneducated fathers and sons, with this contribution falling over time, while a large and growing proportion of the correlation coefficient is due to the top end of college-educated fathers and sons.

Figures 10.3 to 10.5 present the results of a decomposition of the correlation coefficient by cohort in the urban, migrant and rural samples respectively. This decomposition aims to shed light on the *source* of the correlation within the educational spectrum. Based on Equation 10.3, each figure is divided into five stacks, each of which isolates the contribution made by fathers with education

---

13 The focus here on levels of schooling rather than years is necessary to ensure there are enough observations in each level and for ease of exposition; otherwise, we would be looking at a decomposition of 20 by 20 years of education in which many components would be zero and which would be nearly impossible to depict. The reduction to levels also necessitates the focus on just one parent (to avoid the problem of averages lying in between the adopted levels); and following the bulk of the literature, we begin here with the father.

levels beginning with no education (NE) through to college education (C). The vertical sum of all 25 components across the five stacks gives the correlation coefficient ρ for each child cohort.[14]

Figure 10.3 Urban Correlation Decomposition Across Education Levels and Cohorts

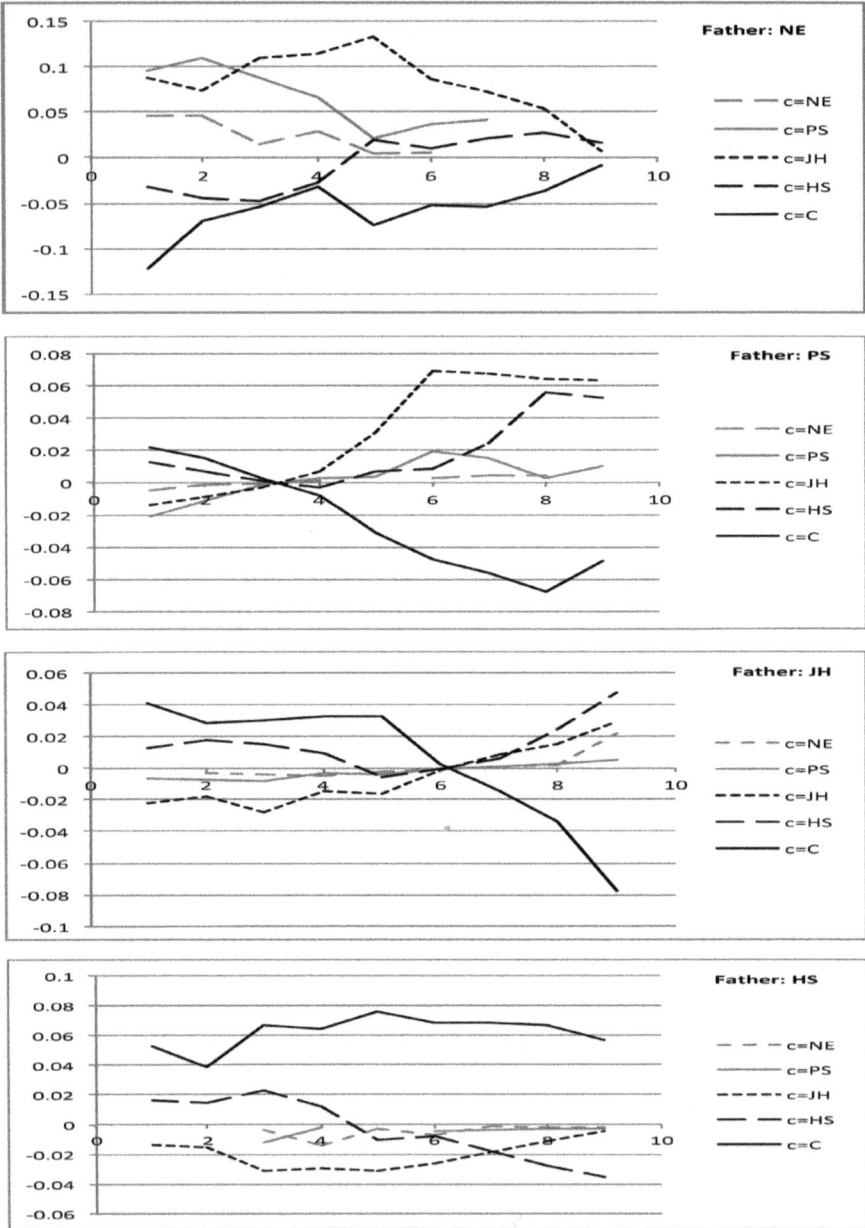

14 These will not exactly match the figures in Table 10.2, because here they are calculated using five levels of education, rather than years.

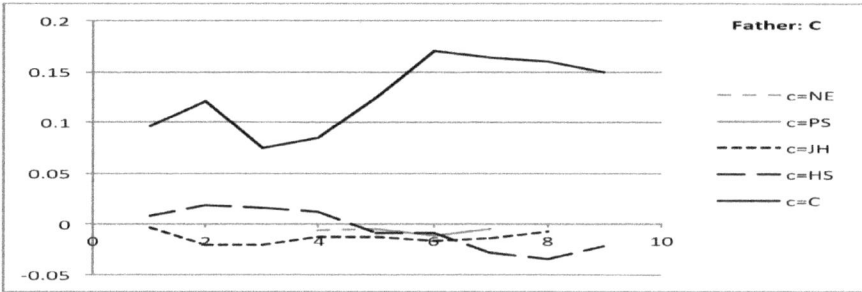

Figure 10.4 Migrant Correlation Decomposition Across Education Levels and Cohorts

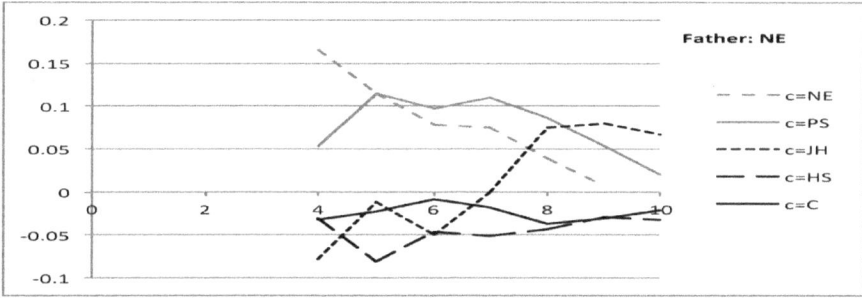

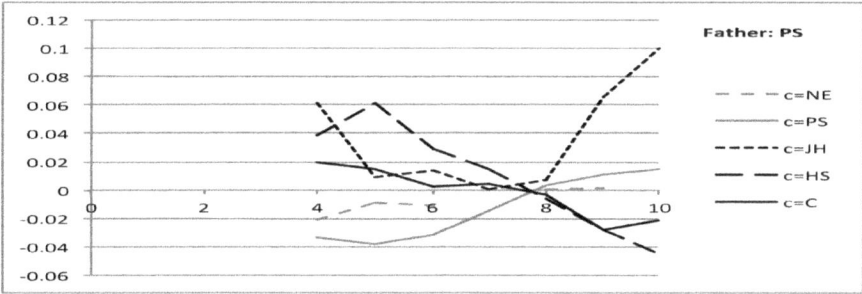

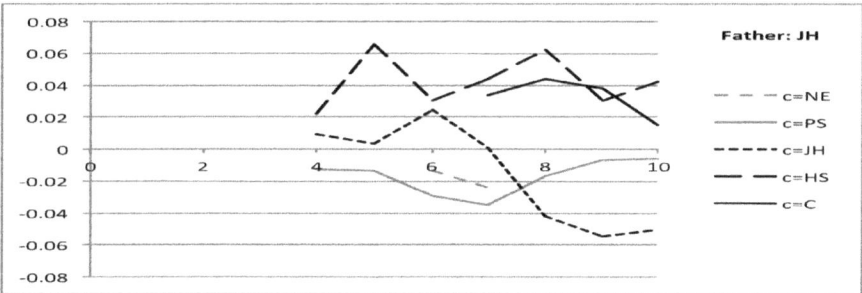

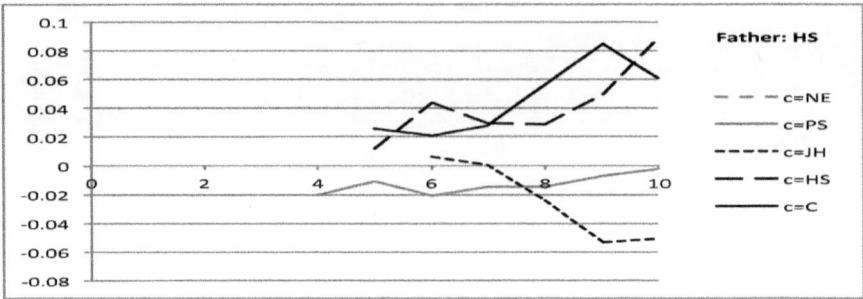

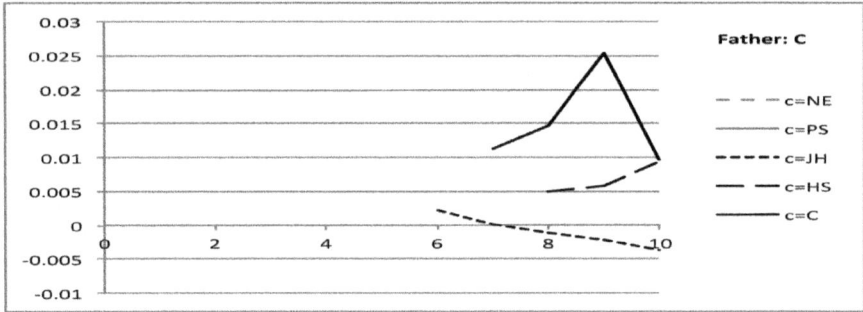

Figure 10.5 Rural Correlation Decomposition Across Education Levels and Cohorts

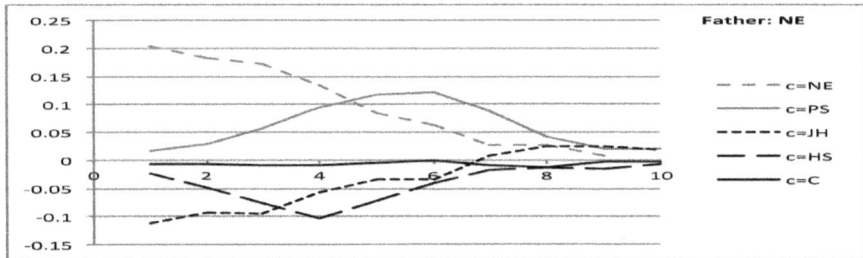

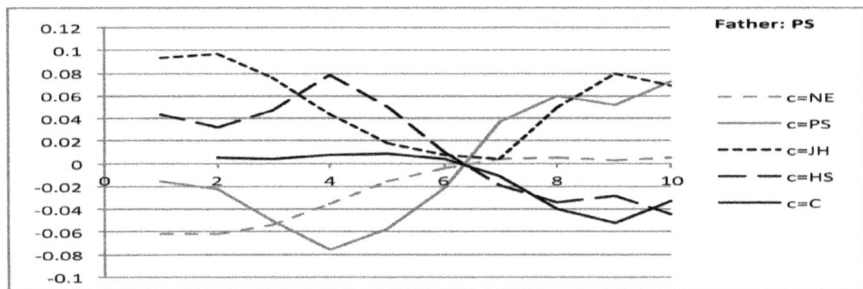

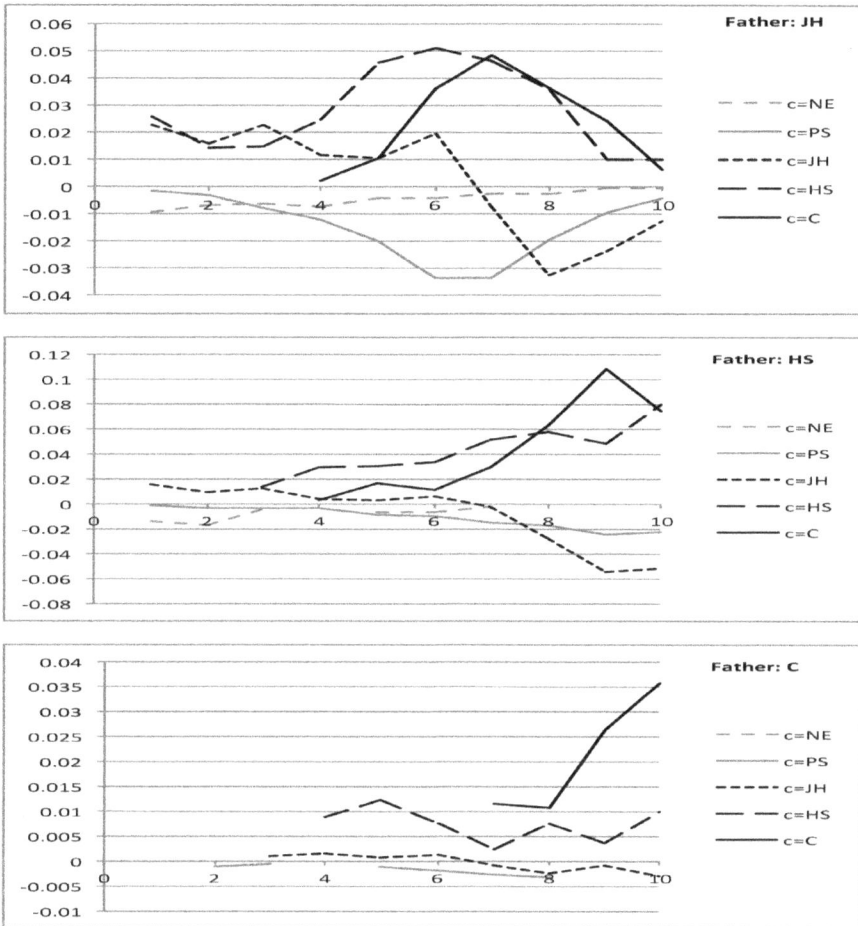

Focusing first on the urban decomposition in Figure 10.3, and to see how the decomposition works, note the positive contributions of the components for fathers with high school and college qualifications whose children obtain college education (the black solid lines in the fourth and fifth stacks respectively); with both parents and children above their mean levels of education, this contributes positively to ρ, or to 'persistence'. Contrast this with the negative contribution of fathers who completed junior high and children who completed college (beyond the sixth cohort, black solid line in the third stack); in this case, fathers below the mean for their cohort have children who achieve above the mean for their cohort, which increases 'mobility' (or reduces persistence). The most obvious point from the urban decomposition is that the correlations between high school and college-educated fathers and their college-educated children dominate the overall correlation for all cohorts, and more so in the younger cohorts than the older ones. By the ninth cohort, of 157 fathers with college education, 90 per cent had children who also completed college with another 9 per cent finishing high school. Of 327 fathers with high school qualifications, 69 per cent of their children went on to complete college and 29 per cent completed high school, leaving just seven children with sub–high school qualifications. And of the 350 fathers who finished junior high, 64 per cent of their children also made it to college and 26 per cent completed high school. In urban China, it seems the only way is up, and once you are up, you stay there.

Turning to the migrant decomposition in Figure 10.4, the first point to note is that the number of migrants with college-educated fathers is small, at less than five for the fourth to eighth cohorts and just 13 and 12 for the ninth and tenth cohorts respectively. For the ninth cohort, six of those children made it to college as well and five completed high school, with both these sets of child–father pairs making positive contributions to the overall correlation. Like their urban counterparts, no migrant children with college-educated fathers in the ninth or tenth cohorts achieved less than junior high qualifications. Given that these college-educated migrants will most likely go on to obtain urban *hukou* status, and that college-educated urban fathers are very likely have college-educated children, these migrants ultimately become part of urban China's intergenerational persistence story.

At the other end of the education spectrum, the *declining* positive contribution of fathers with no education and children with either no education or primary schooling (the dark blue and red lines in stack one) is a good sign—that of decreasing 'persistence' at the low end. But note also the *rising* positive contribution of fathers with no education and children who finish junior high. That is, a jump of two education levels between generations, but with both parents and children below the mean levels of schooling for their own cohorts, contributes to what is interpreted as rising persistence.

Note that the same issue arises for fathers with primary schooling and children with junior high education in stack two, for fathers with junior high and children with high school or college education in stack three, and for fathers with high school and college-educated children in stack four. While these intuitively signal upward mobility across generations in the sense that children out-educate their parents, their positive and rising contribution to ρ results in an interpretation of rising persistence. This is easy to understand mechanically: ρ is rising because children of parents with higher levels of education are increasingly likely to out-educate children of parents with lower levels of education—that is, rising averages with absolute divergence. It is still worth noting here, however, that some kinds of persistence (and mobility) are better than others.

One final point of interest is that the majority of migrants have fathers with either junior high or high school qualifications, and the outcomes of these children are quite different from those of their urban counterparts. In the ninth cohort, for example, of the 508 migrant children with fathers educated to junior high level, 286 (56 per cent) also completed junior high, 257 (31 per cent) completed high school and 53 (10 per cent) completed college degrees. Compare these with the equivalent numbers for the urban survey above and the message is clear: upward mobility is harder for migrants than it is for urban residents. And yet in level terms, observing that the overall correlation in the migrant survey is below the urban one (as shown Figure 10.1b) leads to the suggestion that intergenerational mobility is greater for migrants than for urban residents. Again, this use of language can be somewhat misleading.

The results for the rural survey in Figure 10.5 echo many of the migrant survey results. The number of college-educated fathers is very small, ranging between 15 and 28 for the fifth to tenth cohorts. Despite these small numbers, the message from stack five is clear: college-educated rural fathers are highly likely to have high school or college-educated children, with 13 and six of the 21 in the ninth cohort achieving these levels respectively. At the other end of the spectrum, major contributions to the positive correlation come from child–father pairs with primary school only and from fathers with primary school and children with junior high education—a kind of persistence we would probably rather not observe. For fathers with junior high qualifications— close to 60 per cent of the rural survey from the seventh to tenth cohorts— the majority of their children also reached junior high. For example, of the 1329 fathers with junior high qualifications in the ninth cohort, 61 per cent of children also obtained junior high qualifications, 18 per cent reached high school and 13 per cent completed college. Of the 586 rural fathers with high school qualifications, 45 per cent of their children obtained only junior high qualifications, while 29 per cent and 20 per cent reached high school and college respectively. These percentages are dramatically different from the equivalent urban results reported above. In particular, they indicate that intergenerational mobility in rural China can involve moves both up and down the education ladder.

To illustrate this key point further, Figure 10.6 presents a five-by-five 'mobility' matrix of father–child pairs in the ninth cohort for each of the urban, migrant and rural samples. Each cell, a_{ij}, indicates the conditional probability of a child achieving level of education i given education level j of their father. Thus, for example, the urban matrix reveals that 90 per cent of children with college-educated fathers also made it to college (C-C, bottom right cell), with the remaining 10 per cent moving down the education ladder relative to their fathers. As shown by the figures highlighted in grey, there was a miniscule movement in this direction in the urban survey, particularly in contrast with the migrant and rural surveys.

Figure 10.6 'Mobility' Matrices for Child–Father Pairs in the Ninth Cohort

Urban Survey

Child Father	NE	PE	JH	HS	C
NE	0.00	0.00	0.10	0.50	0.40
PE	0.00	0.02	0.18	0.34	0.46
JH	0.02	0.01	0.07	0.26	0.64
HS	0.00	0.01	0.02	0.29	0.69
C	0.00	0.01	0.00	0.09	0.90

Migrant Survey

Child Father	NE	PE	JH	HS	C
NE	0.01	0.13	0.60	0.21	0.06
PE	0.00	0.03	0.63	0.26	0.07
JH	0.00	0.02	0.56	0.31	0.10
HS	0.00	0.02	0.42	0.38	0.18
C	0.00	0.00	0.15	0.38	0.46

Rural Survey

Child Father	NE	PE	JH	HS	C
NE	0.02	0.14	0.57	0.25	0.01
PE	0.00	0.12	0.63	0.16	0.09
JH	0.00	0.07	0.61	0.18	0.13
HS	0.00	0.06	0.45	0.29	0.20
C	0.00	0.00	0.21	0.36	0.43

In sum, the higher overall correlation between the educational attainments of urban children and their fathers stems largely from the positive contribution of college and high school-educated fathers and their college-educated children, while the lower correlations for the migrant and rural children–father pairs stem from the fact that college-educated fathers hardly exist in the sample, and that the majority of children go on to complete junior high regardless of their fathers' educational achievements. Thus, what looks like greater 'mobility' of children in rural China might instead be a case of limited opportunities for the majority.

Conclusions

Our interest in the issue of the transmission of educational attainment across generations in China commenced with the observation that urban Chinese appear to be investing vast amounts of time, resources and energy to ensure that their children obtain the highest possible educational qualifications—and in the majority of cases they seem to be succeeding: college entry rates among urban Chinese are high by any standards. In contrast, there is plenty of evidence to suggest that rural Chinese are struggling to move beyond junior high. Wang et al.'s (2009) paper on *What is keeping the poor out of college* shows that the college participation rates of the rural poor are low because of barriers to entry that exist throughout the rural education system—a point that is supported by the findings of Luo et al. (2011), whose aptly titled paper 'Behind before they begin: the challenge of early childhood education in rural China', shows that the disadvantages of China's rural children begin at the early childhood education level and are likely to 'hamper their learning experience throughout life'. The implications of this divide for the future trend of rural–urban income inequality in China are both clear and undesirable.

The persistence or mobility of educational attainment across generations, and how this changes over time, is determined by a multitude of factors that interact with each other in complex ways. To the extent that persistence at the top end of the education spectrum reflects high ability, which is transmitted genetically from parents to their children, one might accept the consequential income disparities as being unavoidable, even desirable. The evidence demonstrating the 'rebound' of educational achievements of China's urban and rural 'elites' following their persecution during the Cultural Revolution, and their children (Meng and Gregory 2002; Sato and Li 2008), provides some support for this view; even the policies of the Cultural Revolution could not undermine the educational successes of those who are somehow bound to achieve. To the extent that this persistence reflects anything else, however, there is cause for further thought.

The results presented in this chapter add to a growing literature that suggests that there is more going on in China than the simple line that high-ability parents have high-ability children who achieve high educational outcomes. As Black and Devereux (2010) point out, given that the inheritability of education-related endowments (that is, brains) is unlikely to differ significantly across (or within) countries or over time,[15] the hunt for explanations of cross-country differences tends to focus on differences in returns to education or in government investments, the latter being one of the key determinants of the equality of opportunity. For example, they suggest that the relatively low regression coefficients found in Nordic countries could be explained by compressed earnings distributions (low return to skills) or by social and educational policies that tend to equalise opportunities for children. Similarly, Ichino et al. (2009) find that countries with better public education systems tend to have higher intergenerational mobility, or lower regression coefficients, particularly when focused on primary education.

Applying this logic to our findings here, the relatively low regression and correlation coefficients in rural China are likely to have something to do with relatively compressed earnings there, resulting from ongoing constraints to permanent rural-to-urban migration[16] and segmentation in urban labour markets.[17] Meanwhile, an apparent lack of investment in the rural education system constrains most rural children to a relatively uneducated life, giving the appearance of mobility or of equal opportunity because, regardless of their parents' education, they are most likely to reach only junior high themselves. Only the very brightest rural and migrant students have the opportunity to make it through to college and to ultimately join the majority of urban children who will make up the subsequent generation of educated urban elite. Based on ability alone, and in a country of equal opportunity for all, surely the proportion of this elite originating in rural China would be higher. While our results do not prove any of these claims definitively, they pave the way for ongoing research to deepen our understanding of the factors constraining and facilitating rural and urban children respectively in their climbs up China's educational ladder.

References

Appleton, S., Knight, J., Song, L. and Xia, Q., 2004, 'Contrasting paradigms: segmentation and competitiveness in the formation of the Chinese labour market', *Journal of Chinese Economic and Business Studies*, vol. 2, no. 3, pp. 185–205.

Becker, G. and Tomes, N., 1979, 'An equilibrium theory of the distribution of income and intergenerational mobility', *Journal of Political Economy*, vol. 87, pp. 1153–89.

---

15 Note that the assumption of a uniform (if unknown) degree of 'inheritability' across space is not the same as assuming uniform 'ability' across space.

16 See Cai and Wang (2010); Golley and Meng (2011); Knight et al. (2010); Kong et al. (2010); Meng and Lee (2009); Zhao (1997).

17 See Appleton et al. (2004); Chen et al. (2007); Démurger et al. (2007, 2009); Meng and Zhang (2001).

Becker, G. and Tomes, N., 1986, 'Human capital and the rise and fall of families', *Journal of Labour Economics*, vol. 4, no. 3(2), S1–39.

Black, S. E. and Devereux, P. J., 2010, *Recent developments in intergenerational mobility*, UCD Geary Institute Discussion Paper Series, Prepared for *Handbook of Labour Economics*.

Cai, F. and Wang, M., 2010, 'Urbanisation with Chinese characteristics', in R. Garnaut, J. Golley and L. Song (eds), *China: The next twenty years of reform and development*, ANU E Press and Social Sciences Academic Press, Canberra and China.

Checchi, D., Fiorio, C. V. and Leonardi, M., 2008, *Intergenerational persistence in educational attainment in Italy*, IZA Discussion Paper No. 3622, Institute for the Study of Labor, Bonn.

Chen, Y., Démurger, S. and Fournier, M., 2007, 'The evolution of gender earnings gaps and discrimination in urban China, 1988–95', *Developing Economies*, vol. 45, no. 1, pp. 97–121.

De Brauw, A. and Giles, J., 2006, *Migrant opportunity and the educational attainment of youth in rural China*, IZA Discussion Paper No. 2326, Institute for the Study of Labor, Bonn.

Démurger, S., Fournier, M., Shi, L. and Zhong, W., 2007, 'Economic liberalisation with rising segmentation in China's urban labour market', *Asian Economic Papers*, vol. 5, no. 3, pp. 58–101.

Démurger, S., Gurgand, M., Shi, L. and Ximing, Y., 2009, 'Migrants as second-class workers in urban China? A decomposition analysis', *Journal of Comparative Economics*, vol. 37, pp. 610–28.

Deng, Z. and Treiman, D. J., 1997, 'The impact of the Cultural Revolution on trends in educational attainment in the People's Republic of China', *The American Journal of Sociology*, vol. 103, no. 2, pp. 391–428.

Golley, J. and Meng, X., 2011, 'Has China run out of surplus labour?', *China Economic Review*, vol. 22, pp. 555–72.

Gong, C. H., Leigh, A. and Meng, X., 2010, *Intergenerational income mobility in urban China*, IZA Discussion Paper No. 4811, Institute for the Study of Labor, Bonn.

Hertz, T., Jayasundera, T., Piraino, P., Selcuk, S., Smith, N. and Verashchagina, A., 2007, 'The inheritance of educational inequality: international comparisons and fifty-year trends', *The B. E. Journal of Economic Analysis and Policy*, vol. 7, no. 2, pp. 1–46.

Ichino, A., Karabarbounis, L. and Moretti E., 2010, 'The political economy of intergenerational income mobility', NBER Working Paper 15946, April.

Knight, J., Deng, Q. and Li, S., 2010, *The puzzle of migrant labour shortage and the rural labour surplus in China*, DoE Working Paper Series No. 494, Oxford University, Oxford.

Kong, S. T., Meng, X. and Zhang, D., 2010, 'The global financial crisis and rural–urban migration', in R. Garnaut, J. Golley and L. Song (eds), *China: The next twenty years of reform and development*, ANU E Press and Social Sciences Academic Press, Canberra and China.

Lee, L. and Meng, X., 2010, 'Why don't more Chinese migrate from the countryside? Institutional constraints and the migration decision', in X. Meng and C. Manning, with S. Li and T. Effendi (eds), *The Great Migration: Rural–urban migration in China and Indonesia*, Edward Elgar, Cheltenham, UK.

Liu, X., Park, A. and Zhao, Y., 2010, *Explaining rising returns to education in urban China in the 1990s*, IZA Discussion Paper No. 4872, April, Institute for the Study of Labor, Bonn.

Luo, R., Zhang, L., Liu, C., Zhao, Q., Shi, Y., Rozelle, S. and Sharbono, B., 2011, 'Behind before they begin: the challenge of early childhood education in rural China', *Australian Journal of Early Childhood*, <http://foodsecurity. stanford.edu/publications/behind_before_they_begin_the_challenge_of_ early_childhood_education_in_rural_china/>

Meng, X. and Gregory, R. G., 2002, 'The impact of interrupted education on subsequent educational attainment: a cost of the Chinese Cultural Revolution', *Economic Development and Cultural Change*, vol. 50, no. 4, pp. 935–59.

Meng, X. and Zhang, J., 2001, 'The two-tier labour market in urban China: occupational segregation and wage differentials between urban residents and rural migrants in Shanghai', *Journal of Comparative Economics*, vol. 29, pp. 485–504.

Sato, H. and Li, S., 2008, *Class origin, family culture, and intergenerational correlation of education in rural China*, Global COE Hi-Stat Discussion Paper Series 007, Institute of Economic Research, Hitotsubashi University, Tokyo.

Sicular, T., Yue, X., Gustafsson, B. and Li, S., 2005, The urban–rural gap and income inequality in China, Paper prepared for UNU-WIDER Project Meeting on Inequality and Poverty in China, Helsinki, 26–27 August.

Solon, G., 1999, 'Intergenerational mobility in the labour market', in O. Ashenfelter and D. Card (eds), *Handbook of Labour Economics. Volume 3A*, North-Holland, Amsterdam, pp. 1761–800.

Solon, G., 2004, 'A model of intergenerational mobility variation over time and place', in M. Corak (ed.), *Generational Income Mobility in North America and Europe*, Cambridge University Press, Cambridge.

Teng, M. F., 2005, 'Unequal primary education opportunities in rural and urban China', *China Perspectives*, vol. 60 (July–August).

Wang, X., Liu, C., Zhang, L., Luo, R., Glauben, T., Shi, Y., Rozelle, S. and Sharbono, B., 2010, *What is keeping the poor out of college? Enrollment rates, educational barriers and college matriculation in China*, Working Paper 210, September, Stanford University, Stanford, Calif., <reapchina.org/reap.stanford.edu>

Yang, D. T., 2005, 'Determinants of schooling returns during transition: evidence from Chinese cities', *Journal of Comparative Economics*, vol. 33, no. 1, pp. 244–64.

Zhang, J., Liu, P.-W. and Yung, L., 2007, 'The Cultural Revolution and returns to schooling in China: estimates based on twins', *Journal of Development Economics*, vol. 84, pp. 631–9.

Zhang, J., Zhao, Y. Park, A. and Song, X., 2005, 'Economic returns to schooling in urban China, 1988 to 2001', *Journal of Comparative Economics*, vol. 33, no. 4, pp. 730–52.

Zhang, L., De Brauw, A. and Rozelle, S., 2004, 'China's rural labour market development and its gender implications', *China Economic Review*, vol. 15, pp. 230–47.

Zhang, L., Huang, J. and Rozelle, S., 2002, 'Employment, emerging labour markets, and the role of education in rural China', *China Economic Review*, vol. 13, pp. 313–28.

Zhao, Y., 1999, 'Labor migration and earnings differences: the case of rural China', *Economic Development and Cultural Change*, vol. 47, no. 4, pp. 776–82.

Zhou, X., Moen, P. and Tuma, N. B., 1998, 'Educational stratification in urban China: 1949–94', *Sociology of Education*, vol. 71, no. 3, pp. 199–222.

11. Demographic Transition in Rural China:

A field survey of five provinces

Funing Zhong and Jing Xiang

Introduction

Rural–urban migration and labour mobility are major drivers of China's recent economic growth. Despite the importance of migration to China's continuing economic success there have been few attempts to understand what is happening on the ground.[1] This chapter will look at questions such as how and to what extent China still enjoys the benefits of large-scale internal migration after three decades, and the extent of rising wages in rural areas. Parallel with these questions, the negative impacts of long-term large-scale migration on agriculture and predictions for the future of the rural labor force will be discussed.

The futures of rural–urban migration and of the rural labour force are determined by the remaining rural population and labour force and the demographic structure—for example, the gender and age structures of the population and labour force. It is understandable that, with the same total population, one aged rural society might have a relatively smaller percentage of population of working age, and hence less workers working in agriculture and less labourers looking for off-farm jobs as migrants, compared with another but much younger society. But the demographic structure holds more relative importance. China's population pyramid has been impacted significantly by the 'One Child Policy' since the 1980s and, to a lesser extent, the sustained famine in the early 1960s. The irregularities in China's population pyramid make meaningful analysis of the rural population and labour force more difficult than they would otherwise be. Studies of the demographic dynamics of China's rural population and labour force have been insufficient to date. The sampling procedures generally adopted have not been sufficient to describe the demographic change in rural areas and the official population census data are not released in a timely manner. To fill the gap in the current research, this study has used surveys of whole villages to obtain comprehensive pictures of rural demographic dynamics. The aim of this study is to improve on previous

---

1   More detailed discussions on the impacts of rural–urban migration can be found in a number of publications, such as Chen et al. (2011); Huang (1999); Rozelle et al. (1999).

explanations of rural–urban migration and the projection of future trends. At the same time, we aim to improve understanding of China's rural labour force engaged in agriculture, in terms of total quantity and gender and age.

As a corollary, this study provides insight into China's 'left-at-home' children. China's rural–urban migration has long been characterised by seasonal migration and/or leaving some family members at home. Such migration raises serious issues with children left at home and the impacts on their physical, mental and emotional wellbeing and their education, health and human capital developments. Our study aims to provide a systematic description of the current status of 'left-at-home' children and plausible explanations with regard to the job opportunities their parents face.

Field Survey: Procedures, coverage and reliability

As stated above, the purpose of this survey was to obtain a comprehensive picture of demographic dynamics in rural China that could reveal the impact of rural–urban migration, both permanent and seasonal. The traditional sample procedure does not serve this purpose due to exclusion of those who have already migrated to urban areas; the only way to obtain an accurate picture of rural demographic dynamics is to conduct a village-wide survey, covering all households, including permanent and seasonal migrants.

The survey relied on the cooperation of villagers to provide necessary information regarding absent household members.

The lowest rural community unit (*cunmin xiaozu*) typically consists of 20–30 households, and members are generally close, with a large portion being relatives. In such a social structure, a local student collecting the survey data could obtain necessary demographic information of all households of the village, including those absent, with the help of parents, relatives and village leaders.

Although this approach is considered to provide the fullest picture of rural demographic dynamics, it could (as with all surveys) have some shortcomings regarding the quality and reliability of the survey data especially in regard to information provided on behalf of absent villagers. In order to decrease the potential survey error, we expanded the sample size and reduced the information requirements.

The pilot survey targeted five provinces with high rates of outward migration: Anhui, Hunan, Henan, Sichuan and Jiangsu. Twenty counties in each of the provinces were selected based on per capita income levels. Balanced between the availability of students who could collect the survey data and other considerations, two villages were selected in each of the counties. In the selection procedure, villages close to county centres and/or major towns were avoided to reduce the possible bias of including in the sample an over-proportion of villages/labourers with better migration opportunities.

To ensure reliable information was collected, especially for absent villagers, the survey was restricted to demographic information that was non-sensitive and easily accessible. The demographic information of each individual was recorded—for example, age, education, marital status, occupation, months staying at home in a year, the starting year working outside the village either permanently or seasonally, and residential status outside the village.

The survey covered five provinces, 121 counties, 203 villages, 7317 households and 28 021 people. On average, there are 36 households in a village and 3.83 people in a household.

All students who collected the survey data were trained by the author and conducted the survey during the winter of 2010–11 in their home villages when the number of villagers staying at home was at its peak. After checking completeness and consistency of the information collected, the basic statistics of the effective survey data are summarised in Table 11.1.

Table 11.1 Sample Statistics

Province	Jiangsu	Anhui	Hunan	Henan	Sichuan	Total
County	24	20	21	36	20	121
Villages	51	42	40	39	31	203
Households	2246	1276	929	1305	1561	7317
Persons	8950	4833	3506	5230	5502	28 021

Source: Calculated from field survey data.

The reliability of the survey data was crosschecked with data contained in the *China Statistical Yearbook* and *China Population and Employment Statistical Yearbook* to ensure its accuracy. For example, the average size of the rural household reflected in the survey was 3.83 persons per household at the end of 2010–beginning of 2011; the corresponding figure is 3.98 nationwide, according to the National Rural Household Survey conducted by the National Bureau of Statistics at the end of 2009 (NBS 2010).

A more direct test was undertaken by checking the gender and age structure of our survey data with that for the nation as a whole. Two population pyramids are shown in Figure 11.1—one from our survey (at right) and another from national population and employment statistics (at left) (Department of Population and Employment Statistics of NBS 2010). The two population pyramids are generally consistent.

Figure 11.1 Comparison of Rural Households' Demographic Structures

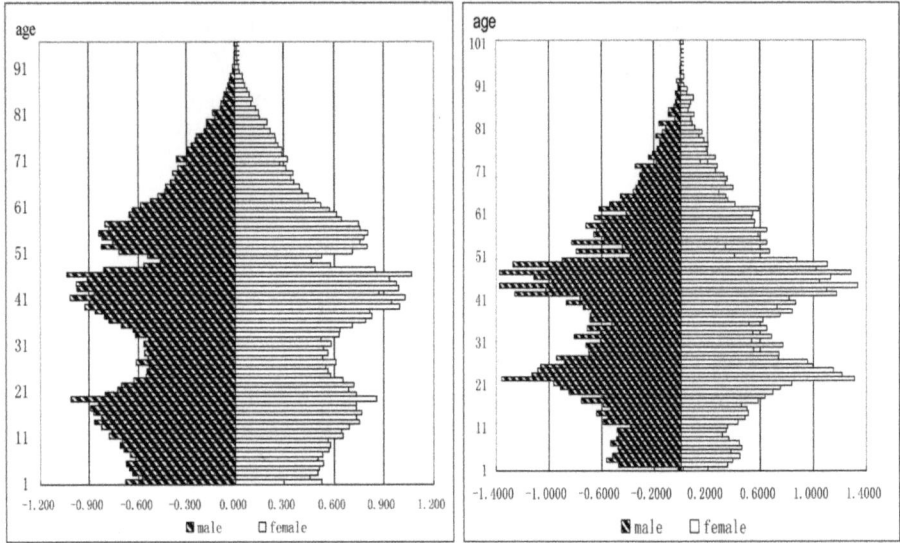

Source: Department of Population and Employment Statistics of NBS (2010); field survey.

Considering the time difference in survey conducting, the similarity might increase if the pyramid generated from the survey moves down one or two years; however, there are two features requiring further explanation: the first gap is rather smaller in our survey compared with the national population and employment statistics data. A plausible explanation is that all five provinces have been major grain producing and exporting areas for a long time and the rural population might have relatively better access to food compared with those living in food-deficit regions, which could lead to relatively higher birth rates as a result, even during times of famine. The second point of inconsistency is that the population reproduction cycle seems to extend based on our survey. The second gap centres on the group of those aged thirty-five, but the third gap does not show a clear sign of ending or bouncing back. One of the plausible explanations for this could be that rural young people have delayed their marriage and reproduction due to uncertainty associated with migration.

Basic Features of Rural Demographic Dynamics

As mentioned above, to ensure the quality of the data, the questionnaires were short and straightforward, focusing primarily on demographic information.

After preliminary work cleaning the data, some useful information was organised to show three aspects of the rural demographic dynamics: the residential and employment status, the demographic structure of the rural labour force and the custody status of the 'left-at-home' children.

Residential and Employment Status

In our study, all persons with local residence registration status are classified into five groups based on their length of stay at home in a calendar year: none—that is, already migrated; less than three months; more than three months but less than six months; more than six months but less than 10 months; and more than 10 months. The official statistical criterion for permanent residence is living in a place for more than six months in a calendar year. We specify two much longer periods—that is, between six and 10 months and more than 10 months—in an effort to separate farmers more precisely according to their major employment by working place.

The survey was conducted in the winter of 2010–11, and preliminary findings are presented in this chapter.

Among the 28 021 respondents, 13 169 people live more than 10 months at home per year; however, a significant portion of this population has already found off-farm employment to supplement their income. The number of villagers who had already migrated was 8020 (28.6 per cent); if these respondents are added to those who are at home less than three months per year (18.5 per cent), those who might be considered not staying at home account for another 47 per cent of the total rural population. The number of persons who move between home and work more frequently—that is, stay home between three and 10 months a year—is relatively smaller, at less than 6 per cent of the total (see Table 11.2).

Table 11.2 Residency Status of Total Population Surveyed

Time staying at home	Persons	Percentage of total
Already migrated	8020	28.62
Less than 3 months	5174	18.46
Between 3 and 6 months	899	3.21
Between 6 and 10 months	759	2.71
More than 10 months	13 169	47.00
Total	28 021	100.00

Source: Calculated from field survey data.

In Jiangsu Province, more than 47 per cent of the rural population has migrated to urban areas, and 11 per cent of the population returns home less than three months each year; the number of rural residents who are considered to have migrated to an urban area has reached more than 58 per cent and more than 37 per cent of the population stays at home for more than 10 months per year. The number of persons leaving home between three and 10 months a year is small—just more than 4 per cent of the total. There is a rather similar distribution of residence status in Sichuan, where the number of population left home is roughly short by 9 percentage points, while the number staying at home is about 6 percentage points more than that in Jiangsu. In comparison, the proportions of those who have migrated are relatively smaller in Anhui, Hunan and Henan, at about one-quarter, one-third and one-fifth of the level in Jiangsu respectively, with the proportions of population staying at home greater by 13–19 percentage points (Table 11.3).

Table 11.3 Residency Status by Province (per cent)

Time staying at home	Jiangsu	Anhui	Hunan	Henan	Sichuan	Total
Already migrated	47.31	12.48	16.69	9.16	38.51	28.62
Less than 3 months	11.04	24.73	26.30	24.24	14.56	18.46
Between 3 and 6 months	1.9	3.06	3.85	6.44	1.98	3.21
Between 6 and 10 months	2.37	2.79	2.88	4.13	1.73	2.71
More than 10 months	37.39	56.94	50.29	56.02	43.22	47.00
Total	100	100	100.00	100	100	100.00

Source: Calculated from field survey data.

From comparison of the residence status among the five provinces, the rate of rural–urban migration is dependent on economic development due to associated opportunity costs, including the financial costs directly incurred during the migration process, and the human and social capital required for looking for appropriate employment.

The actual speed of migration at any time is partly determined by the gender and age structure of the remaining population. Given total rural population, ageing indicates fewer people seeking migration opportunities hence less mobility of the population. In order to understand past demographic dynamics in relation to rural–urban migration and, more importantly, to understand the future trend, it is necessary to know the demographic structure of the rural population (Figure 11.2).

Figure 11.2 Rural Demographic Structures by Residence Status

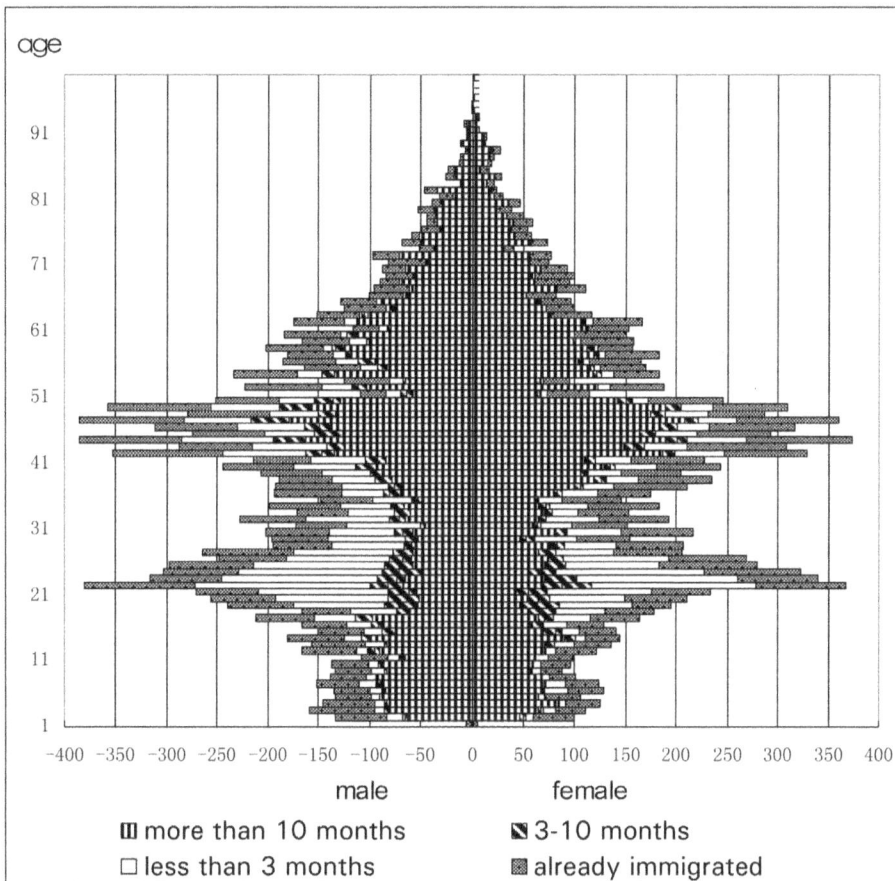

Figure 11.2 Rural Demographic Structures by Residence Status

Source: Calculated from field survey data.

The data show that most of the 'permanent' rural population who live in home villages more than 10 months a year are either elderly or youngsters with a dependency ratio close to 0.42; the proportions of the 'left-home' population are quite high among those aged sixteen to fifty, peaking about the group of those aged twenty, and declining afterwards; and the ratio of women staying at home is relatively higher, and increasing with age.

If migrants are excluded from the data, the relationship between age and working place is higher. Seasonal migration is common in China from the age of sixteen and increases with age. By age twenty-five, only about one-quarter of the rural population still lives in home villages more than 10 months a year, while the proportion staying home less than three months is as high as 60 per cent. The ratio of seasonal migration declines after age thirty, but even for those aged over fifty, more than 30 per cent of the rural population is still temporarily moving between rural and urban areas.

Demographic Structure of the Rural Labour Force

For agricultural production, the demographic structure of the remaining rural labour force, especially those primarily engaged in agriculture, is more important than that of the total population with formal rural registration status. There are two steps in presenting a clear picture of the status of the remaining rural labour force and its employment distribution. The first step is to clarify who is considered as a remaining, or permanent, rural worker, and to draw the demographic structure of such a rural labour force. Following international standards,[2] age groups between sixteen and sixty-five are taken as criteria to clarify the labour force. Further, only those who stay home for more than 10 months a year are considered 'remaining' or 'permanent' rural workers. The data from our survey are summarised in Table 11.4.

Table 11.4 Demographic Structure of Permanent Labour Force

Age	Male (persons)	Female (persons)	Total (persons)	Male (%)	Female (%)	Total (%)	Gender ratio (female = 100)
16–25	610	602	1212	6.57	6.49	13.06	101.33
26–35	575	667	1242	6.20	7.19	13.39	86.21
36–45	1094	1434	2528	11.79	15.45	27.24	76.29
46–55	1130	1295	2425	12.18	13.96	26.13	87.26
55–65	972	900	1872	10.48	9.70	20.17	108.00
Total	4381	4898	9279	47.21	52.79	100.00	89.44

Source: Calculated from field survey data.

It is shown that, if staying home more than 10 months and being aged between sixteen and sixty-five are taken as the criteria for the sub-sample, aged and female participation become more important parts of the permanent rural labour force. The absolute number of the permanent rural labour force in either the sixteen–twenty-five or the twenty-six–thirty-five age groups is about half that for older age groups and the gender ratio is significantly biased towards females.

A further step is to discompose employment structure among the permanent rural labour force, and a preliminary picture is shown in Table 11.5.

---

2 There are slight differences in defining working age, or the economically active age, among countries and organisations. For example, the International Labor Organisation statistics for the economically active population (ILO 2011) cover age groups from fifteen–sixty-five and over, which are similar to the same standards used in many countries. China has a formal retirement age based on gender and occupation in urban sectors, but this is not applied to farmers, and the legal age to start work is set at sixteen, so the working age is taken as being between sixteen and sixty-five in this chapter.

Table 11.5 Employment Structure of Permanent Labour Force

Age	Farm		Non-farm		Both		No-work		Total	
	No.	%	No.	%	No.	%	No.	%	No.	%
16–25	154	1.66	240	2.59	458	0.49	360	3.88	1212	13.06
26–35	286	3.08	268	2.89	633	0.68	55	0.59	1242	13.39
36–45	881	9.49	260	2.80	1322	1.42	65	0.70	2528	27.24
46–55	967	10.42	164	1.77	1202	1.30	92	0.99	2425	26.13
55–65	908	9.79	67	0.72	725	0.78	172	1.85	1872	20.17
Total	3196	34.44	999	10.77	4340	4.68	744	8.02	9279	100.00

Source: Calculated from field survey data.

By comparing Table 11.4 and Table 11.5, it is clear that ageing is an even more serious problem in agricultural production than in the rural economy as a whole. Among the 3196 permanent rural workers primarily engaged in farm work, only 154 persons were aged sixteen–twenty-five and 286 persons were aged twenty-six–thirty-five—about one-sixth or one-third of that for older age groups, respectively. The situation is a little better in terms of the numbers working in both the farm and the non-farm sectors, but the figures for younger generations are still significantly lower than those for older generations. If such a structure is maintained, even without further out-migration of young farmers, the total number of those in the rural labour force primarily engaged in agriculture will sharply decline in 20–30 years when those currently aged over thirty-five retire or die.

Custody Status of 'Left-at-Home' Children

According to our survey, about 28 per cent of rural residents have left home with all members of their families; there were no so-called 'left-at-home' children for those families. For those who have not left with their whole family, about 20 per cent of children under the age of fifteen are staying home less than 10 months a year, possibly going out with their parents (or one of the parents) seasonally. Education and other welfare issues exist for these children too but they are not classified as left-at-home children.

In the sample covered by our survey, there are 3169 rural children under the age of fifteen staying at home for more than 10 months a year. About half the total, 1595 children, are living with both parents at home. The remaining 1574 children are categorised as 'left at home': 685 with mothers alone, 54 with fathers alone, 815 with one or more grandparents, and 20 in the custody of other persons. Detailed custody information of those children staying at home for more than 10 months a year, including regional variations, is listed in Table 11.6.

Table 11.6 Custody Status of Rural Children by Province (per cent)

Custodians	Jiangsu	Anhui	Hunan	Henan	Sichuan	Total
Parents	40.63	47.98	50.00	53.43	64.36	50.33
Mother	25.19	22.94	16.15	28.52	7.13	21.62
Father	2.78	2.10	1.55	0.96	0.84	1.70
Grandparents	29.87	26.17	32.08	16.85	27.67	25.72
Others	1.52	0.81	0.22	0.24	0.00	0.63
Total	100.00	100.00	100.00	100.00	100.00	100.00

Source: Calculated from field survey data.

Table 11.6 indicates that the percentage of children in the custody of both parents reaches its lowest level of 41 per cent in Jiangsu, and then increases to 48 per cent in Anhui, 50 per cent in Hunan, 53 per cent in Henan and 64 per cent in Sichuan. This regional difference might suggest a relationship between the decision to work outside and that of child care. As the destinations of outgoing migrant workers are concentrated in the south-east coastal regions, the distance between the working place and home is much further for farmers from Sichuan compared with those from the other four provinces. The travel costs will be much higher for Sichuan farmers, not only because of the distance but also because of geographic conditions, so seasonal migrants might come back only once a year. As more and more young couples are not willing to suffer long-term separation, they tend to migrate together or stay at home together. The high proportion of single-mother custody in Jiangsu, Anhui and Henan could be explained by the same reason: with better job opportunities in nearby locations, the husbands might commute between working places and home more frequently, hence the suffering of separation is largely reduced.

Summary and Policy Implications

The above is an analysis of demographic structure in rural China based on a survey conducted in the winter of 2010–11 covering five provinces with a large rural population and a large proportion of rural–urban migration. While in-depth study is yet to be formulated and carried out, some preliminary results can be summarised.

Rural–Urban Migration Will Continue, but the Speed Will Reduce

The rural population pyramid (Figure 11.1) indicates that the gap in the pyramid is getting larger with an extended cycle, and the number of children under the age of fifteen is about 30 per cent less than that for those in the twenty-five–forty age group. As a result, even as the One Child Policy is phased out in the near future, the number of annual births might not exceed the current level, so the rural population will shrink purely due to lower birth rates.

The current rural demographic structure (Figure 11.2) further indicates that most young people have at least seasonally migrated (80 per cent about the age of twenty). As young urban migrants are eager to settle down with their whole families, more children will move out before reaching working age. As the number of children under age fifteen is smaller than the number of those in the older generation, a further reduction of this number could lead to lower migration levels by those of working age.

Due to demographic dynamics, rural–urban migration will continue in the near future, while the speed might reduce significantly; however, if measured by official statistics, the index of urbanisation might significantly increase in the next 20–30 years, even without large-scale rural–urban migration. The reason is simple: ageing in rural China. As the population ages due to the out-migration of young generations—pine-shaped, and possibly mushroom or umbrella-shaped—the rural population will dramatically shrink when all those elderly pass away. Urbanisation will appear to progress as the number of rural residents reduces by more than half in 20–30 years, but it will be mainly due to demographic changes and not an increase in migration.

The Number of Agricultural Workers Ageing Will Continue to Increase Rapidly and then Decline Sharply

Table 11.5 indicates that, among those engaged mainly in agricultural production, the number in the twenty-six–thirty-five age group is only about one-third that for the thirty-six–forty-five, forty-six–fifty-five and fifty-six–sixty-five age groups. The same number is even smaller for the sixteen–twenty-five age cohort: only about one-sixth. There is no reason to expect that children under the age of fifteen will participate in agriculture in greater numbers than the older generation when grown up. On the contrary, the number of children permanently staying at home is already below that for the older generation currently, and is likely to reduce further as more parents settle in urban areas.

In general, looking at the permanent rural labour force engaged mainly in agriculture, the age structure looks like a spindle with a tail at the bottom. As the elderly leave employment and youngsters move out, the 'spindle' will become thinner and thinner, with the top shrinking much faster. As a result, the ageing of the agricultural labour force could speed up, followed by a sharp decline in the total number of those aged twenty–thirty years.

Decisions Regarding Migration Interact with Those Regarding Child Care

Table 11.6 suggests that the issue of left-at-home children is interrelated with off-farm job opportunities. If off-farm jobs are easily accessible in nearby regions, more children will be left at home with a single parent. Otherwise, more children will be taken with both parents or both parents will stay at home. The figures in Table 11.6 are, however, in percentage terms, and provide only a comparison of custody status for children staying at home for more than 10 months a year among the five provinces covered by the study. One cannot directly infer the percentage of children left-at-home and its relationship with out-migration decisions.

Nevertheless, the relationship between child care and out-migration suggested by such a comparison is still important as it raises some interesting yet inconclusive issues looking into the future. If the local economy in Sichuan and other inland provinces is to be boosted by the Western Development Strategy,[3] will more children in western regions be left at home as off-farm jobs are increasingly available nearby? Or, will more children move out with their parents instead? In either case, the movement of children will have some important implications for future development in social security and service systems.

Finally, the above analysis opens up a lot of issues for further study. For example, one could apply the collected data containing gender and age information of the rural population to more rigorous demographic models, systematically simulating and projecting future trends of rural population along with its changing structure. The same data could also be applied to study the timing of each migrant moving out for the first time, re-establishing models of rural–urban migration and systematically simulating and projecting future trends of the migration; to establish a model to explain the relationship between

---

3 The Western Development Strategy was first formally raised in the Tenth Five-Year Plan (People's Congress of China 2001), aiming to speed up economic development in the vast western regions with greater allocations of the state budget, along with induced funds from other sectors directed to infrastructure and other investment. More detailed investment plans submitted by the State Development and Reform Commission were approved by the State Council in 2007 and 2012.

the general welfare status of left-at-home children and the employment of their parents; and to explain the different trends of ageing among provinces, and identifying the potential economic and social factors impacting on the ageing status.

References

Chen, X., Yiyang, C. and Jianjun, Z., 2011, 'An analysis of rural population ageing's effect on agricultural output in China', *Chinese Journal of Population Science*, no. 2, pp. 39–46.

Department of Population and Employment Statistics of National Bureau of Statistics of China, 2010, *China Population and Employment Statistical Yearbook 2010*, China Statistics Press, Beijing.

Huang, P., 1999, 'When young farmers leave the land', in C. Lindqvist et al. (eds), *Globalization and Its Impact*, FRN, Stockholm.

International Labor Organisation (ILO), 2011, *ILO Estimates and Projections of the Economically Active Population: 1990–2020*, October, [Sixth edition], International Labor Organisation, Geneva, <http://laborsta.ilo.org/applv8/data/EAPEP/v6/ILO_EAPEP_methodology_2011.pdf>

National Bureau of Statistics of China (NBS), 2010, *China Statistical Yearbook 2010*, China Statistics Press, Beijing.

People's Congress of China, 2001, *Outline of the 10th Five-Year Plan of National Economic and Social Development*, Approved by the Fourth Plenary Session of the Ninth National People's Congress of China, Beijing, 18 March 2001, <http://ghs.miit.gov.cn/n11293472/n11294974/n11296707/n11640313.files/n11754020.pdf>

Rozelle, S., Taylor, J. E. and de Brauw, A., 1999, 'Migration, remittances and agricultural productivity in China', *American Economic Review*, vol. 89, no. 2, pp. 287–91.

12. Building Social Welfare in China:

Providing retirement incomes in a transforming economy

Andrew Watson

Introduction

Rapid growth and structural reforms since 1978 have transformed the economic and social basis of China's welfare system. A sedentary population serviced through the unit of employment has been replaced with a mobile labour force, a market economy and greater reliance on user-pays principles. Until the 1980s, China's welfare provision was based on the planned economy model, whereby the employer was responsible for all aspects of the employee's welfare, including old-age retirement income. In urban areas this revolved around the work unit—be it enterprise or government organisation—and in the countryside the people's communes provided for their members (Dixon 1981). Once the market reforms were introduced, such a system could no longer be sustained. Labour became mobile, enterprises became profit oriented, the people's communes disappeared and the sources of poverty and disadvantage changed. China thus faced the need to rebuild its welfare system by creating services that are more standardised across society as a whole, are accessible to all citizens, are linked to the government's budget and are operated through specialised service providers. In effect, the work unit could no longer supply employees and retirees with the full range of housing, medical, welfare and retirement benefits that had been the norm. China had to build a social welfare system with the familiar range of services found in market economies: unemployment benefits, health insurance, work injury cover, maternity support and old-age retirement incomes.

Alongside its role in maintaining social justice, equity and stability, the provision of social welfare can be seen both as a basic safety net to provide *ex-post* support to citizens in need and as developmental to provide *ex-ante* preparation for the challenges created by structural economic change (Cook et al. 2003). In other words, by providing citizens with the resources to withstand shocks and build resilience, it can help cushion the adjustments that rapid growth and structural economic change bring and sustain the human resources needed for new growth. In China's case, the development of an equitable and reliable social welfare system can also be seen as a small but important part of the effort to rebalance the economy away from its high investment and high savings rates towards greater consumption and greater income equity.

This brief study will first review a number of reasons why the development of a new social security system is a critical part of rebalancing and sustaining growth in China over the next phase of economic development. It then focuses on the issue of old-age retirement incomes and discusses the choice of model, the evolution of policy and the current operation of the system. It will conclude with a few comments on the lessons to be drawn and the challenges for further development.

The Underlying Challenges

In market economies, social security is a form of risk sharing and of managing market failures. It creates social equity and stability by ensuring basic incomes and services for citizens in need. It redistributes income across sectors and generations. In China's case, the planned economy model sought to achieve that within the unit of employment, with the result that the levels of service obtained by individuals depended on the resources available to their unit. A commune in a poor area had little to offer its farmers; one in a rich area could ensure a better quality of life. A well-endowed state enterprise could provide quality housing and retirement incomes. An inefficient and low-income factory had much less to offer. The shift to a market system with a large private sector inevitably required China to make the transition from a unit-based system to a socialised and government-managed system. Since the mid-1980s, therefore, China's social security system has gradually evolved towards local pooling of social security funds at county and urban levels and then towards higher levels of regional and national integration (Saunders and Shang 2001; Wang 2001:3–12). In that process, a number of key issues have emerged as drivers of the need to build an integrated national system.

First, there is the contradiction between labour market integration and the operation of a social security system based on place of employment and locality. The latter was originally designed for a sedentary population, with resources allocated through the bureaucratic distribution system. Economic reforms liberated the labour force and required labour flexibility and mobility in order to respond to changing market and production conditions. The most obvious sign of this has been the emergence since the 1980s of the huge flow of rural-to-urban migration. Though their mobility makes it difficult to produce accurate and reliable statistics, it was reported that in 2011 there were about 252 million such 'farmer-workers' in China, consisting of 94 million who were working in off-farm enterprises in their locality and 158 million who had migrated elsewhere (SSB 2012). Their contribution to economic growth and structural change has been huge, but because of their rural household registration they are excluded from the urban social security system (Watson 2009). The fact that they can slip between the two categories adds to the complexity of designing social security systems for them. This problem of mobility, however, is not exclusive to migrants. The creation of urban social security pools helped share obligations and create mobility at the local level, but residents seeking to move between cities and provinces still face the challenge of transferring their social security registration and entitlements between different pool areas. In effect, by forming an obstacle to the flexible movement of labour, the social security system has risked becoming a barrier to further structural change.

A second issue requiring urgent change to the social security system is the ageing of the population. The need to provide retirement pensions, health care for the old and other support services for the ageing has long been a major challenge for public policy and social security systems in most developed economies. China's rapid social and economic changes combined with its family planning policies have meant that it has entered the phase of demographic transition to an ageing society much more rapidly than most countries (Wang 2011). According to estimates by the United Nations (UN 2011a:103), the Chinese population aged over sixty was nearly 12.8 per cent in 2010 and will grow to 33.9 per cent in 2050, and remain at more than 34 per cent by 2100. The same study (UN 2011b:327) estimates a rising dependency ratio from 12.7 per cent in 2010 to 18.4 per cent in 2020 and 40.1 per cent in 2040. Whatever the reliability of such estimates— and work by others has suggested that previous UN calculations might be underestimates (Zhao and Guo 2007)—even if population policies were to change today, the demographic momentum implies that the era of a plentiful, young workforce is coming to an end, the ratio of old to young will increase and the proportion of working-age people able to support the old will decline. This reality means that the design and implementation of an effective social security system and especially a set of policies to provide for old-age retirement incomes have become urgent priorities. Failure to prepare now would create a huge fiscal burden for the government in the future.

The issue of funding social security is thus another urgent challenge facing China's social security reform. Furthermore, while many aspects of social security such as unemployment, work injury, maternity and health are needed for only specific periods for each individual and can be managed through forms of insurance, the provision of old-age retirement incomes is something that lasts over many years and requires both a period of accumulation before retirement in order to prepare for the post-retirement obligation and a period of payout until death. In an ageing society, where the declining numbers of young are no longer able to pay for the growing numbers of the old while at the same time saving for their own ageing, the need to make financial preparations is obvious. If the government decides to rely on paying pensions from fiscal revenue, the fiscal burdens become substantial. Furthermore, if accumulation through contributory insurance or superannuation schemes is adopted, the design has to be reliable and transparent, and the accumulated contributions have to be able to preserve and grow value. What is more, the total amount of funds in such schemes for a large population will be very large. They can provide a significant growth of capital resources and can play an important role in capital markets. They also require strong regulatory mechanisms to ensure the safety of the accumulation.

Finally, a further important dimension for the development of social security systems in China is their role in helping economic rebalancing. The need to rebalance China's economic growth model has long been recognised (Dollar 2007; Kuijs and Wang 2006; Pettis 2011). Growing income and regional inequalities, heavy reliance on investment in export manufacturing, a declining share of consumption and wages, high savings rates with low financial returns to savers and poor social security systems have all been identified as indicators of a need to change. A shift towards higher levels of wages and domestic consumption, increased growth of the service sector and small enterprises, and better social welfare are all seen as part of this process. Within that context, the introduction of a more equitable and accessible social security system would not only generate better social welfare outcomes, but would also reduce the need for individual saving, help increase the consumption of the disadvantaged and contribute to the redistribution of income.

Given these factors, it is not surprising that the development of social security has emerged as a key policy goal for the Chinese Government. Opinion surveys show that it has also become a major issue of concern for the average citizen (*China Daily*, 22 February 2011). While, as discussed below, the political economy is complex and implementation has faced many challenges, the issue has received a lot of attention in leaders' speeches over the past 10 years, and was given considerable prominence in the Twelfth Five-Year Plan (Xinhua 2011). The *Government Work Report* delivered by Wen Jiabao at the National People's Congress (NPC) on 5 March 2012 claimed that significant expansion of the system was taking place.

The administration of China's social security is entrusted to the Social Insurance Administration (SIA), a public service unit under the Ministry of Human Resources and Social Security (MOHRSS). The SIA has a hierarchy of bureaus at central, provincial, urban and county levels, each of which manages their local social insurance pools. It is responsible for drafting and implementing legislation and for the management and regulation of the system. In October 2010, the NPC approved the Social Insurance Law, which had been in preparation for a number of years, and it was implemented on 1 July 2011 (NPC 2010). The overall model is based on contributory insurance and covers health, unemployment, work injury, maternity and old-age insurance. Against this overall background, this study now turns to examine the old-age insurance system, which because of its complexity provides clear insights into the challenges faced.

The Choice of Model for Old-Age Retirement Incomes

For many years, international economic institutions such as the World Bank, the Asian Development Bank (ADB) and the Organisation for Economic Cooperation and Development (OECD) have devoted considerable resources to studying the policy choices facing governments in providing for the old (World Bank 1994; World Bank and OECD 2008). They have supported policy-related research in many countries. These studies suggest that the key policy choices for old-age retirement incomes are

- the extent to which the state should provide for the old
- the extent to which individuals should provide for themselves
- the target levels of retirement income to be achieved
- the merits of 'pay-as-you-go' schemes, in which pensions are paid from current income, compared with 'fully funded' schemes, in which funds are accumulated from current income to pay for retirement incomes in future
- the mechanisms used to accrue funds for pension payments
- the mechanisms for the distribution of benefits.

In most countries, models of 'pay-as-you-go' schemes that provide the old with a defined benefit from current revenue are giving way to defined contribution schemes, in which contributions from employers and individuals are accumulated during their working life in order to provide the retirement incomes. In other words, what a person will get in retirement will depend on what is saved and will not be a defined proportion of final salary paid from current revenue after retirement. This trend has driven retirement income reform in Australia and many European countries.

Associated challenges include pressures to increase the retirement age so that people work longer and the number of retirement years is reduced, equalising retirement ages for men and women, and closing existing defined benefit schemes whereby retirees are entitled to a defined benefit as a proportion of their final salary. These last schemes are common for public service workers and government employees and tend to be pay-as-you-go schemes funded from fiscal revenue.

Overall, the consensus in market economies focuses on building a three-pillar model.

1. *A state pension.* This generally gives a low level of income paid from fiscal revenue. It provides a basic safety net for those who do not have enough accumulation or income from other sources.

2. *A compulsory contributory scheme.* Such schemes are funded by contributions from employers and/or employees. The contributions are paid into an accumulation account held in each member's name and are eventually paid out after retirement in the form of annuity insurance or superannuation.

3. *A voluntary contributory scheme.* Individuals are encouraged to supplement the compulsory scheme by contributing more of their own funds to their retirement savings. Such schemes may also attract tax concessions or incentives from the state.

The aim of this model is to increase individual accumulation for old age and to reduce the burden on state revenue, especially in a context in which an ageing society means that there are declining numbers of people of working age paying taxes to support the old.

As discussed above, China's planned economy model was essentially a defined benefit scheme that operated at the unit of employment level. People's benefits thus varied by location and employment, with a major difference between the urban and the rural systems. During the reform period, the need for change was shaped by the key drivers listed above, and it has resulted in a move towards defined contribution schemes that embody the principles of the three-pillar model. This has been reflected in the transition from the unit-based system to local and regional pools and a gradual raising of the level of the pool from county and town to province, with the eventual goal of creating an integrated national scheme.

As yet, there is no *first pillar* in the form of a state pension, and a basic social safety net is provided by the guaranteed minimum income scheme launched in 1993 and operated through the Ministry of Civil Affairs. The extent of coverage is, however, patchy, especially in rural areas, there is considerable regional variation, and studies suggest it is not yet very effective (Chen et al. 2006; Tang 2012). The *second pillar* is provided by a combination of the basic urban old-age insurance for enterprise employees, the new rural pension plan that was introduced in 2010 and is gradually spreading across the countryside, and the other emerging schemes for unemployed and self-employed urban residents. Public servants for the moment continue to receive defined benefit pensions paid from government revenue that are generous and indexed for wage increases (Chen 2008), but mooted reforms to public service units indicate that these might also eventually be changed into defined contribution schemes as well. The *third pillar* is left to the individual and to enterprise annuity schemes voluntarily established by employers.

The Evolution of Policy

As noted above, during the early phase of economic reform in the 1980s, China's unit-based system of social security gave way to a social pooling system based on county or urban administrations that brought the obligations of the local state-owned enterprises within an administrative area together. By the mid-1990s, as the urban reforms intensified, state-owned enterprises were reformed, merged or closed and the market and private economy grew, any remnants of the old model became unsustainable. There was no accumulated provision to fund pension obligations, and the ratio of pensions to wages was increasing (Zhao et al. 2006). In loss-making state enterprises, it was no longer possible to guarantee a fixed percentage of an individual's final wage as a pension, and the government had to look for alternative ways to smooth income over time in order to provide for peoples' old age. Given the growing number of people dependent on pensions, the ageing of the population underlined the urgent need for change. After 1990, therefore, China began to develop a new set of policies.

Between 1991 and 1998, the government progressively elaborated a system of basic old-age insurance for enterprise employees (Wang 2001, 2002:4–9; Zhao et al. 2006). Employers were required to pay the equivalent of a percentage of the wage into the old-age insurance fund and the individual worker also contributed a percentage. These two elements created the common social pool and the individual account. These developments were extended in August 1998 in the decision to work towards raising social pooling to provincial level and to merge 11 existing industry-based pension funds into the social insurance pools (SC 1998). Subsequently, regulations and decisions sought to clarify the management of the system and its requirements and entitlements, to increase the level of contributions to 20 per cent from the employer and 8 per cent from the employee, and to enable self-employed people to join (SC 2005). Ultimately, the basic principles of the scheme were incorporated into the Social Insurance Law of the People's Republic of China (NPC 2010) and further refinements were introduced to bring in migrant workers and to make transfers between pool areas by people with urban household registration easier (Watson 2009).

An important aspect of this process, however, was that existing retirees or those close to retirement were brought in as members, even though they did not bring any accumulated contributions with them. The funds thus had to cover old members (with 'empty accounts' and no accumulation), middle members (with partial accumulation) and new members (those making full contributions from the time of joining) (Wang 2005). There was thus an unfunded obligation that threatened funds with deficits and created pressures on local governments to defend their pools.

Because this scheme was designed for enterprise employees, unemployed urban residents did not have access to it. The State Council recognised this in its 2000 policy document on improving the urban welfare system, when it called for special provisions for such people (SC 2000). Given the difficulty that residents would have in paying both the pool levy and the individual payment, it was necessary to develop a different scheme for this category of people. Consequently, experiments began with establishing pensions through an insurance scheme based on individual contributions and government subsidies. These schemes paralleled the emerging new rural pension plan discussed below, and a number of cities introduced combined provisions for unemployed urban residents and for local landless farmers who had been displaced by urban expansion (Chen and Li 2012; State Council 2011; Yang 2012).

The rural system was much slower to replace the old collective structures. Until the recent innovations, rural social welfare continued to rely primarily on what the village or individual could provide. Initially there were a number of local experiments that attempted to provide insurance cover for farmers and, after central guidelines were issued in 1992, some provinces and localities introduced contributory old-age insurance schemes run by the Ministry of Civil Affairs (Luo and Lü 2006; Song 2008:436–8; Su 2009:53–61; Zhao et al. 2002:120–33). Collectively known as the 'old rural pension plan', these experiments suffered from reliance on individual contributions, low rates of return, poor administration and combined government and commercial operation with the associated high risks. It was estimated that by the end of 1997 they covered only about 80 million farmers, and the schemes subsequently tended to languish.

Given the increasing urban–rural inequalities, the lack of welfare provisions for farmers and the decline of rural family support systems with the growth of rural-to-urban migration, the need to improve the scheme was becoming increasingly urgent. In 2007 the Central Government re-emphasised the need to develop a rural pension system (Institute of Economics, Chinese Academy of Social Sciences 2010:353). At its Seventeenth Congress in 2007, the Chinese Communist Party (CCP) called for 'exploring the establishment of a rural old-age insurance system', and in October 2008 proposed building 'a new rural pension system requiring a combination of individual contributions, collective subsidies and government subsidies'. This statement established the principle of direct government fiscal support for the rural scheme. The new national system was formally announced in August 2009, with trial implementation to begin in 10 per cent of counties in 2010 and national coverage to be achieved by 2020 (SC 2009). In practice, however, the scheme expanded rapidly and, by March 2012, Premier, Wen Jiabao, stated in the *Government Work Report* to the National People's Congress that trials of the system operated in 60 per cent of counties and embraced some 358 million people, of whom nearly 99 million received pensions. While, as discussed below, the level of benefit is not high and there are many challenges of implementation, this new rural pension plan marks a substantial development in rural welfare policy.

The other major group that had to be addressed in the development of old-age insurance policy was the rural-to-urban migrant workers (for a full discussion of the issues below, see Watson 2009). Since the basic urban system was built around one's place of household registration, migrant workers were excluded because of their rural registration; however, including those in township and village enterprises, there are now about 252 million of them, and they make up the major proportion of the total manufacturing workforce. They are characterised by relative youth (average age about twenty-nine), high mobility, low incomes and a high proportion of informal employment. Apart from the basic obstacle created by their household registration, there are a number of systemic and political economy challenges to bringing them within the basic urban system. Their mobility conflicts with the fragmented structure of the social pooling system and with regulations that require 15 years' contributions with the final five years to be in the same location. There are many technical and administrative difficulties of managing interregional transfers of registration. There is resistance from employers who are unwilling to increase their labour costs by paying social insurance. And local governments are happy to use any social contributions made on the migrants' behalf to bolster their pool funds and counteract implied deficits but reluctant to allow these contributions to be transferred out when the migrants move on. As a result, a major segment of the young workforce has been excluded from basic insurance at a time when they are most able to contribute.

Initially, some areas experimented with allowing migrants to join local schemes or established special programs of their own (Han 2009:480–2; Liu and Xu 2008:209–43). Eventually, however, the need to provide social security services for migrants and to combat discrimination against them was recognised at the national level. Document Five in 2006 called for a comprehensive review of migrant issues and for the establishment of an old-age insurance scheme to suit their needs (SC 2006). Subsequently, the Ministry of Human Resources and Social Security issued a discussion draft of a separate scheme for migrants that allowed for lower levels of contribution and greater flexibility of transfers. Plans to develop this scheme, however, were rapidly overtaken by the introduction of the new rural pension plan. The proposed separate migrant worker scheme implied increased fragmentation of the social insurance system. It seemed that migrants might eventually have the choice of joining the basic urban scheme, the special migrants' scheme or the rural pension plan. The administrative complexity of managing transfers between several schemes also loomed large. In the face of these challenges, the decision was made in late 2009 to require the migrants to join the basic urban scheme, to have the right to transfer back to the rural pension plan if they wished and to improve the mechanisms for the transfer of social security registration between pool areas. Subsequently, the policy focus shifted to developing mechanisms for managing the migrants' transition to the integrated urban scheme, for making membership transfers between the rural and urban schemes and for the transfer of registration between pool areas.

This discussion of the process of policy development has illustrated the two interlinked features that have dominated the development of China's social welfare. The first is that the reforms have been profoundly shaped by the inheritance of the plan period. The second is that the new system is fragmented by location and by category. The division between urban and rural welfare based on household registration has continued to have a profound influence, and the practice of different categories of people in different localities obtaining different types of access and benefits remains embedded within the operation of local pools. The overall framework thus maintains separate systems for enterprise employees, migrants, non-employed residents, farmers and government employees. It is perhaps inevitable that a transitional system has to build on pre-existing practices and expectations. As in many other aspects of the gradual reform process, therefore, the political economy of the existing set of vested interests, understandings and obligations has made it difficult to sweep everything aside and start again. The result, however, is that the social security system remains fragmented by place and by employment status, and this is the core challenge facing its evolution.

The Operation of the System and its Challenges

Social insurance policies are implemented through the SIA. This has a hierarchy of offices from central to local levels at provincial, urban, county and district offices. As is common in the Chinese system, professional management comes through the ministerial hierarchy but local government handles the administrative responsibilities. Each level has its Social Security Bureau, which manages the registration of members and the operation of the insurance. It has service centres that deal with both employers and members. Membership requires the employer to register the employee. After registration, the monthly contributions due from the employer and employee are calculated by the social security department and collected from the employer, who deducts the employee amount from the wage. The contributions are paid to the bureaus (in some localities the payments are made to the tax bureaus but the records are kept by the social security system). The funds are placed in a special account operated through the fiscal offices and subject to strict and conservative management rules in an effort to ensure their security. In this context, it is important to recognise that the definition of 'local' is complex. Enterprises register their employees at the level at which they operate. A provincial-level enterprise would register with the provincial bureau and an urban one at the urban level. The bureaus manage the collection of funds and the distribution of benefits.

During the 1990s, much of the record-keeping and administration was on paper, but the elaboration of the system required substantial improvement in management and information systems and in computerisation. This is an inevitable precondition for the introduction of an integrated national system. In 1999, the ministry began to introduce social security cards, and these now operate as smart cards in the more developed regions. In 2002, when the government announced a major drive to develop information systems for government, the Jinbao Project was launched to build up information technology (IT) for social security (State Council 2002). This project is operated by the MOHRSS. It aims to be a single, integrated platform with two sections: one for social security and one for employment. It operates at three levels: central, provincial and urban. The system includes the development of computerised systems for providing services, internal management, fund management and access for individuals to consult their own records through the Internet. Since computer systems are not yet nationally standardised and links between regional databases are still developing, there is some distance to go before a truly integrated system can be built. These technical challenges are also magnified by disparities in the capacity of local administrations; however, considerable investment is taking place and the infrastructure to enable an integrated national system is emerging.

The operation of the *basic urban old-age insurance scheme* is straightforward, though there can be much local variation in the details. Employers and employees contribute at a rate of 20 per cent and 8 per cent of the wage respectively. The employer contribution goes to the local social pool and the employee contribution goes to the individual account. Individuals are able to apply for a monthly pension after reaching the retirement age (currently fifty-five for women and sixty for men). The pension has two parts: the social pool payment and the individual account payment. The social pool payment is set at 60 per cent of the local social average wage, provided there has been a minimum of 15 years' contributions, with the last five being continuous in the pool area. This payment is therefore based on the local average and not on the actual wage of the individual. It is adjusted over time to take account of wage changes. The individual account payment depends on the amount of accumulation in the individual account. It is paid at a monthly rate of 1/139 of the total accumulation (that is, it assumes an actuarial life of 139 months after retirement). Overall, the scheme has a number of characteristics that add to its complexity and underline its fragmented structure at the current stage of development.

1. While national integration is the long-term goal, it is not yet operated as a unified system but as a set of parallel local pools. These are managed as separate funds and can have their own specific features, such as variations to the national standards, depending on local average wages, and extra subsidies depending on the strength of local finances. As a result, the levels of contributions and benefits will vary by location. Although a growing number of provinces are developing provincial-level pooling, in practice many pools remain at city or county level. Transfers of contributions and benefits between cities and regions thus present problems.

2. The coexistence of the common social pool and the individual account means that the two elements are managed separately. Local authorities see the social pool as a local resource and rely on it to ensure that they can meet their obligations to their members. They therefore have an incentive to retain as much of it as they can when an individual moves to employment in a different pool area. This pressure was recognised in the 2009 transfer regulations, which allow local pools to retain some 40 per cent of the employer's contribution when an employee moves elsewhere, and only 60 per cent is transferred to the destination pool.

3. This strong sense of local interest is linked to the fact that when the system was introduced in 1996, no provision was made for existing retirees or for those approaching the end of their working life. The social pools thereby inherited unfunded liabilities from the pre-existing system. Areas with lots of failing state-owned enterprises faced large deficits, whereas new-economy areas with a smaller legacy and growing new industries had a much healthier financial position.

4. The system differentiates among different categories of people. As discussed above, employees in government agencies, public welfare units and similar institutions still receive the old planned economy defined benefits pensions and do not participate in these schemes. Self-employed people may join, provided they contribute to both the pool and the individual account. Unemployed urban residents have access to a different scheme.

The above characteristics highlight the barriers the design of the scheme presents to *migrant workers*. The high individual costs relative to low incomes, the operation of local pools and barriers to portability, the lack of formal employment contracts for most migrants and the retention of enterprise contributions in the local pool all combine to mean that migrants lack incentives to join the urban scheme. Their mobility, their frequent changes of job and their employment in the informal sector add to the obstacles. Migrants cannot guarantee that they will be able to make 15 years' worth of contributions to the fund (including the required five consecutive years of contributions in the final years of employment), and it is therefore difficult for them to qualify for a retirement benefit in a particular pool area. Until 2009, these barriers to transfers between pool areas were a major challenge. As a result, when migrants were allowed to join, they could withdraw their contributions to their individual account only when they moved elsewhere. The employer's social contribution made on their behalf was retained in the local pool. In effect, these contributions helped maintain the fund balance and reduced any funding deficits for the payment of pensions to the local population. The migrants' individual account contributions represented an enforced saving of a proportion of their wages until they changed jobs, when they were allowed to withdraw it. The 2009 procedures for transfers are intended to resolve this problem by guaranteeing transfers of pool contributions, but many technical issues of implementation remain to be resolved. For employers, registering migrant workers means increasing their labour costs. For the social security system, constant movement adds to the complexity of maintaining records and managing funds. These issues are magnified for female migrants who have greater job mobility, higher levels of informal employment and more inconsistent employment records because of childrearing and family responsibilities. Not surprisingly, therefore, migrants lack incentives to join and have little faith in the system.

The 2009 regulations requiring migrants to join the urban scheme were intended to address some of these issues. The new policy required: 1) compulsory participation with no withdrawals; 2) reducing the entry threshold for migrants by allowing lower contributions; 3) maintaining sealed accounts in local pools when migrants moved; 4) establishing a national database for migrant records; 5) developing a mechanism for pooling lifetime contributions at the place of final residence; and 6) designing procedures for linking the urban scheme to the rural pension plan should the individual decide to retire back to the countryside. Designing mechanisms to implement these goals requires flexible, accurate and integrated information management systems, and good record-keeping to ensure that fund contributions are preserved in the various pools, combined and transferred to the place of final residence when the individual retires.

The *rural pension plan* mandates a minimum monthly cash pension of RMB55 to all rural residents, male and female, over the age of sixty. This payment is guaranteed by the government and funded by a combination of central, provincial and collective-level contributions. Individual farmers may join voluntarily while they are still working and make an annual payment into the scheme. If they do so, when they reach the pensionable age they become eligible to receive both the government pension and an additional monthly amount calculated at the actuarial rate of 1/139 of the total funds in their individual contribution account (that is, the same actuarial assumption as the urban scheme). As the scheme matures, it would therefore have two components like the basic urban insurance: the pension and the individual account. The difference is that in this case the basic pension is a guaranteed payment from government finances. All farmers aged sixteen and over who are not migrant workers and therefore do not belong to urban schemes are eligible to join in their home villages.

The basic design of this scheme is simple, and the payment of the government subsidy from the budget marks an important innovation in old-age income payments. This innovation has also been extended to unemployed urban residents who have a similar subsidy. There is also gender equity, since both males and females get the same pension. While the total amount of RMB55 per month per person is not large, it is in cash, which can be important in poor rural areas. There are also expectations that the pension level will rise over time.

Trial implementation of the new scheme during 2010 allowed a number of local policy variations.[1] The government subsidy was provided 100 per cent from the Central Government in the poor western provinces and 50 per cent from the centre and 50 per cent from provincial governments in the richer east. Further variations were then developed within provinces. For example, in Fujian, several ways of providing the 50 per cent local component of the subsidy were used. In poor counties, the province provided 30 per cent and required the counties to supply the remaining 20 per cent. In intermediate-level counties, the ratio became 10 per cent provincial and 40 per cent county. Rich counties had to provide the full 50 per cent themselves. In addition, if they wished, rich counties could add an amount so that the monthly pension

---

1 The following discussion draws on interviews with the Fujian Social Insurance Centre, 29 March 2010.

might be RMB10 higher than the national guideline. A further variation was in the contributory individual account amount to be paid by working farmers. The national guidelines proposed five levels from RMB100 to RMB500 per person per year. Recognising the capacity of its richer areas to accumulate more, Fujian introduced 12 levels ranging from RMB100 to RMB1200. Furthermore, to encourage farmers to join, it experimented with paying a RMB30 state subsidy to the individual account of farmers who started at the basic level. Administrative villages were also allowed to contribute an additional amount to the basic pension if they had the resources. It was therefore possible for the guaranteed pension in rich areas to be higher than the norm and for richer farmers to accumulate more in their account.

The implementation of the trial program also highlighted some of the difficulties and teething problems. Issues included

- identifying all the people who were eligible (some old farmers do not have ID cards or reliable records of their age)
- maintaining up-to-date records so that new entrants and exits through death can be accurately recorded each month
- having staff available at the basic level to manage the scheme
- enabling old people to have bank accounts through which the pension can be paid, in a context in which many old people are barely literate and many villages do not have a local financial institution
- persuading young farmers to join and ensuring that families will also pay contributions for female members
- experiments with a system of 'binding' that requires young family members to join the scheme and make contributions before their old parents can qualify for a pension, thereby changing a voluntary scheme into a compulsory one.

Practical issues of this kind can be expected as the new scheme is developed; however, it represents a major innovation for rural welfare and the rural elderly. Furthermore, the introduction of the new rural pension plan also created a challenge for migrant workers and for the operation of their old-age insurance schemes. They now face a range of choices. They may opt to join the local rural pension in their home village, to enrol in local insurance schemes for township and village employees, to enrol in any remaining special schemes for migrants in some cities or to join the basic urban scheme. They might also need to shift between these as their employment changes. The fragmentation of the schemes and the uncertainty about the differences in final outcomes for each of them makes a clear choice difficult. From the administrative point of view, maintaining reliable and accurate records of highly mobile migrants and calculating the ratios for the transfer of entitlements and benefits between schemes that operate with different standards are both very difficult. These challenges for migrant workers underline the fact that, in the long term, the need is to move towards a standard, integrated national scheme for all citizens, regardless of where they live and work.

A further key issue facing the old-age insurance system is the management of the accumulated funds. Contributory old-age insurance schemes have a lifetime of up to 60 or more years for each member in order to cover both the period of accumulation and the period of payment of benefits. Commitment to long-term participation requires trust in the security of the fund and a belief that value will be preserved and will grow. If the system is not transparent and accountable or there is a fear of corruption and misuse then support for it is low. Members also need to have access to information on the performance of the fund and their individual accounts. Given that China's transitional structure means that there are still many retirees with unfunded 'empty accounts', the security of the fund remains an issue. According to Zhao et al. (2006:55), in 1999, 26 provinces operated with a deficit and in 2001 a number of provincial fund outgoings exceeded income by close to 30 per cent. One estimate put the national shortfall between accumulation and liabilities at RMB2.5 trillion (Wang 2005:8). Another recent estimate by expert commentator Zheng Bingwen (*Dongfang Zaobao*, 16 March 2012:A30) suggested a total of RMB1.7 trillion of such empty accounts. Some studies also suggest that these figures will blow out over the next 50 years. While the reliability of such claims can be questioned, the size indicates the scale of the challenge. It is not surprising therefore that Article 56 of the Social Insurance Law states that 'the balance between income and expenditure of the social insurance funds will be realized through the budget' and that governments at the county level and above will subsidise any deficits. Furthermore, the China Social Insurance web site takes pains to underline that the empty accounts may be managed through government subsidies (CNSS 2012). In effect, the system as a whole is not yet fully funded and in many ways operates as a pay-as-you-go fund.

The amount of capital involved is substantial. In 2010, the *Renmin Ribao* reported that the current size of the social security fund was about US$130 billion and by 2015 it would grow to US$300 billion (*Renmin Ribao*, 11 April 2010). The MOHRSS reported that in 2010, total income in the old-age insurance fund was some RMB1.35 trillion (including RMB1.95 billion of fiscal subsidies) (MOHRSS 2011). These funds represent a large and growing source of capital. At present, however, fund management is very conservative and is regulated to rely only on bank deposits and government bonds. There is no investment in stocks, property or other assets. Given the many risks of corruption and misuse, these restrictions are understandable. This does, however, mean that the potential to preserve value against inflation and to grow value to match rising incomes and expectations is very limited. Not surprisingly, the ministry is now considering some experiments to improve investment performance, though the security of the funds remains a paramount concern (*China Daily*, 26 October 2011).

The above discussion has highlighted the many challenges facing the development of China's old-age insurance system. These include

- the legacies of the old system and its expectations
- the complexities of overcoming the fragmented structure
- the burdens of the transition to a fully funded scheme
- the significant improvements in the management and information systems that are needed
- the political economy of the conflicts of interests involved—the local governments, the employers, the local residents, the migrants and the different levels of government all have competing stakes in the way the system operates.

Nevertheless, the system as a whole continues to develop. Table 12.1 lists some recent statistics on the growth in membership of old-age insurance schemes, drawn from a number of sources. While the figures must, inevitably, be treated with caution, the reports indicate that the extent of coverage is growing and the system is becoming more elaborated. They also show that many people in each category are yet to become members and also that migrant workers continue to be excluded. Nevertheless, the issues are a major public concern. A web search of Chinese sources with such questions as: 'how do I claim my old-age benefits', 'can I still get medical benefits when I am drawing unemployment insurance', and so forth will yield a lot of discussion of the rules and their implementation.

While the distance between policy and implementation remains large and coverage still has many gaps, the significance of the issues facing an ageing society appears to have been recognised. As a result, the Twelfth Five-Year Plan adopted in March 2011 calls for

- all-round implementation of the rural pension plan
- further improvement of the basic urban insurance and unemployed resident insurance schemes
- realisation of provincial-level pooling
- national integration of the age funds
- realisation of better transfer and portability mechanisms
- gradual extension of the linkages between urban and rural schemes

• reform of government and public welfare enterprise pension systems.

This agenda is extensive, but failure to realise it would have major implications for China's sustainable development.

Table 12.1 Membership of Old-age Insurance Schemes (millions)

Item	2009	2010	2011
Total population	1334.7	1341	1347.4
Urban employment	311	347	359
Total number of migrant workers	230	242	253
Members of basic urban old-age insurance	235.5	257	284
Of which:			
pensioners	58	63	68.2
migrants	26.5	32.8	
Members of rural pension plan	86.9	102.8	326
Of which:			
pensioners	15.6	28.6	98.8
Members of non-employed urban residents scheme			13.34
Of which:			
pensioners			6.4

Source: Ministry of Human Resources and Social Security 2009 and 2010 Statistical Reports, Wen Jiabao's 2011 Government Work Report, March 2012 State Statistical Bureau, Annual Communiques on Economic and Social Development 2009/2010/2011.

Lessons and Conclusions

This study has outlined the main features of the development of China's social security system, and especially its old-age insurance schemes. It has emphasised the importance of these reforms for social justice and equity on the one hand and for sustaining growth and rebalancing the economy on the other. It suggests that there are a number of features that are now needed for successful and sustainable policy development in China. First, an integrated national system with equal access to all citizens is most likely to provide both social equity and efficiency of management. It would reduce barriers to labour mobility and simplify the complexities of service provision. Second, it will be important for the state to continue to provide system guarantees and to sustain a social safety net to cover retirement incomes for those who are disadvantaged or fall outside the system. Third, portability and flexibility of design and operation are essential. The system needs to be able to respond to the many adjustments that will take place in an individual's circumstances as structural economic change continues and the economic and demographic changes in an ageing society. This challenge is thrown into stark relief by the needs of migrant workers. They represent the bulk of China's young labour force and preparations for their retirement are urgently required while they are still working. Fourth, it is necessary to design ways in which accumulated funds can preserve and grow value, while at the same time reducing or offsetting the risks created by exposure to market changes. Fifth, given the different life expectations and experiences of women and men, a gender perspective is needed when policy is being designed. Otherwise, there is the prospect of a growing cohort of old but poor women. Finally, the most successful public policy development and management require open, transparent and consultative processes. Citizens need to understand and trust the system. The ways competing interests are balanced against each other need to be debated and articulated. In this way, public confidence can be built and policy can be broadly supported and implemented.

References

Chen, C. and Li, W., 2012, 'Chengzhen jumin jiben yanglao baoxian zhidu: moshi yu pingjia [The basic old-age insurance system for urban residents: an evaluation of the models]', *Shehui Baozhang Yanjiu*, no. 1, pp. 177–86.

Chen, J., 2008, 'Gongwuyuan yanglao baoxian zhidu gaige yanjiu [Research on the reform of the system of old-age insurance for public servants]', *Fuzhou Daxue Xuebao*, no. 2, pp. 59–62.

Chen, S., Ravallion, M. and Wang, Y., 2006, Di Bao: *a guaranteed minimum income in China's cities?*, World Bank Policy Research Working Paper, WPS3805, The World Bank, Washington, DC.

CNSS, 2012, 'Yanglao baoxian kongzhang 1.7 wan yi shi zenme hui shi? [What is the 1.7 trillion of empty accounts in the social insurance fund?]', CNSS, 26 March, viewed 3 April 2012, <http://www.cnss.cn/new/bjzm/xjj/201203/t20120326_252923.htm>

Cook, S., Kabeer N. and Suwannarat, G., 2003, *Social Protection in Asia*, Har-Anand Publications, New Delhi.

Dixon, J., 1981, *The Chinese Welfare System 1949–1979*, Praeger, New York.

Dollar, D., 2007, *Poverty, inequality and social disparities during China's economic reform*, World Bank Policy Research Working Paper, WPS4253, The World Bank, Washington, DC.

Han, J. (ed.), 2009, *Diaocha Zhongguo Nongcun* [Surveying the Chinese Countryside], 2 vols, Zhongguo Fazhan Chubanshe, Beijing.

Institute of Economics, Chinese Academy of Social Sciences, 2010, 'Xinxing nongcun shehui yanglao baoxian yu nongcun nüxing de xuqiu yanjiu [Research on the new rural social old-age insurance and the needs of rural women]', in Ministry of Human Resources and Social Security, *Nongmingong yanglao baoxian yanjiu chengguo huibian* [*Collection of research results on old-age insurance for migrant workers*], Reports on the China–Australia Governance Program Project, Internal Publication, September, pp. 352–72.

Kuijs, L. and Wang, T., 2006, 'China's pattern of growth: moving to sustainability and reducing inequality', *China and the World Economy*, vol. 145, no. 1, pp. 1–14.

Liu, C. and Xu, J., 2008, *Zhongguo nongminggong shiminhua jincheng yanjiu* [*Research on the Process of Urban Transformation of China's Farmer-Workers*], Renmin Chubanshe, Beijing.

Luo, Z. and Lü, J. (eds), 2006, *Nongcun Shehui: Yanglao Baoxian Shouce* [*Rural Society: Handbook on Old-age Insurance*], Zhongguo Shehui Chubanshe, Beijing.

Ministry of Human Resources and Social Security (MOHRSS), 2011, *2010 niandu renli ziyuan he shehui baozhang shiye fazhan tongji gongbao* [*2010 statistical report on the development of human resources and social insurance*], 20 July, Ministry of Human Resources and Social Security, Beijing, viewed 3 April 2012, <http://www.mohrss.gov.cn/page.do?pa=40288020240500280124088 2b84702d7&guid=e60c0ef72ddd4e8eb968ac5f11900f59&og=8a81f0842d0d 556d012d111392900038>

National People's Congress (NPC), 2010, *Zhonghua Renmin Gongheguo Shehui Baoxian Fa* [*The Social Insurance Law of the People's Republic of China*], 28 October, National People's Congress, Beijing, viewed 6 March 2012, <http://www.china.com.cn/policy/txt/2010-10/29/content_21225907.htm>

Pettis, M., 2011, 'The contentious debate over China's economic transition', *Carnegie Endowment for International Peace Policy Outlook*, 25 March, viewed 5 March 2012, <http://www.relooney.info/SI_FAO-Asia/0_Important_42.pdf>

Saunders, P. and Shang X., 2001, 'Social security reform in China's transition to a market economy', *Social Policy and Administration*, vol. 35, no. 3, pp. 274–89.

Song, H. (ed.), 2008, *Zhongguo Nongcun Gaige Sanshi Nian* [*Thirty Years of Rural Reform in China*], Zhongguo Nongye Chubanshe, Beijing.

State Council of China (SC), 1998, *Guanyu shixing qiye zhigong jiben yanglao baoxian shengji tongchou he hangye tongchou yijiao defang guanli youguan wenti de tongzhi* [*Circular concerning issue related to the raising of pooling for basic old-age insurance for enterprise employees to provincial level and the transfer of industry pools to the administration of local government*], State Council of China, Beijing, viewed 12 March 2012, <http://www.gdsi.gov.cn/upload/resource/zcfg_content.jsp?contentId=647>

State Council of China (SC), 2000, *Guanyu yinfa wanshan chengzhen shehui baozhang tixi shidian fangan de tongzhi* [*Circular on the distribution of the program of the experimental sites for the improvement of the urban social insurance system*], 15 December, State Council of China, Beijing, viewed 3 April 2012, <http://www.51labour.com/lawcenter/lawshow-19332.html>

State Council of China (SC), 2002, *Guanyu zhuanfa 'Guojia Xinxihua Lingdao Xiaozu guanyyu woguo dianzihua zhengwu jianshe zhidao yijian' de tongzhi* [*Circular on the transmission of 'The National Leading Group for Informatisation's Guidance on Developing Electronic Government Business'*], August, State Council of China, Beijing, viewed 4 April 2012, <http://www.hbzx12333.gov.cn/look.asp?vid=88>

State Council of China (SC), 2005, Guanyu wanshan qiye zhigong jiben yanglao baoxian zhidu de jueding [Decision on Improving the Basic Old-Age Insurance System for Enterprise Employees], State Council of China, Beijing, viewed 12 March 2012, <http://www.china.com.cn/chinese/PI-c/1061304.htm>

State Council of China (SC), 2006, *Guanyu jiejue nongmingong wenti de ruogan yijian* [*Some Proposals for Resolving the Problems of Migrant Workers*], 31 January, State Council of China, Beijing, viewed 3 April 2012, <http://www.gov.cn/jrzg/2006-03/27/content_237644.htm>

State Council of China (SC), 2009, *Guanyu kaizhan xinxing nongcun shehui yanglao baoxian shidian de jidao yijian* [*Guidance on the trial sites for the new rural social old-age insurance*], Document 32, September, State Council of China, Beijing, viewed 4 January 2011, <http://www.gov.cn/zwgk/2009-09/04/content_1409216.htm>

State Council of China (SC), 2011, *Guanyu kaizhan chengzhen jumin shehui yanglao baoxian shidian de zhidao yijian* [*Guidance on Developing Experimental Sites for the Old-Age Insurance of Urban Residents*], June 2011, State Council of China, Beijing, viewed 3 April 2012, <http://www.gov.cn/zwgk/2011-06/13/content_1882801.htm>

State Statistical Bureau (SSB), 2012, *2011 nian Zhongguo nongcun jumin shouru zengsu kuai yu chengzhen* [*The Rate of Increase of Rural Residents' Income in 2011 was Faster than that of the Cities*], 17 January, State Statistical Bureau, Beijing, viewed 10 April 2012, <http://www.gov.cn/jrzg/2012-01/17/content_2046902.htm>

Su, B., 2009, *Zhongguo Nongcun Yanglao Wenti Yanjiu [Research on China's Rural Old-Age Insurance]*, Qinghua Daxue Chubanshe, Beijing.

Tang, J., 2012, 'Cheng-xiang dibao zhidu: lishi, xianzhuang yu qianzhan [The urban and rural guaranteed minimum income system: history, current state and prospects]', China Sociology web site, viewed 12 March 2012, <http://www.sociology.cass.cn/shxw/shzc/P020051002830994538742.pdf>

United Nations (UN), 2011a, *World Population Prospects: The 2010 revision, highlights and advance tables*, United Nations, New York, viewed 5 March 2012, <http://esa.un.org/unpd/wpp/Documentation/pdf/WPP2010_Highlights.pdf>

United Nations (UN), 2011b, *World Population Prospects: The 2010 revision. Volume II. Demographic profiles*, United Nations, New York, viewed 5 March 2012, <http://esa.un.org/unpd/wpp/Documentation/pdf/WPP2010_Volume-II_Demographic-Profiles.pdf>

Wang, D., 2005, *China's urban and rural old age security system: challenges and options*, Working Paper Series No. 53, October, Institute of Population and Labor Economics, Chinese Academy of Social Sciences, viewed 16 November 2009, <http://iple.cass.cn/file/dw17.pdf>

Wang, F., 2011, 'The future of a demographic overachiever: long-term implications of the demographic transition in China', *Population and Development Review (Supplement)*, vol. 37, pp. 173–90.

Wang, M. (ed.), 2001, *Zhongguo Shehui Baozhang Tizhi Gaige [Restructuring China's Social Security System]*, Zhongguo Fazhan Chubanshe, Beijing.

Wang, M. (ed.), 2002, *Restructuring China's Social Security System*, Foreign Languages Press, Beijing.

World Bank, 1994, *Averting the Old-Age Crisis: Policies to protect the old and promote growth*, Oxford University Press, Oxford.

World Bank and Organisation for Economic Cooperation and Development (OECD), 2008, *Pensions at a Glance: Asia Pacific edition*, World Bank and Organisation for Economic Cooperation and Development, Washington, DC, viewed 16 November, 2009, <http://www.oecd.org/dataoecd/33/53/41966940.pdf>

Watson, A., 2009, 'Social security for China's migrant workers—providing for old age', *Journal of Current Chinese Affairs*, vol. 38, no. 4, pp. 85–115.

Xinhua, 2011, *Zhongguo Renmin Gongheguo Guomin Jingji he Shehui Fazhan Di Shi'erge Wunian Guihua Gangyao [Twelfth Five-Year Plan of the People's Republic of China]*, 16 March, Xinhua, Beijing, section 33.

Yang, C., 2012, 'Chayi yu gongxing: difang chengxiang jumin shehui yanglao zhengce de bijiao yu fenxi—jiyu dui 6 ge chengshi shidian fangan de kaocha [Differences and commonalities: comparison and analysis of local old-age policies for urban residents—based on a survey of experimental plans in 6 cities]', *Sichuan Xingzheng Xueyuan Xuebao*, no. 1, pp. 67–70.

Zhao, R., Lai, D. and Wei, Z., 2006, *Zhongguo de Jingji Zhuanxing he Shehui Baozhang Gaige* [*The Transformation of the Chinese Economy and the Reform of Social Security*], Beijing Shifandaxue Chubanshe, Beijing.

Zhao, R., Wang, A. and Ren, L., 2002, *Zhongguo Nongmin Yanglao Baozhang zhi Lu* [*The Road to Old-Age Security for China's Farmers*], Heilongjiang Renmin Chubanshe, Harbin.

Zhao, Z. and Guo, F. (eds), 2007, 'Introduction', *Transition and Challenge: China's population at the beginning of the 21st century*, Oxford University Press, Oxford.

13. An Empirical Study of China's High-Tech Industry Innovation Capability in Transition

Zhiyun Zhao and Chaofeng Yang

Introduction

Since the reform and opening up, the growth mode of China's economy has essentially featured a heavy reliance on investment and exports and intense input of low-cost resources and factors. Such a mode was reasonable to some extent when China lagged behind in economic development and its economic aggregate accounted for a relatively small proportion of the world economy. With China's continuous economic growth, however, the costs of this growth mode have become increasingly large, including resource depletion, environmental damage, a gradually widening wealth gap, significantly increased social conflicts and more frequent international trade friction. The international financial crisis and the severe recession that it triggered spelt an end to the rapid economic growth experienced since the 1980s, and especially since the turn of the new century, which caused a profound adjustment of the global economy. Consequently the external environment for China's development has changed deeply and extensively. Urgent demands are thus generated for China to transform its economy as soon as possible from the traditional economic growth mode based on resources, capital and labour to the new mode based primarily on innovation.

The high-tech industry, with characteristics of high growth, large driving forces and high value added, is a strategically leading industry in the national economy, playing an important role in industrial restructuring and transformation of the economic development pattern. In 2010, the total output value of China's high-tech industry reached RMB7.47 trillion, accounting for 10.56 per cent of the total output value of the large and medium-sized enterprises in that year. China has become the world's major manufacturing base for high-tech products, with an important role in the international high-tech production chain. During the development process, however, there have been several problems in China's high-tech industry, including weak innovation capacity, low technology intensity and poor economic efficiency. A top agenda item for China's government, high-tech industry and academia is to improve the innovation capability of China's high-tech industry and make it play a greater role in China's ongoing economic transformation.

In recent years, some scholars have carried out empirical research on innovation performance in China from the regional and industrial points of view. The major studies from a regional perspective of innovation efficiency in China are summarised as follows. Shi and Zhao (2009) calculate the regional innovation efficiency in China and analyse its spatial discrepancy using the stochastic frontier approach. Li (2007) conducted an empirical analysis of the efficiency factors influencing the regional innovation capability differences in China, taking the number of invention patent applications granted as indicators of innovation output. Guo et al. (2007) analysed the ability of technology innovation and its influencing factors for the six provinces of central China by establishing a knowledge production function model with fixed effects and variable intercept. Yang (2008) studied the technological innovation capacity of large and medium-sized enterprises in different regions and conducted a comprehensive evaluation using the factor analysis method. The major literature on Chinese innovation efficiency from an industrial perspective is summarised as follows. Zhang and Feng (2007), through their panel data analysis of 28 sectors in China's high-tech industry, discussed the relationship between market structure, research and development (R&D) investment and economic performance under different industrial characteristics. Zhi (2009) used the stochastic frontier method to analyse the technological innovation performance of China's electronic information industry. Han (2010) also applied the stochastic frontier method to conduct an empirical analysis of the innovation efficiency of China's high-tech industry. These studies have contributed a lot to this research field and provide a number of policy ideas to promote China's innovation capacity; however, there are also some shortcomings in previous studies, which can be viewed from the following three aspects. First, the majority of scholars selected sales revenues of new products and the number of patent applications as the output indicators of innovation. Though it is generally believed that the number of patents—information for which is relatively easy to obtain and use in statistical analyses—is a good indicator of innovation output, there are still some limitations. On the one hand, not all innovation will be registered as patents. On the other hand, the tendency to apply for patents varies with enterprises' size. Large enterprises often rely on a monopoly of market and technology to protect innovation while small companies are more willing to apply for patents in order to protect their innovation from infringements by other companies with more resources (Comanor and Scherer 1969). These are issues that should be addressed in future research. Second, when choosing indicators of innovation, most scholars do not take the knowledge stock into account. The generation of new knowledge depends not only on investment in R&D and personnel, but also on the existing knowledge stock. Third, when choosing the factors affecting innovation efficiency, most scholars consider market structure and government support for innovation activities. These factors are very important when examining the innovation efficiency of different countries, but they are not necessarily differentiating across industries in the one country. For China, as an economy in transition, factors that affect innovation efficiency should be determined by taking into consideration the characteristics of regional or industrial development during the transition period.

This chapter strives to achieve a breakthrough in the above aspects. An analytical model is established to evaluate the innovation capability of high-tech industries in China, and the influencing factors of innovation capability are discussed. The chapter is organised as follows: the first section is the introduction; the second section briefly analyses the characteristics of China's high-tech industries during the transition period; the third section introduces the model and accounts for the variable selection; the fourth section details the empirical analysis; and the final section contains the conclusions and policy recommendations.

Characteristics of China's High-Tech Industry During the Transition Period

Since its entry into the World Trade Organisation (WTO), China has witnessed rapid growth in its high-tech industry and has leapt into the front ranks of the world in terms of scale through taking an active part in economic globalisation. But, unlike developed countries, China's economic system is in a transitional period. In such a special period, the development of China's high-tech industry is significantly distinct from that of developed countries.

Significantly Increased R&D Activities

In recent years, investments in R&D activities and personnel for China's high-tech industry have increased dramatically. R&D expenditures expanded rapidly from RMB36.25 billion in 2005 to RMB96.78 billion in 2010, increasing 170 per cent in six years. R&D personnel rose from 173 000 people (full-time equivalent) in 2005 to 399 000 people in 2010—an increase of 130 per cent in six years (Figure 13.1).

Figure 13.1 R&D Investments of China's High-Tech Industry, 2005–10

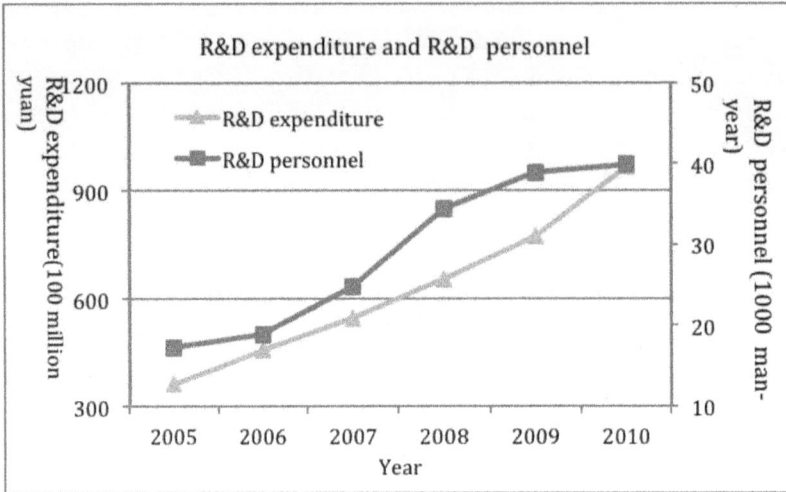

Source: Authors' own calculation using the data from *China Statistical Yearbook on Science and Technology*.

Driven by these investments, the R&D output of the high-tech industry in China has grown rapidly. There were less than 10 000 invention patent applications in China's high-tech industries in 2005, but there were 35 000 applications in 2010, increasing at an average annual growth rate of 29.7 per cent. Such a growth rate is rare even in developed countries. At the same time, the number of invention patents in force owned by China's high-tech industries had soared to more than 50 000 in 2010 (Figure 13.2).

Figure 13.2 Number of Invention Patents in China's High-Tech Industry, 2005–10

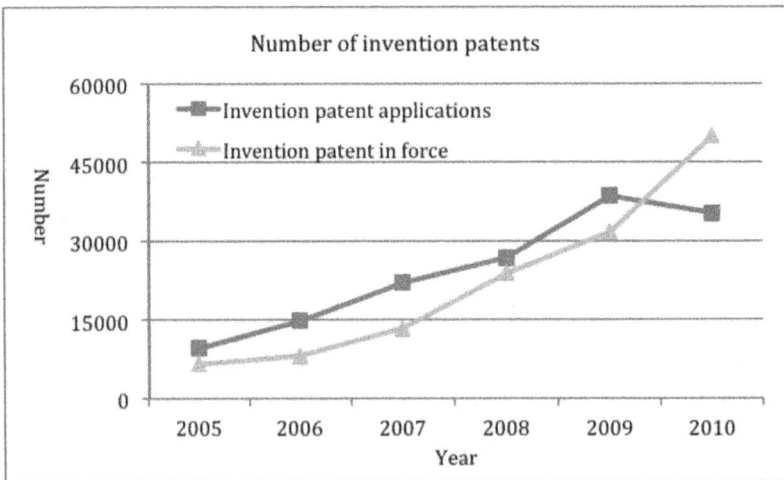

Source: Authors' own calculation using the data from *China Statistical Yearbook on Science and Technology*.

Low R&D Intensity and Productivity

Technology intensity is a basic international standard for high-tech industry. Only those industries with technology intensity significantly higher or several times higher than the average intensity of all manufacturing industries can be defined as high-tech industries. R&D expenditure intensity is an important indicator of technology intensity. In the United States, Germany, France, Britain and other developed countries, the R&D intensity of the high-tech industries is three or four times higher than the average level of manufacturing industries. In contrast, the R&D intensity of China's high-tech industry (1.3 per cent) was only about two times that of the manufacturing industry (0.62 per cent) in 2010—far lower than the level of the abovementioned countries (Figure 13.3). This indicates that the technology intensity of China's high-tech industries is still low and the innovation capacity of enterprises is relatively poor.

Figure 13.3 R&D Intensity of China's High-Tech Industry, 2006–10

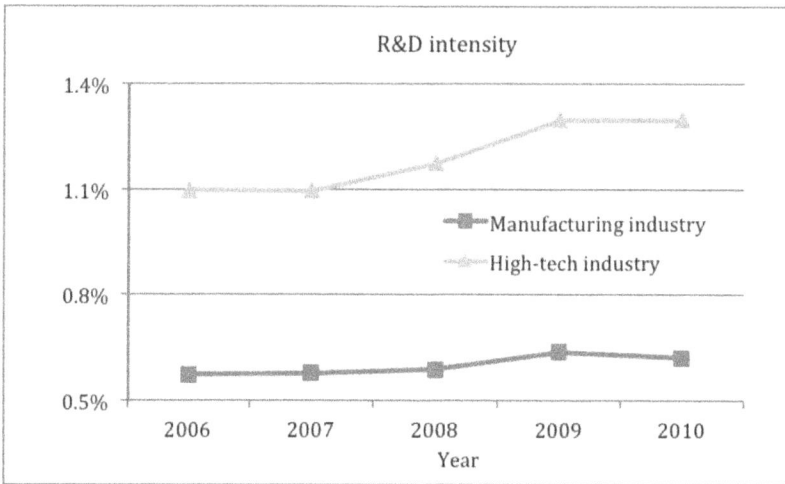

Source: Authors' own calculation using the data from *China Statistical Yearbook on Science and Technology*.

Paradoxically, 'low-tech' is a more appropriate description of China's 'high-tech' enterprises. Although the products they produce are called 'high-tech products', they assemble such products rather than design and build them completely. The rapid expansion of China's high-tech industry in the past six years was based on scale expansion more than on industrial upgrading. The overall labour productivity of China's manufacturing industry was RMB726 400 per capita in 2010—an increase of 100 per cent compared with that of 2005; meanwhile, the overall labour productivity in high-tech industry increased by only 32 per cent. The labour productivity of China's high-tech industry in 2010 was even lower than the overall level of the manufacturing industry, reflecting the slow improvement of production efficiency in China's high-tech industry (Figure 13.4).

Figure 13.4 Labor Productivity of China's High-Tech Industry and Manufacturing Industry, 2005–10

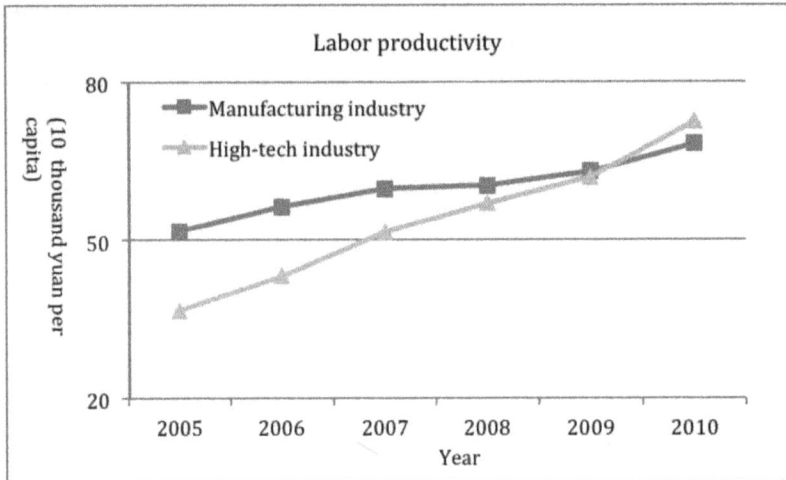

Source: Authors' own calculation using the data from *China Statistical Yearbooks* and *China Statistical Yearbook on Science and Technology.*

Acquiring Technologies Mostly from Domestic Providers

The external channels of technology acquisition for China's high-tech industry mainly include acquisition of foreign technologies and the purchase of domestic technologies. During the period 2005–10, China's high-tech industry experienced an increase and then a decrease in its expenditures for acquisition of foreign technologies, with the peak—RMB13 billion—in 2007. Since then, it has decreased continuously, to RMB6.88 billion in 2010—almost half of that in 2007 and RMB1.6 billion less than in 2005 (Figure 13.5). At the same time, the funds for purchasing domestic technologies of high-tech industries in China increased steadily, from RMB950 million in 2005 to RMB2.13 billion in 2010. This indicates the gradual change in the technology sources of China's high-tech industries from foreign channels towards domestic providers.

Figure 13.5 Expenditure for Acquisition of Foreign Technology and Purchase of Domestic Technology of China's High-Tech Industry, 2005–10

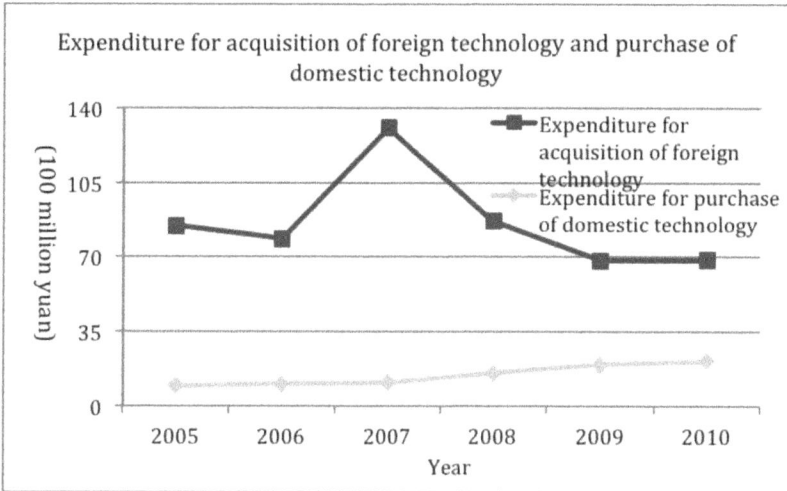

Source: Authors' own calculation using the data from *China Statistical Yearbooks* and *China Statistical Yearbook on Science and Technology.*

Research Methods and Data

As innovation is a process of knowledge production and commercialisation, we can explore the industry's innovation capability through the knowledge production function. The knowledge production function was initially proposed by Griliches (1979) when he estimated the contribution of R&D to economic growth using the production function. Improved by Jaffe (1989), the Griliches–Jaffe knowledge production function model was developed. The knowledge production function connects the inputs and outputs of innovation, thus, we can get a better understanding of the driving forces, nature and influencing factors of knowledge production through the study of it, and furthermore promote knowledge production and innovation. A large body of empirical research has found that a knowledge production function does exist in the real world and that it is a good statistical model for the study of knowledge and innovation. It has been proven by most empirical studies at the national or industry level (Anselin et al. 1997; Blind and Grupp 1999; Bode 2004). The Griliches–Jaffe knowledge production function in Cobb-Douglas form can be described as follows (Equation 13.1).

Equation 13.1

$$K_i = RD_i^\alpha Z_i^\delta e_i$$

In Equation 13.1, K denotes the innovation output; RD denotes R&D investment; Z is the series of factors that affects innovation output (such as knowledge stock); e is random disturbances; and i are decision-making units in high-tech industries.

Given the shortcomings we have identified regarding the use of the number of patents to measure innovation output, we use the number of new product development projects and sales revenue of new products to measure the innovation output in this study. According to the definition in the *China Statistical Yearbook on Science and Technology* (NBS 2009), the new product time series captures 'new products developed and produced by adopting new technological principles and new design concepts, or products with performance obviously enhanced or functions expanded through significant improvement in structure, material or techniques of the original products'. The new products include both those that have applied for patents and those that have not yet applied. Using the number of new product development projects can overcome the estimation bias caused by the differences of tendency to apply for patents across industries. In addition, in order to make up for the weakness of the number of new product development projects in measuring the direct contribution of innovation to economic growth, we also use the sales revenue of new products to measure the innovation output. It should be noted that it is also inappropriate to measure the innovation output with the sales revenue of new products only, because the industry's innovation capability is not necessarily strong when the sales revenue of new products is high considering the market size of different industries. Thus, it is better to use both indicators.

Compared with the measurement of innovative output, the measurement of innovation is relatively easy. Considering the characteristics of knowledge production, in addition to the R&D expenditure and R&D personnel, we regard the knowledge stock as an important input factor of knowledge production, for the knowledge stock could reflect the knowledge production status quo and development potential of technological innovation of an industry or a region. It is also a key measure of industrial or regional innovation capability. There have been no uniform standards for the estimation of knowledge stock. Following the approach used by Acs et al. (2002), the number of effective invention patents is used to measure the knowledge stock here.

For the factors affecting innovation output, combined with the characteristics of the transitional economy, we consider three factors: the expenditure for acquisition of foreign technology, the purchase of domestic technology and enterprise size. In developed countries, innovation is mainly performed through R&D activities; but in an economy in transition, innovation is based more on technological learning, mainly through the absorption of external technologies instead of independent R&D efforts (Gil et al. 2003). In addition, with regard to the impact of enterprise size on innovation output, it is commonly agreed that such an impact exists, though views differ on whether the innovation efficiency is higher in small enterprises or in large enterprises. In this chapter, the average output value per enterprise in the industry is adopted to measure the size of the enterprise in the high-tech industry.

A defect in using traditional regression analysis to estimate a knowledge function is the assumption that production is carried out on the production possibility frontier. But in fact, most producers often deviate from the optimal production plan, resulting in inefficiency to some extent. There are usually two types of methods to identify inefficient items: parametric and non-parametric methods. Data envelope analysis is the main non-parametric method. It establishes the production frontier through linear programming and uses the distance function to calculate the efficiency of the production unit. The advantage of this method is that there is no need to assume a particular form of production function or make an assumption of the distribution of inefficiency in the sample(s). Its flaw is its assumption that there are no random errors affecting the output. Stochastic frontier analysis is the main parametric method. It is based on the idea of dividing the deviation of the actual production unit from the frontier into random error and inefficiency, estimating the frontier production function using the metric method. Compared with data envelope analysis, stochastic frontier analysis has a more solid theoretical foundation and can separate the potential impact caused by random errors and provide a variety of statistical tests to judge the quality of model fit. So, we choose the stochastic frontier model for our estimation.

The stochastic frontier model was first put forward by Aigner et al. (1977) and Meeusen and van den Broeck (1977), then expanded and developed by Jondrow, Battese and Coelli and other researchers with the flexibility and applicability improved. According to the definition of the stochastic frontier production function by Battese and Coelli (1995), we set up the stochastic frontier knowledge production function model as follows (Equations 13.2–5).

Equation 13.2

$$y_{it} = \alpha^0 \cdot RDK_{it}^{\alpha^1} \cdot RDL_{it}^{\alpha^2} \cdot KS_{it}^{\alpha^3} \cdot \exp(v_{it} - u_{it})$$

Equation 13.3

$$v_{it} \sim N(0, \sigma_v^2)$$

Equation 13.4

$$u_{it} \sim TN(m_{it}, \sigma_u^2)$$

Equation 13.5

$$m_{it} = \delta_0 + \delta_1 TIF_{it} + \delta_2 TID_{it} + \delta_3 ES_{it}$$

RDK denotes R&D expenditure; RDL denotes R&D personnel; KS is the knowledge stock measured by the number of invention patents in force; v_{it} is the random observation error normally distributed and independent of u_{it}, the inefficient error, which is a random variable from a truncated normal distribution with its mean as m_{it} and variance as σ_v^2; m_{it} is expressed as a linear combination of a set of influencing factors; TIF is the expenditure for acquisition of foreign technologies; TID is the expenditure for purchase of domestic technologies; and ES is the enterprise size.

Compared with more traditional estimation methods, the advantages of stochastic frontier analysis lie in its consideration of the inefficiency item. How then to determine the effectiveness of the stochastic frontier function? If there is no inefficient item in the model or the inefficient item is not obvious, it would be more appropriate to use the traditional method. According to Battese and Corra (1977), the coefficient of variation can be used to determine the effectiveness of the frontier function model. The coefficient of variation is defined as follows (Equation 13.6).

Equation 13.6

$$\gamma = \frac{\sigma_u^2}{\sigma_u^2 + \sigma_v^2}, 0 \leq \gamma \leq 1$$

When Y is close to one, indicating that the inefficient item accounts for the main part of the deviation of the production units from the frontier, it is appropriate to use the frontier function model; if Y is close to zero, indicating that the random error is the main component, it is better to use traditional estimation methods.

After the effectiveness of the model is tested, the estimated value of innovation efficiency can be calculated by the following formula (Kumbhakar and Lovell 2000) (Equation 13.7).

Equation 13.7

$$IE_{it} = E\{\exp(-u_{it}) \mid (v_{it} - u_{it})\}$$

The data in this chapter come from the *China Statistical Yearbook* and *China Statistical Yearbook on Science and Technology*. According to the related statistical indicators of the National Bureau of Statistics, China's high-tech industry is divided into five major categories (namely, medicine manufacturing industry, aircraft and spacecraft manufacturing industry, electronic and communication equipment manufacturing industry, computers and office equipment manufacturing industry, and medical equipment and meters manufacturing industry), which are further divided into 17 classes. Each class of industries is treated as a decision-making unit. The sample period is 2005–10. The descriptive statistics for all variables are shown in Table 13.1.

Table 13.1 Descriptive Statistics of Variables

	Maximum	Minimum	Mean	Standard deviation
Sales revenue of new products (RMB10 000)	42 748 772.6	37 857.00	6 742 440.14	8 750 481.42
Number of new product development projects (10 000)	9316.00	57.00	2179.94	2162.41
R&D expenditure (RMB10 000)	3 047 068.40	14 160.00	382 918.57	491 888.58
R&D personnel (man-years)	98 637.00	341.00	16 845.96	19 518.94
Number of invention patents in force	23 979.00	2.00	1428.87	3040.46
Expenditure for acquisition of foreign technologies (RMB10 000)	335 532.00	0.00	50 658.77	76 498.78
Expenditure for purchase of domestic technologies (RMB10 000)	222 193.00	0.00	10 357.91	24 574.96
Enterprise size (0.1 billion/ enterprise)	64.48	0.44	4.06	9.72

Source: Authors' own calculation based on data from *China Statistical Yearbook on Science and Technology*.

Empirical Results and Analysis

Estimation Results

The estimation software we used is FRONTIER4.1. In order to reduce the impact of outliers on the estimated results and make the estimated coefficient easier to explain (as a coefficient of elasticity), all variables were converted to natural logarithms. In addition, in terms of the input/output delay that must be dealt with in the model estimation, most researchers set it as long as one year when facing direct R&D output (such as the number of patent applications), and two years when facing indirect R&D output (such as the contribution of R&D investments to economic growth). According to the above tradition, the input/output delay is set to two years when the sales revenue of new products is used as an innovation output indicator, and one year when the number of new product development projects is used as an innovation output indicator. Table 13.2 shows the estimation results under different conditions.

Table 13.2 Estimation Results

Variables	Number of new product development projects			Sales revenue of new products		
	Coefficient	Standard deviation	T value	Coefficient	Standard deviation	T value
Factors affecting the function frontier						
Constant	0.57993	0.92501	0.62694	5.04503**	2.43261	2.07392
RDK	0.40839**	0.18123	2.25345	1.41651*	0.25939	5.46102
RDL	0.20830**	0.20996	1.99205	0.71739*	0.22210	3.22998
KS	0.11571**	0.06575	1.75985	0.02347	0.11030	0.21274
Factors affecting the efficiency						
Constant	0.97835	0.62917	1.55498	4.28012*	1.49926	2.85482
TIF	−0.03579	0.03065	−1.16755	−0.14040	0.13325	−1.05366
TID	−0.12382*	0.03564	−3.47410	−0.21459	0.19943	−1.07600
ES	0.34534*	0.10922	3.16196	−0.78163***	0.65169	−1.29939
Model test and other settings						
Coefficient of variation	0.82484	0.11044	7.46872	0.89179	0.08528	10.45677
Delay			1			2
Sample size			85			68

* statistically significant at the 1 per cent level

** statistically significant at the 5 per cent level

*** statistically significant at the 10 per cent level

Source: Authors' own estimation.

It can be seen from the coefficient of variation estimated through the stochastic frontier model in the antepenultimate row of Table 13.2 that a considerable part of the variance can be attributed to the efficiency factor under both assumptions. It strongly supports our use of the stochastic frontier analysis model.

Known from Table 13.2, the number of new product development projects is significantly correlated with the R&D expenditure and R&D personnel, as well as the knowledge stock, while the sales revenue of new products is significantly correlated with the R&D expenditure and R&D personnel, but not with the knowledge stock. One possible reason for this difference is the lower quality of R&D outputs in China's high-tech industry; many R&D outputs can be used for further R&D activities and produce patents, but only a relatively small proportion of them can be successfully commercialised. In terms of the size of the coefficients, the estimation results show that, if the R&D expenditure increases by 1 per cent, the number of new product development projects will increase by 0.41 per cent and sales revenue will increase by 1.42 per cent, assuming that other variables are constant; if the number of R&D personnel increases by 1 per cent, the number of new product development projects will increase by 0.21 per cent and sales revenue will increase by 0.72 per cent. The direct R&D output/input coefficient is large while the final output/input coefficient is small, which, to some extent, confirms the view previously mentioned that the rapid expansion of China's high-tech industries is more a scale expansion at low technical level without the quality of economic growth improving accordingly.

As to the factors affecting the innovation efficiency of China's high-tech industry, the expenditure for acquisition of foreign technologies is statistically significant neither with the number of new product development projects nor with sales revenue of new products, indicating that the acquisition of foreign technologies had no important influence on the innovation capability of China's high-tech industry during the sample period. One possible reason for this result is that, compared with other industries, developed countries impose more strict limits on high technology exports against developing countries due to intellectual property concerns so that China's high-tech industries might benefit from the introduction of foreign technologies in a very limited way.

When using the number of new product development projects as the measure of innovation output, the estimated coefficient of expenditure for the purchase of domestic technologies is negative and statistically significant. It indicates that the mean of inefficiency level u_{it} will decrease with the increase of expenditure for the purchase of domestic technologies and thereby the innovation efficiency will increase. This shows that the R&D achievements of China's R&D institutions other than high-tech enterprises play a significant role in promoting the R&D activities in high-tech industry. When using the sales revenue of new products as a measure of innovation output, the estimated coefficient of expenditure for the purchase of domestic technologies is negative but statistically insignificant. It shows the introduction of domestic technologies by high-tech industry has no significant impact on its final innovation output. To some extent, this result suggests that high-tech enterprises in China focus more on the introduction of assembly lines than on the absorption and commercialisation of technology.

When using the number of new product development projects as the measure of innovation output, the estimated coefficient of enterprise size is positive and statistically significant. This means the enterprise size has a negative impact on the innovation output of China's high-tech industry. When using the sales revenue of new products as the measure of innovation output, the coefficient of enterprise size is negative and statistically significant, indicating that the enterprise size has a positive impact on the innovation output of China's high-tech industry. This apparently confusing result is not necessarily contradictory. It is a general problem that China's large-scale enterprises pay little attention to R&D, but these enterprises can acquire more economic benefits (extract higher margins) from a small number of innovations through their market power.

Comparison of Innovation Efficiency

Using the model estimation results, we can calculate the estimated innovation efficiency of the 17 industries in each year (see Tables 13.3 and 13.4).

Table 13.3 Estimated Innovative Efficiency (with the number of new product development projects as the indicator of innovation output)

Industry	2006	2007	2008	2009	2010	Mean
Chemical medicines	0.732	0.661	0.807	0.791	0.622	0.723
Finished traditional Chinese medicines	0.706	0.617	0.750	0.714	0.447	0.647
Biological and biochemical products	0.426	0.475	0.702	0.664	0.274	0.508
Aeroplane making and repair	0.575	0.642	0.497	0.463	0.447	0.525
Spacecraft	0.222	0.391	0.172	0.077	0.046	0.181
Communications equipment	0.210	0.223	0.386	0.442	0.199	0.292
Radar and its fittings	0.592	0.541	0.503	0.398	0.484	0.504
Broadcasting and television equipment	0.711	0.270	0.570	0.487	0.185	0.445
Electronic appliances	0.534	0.707	0.746	0.706	0.392	0.617
Electronic components	0.898	0.724	0.827	0.763	0.594	0.761
Domestic televisions and radios	0.688	0.679	0.634	0.506	0.495	0.600
Other electronic equipment	0.374	0.321	0.808	0.474	0.272	0.450
Computers	0.250	0.136	0.142	0.110	0.555	0.239
Computer peripherals	0.235	0.247	0.324	0.279	0.372	0.291
Office equipment	0.152	0.310	0.293	0.307	0.180	0.248
Medical equipment and appliances	0.314	0.357	0.685	0.619	0.227	0.440
Measuring instruments	0.698	0.721	0.894	0.852	0.456	0.724
Mean	0.489	0.472	0.573	0.509	0.367	0.482

Source: Authors' own estimation.

It can be seen from Table 13.3 that, when using the number of new product development projects as the indicator of innovation output, the electronic components industry, measuring instruments industry and chemical medicines industry were significantly better than others in innovation efficiency. This could be closely associated with their greater experience in global competition and deeper integration into the global value chain than other industries. The innovation efficiency of the manufacture of spacecraft was the lowest—only 0.181, which is greatly below that of the electronic components industry (0.761). The innovation efficiency of the computer industry was also relatively low. These two industries are related with a state's security. Obviously, there is still a long way to go to improve the innovation capability of high-tech industry.

From the perspective of the dynamic trends, the innovation efficiency of China's high-tech industry remained low during 2006–10. It reached its peak in 2008 and then declined dramatically. Such a dividing line indicates that the international financial crisis changed the dynamics in many industries. Overall, the innovation efficiency of China's high-tech industry increased slowly in the past five years, leaving much room for further improvement.

Table 13.4 Estimated Innovative Efficiency (with the sales revenue of new products as the indicator of innovation output)

Industry	2007	2008	2009	2010	Mean
Chemical medicines	0.591	0.695	0.743	0.730	0.690
Finished traditional Chinese medicines	0.387	0.444	0.507	0.563	0.475
Biological and biochemical products	0.381	0.627	0.573	0.312	0.473
Aeroplane making and repair	0.776	0.762	0.369	0.404	0.578
Spacecraft	0.038	0.104	0.067	0.064	0.068
Communications equipment	0.833	0.825	0.878	0.846	0.846
Radar and its fittings	0.551	0.231	0.149	0.375	0.326
Broadcasting and television equipment	0.531	0.400	0.481	0.305	0.429
Electronic appliances	0.721	0.767	0.800	0.729	0.754
Electronic components	0.726	0.619	0.738	0.770	0.713
Domestic televisions and radios	0.694	0.710	0.777	0.733	0.729
Other electronic equipment	0.590	0.869	0.781	0.520	0.690
Computers	0.905	0.884	0.809	0.874	0.868
Computer peripherals	0.865	0.866	0.670	0.894	0.824
Office equipment	0.804	0.480	0.385	0.681	0.587
Medical equipment and appliances	0.264	0.444	0.445	0.174	0.332
Measuring instruments	0.691	0.828	0.801	0.613	0.733
Mean	0.609	0.621	0.587	0.564	0.595

Source: Authors' own estimation.

It can be seen from Table 13.4 that, when using the sales revenue of new products as the indicator of innovation output, computers, communications equipment and computer peripherals were significantly better than other industries in innovation efficiency. This could be a result of the huge consumer market for these industries in China. The average innovation efficiency of the manufacture of spacecraft industry was the lowest—only 0.068—significantly lower than that of the computer industry, with the highest innovation efficiency (0.868). It is clear that there are enormous obstacles for the commercialisation of the R&D results in China's spacecraft industry.

Though different indicators are used to measure innovation output, we can see the trend of the changes in the innovation efficiency of China's high-tech industry is consistent—that is, an inverted U-shape.

Conclusions

A country's international competitiveness and its role in the world economy depend on its innovation capability in high-tech industry, which is also an important indicator for developing countries to graduate to developed status. In this chapter, the stochastic frontier knowledge production function model is applied to conduct an empirical analysis of innovation efficiency of China's high-tech industry in transition. The results show that, during the period 2005–10

1. the knowledge stock did not play a major role in China's high-tech industry innovation

2. the effects of acquisition of foreign technology on innovation capability in China's high-tech industry were not statistically obvious

3. the effects of the purchase of domestic technology on the R&D output of China's high-tech industry were obvious, but the economic benefits due to the purchase of domestic technology were not statistically obvious

4. the scale of enterprises in China's high-tech industry had a negative impact on their innovation capability.

The above conclusions have important implications for the development of China's high-tech industry.

First, due to the technological 'blockade' imposed by developed countries, the role of acquisition of foreign technologies in promoting China's high-tech industry is far weaker than that in China's non-high-tech manufacturing industries. With the continuous increase of the share of China's economy in the world economy, we can expect an even stricter technological 'blockade' from the developed countries. Therefore, the main way to enhance the innovation capability of China's high-tech industry is via local innovation, with the importation of foreign technologies as a complementary trend. More preferential policies and public funds should be invested in the high-tech industries, especially in the enterprises that have already exhibited innovative ability in strategic high-tech industry. Through this channel, China's high-tech industry can enhance its innovation capacity and international competitiveness more quickly and occupy the high end of the global industry chain.

Second, as to the poor quality of China's high-tech industrial development, China should change the practice that evaluates regional economic restructuring mainly by the output of high-tech industry, and construct a scientific evaluation system to guide local governments to pay more attention to the quality of the high-tech industry's development. It will greatly reduce the phenomenon in which high-tech industry is treated as the Government's 'achievement projects' when promoting economic transformation. At present, many technological breakthroughs in China cannot be commercialised and receive returns from the market, which greatly reduces the enthusiasm of enterprises for technological innovation. Thus, it is necessary for the Government to regulate monopolies to create a favourable environment for innovation and enable the innovator to realise market value more easily. China must make great efforts to establish various types of intermediaries and create a complete business model that can commercialise the major technologies. Only in this way can China fundamentally address the problems of poor-quality industrial development in its high-tech industry.

Third, the empirical result that the effects of purchasing domestic technology on the R&D output of China's high-tech industry was obvious, but the economic benefits due to the purchase of domestic technology were not statistically obvious shows that technology transfer and cooperation between China's enterprises does help to promote the R&D activities of high-tech industry. Without technological barriers, enterprises can make their cooperative R&D on key technologies more efficient through the technology transfer between them. It also confirms the effectiveness of industrial technology innovation alliances among enterprises. It is a good way to accelerate the integration of enterprises' technologies and overcome the key and common technological challenges constraining the development of the industry under the guidance of the Government. But, on the other hand, the lack of obvious measurable economic benefits reveals that there is room for further improvement in the back-end operations of the technology innovation alliance among enterprises. In addition to improving the business model, it is also very important to coordinate different types of enterprises to take on appropriate responsibilities and work together to develop technological applications with greater commercial value after achieving breakthroughs in key and common technologies. This will ensure that the enterprises in the same alliance can position themselves correctly in cooperative R&D according to the location of their products in the industrial chain, and carry out strategic arrangements to occupy the corresponding market. In this process, the market mechanism is the principal determinant, while the Government plays only a guiding role. Intermediary organisations such as industrial associations and professional investors could exert a greater influence; this is the third force to promote innovation that China needs to cultivate and develop in the future.

Fourth, according to the empirical result that the size of enterprises in China's high-tech industry had a negative impact on their innovation capability, we would make two points. On one hand, it shows once again that being state-owned is an institutional barrier that has been an important factor hindering the functioning of enterprises' innovation capability, as most of the large high-tech enterprises in China are state-owned. It has been a prominent issue during China's current economic restructuring and institutional reform that the state-owned enterprises have insufficient motives for innovation. How can an effective incentive mechanism be established to stimulate the innovation of state-owned enterprises? It is a problem highlighted in the current pattern of reform and changing economic development that requires great attention from relevant departments and is critical to the success of transition to some extent. On the other hand, the empirical result further argues for the important role of small and medium-sized high-tech enterprises in the process of economic restructuring and changing development mode. It is a crucial issue for the successful transformation of China's economic development mode in the future: how to enhance the innovative enthusiasm and capability of small and medium-sized high-tech enterprises? For the large number of small and medium-sized enterprises (SMEs) in China, due to their small size, the transformation is relatively easy for them and the opportunity cost of transformation is also relatively low. This reinforces the point that it is appropriate to set as key policy priorities the solution of SMEs' financing difficulties and improving SMEs' innovation capacity. This policy should absolutely be maintained.

Fifth, through the above analysis, in our opinion, over a long period, China should insist on its development strategy of innovation and building an innovation-oriented nation, further increase R&D investments in enterprises, boost their innovation capability to occupy the high-end of the global value chain in the favourable period of global industrial adjustment, and drive the economic restructuring and change of economic development mode through improvement of high-tech industry's innovation capability. Meanwhile, China should further promote the cooperation of industry, colleges and institutes through policy guidance to catalyse the commercialisation of new technologies and to promote their ability to realise the market value of new technologies. China should also carry out various initiatives to speed up technology incubation, create new business models to enhance the value added of high-tech industry's products, combine technological innovation, financial innovation, industrial innovation and business model innovation to form a strong power to improve the overall innovation capability of China's high-tech industry, provide support and play a leading role in accelerating China's transformation of economic development modes.

Finally, it should be noted that there are still shortcomings in this study. For example, when determining the factors affecting innovation efficiency, due to the availability of data, only the expenditure for acquisition of foreign technology and purchase of domestic technology and enterprise size are taken into consideration, with industrial market structure, profitability and other factors being ignored. In this sense, the conclusions in this chapter are limited. These issues should be overcome and improved in our future research.

References

Acs, Z. J., FitzRoy, F. R. and Smith, I., 2002, 'High-technology employment and R&D in cities: heterogeneity vs specialization', *The Annals of Regional Science*, vol. 36, no. 3, pp. 373–86.

Aigner, D., Lovell, C. A. K. and Schmidt, P., 1977, 'Formulation and estimation of stochastic frontier production function models', *Journal of Econometrics*, vol. 6, no. 1, pp. 21–37.

Anselin, L., Varga, A. and Acs, Z. J., 1997, 'Local geographic spillovers between university research and high technology innovations', *Journal of Urban Economics*, vol. 42, pp. 422–48.

Battese, G. E. and Coelli, T., 1995, 'A model of technical inefficiency effects in stochastic frontier production for panel data', *Empirical Economics*, vol. 20, pp. 325–32.

Battese, G. E. and Corra, G. S., 1977, 'Estimation of a production frontier model: with application to the pastoral zone of eastern Australia', *Australian Journal of Agricultural Economics*, vol. 21, no. 3, pp. 169–79.

Blind, K. and Grupp, H., 1999, 'Interdependencies between the science and technology infrastructure and innovation activities in German regions: empirical findings and policy consequences', *Research Policy*, vol. 28, no. 5, pp. 451–68.

Bode, E., 2004, 'The spatial pattern of localized R&D spillovers: an empirical investigation for Germany', *Journal of Economic Geography*, vol. 4, pp. 43–64.

Comanor, W. S. and Scherer, F. M., 1969, 'Patent statistics as a measure of technical change', *Journal of Political Economy*, vol. 77, pp. 392–8.

Gil, Y., Bong, S. and Lee, J., 2003, 'Integration model of technology internalization modes and learning strategy: globally late starter Samsung's successful practices in South Korea', *Technovation*, vol. 23, pp. 333–47.

Griliches, Z., 1979, 'Issues in assessing the contribution of research and development to productivity growth', *Bell Journal of Economics*, vol. 10, pp. 92–116.

Guo, G. F., Wen, J. W. and Sun, B. Y., 2007, 'The affected factor analysis of the ability of technology innovation for the six provinces of central China', *Journal of Quantitative & Technical Economics*, vol. 9, pp. 134–43.

Han, J., 2010, 'An empirical analysis on China's high-tech industry innovation efficiency based on SFA', *Studies in Science of Science*, vol. 3, pp. 467–72.

Jaffe, A. B., 1989, 'Real effects of academic research', *American Economic Review*, vol. 79, no. 5, pp. 957–70.

Kumbhakar, S. C. and Lovell, C., 2000, *Stochastic Frontier Analysis*, Cambridge University Press, Cambridge.

Li, X. B., 2007, 'An empirical study on the transition of China's regional innovation capacity: based on the view of innovation system', *Management World*, vol. 12, pp. 18–30.

Meeusen, W. and van den Broeck, J., 1977, 'Efficiency estimation from Cobb-Douglas production functions with composed error', *International Economic Review*, vol. 18, pp. 435–44.

National Bureau of Statistics of China (NBS), 2009, *China Statistical Yearbook on Science and Technology, 2009*, China Statistics Press, Beijing.

Shi, X. S. and Zhao, S. D., 2009, 'Analysis of regional innovation efficiency and spatial discrepancy in China', *Journal of Quantitative & Technical Economics*, vol. 3, pp. 45–55.

Yang, Y., 2008, 'Synthetic evaluation on self-innovation ability of enterprises: an empirical research from the perspective of the input–output efficiency', *The Study of Finance and Economics*, vol. 6, pp. 30–40.

Zhang, G. Q. and Feng T., 2007, 'An empirical study on the market structure, R&D investment and economic performance: evidence from China's high-tech industry', *Science and Technology Management Research*, vol. 12, pp. 42–7.

Zhi, Y., 2009, 'Innovation ability, technology transformation and innovation performance: an empirical analysis of China's electronic industry's listed companies', *Science of Science and Management of S. & T.*, vol. 3, pp. 96–9, 131.

14. The Impact of China's Economic Growth on its Water Resources:

A regional and sectoral assessment

Hong Yang, Zhuoying Zhang and Minjun Shi

Introduction

With the astonishing speed of its economic growth during the past four decades, China has made unprecedented progress in national development and improvements in the living standard of its people. Alongside this achievement, however, there has been a continued intensification of water shortages and deterioration of water quality. Between 1980 and 2010, total water use increased by 35.8. per cent, from 443.7 billion cubic metres to 602.2 billion cu m (Liu and Chen 2001; MWR 1997–2010). Total industry and household wastewater discharge doubled during the same period.

China's water endowments are, overall, unfavourable. Average water resources per capita are a mere one-quarter of the world average. The uneven spatial and temporal distribution of water resources exacerbates the quantity problem. The bulk of water resources are concentrated in the southern part of the country, whereas the northern part has a much smaller share of the total water resources compared with its proportion of land. China is dominated by the East Asian monsoon climate, and a majority of its annual precipitation is concentrated in the summer months, leaving the rest of the year with little rainfall. Since the late 1980s, water shortages have emerged in many areas in China, particularly in the north. The problem has been worsening over the years in terms of intensity and coverage. It is reported that in some northern cities, the current water supply can barely meet 70 per cent of demand during the dry season. Out of 600 medium to large-sized cities, more than half of them have insufficient water supplies, and more than 100 of them are experiencing severe water shortage (Jiang 2009). Lacking water has caused hardships to people's livelihoods and losses of economic activity. In many northern cities, water scarcity has become a bottleneck to the continuation of economic growth. Competition for limited water resources has led to a reallocation of agricultural water to urban sectors, putting irrigation under great pressure in many areas in the north. Food production—a sector heavily dependent on irrigation—is facing the challenge of producing more food with less water. The water that is needed for maintaining healthy environmental and ecosystem functions has been held back to give priority to meeting the demands of the economic sector.

Along with the intensification of water shortages, water pollution and environmental degradation have been serious across the country. Currently, many rivers and lakes in the eastern part of the country have water quality below Grade V, meaning that the water is too polluted to be suitable for any use. Degraded water quality further aggravates the problem of water shortages. In the North China Plain, most rivers are now dry either completely or seasonally. The ones with water are all heavily polluted and often cannot be used.

Water scarcity and pollution problems have drawn increasing attention in China since the late 1990s. Many measures aimed at increasing water supply and curbing demand have been put forward; yet the problems remain severe, and in many places are worsening. The serious water situation in China has raised questions about water and environmental sustainability. How China will deal with its water shortage and pollution problems will have significant implications for its long-term economic development.

China's water problems are also of global concern given the increasing connection of China with the rest of the world through the international trade of goods and services. International trade between countries entails flows of virtual water—that is, the water used for the production of traded products (Allan 1997; Yang and Zehnder 2007). An inflow of virtual water through trade reduces the pressure on household water resources, whereas an outflow of virtual water adds to the pressure. As the 'world's manufacturing factory', China uses a large portion of water for the production of its exports. Currently, China as a whole is a net 'virtual water exporter'—that is, the amount of water used for the production of exported products is greater than the amount saved on imported products. The intensification of water scarcity in China could impact on its international trade, which has been an important pillar of its rapid economic development since the late 1970s.

As China struggles to develop effective approaches to alleviate water shortages and pollution, a clear understanding of the water situation and its implications for economic development is important. The related questions include: how much water is available and in what quality across regions? How much water is used and for what purposes? Which economic activities are the major polluters of water? To what extent has China's international trade influenced its water uses? This chapter addresses these issues.

The Status of China's Water Resources with Respect to Quantity and Quality

Water Resources and their Spatial Distribution

The annual average volume of renewable water resources in China is approximately 2812 billion cu m per year, including surface and groundwater (MWR 1997–2011). Dividing this volume by the total population of 1.33 billion in 2010, average water availability stands at approximately 2100 cu m per capita. This figure is roughly one-quarter of the world average and one-sixth of the figure for the United States. Thus, China as a whole can be said to be a water-poor country by world standards.

China's water resources are geographically divided into nine major watersheds/ river basins: the Yangtze, Yellow (Huang), Hai-Luan, Huai, Song-Liao, Pearl, South-East, South-West and North-West (Table 14.1). The spatial distribution of water resources is highly uneven. The Yellow (Huang) River Basin, Hai-Luan River Basin and Huai River Basin (hereinafter, the HHH region) have average water resources of between 300 cu m/year and 700 cu m/year—substantially below the water-scarcity threshold of 1700 cu m/year defined by Falkenmark (1995). The Inland region is dominated by arid and semi-arid climates where water is extremely scarce. The relatively large volume of per capita water resources in the region is mainly because of the sparse population relative to the vast territory. The South-West watershed is endowed with abundant water resources. Several international rivers originate here, including the Mekong, Thanlwin and Brahmaputra; however, most of the water in the south-west is not accessible to the rest of the country due to geographical barriers and, to a lesser extent, international political sensitivities over shared waters.

The ratio of water withdrawal to water availability is an indicator of the intensity of water use and the pressure on the ecosystem. Forty per cent (or 0.4) is a rule-of-thumb ratio commonly used as a benchmark for water criticality (Alcamo et al. 1999). The higher the ratio, the greater is the pressure of water withdrawal on the available water resources and dependent ecosystems. Table 14.1 shows the ratio of water withdrawal to water resource availability in the major river basins in China.

Table 14.1 Water Resources Availability and Water Withdrawal in the Major River Basins (average 2006–10)

Basins	Per capita water resources availability	Water resources availability	Water use	Ratio of withdrawal to availability
	cu m/capita	billion cu m	billion cu m	%
Song-Liao	1704	172.07	64.38	37.42
Hai	358	29.75*	37.00	124.37
Huang	749	61.06	46.67**	76.43
Huai	505	89.06*	63.97	71.83
Yangtze	2388	839.60	197.04	23.47
Pearl	3327	453.62	87.68	19.33
South-East watershed	2962	173.52	34.36	19.80
Inland watershed	5270	132.34	64.13	48.46
South-West watershed	31 914	594.44	11.18	1.88
Nation	2100	2475.52	596.52	24.10

* including water transfer into the Hai River Basin and the Huai River Basin
** including water transfer out of the Yellow River Basin
Sources: MWR (1997–2011).

Currently, the ratios of water withdrawal to water resources availability in the Hai, Yellow and Huai Rivers are excessively high compared with the internationally recommended sustainable ratio of 40 per cent, indicating severe water stress in these basins. The Hai River Basin has a ratio of 124 per cent, meaning that the basin is using more water than it has. This is possibly mainly due to the exploitation of non-renewable deep aquifers in the North China Plain, supplemented with a small amount of desalinated seawater. The result has been a drop of the groundwater table at an alarming rate and a depletion of water resources in the region. It is estimated that the accumulated overdraft of groundwater during the past two decades in the North China Plain has exceeded 90 billion cu m (Yang and Zehnder 2005). The depletion of groundwater has serious consequences, including land subsidence, seawater intrusion and loss of ecosystem functions. With the excessively high level of water withdrawal, many rivers and their tributaries in the north have had extremely poor ecological status. The Yellow River has become a seasonal river, and sent little or no water to the sea for most of the late 1990s (MWR 1997–2011).

State of Water Quality

The rapid economic growth in China during the past four decades has been accompanied by a continuous deterioration of its water quality. In China, water quality is divided into five categories that can be described as 'good' (grades I, II and III) or 'poor' (grades IV and V or V+). As shown in Figure 14.1, China's water quality is characterised by extended sections of water of poor quality. At the national level, more than 40 per cent of river sections currently have poor water quality. In northern China, water-quality degradation is severe in all major rivers with the percentage of monitored water sections ranked poor exceeding 60 per cent. In the Yangtze and Pearl River Basins in the south, more than 30 per cent of the monitored water sections have poor water quality. Water-quality status presents a serious situation in China, where water shortages and degraded quality interact and reinforce the negative effects of each other.

It should be mentioned that the water-quality issue has drawn much attention in China and huge investment has been poured into the construction of wastewater treatment facilities since the late 1990s; however, little improvement has been made so far. In many areas, water quality has been deteriorating. This situation is of particular concern for the southern rivers. During the past two decades, there has been a clear trend of water-quality degradation in the Yangtze and Pearl River Basins (MWR 1997–2011).

Figure 14.1 Water Quality in the Monitored Sections of the Major Rivers in China, 2010

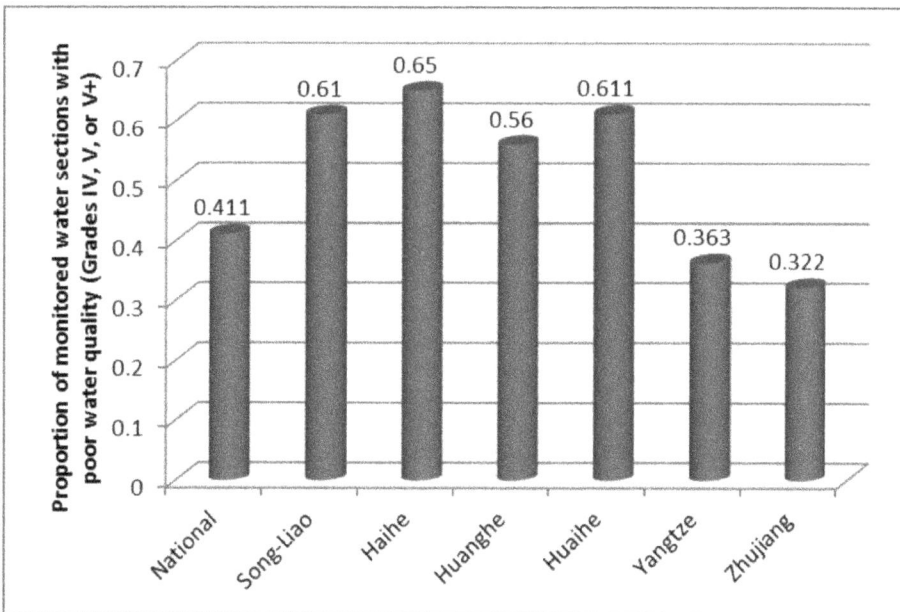

Source: MWR (1997–2011).

While the water quality in rivers is bad, the situation in lakes is generally worse because of the slow circulation of water and the high concentration of pollution sources in surrounding areas. Among 44 major lakes in China, 56 per cent have water quality of grades IV, V and V+. The water quality for the entirety of Tai Lake is below Grade III. In the Dianchi and Chao Lakes, water quality is below Grade V. The huge investment in the past decade in the improvement of water quality in the Tai, Dianchi and Chao Lakes has so far achieved hardly any result (MWR 1997–2011).

Changes in Water-Use Quantity and Value in Different Sectors

Trends in Water Use in Different Sectors

Rapid economic development together with continuous population growth have generated an increased demand for water. Figure 14.2 shows the changes in water use in different sectors between 1980 and 2010.

Figure 14.2 Trends in Water Use by Industry, Domestic (Households) and Agriculture, 1980–2010

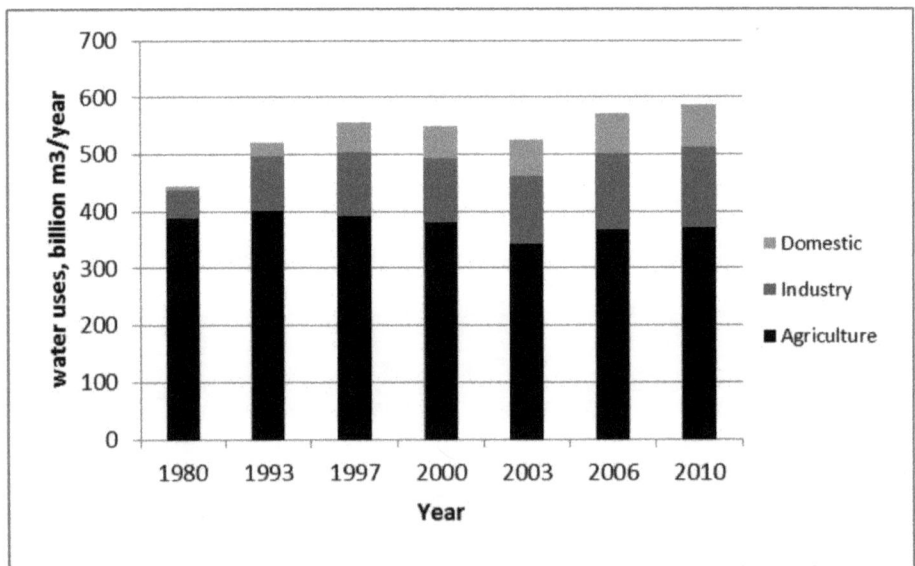

Sources: Liu and Chen (2001); MWR (1997–2011).

Between 1980 and 2009, total water use in China increased by 34 per cent. The increase, however, is solely from the industrial and household sectors. The quantity of water use in the industrial sector increased from 45.7 billion cu m to 139.1 billion cu m, or threefold. The household sector had a much faster increase, from 6.8 billion cu m to 74.8 billion cu m, or elevenfold. In contrast, agricultural water use has experienced a decrease of 5 per cent, from 391.2 billion cu m to 372.3 billion cu m. About 19 billion cu m of the agricultural water was reallocated to the industrial and household sectors during this period.

Despite the decrease in agricultural water use, the total irrigated area in China expanded by 34 per cent between 1980 and 2010, from 44.89 million hectares to 60.35 million ha (SSB various years). This has been achieved with improvements in water-use efficiency in irrigation. On average, water use per hectare of irrigated land decreased from 8240 cu m/ha (549 cu m/mu)[1] to 6280 cu m/ha (417 cu m/mu). The North China Plain has been leading the trend, with current irrigation water use of between 3000 cu m/ha and 4000 cu m/ha. In Beijing, irrigation water use efficiency is reported to be as high as 0.8 (*China Daily*, 2011). In most other regions, however, irrigation water-use efficiency remains low. In the upper and middle reaches of the Yellow River and the north-west inland areas, it is below 0.5. Hence, the potential for improving irrigation water-use efficiency is considered to be high.

The need to allocate (or reserve) water for environmental uses has received attention in recent years. There is some confusion/disagreement about the appropriate amount of water required for maintaining healthy ecosystem status and functions. This is partly because of the complexity of measuring the ecosystem's water use and partly because of the close relations between the ecosystem water requirement and the society's demand for the quality of the aquatic environment. The latter evolves with economic development, as described by the Environmental Kuznets Curve (Jia et al. 2006). Despite the difficulty of determining the appropriate amount of water for the environment, it is clear that with competition for water from the economic sectors, little water has been left in the rivers of the northern regions. As the environment cannot represent itself in the competition for water, it is ultimately the responsibility of the government to ensure the allocation of water for maintaining ecosystem health at a level that is acceptable to (and demanded by) the society.

Changes in Water-Use Values

The quantity of water use per RMB10 000 gross domestic product (GDP) value is an indicator used in China to measure the water-use value of the economic sectors. Hereinafter, this metric will be referred to as 'water intensity'. Figure 14.3 shows the changes in this metric from 1993 to 2010. Water intensity decreased from 771 cu m in 1993 to 382 cu m in 2010. In the industrial sector,

---

1 'Mu' is a measure of land area in China. 1 mu is equivalent to 1/15 ha.

the figures are 363 cu m and 230 cu m, respectively (note that the GDP figure comes from a constant price series based on the year 2000). The decrease in water intensity is rather slow. This concurs with the generally low efficiency of resource use in China.

Figure 14.3 Sectoral Water Use Per RMB10 000 GDP Values, 1993–2010

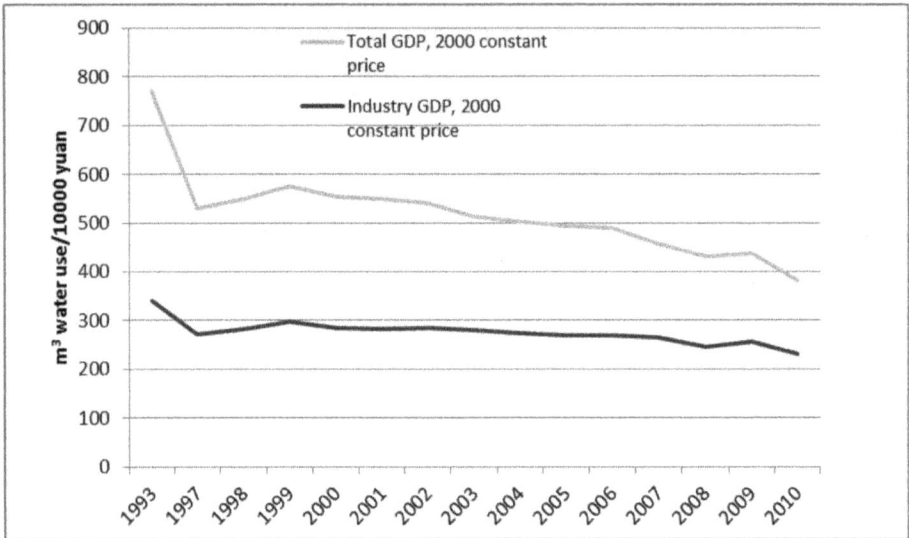

Sources: The data for 1993 are from Liu and Chen (2001). The rest of the data are from SSB (various years).

Quantifying water intensity for individual economic sectors is complex because of the interconnection of water uses between sectors through the input–output relations. For example, the water used for a product in the textile industry might come partially from the agricultural sector through the raw materials it provided. Hence, the water-use value in the individual sectors can be accounted for by the direct water-use coefficient (DWUC) and the total water-use coefficient (TWUC), both of which are measured in the same fashion as aggregate water intensity. DWUC reflects the direct water intensity at the last stage of the production chain (the operational stage for a business or a factory), whereas TWUC reflects the water use throughout the whole production chain— for example, from cotton production to the final production of, say, a pair of jeans. Hence, it is also called the 'life cycle water-use coefficient'. DWUC is the conventional measure for the sectoral water intensity; however, it does not reflect the total water embodied in final outputs because a large amount of water used is in the upstream supply chain. To this end, TWUC provides a more complete picture of water use. Based on China's provincial input–output tables for 2002 and 2007 and the water-use quotas in individual economic sectors, DWUC and TWUC can be estimated. For simplicity, the full industrial classification has been compressed into 20 sectors. Table 14.2 shows DWUC and TWUC estimates for the individual sectors in 2002 and 2007.

Table 14.2 Water-Use Coefficient for 2002 and 2007 (cu m/RMB10^4)

Sectors		2002		2007	
		DWUC	TWUC	DWUC	TWUC
1	Agriculture	1582	2068	924	1181
2	Coalmining and processing	38	268	22	140
3	Food and tobacco processing	39	991	23	523
4	Textile goods	37	652	21	520
5	Clothing	7	543	4	306
6	Sawmills and furniture	3	543	2	279
7	Paper and products	109	506	64	320
8	Petroleum processing	30	257	18	144
9	Chemicals	58	417	34	239
10	Non-metal mineral products	27	351	16	184
11	Metal smelting and products	49	386	29	217
12	Machinery and equipment	6	270	3	152
13	Transport equipment	7	291	4	147
14	Electrical equipment, telecommunications equipment	4	246	2	140
15	Other manufacturing	6	288	3	165
16	Electricity, gas and water production and supply	985	1251	575	840
17	Construction	5	271	3	159
18	Wholesale and retail trade and passenger transport	48	226	28	124
19	Restaurants and hotels	206	785	120	441
20	Other services	28	196	16	114

Sources: Zhang et al. (2011, 2012).

The difference between DWUC and TWUC is small in some sectors and large in others, reflecting different characteristics of water use in the production chain of each sector. In general, 'Agriculture' and 'Electricity, Gas and Water Production and Supply' (hereinafter, utilities) are direct water-use–dominated sectors, reflected by the high proportions of DWUCs in TWUCs. In contrast, most manufacturing sectors have large indirect water uses. In the sectors of 'Food and Tobacco Processing', 'Clothing', 'Sawmills and Furniture', 'Machinery and Equipment', 'Transport Equipment', 'Electrical Equipment' and 'Telecommunications Equipment', more than 95 per cent of the water use takes place in an indirect way—that is, in the processing stages prior to the final stage. For example, clothing had a DWUC of 7 and a TWUC of 543 in 2002. This means that about 99 per cent of water use took place in the upstream supply chain of the industry.

For both 2002 and 2007, agriculture had the highest water intensity, with a TWUC of 2068 cu m per $RMB10^4$ in 2002 and 1181 cu m/$RMB10^4$ in 2007. This was followed by utilities, which had a TWUC of 1250 in 2002 and 840 in 2007. The other sectors with relatively high TWUCs are 'Food and Tobacco', 'Textiles' and 'Restaurants and Hotels', which are indirect water-use dominated. Their main water uses were incurred in the upstream supply chain, typically through raw materials from the agricultural sector.

Compared with 2002, in 2007, all the sectors showed notable reductions in both DWUC and TWUC. The scale of the reduction is mostly between 20 per cent and 50 per cent, indicating that considerably less water was used in the production of one unit of output in 2007 compared with that in 2002. The sectors with the largest reductions in TWUC are 'Sawmills and Furniture', 'Transport Equipment', 'Coalmining and Processing' and 'Non-Metal Mineral Products', where the reductions amounted to 49 per cent, 49 per cent, 48 per cent and 48 per cent respectively. The pace of the reduction in DWUC and TWUC, however, was not fast enough to offset the incremental water use due to the expansion of production. Total water use at the national level increased from 549.7 billion cu m in 2002 to 581.8 billion cu m in 2007.

Major Sources of Water Pollution

Sources of water pollution are mainly wastewater discharge from industrial and household sectors and non-point source pollutants from agriculture (for example, from fertiliser, pesticide, processing residuals, and so on). The official statistics on wastewater discharge include only industrial and household wastewater. In the industrial sector, statistics for wastewater discharge account for only the enterprises at and above county level. Enterprises at the township level and below are not included. No information on agricultural water pollution is reported partly because of the difficulty of measuring the non-point source pollution from agriculture. Figure 14.4 shows the trend in wastewater discharge from the industrial and the household sectors during 1981 and 2010.

Figure 14.4 Trends in Industry (Enterprises at or Above the County Level)
and Domestic (Household) Wastewater Discharge, 1981–2010

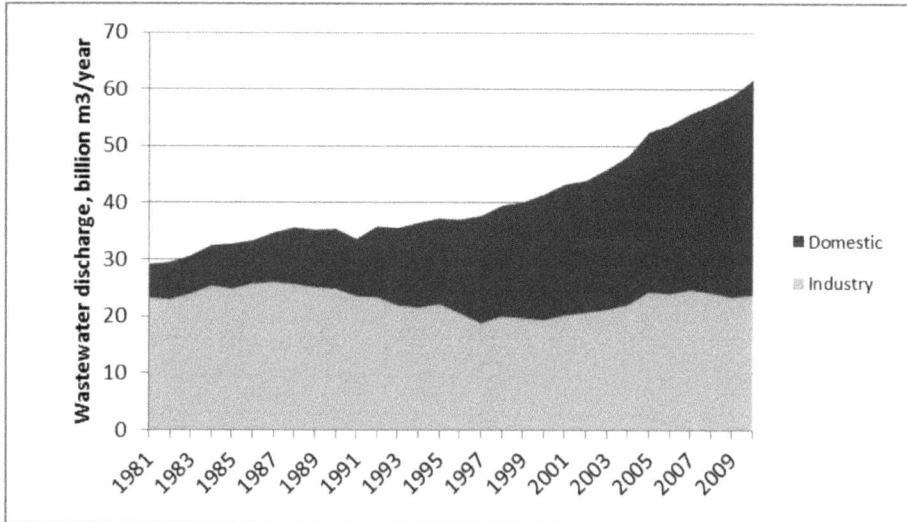

Source: SSB (various years).

The quantity of industrial wastewater discharge has not changed significantly over the years, while household wastewater discharge has increased rapidly. In the 1980s, industrial wastewater dominated the total wastewater discharge. The household wastewater discharge surpassed the level from industry in the 1990s to become the major source of wastewater discharge. Part of the discharged wastewater from industry and households is after treatment and meets the state discharge quality requirement. According to the official Chinese statistics, the proportion of the wastewater discharge meeting the effluent standard has increased steadily in the industrial sector. Currently, about 92 per cent of industrial wastewater discharge meets the requirement (SSB various years); however, as the wastewater discharge and the treatment rates are reported by local government agencies, there is a high possibility of underreporting in the official statistics. This is because of a strong incentive for reporting smaller wastewater discharges, especially of the amount below the effluent standard. In reality, the treatment rates for both industrial and household wastewater are probably much lower.

Adding to the problems of measurement is pollution from rural enterprises that is not accounted for in the official statistics. It must be pointed out that the exclusion of wastewater discharge from these enterprises substantially understates the intensity of industrial water pollution. Small scale and low technology are the common features of rural enterprises. They are notorious for releasing heavily polluted wastewater without any treatment.

Unlike industrial wastewater discharge, which in general requires treatment within the system before release into waterways, household wastewater is collected and treated on site or transferred to centralised wastewater treatment plants. In reality, due to the lack of collection networks and treatment facilities/ capacities, as well as the generally poor economic returns of the wastewater treatment business, a high proportion of household wastewater is released to water bodies without treatment. In small cities, the untreated component of household wastewater can be as high as 90 per cent (SEPA 2010).

Table 14.3 Major Polluting Sectors and their GDP Values, 2010

Sector	Industrial wastewater discharge	Gross industry output value	Wastewater/ output value
	10^4 tonnes	RMB10^8	cu m/RMB10^4
Mining and washing of coal	80 235.5	16 404.27	48.91
Mining and processing of non-ferrous metal ores	37 307.31	2814.67	132.55
Processing of food from agricultural products	143 837.66	27 961.03	51.44
Manufacture of foods	52 699.09	9219.24	57.16
Manufacture of textiles	239 115.6	22 971.38	104.09
Manufacture of leather, fur, feather and related products	24 964.32	6425.57	38.85
Manufacture of paper and paper products	392 604.14	8264.36	475.06
Manufacture of raw chemical materials and chemical products	297 061.66	36 908.63	80.49
Manufacture of medicines	52 718.39	9443.3	55.83
Manufacture of chemical fibres	43 854.81	3828.32	114.55
Smelting and pressing of ferrous metals	125 978.31	42 636.15	29.55
The sum of the above sectors	1 490 376.79	186 876.92	
Average			79.75
Percentage of national total	71	34	

Source: SSB (various years).

The wastewater discharge intensity varies among industrial sectors. Table 14.3 shows the large contributors to industrial wastewater discharge. At the national level, the sectors encompassed in Table 14.3 account for 34 per cent of the total gross industrial output value, whereas they produce 71 per cent of the total industrial wastewater discharge. The sectors with very high wastewater discharge intensity are Mining, Textiles, Paper and Chemical-related industries. Bearing in mind that small rural enterprises are highly concentrated in these sectors, the untreated wastewater discharge from these enterprises has a significant impact on water quality. This perhaps partially explains the situation that the observed water quality is often worse than that reported in the official statistics.

The Impact of China's International Trade on its Water Resources

International trade between countries entails flows of virtual water—that is, the water used for the production of traded products. With world markets filled with 'made in China' products on the one hand and the increasingly severe water stress and pollution endured in most parts of China on the other, the impact of China's international trade of goods and services on its water resources warrants scrutiny. The input–output tables for the 30 provinces (excluding Tibet) in 2002 and 2007 are used for the investigation.

Sectoral Assessment

The virtual water trade by sector is quantified for the whole production chain, instead of just the final stage of the process—that is, these are comparable in breadth with the TWUCs estimated above. In so doing, the total water use for the final products in individual sectors can be better reflected. The virtual water associated with the trade of the products in individual sectors includes the water used for the production of the input materials that are from other sectors—typically from the primary sectors. Table 14.4 shows the estimated virtual water flows associated with China's international trade.

China as a whole is a net virtual water exporter. The annual net virtual water export was estimated at 39.04 billion cu m in 2002 and 68.18 billion cu m in 2007. This represents an increase of 74 per cent over five years. The situation coincides with the trend seen in the national total water use mentioned earlier. The improvement in water-use efficiency in individual sectors has not been able to offset the additional virtual water exported due to the expansion of international trade during this period.

Of the 20 sectors in the study, only Agriculture, Petroleum Processing, Machinery and Equipment and Utilities are net importers of virtual water. The remaining sectors are net exporters. Textiles, Clothing, Electrical Equipment, Telecommunications Equipment, Wholesale and Retail Trade, Passenger Transport and Metal Smelting and Products are the five major net virtual water exporters. Their net virtual water export accounts for more than 85 per cent of the national total. These sectors are also mainstay industries in China, greatly contributing to China's role as the 'world's factory'.

Table 14.4 Sectoral Virtual Water Trade in 2002 and 2007 (10^6 cu m)

Sectors		2002			2007		
		Virtual water export	Virtual water import	Net virtual water export	Virtual water export	Virtual water import	Net virtual water export
1	Agriculture	7080	10 247	-3167	18 212	21 137	-2924
2	Coalmining and processing	273	27	246	678	123	555
3	Food and tobacco processing	5595	2783	2812	7288	5137	2151
4	Textile goods	11 644	829	10 815	6329	313	6015
5	Clothing	8375	700	7675	19 392	1363	18 029
6	Sawmills and furniture	2833	469	2364	5239	402	4837
7	Paper and products	3446	785	2661	4928	753	4175
8	Petroleum processing	499	1536	-1037	1139	3167	-2028
9	Chemicals	6635	4107	2528	10 430	4653	5777
10	Non-metal mineral products	1383	390	992	2170	434	1736
11	Metal smelting and products	4059	2321	1738	13 278	4493	8785
12	Machinery and equipment	2286	5858	-3572	6085	6990	-905
13	Transport equipment	1344	1337	7	3735	1334	2400
14	Electrical equipment, telecommunications equipment	12 575	5011	7564	32 067	10 028	22 039
15	Other manufacturing	2802	1761	1042	1532	736	796
16	Electricity, gas and water production and supply	60	3193	-3133	1325	7090	-5765
17	Construction	124	89	35	481	2352	-1871
18	Wholesale and retail trade and passenger transport	6449	375	6074	5074	1431	3643
19	Restaurants and hotels	1749	18	1730	1184	291	893
20	Other services	3430	1765	1665	2067	2229	-163
	Total	82 641	43 602	39 038	142 634	74 457	68 177

Sources: Zhang et al. (2011, 2012).

It is worth noting that Food and Tobacco Processing and Textiles and Clothing are typical downstream industries of agriculture—that is, using raw materials from agriculture as inputs. Although the agricultural sector is a net importer of virtual water, its downstream industries are not. The situation implies that part of the imported virtual water in agriculture is re-exported through the exports of products in its downstream sectors.

Net virtual water exports are highly concentrated in Textiles, Clothing and Electrical Goods and Communication Equipment. These sectors are typically labour intensive, employing a large number of rural migrant workers. In terms of water use, Textiles and Clothing are rather water-intensive sectors with high TWUCs. The share of these sectors is often high in water-scarce regions, such as Tianjin, Hebei and Shandong. The impact of international trade on water resources in the water-scarce provinces is therefore more significant.

In addition to the impact on the quantity of water resources, China's international trade also impacts on its water quality. The wastewater discharge from Food and Tobacco Processing, Textiles, Clothing, Paper and Products, and Metal Smelting and Products accounts for a large percentage of the total industrial wastewater discharge (Table 14.3). Small-scale and low-technology rural enterprises are mostly concentrated in these sectors. Hence, China is exporting a large amount of virtual water to other countries while keeping heavy water pollution to itself.

Regional Assessment

With total water resources of 2812 billion cu m per year in China, the net virtual water export of 68.2 billion cu m/year (in 2007) is about 3.1 per cent of its total water resources. As a large portion of the country's water resources are not accessible to the water-poor regions due to geographical barriers, the impact of China's international trade on water resources is, however, much more significant when viewed at the regional level. In the extremely water-scarce Huang–Huai–Hai (HHH) region, 5.1 per cent of the region's water resources are forgone due to virtual water exports.

Total water use in China was approximately 526 billion cu m in 2007 (SSB 2008). The net virtual water export accounted for 11.5 per cent of total water use (Table 14.5). In the water-scarce HHH region, roughly 7 per cent of the total water use was for export. The share in Tianjin—an extremely water-scarce city in this region—was 63 per cent. In Beijing and Shandong, the shares were 17.9 per cent and 20 per cent, respectively. The results suggest that China's economic gains from being the 'world's manufacturing powerhouse' (McKay and Song 2010) have been attained at a high cost to its water resources and environment, particularly in the northern regions.

Table 14.5 Water Resources (WR), Water Use (WU) and Net Virtual Water Export (NVWE) in Different Regions, 2007

Regions	Provinces	NVWE 10⁶ cu m	NVWE/WR %	NVWE/WU %
North China Plain	Beijing, Tianjin, Hebei, Shanxi, Shandong and Henan	5240	5.1	6.9
North-East	Liaoning, Jilin and Heilongjiang	378	0.3	0.7
East and Middle	Shanghai, Jiangsu, Zhejiang, Anhui, Jiangxi, Hubei and Hunan	21 662	3.5	10.8
South	Fujian, Guangdong, Guangxi and Hainan	26 044	5.2	25.7
South-West	Chongqing, Sichuan, Guizhou and Yunnan	423	0.1	0.8
North-West	Inner Mongolia, Shaanxi, Gansu, Qinghai, Ningxia and Xinjiang	14 429	5.6	14.2
Nation		68 177	3.1	11.5

Sources: Data for WR and WU are from SSB (2008); data for NVWE are from Zhang et al. (2012).

Balancing Water Needs Between Society and Nature

China's water problems are characterised by insufficient quantity and poor quality. Rapid economic development and urbanisation combined with population growth continue to intensify the conflict between water supply and demand; and adverse future climate change is expected to increase China's vulnerability to water scarcity.

Poor management is one of the important factors responsible for the water problems in China. Hence, improving water resource management is crucial for alleviating China's water vulnerability. Addressing China's water problems requires a holistic, integrated and scientific approach with long-term and coordinated efforts. In recent years, some efforts have been made to improve water resource management to support long-term economic growth and restore aquatic ecosystem functions.

China is making efforts to improve institutional systems that regulate water withdrawal and uses. River basin conservation commissions, under the Ministry of Water Resources, have been entrusted with more power over the administration and management of the water defined by basin boundaries and consistent with the hydrological cycle of water resources. Issuing water withdrawal permits has been gradually implemented in some river basins. In this respect, the Yellow River Conservancy Commission (YRCC) has been at the forefront. The current Yellow River water allocation plan is enforced with both total quantity control and cross-provincial border discharge monitoring. In recent years, a so-called 'investment for water saving and water rights transfer measure' has been put forward in the Yellow River Basin. It mainly concerns water reallocation from agriculture to industry. As obtaining additional water in the water-scarce basins has been difficult, the increase in industrial water demand has to be met with the transfer of water from the agricultural sector. Given the widespread low efficiency in irrigation, the potential for water saving is considered high (Yang and Jia 2008). Industries, especially large enterprises, are encouraged to invest in water-saving projects in the existing irrigation schemes in exchange for the rights for the use of part of the saved water. The measure is regarded as a 'win-win' solution for low water-use efficiency and water shortages in water-scarce regions. So far, however, all the water rights transfers have been conducted within individual provinces. Cross-provincial water rights transfers have not taken place. In general, provinces are not willing to give up their entitled shares of water. This is partly because of the increased administrative complexity in water rights transfer across provincial boundaries. More importantly, recognising that water scarcity is a long-term trend in many parts of China, individual provinces all want to hold their shares of water for their own economic development. Water rights transfer is still in its infancy. Its scale and overall effect on improving water use efficiency remain to be seen.

Since the late 1990s, economic incentive-based approaches—typically water pricing and wastewater charges—have been given much emphasis in the effort to build a 'water-saving' society. With the exhaustion of suitable sites for water projects on the major rivers, as well as the very high withdrawal ratios from the northern rivers, augmentation of water supply becomes more and more difficult and costly. The economic incentive-based approaches are implemented to allow the market to adjust water demand and supply. Increasing water prices have been a general trend seen in all economic sectors; however, the pricing mechanism alone has not been effective in capping total water use within a sustainable amount. In many places, total water use has been rising continuously while water pollution has been worsening. The situation suggests that integrated approaches, including economic and non-economic measures, are necessary to tackle the water shortage and pollution problems, which are often interconnected.

Environmental water use and ecosystem water requirements have received increasing attention since the late 1990s. The criteria used for estimating ecosystem water demand are often subjective. Thirty per cent of the average river flow is commonly used as a rule-of-thumb percentage for the amount of water required to maintain healthy aquatic ecosystems. As mentioned earlier, the ratios of water withdrawal to water resources in the major northern rivers all exceeded 70 per cent, meaning that less than 30 per cent of water is left for ecological maintenance. In the Hai River Basin, where the ratio exceeded 100 per cent, the environment is left with essentially no water. It is interesting to note that the argument for the need to meet the ecosystem's water demand in the rivers of the North China Plain has been an important factor in the decision on the construction of the South–North Water Transfer Project (Yang and Zehnder 2005).

Facing the enormous challenges of water shortages and pollution, the Chinese Government has been implementing more stringent controls over water uses and wastewater discharges. In January 2012, the State Council released a 'Red Head' document (No. 3), in which several ambitious controlling Red Lines are set. For the year 2030, total water use will be capped at 700 billion cu m, compared with approximately 600 billion cu m in 2010. Water intensity will be reduced to 40 cu m (GDP being measured at 2000 prices). Agricultural irrigation water-use efficiency will be lifted to above 0.6, compared with the current 0.5. Water quality will be 'good' in 95 per cent of water bodies (SC 2012). There are many challenges to surmount before these targets can be reached. It requires the establishment of accountable water resource management and evaluation systems, sound monitoring systems, investment mechanisms, regulations and laws, enforcement agencies and social scrutiny. How successful China will be in achieving these goals remains an open question.

Conclusion

China's water endowments are unfavourable in terms of both the quantity (relative to its population) and spatial distribution. Water pollution due to the rapid pace of industrialisation and urbanisation has also aggravated the physical scarcity by reducing the availability of useable water. In many regions, water shortage has become a bottleneck to economic development, while water pollution has posed an increasingly high risk to human health as well as threatening environmental sustainability. As the major exporter of low value-added and high water-use intensity manufactured products, China has been exporting a large amount of virtual water, while keeping heavily polluted water to itself.

The low efficiency of water use in China concurs with the generally low efficiency of resource use and the dependence of economic growth on the expansion of resource supply. This calls for an integrated approach, including economic (such as water pricing) and non-economic measures. An integrated approach is necessary to tackle the water shortage and pollution problems simultaneously. Decoupling economic growth from increasing water use and pollution is important for long-term economic development. A regional economic structural adjustment taking into consideration water resource endowments would be conducive to reducing pressure on the limited water resources in the water-scarce regions. Also important is the establishment of enabling institutions that can ensure the effective enforcement of the required measures for improving water resources management.

Water shortages and water pollution are serious problems. How China deals with these challenges will be vital for its long-term economic development and environmental sustainability. Given its central position in the world economy, China's degree of success in overcoming these challenges will have material implications for the rest of the world.

Bibliography

Alcamo, J., Henrichs, T. and Rosch, T., 1999, *World water in 2025. Global modeling and scenario analysis for the World Commission on Water for the 21st century*, Kassel World Water Series Report 2, University of Kassel, Germany.

Allan, J. A., 1997, *'Virtual water': a long term solution for water short Middle Eastern economies?*, Occasional paper, Water Issues Group, School of Oriental and African Studies, London.

China Daily, 2011, Boost in capital's water efficiency, <http://www.chinadaily.com.cn/cndy/2011-04-28/content_12409302.htm>

Falkenmark, M., 1995, 'Land–water linkages—a synopsis. Land and water integration and river basin management', *FAO Land and Water Bulletin*, no. 1, pp. 15–16.

Jia, S. F., Yang, H., Zhang, S. F., Wang, L. and Xia, J., 2006, 'Industrial water use Kuznets Curve: evidence from industrialized countries and implications for developing countries', *Journal of Water Resources Planning and Management*, vol. 132, no. 3, pp. 183–91.

Jiang, Y., 2009, 'China's water scarcity', *Journal of Environmental Management*, vol. 90, pp. 3185–96.

Liu, C. M. and Chen, Z. K., 2001, *China Water Resources Status Assessment and Supply and Demand Trend Analysis*, China Hydro-Engineering Publishing House, Beijing.

McKay, H. and Song, L., 2010, 'China as a global manufacturing powerhouse: strategic considerations and structural adjustment', *China and World Economy*, vol. 18, no. 1 (February), pp. 1–32.

Ministry of Water Resources (MWR), 1997–2011, *Water Resources Bulletin*, Ministry of Water Resources, Beijing, <http://www.chinawater.net.cn>

Shen, D. J., 2010, 'Climate change and water resources: evidence and estimates in China', *Climate Change and Water Resources*, vol. 98, no. 8, pp. 1063–128.

State Council of China (SC), 2012, *State Council Proposal for Implementing the Most Strict Water Resources Management Systems*, State Council of China, Beijing, viewed 15 February 2012, <http://www.mwr.gov.cn/slzx/slyw/201201/t20120119_312981.html>

State Environmental Protection Administration (SEPA), 1994, *China Environmental Statistical Data Compilation. 1981–1990*, China Environmental Science Publishing House, Beijing.

State Statistical Bureau (SSB), various years, *China Statistical Yearbook*, China Statistics Press, Beijing.

State Statistical Bureau (SSB), 2008, *Regional Input–Output Table of China, 2002*, China Statistics Press, Beijing.

State Statistical Bureau, 2009, *Input–Output Table of China, 2007*, China Statistics Press, Beijing.

Yang, H. and Jia, S. F., 2008, 'Meeting the basin closure of the Yellow River in China', *International Journal of Water Resources Development*, vol. 24, no. 2, pp. 265–74.

Yang, H. and Zehnder, A., 2007, '"Virtual water": an unfolding concept in integrated water resources management', *Water Resources Research*, vol. 43, <doi:10.1029/2007WR006048>

Yang, H. and Zehnder, A. J. B., 2005, 'The South–North Water Transfer Project in China: an analysis of water demand uncertainty and environmental objectives in decision making', *Water International*, vol. 30, no. 3, pp. 339–49.

Zhang, Z. Y., Shi, M. J., Yang, H. and Chapagain, A., 2012, 'An input–output analysis of trends in virtual water trade and the impact on water resource and uses in China', *Economic Systems Research*, vol. 23, no. 4, pp. 431–46.

Zhang, Z. Y., Yang, H. and Shi, M. J., 2011, 'Analyses of water footprint of Beijing in an interregional input–output framework', *Ecological Economics*, vol. 70, pp. 2494–502.

15. Why Are the Stakes So High?:
Misconceptions and misunderstandings in China's global quest for energy security

ZhongXiang Zhang

Introduction

China was the world's second-largest carbon emitter behind the United States for years. On the trends of the 1980s and 1990s, the US Energy Information Administration (USEIA 2004) estimated that China's carbon dioxide emissions would not catch up with those of the United States until 2030. China's energy use has surged, however, since the turn of this century, almost doubling between 2000 and 2007. Despite similar rates of real economic growth, the rate of growth in China's energy use during this period was more than twice that of the last two decades of the twentieth century (NBS 2009). As a result, China became the world's largest carbon emitter in 2007, instead of being number two 'until 2030' as estimated as late as 2004.

Confronted with rampant environmental pollution problems and health risks, and rising greenhouse gas emissions and the resulting climate change, the mounting challenge for China is how to keep its energy consumption and carbon dioxide emissions under control while sustaining its rapid economic growth (Zhang 2010a, 2011c). Another enormous challenge that China needs to deal with is a huge increase in its oil imports, which is accompanying its rapid economic growth, and the resulting carbon emissions. This has raised great concern about China's energy security because its rapidly increasing oil imports come mainly from politically unstable regions and are shipped through lengthy sealanes over which China has little influence. Given that global oil markets are very volatile and China's incremental oil demand dwarfs that of any other single country, China's responses to growing energy security concerns have been brought into the spotlight. In this context, China's global quest for resources—in particular, oil and natural gas—has received unprecedented worldwide attention and scrutiny. This is partly because of China's own high-profile, active state diplomacy and its national oil companies' acquisitions in the key exporting regions of oil and natural gas. But, in my view, the stakes are raised unnecessarily high mainly because of the growing politicisation of Chinese energy security as a result of misconceptions and misunderstandings of China's quest for energy security both inside and outside China. Inside China, these relate to the perceived US-led oil blockade against China and China's illusion that its investments in oil fields overseas are able to help strengthen its energy security. Western political rhetoric characterises China's efforts to secure energy supplies overseas as a major threat. That rhetoric further intensifies China's mistrust of global oil markets, sparking fears that the energy establishment will seek to deny China's access to the oil it needs for development. Outside China, there are wide misconceptions and misunderstandings of how Chinese policy banks operate and their oil and natural gas-based loans. China's loans are often misrepresented as asking borrowers to sell a fixed quantity of oil to China during the contract period at a predetermined price so that China can capture windfall gains as oil prices rise.

This chapter aims to depoliticise the debate on China's global quest for energy resources and to put discussions on that issue into perspective. To that end, the chapter first categorises the main features of China's energy mix and discusses why energy security in China equates to a large extent to oil security. The chapter then pays special attention to misconceptions and misunderstandings regarding the hypothesised US-led 'oil blockade' against China; the Chinese policy banks and their oil and natural gas-based loans; and the role of Chinese investments in oil and gas fields overseas in discussions on China's global quest for energy resources. The chapter ends with some concluding remarks on a more constructive way forward.

Energy Security in the Chinese Context

China's energy security issues cannot be well understood without a better understanding of its energy mix. This section will categorise the main features of China's energy mix and discuss why energy security in China equates to a large extent to oil security.

Main Reliance on Domestic Energy Resources

China is self-sufficient in energy. Even in the 1950s when almost all oil was imported, 97 per cent of energy supply was still from domestic sources (Zhang 1998). China's energy balance was also unaffected by the first rise in world oil prices. China is indeed a large energy consumer. With rapid economic growth fuelled by increasing energy consumption, China is now the world's largest energy consumer, with an increasing dependence on imported oil. At the same time, however, China is also the world's largest energy producer. With total domestic primary energy production of 2960 million tonnes of coal equivalent (mtce)[1] and total domestic energy consumption of 3250 mtce in 2010 (Hua 2011), domestic supply provides about 91 per cent of the total energy consumption in China, meaning that overall energy dependence (namely, the ratio of the energy that a country imports to the total it consumes) is about 9 per cent. With a variety of policies and investments in place that will further expand domestic supply capacity, China will continue to rely mainly on domestic supply to meet its growing energy demand in the future.

Heavy Reliance on Coal as a Major Source of Energy

A country's choice of fuels and technologies depends to a large extent on its resource endowments and their relative prices. China is abundant in coal resources (BP 2011). This abundant supply of coal and its relatively lower price compared with its more environmentally friendly substitutes make China far more reliant on coal for its primary energy needs than any other major economy. As the world's largest coal producer and consumer, China produces and consumes about twice as much coal as the United States, the world number two, and China was responsible for almost half of global coal consumption in 2010 (USEIA 2011a). Coal has accounted for more than two-thirds of China's primary energy consumption for several decades. For a considerable period to come, China's energy mix will remain dominated by coal (IEA 2010, 2011; Zhang 1990).

China displaced Japan as the world's top coal importer in 2011—a position Japan had held since at least 1975. This raised concerns about whether China can meet its own coal demand. In my view, this is an over-interpretation. China imported 182.4 million tonnes of coal in 2011. That is a very small amount when compared with China's total coal consumption. The move into the position of number-one importer can be attributed to some special factors. On the Japanese side, the Fukushima Daiichi nuclear power plant accident in Japan on 11 March 2011 led to a power shortage. This, combined with strong Japanese currency appreciation, led to slack demand for coking coal as steelmakers curbed production. Moreover, as the magnitude 9.0 earthquake damaged coal-fired power plants along the country's north-east coast, this led to a reduction in Japan's imports of thermal coal used for power generation. On the Chinese side, with robust demand for coal for power generation and cement production and rising costs of domestic coal production, foreign coal was particularly attractive to those regions far from domestic coal production bases (Tsukimori 2012).

---

1   China still uses mtce as its benchmark, whereas the international standard has moved towards oil equivalents (mtoe). Multiplying mtce by 1.43 will convert to mtoe.

Imports of Natural Gas Set to Rise, but Much Less Concerning than the Oil Situation

Since 2006 China has been an importer of natural gas. China's imports of natural gas are set to increase as its overall energy consumption rises. China hopes to expand its domestic natural gas output to 150–180 billion cubic metres (bcm) a year by 2020, while imports would amount to 120–150 bcm per annum (Oxford Analytica 2012). Even by then, its gas dependency rate is much less than that of oil. Moreover, the majority of natural gas is used for chemical feedstock and power generation in China. There are a number of alternatives to natural gas for those uses. Furthermore, China's unconventional gas reserves suggest that gas use can expand faster than expected without creating huge new import dependency. According to the US EIA (2011b), China is believed to have the world's third-largest coal-seam gas reserves, and 36 trillion cu m of recoverable shale-gas reserves—the largest in the world.[2] China has significantly increased its expectations for unconventional gas production, announcing in February 2012 a plan to invest RMB116.6 billion to raise coal-seam gas production to 30 bcm per annum by 2015—up from 15 bcm per annum in 2010. Expectations regarding shale-gas output range from 15–30 bcm per annum to 60–100 bcm per annum by 2020 (NDRC et al. 2012; Oxford Analytica 2012). If unconventional gas production meets even the lower bound of expectations, this will significantly cut China's imports of natural gas and its future dependency rate.

China's attempts to achieve a commercial scale of shale-gas production have, however, so far been hindered by the lack of expertise and difficult geology. China's shale-gas is situated in deeper and more difficult terrain than North American formations. Moreover, Chinese companies have struggled to master the hydraulic fracturing and horizontal drilling techniques used to exploit these resources. To that end, Chinese national oil companies (NOCs) establish strategic partnerships with other NOCs and international oil companies (IOCs) to gain technical know-how in areas where Chinese NOCs lack technical expertise. PetroChina, a Hong Kong-listed unit of China National Petroleum Corporation (CNPC), bought in February 2012 a 20 per cent stake in Shell's Groundbirch natural gas development in north-eastern British Columbia, hoping to gain shale-gas experience from Shell (Welsch and Lee 2012). In January 2012, Sinopec signed a deal with Devon Corporation to invest US$2.2 billion for a one-third stake in five US shale and oil-and-gas fields controlled by Devon (Xinhua 2012). China National Offshore Oil Corporation (CNOOC) is working with TOTAL in Nigeria's Akpo and Egina deepwater fields (Jiang and Sinton 2011). PetroChina partnered with Shell in March 2010 to acquire a 100 per cent stake of Australian coal-bed methane producer Arrow Energy. The recent flurry of Chinese NOCs'

---

2 China's own estimate puts its recoverable shale-gas reserves at 25 trillion cu m (NDRC et al. 2012).

deal-making is more about gaining access to technology than the commodity itself so that Chinese NOCs will be better positioned to explore and develop similar resources (deepwater reserves, coal-bed methane and shale-gas) within China.

Moreover, to achieve the aforementioned ambitious target for shale-gas, from virtually zero in 2012, China allows foreign partners in this sector. In March 2012, Royal Dutch Shell PLC and CNPC signed the first production-sharing contract to explore, develop and produce shale-gas in China. This deal marks a milestone in the development of China's shale-gas reserves and fits in with China's overall strategy to bring technical and operational know-how to the development of its untapped reserves of shale-gas. Under the agreement, Shell will apply its advanced technology, operational expertise and global experience to jointly develop shale-gas with CNPC over a 3500 sq km area in the Fushun-Yongchuan block in the Sichuan Basin (W. Ma 2012). This pact will serve as a template showing how production-sharing contracts between foreign and domestic companies might work to help China tap this unconventional fuel.

Increasing Dependence on Imported Oil and China's Concerns about the Strait of Malacca

China's appetite for oil has been soaring over the past two decades. Its oil demand grew from 2.3 million barrels per day (mbpd) in 1990 to 4.4 mbpd in 2000 (IEA 2000). By 2010, China's demand had jumped to 8.9 mbpd (IEA 2011). The IEA (2011) estimates that by 2035, China's oil demand will reach 14.9 mbpd, overtaking the United States (14.5 mbpd) as the largest oil consumer in the world.

China was self-sufficient in oil for most of the 60 year history of the People's Republic, but since 1993 it has been a net oil importer. China's economic boom and its stagnating domestic production of oil have produced a growing hunger for imports. As of 2003, China emerged as second only to the United States in terms of oil imports. In 2009, China imported 4.3 mbpd, or 51.3 per cent of its demand (IEA 2010). This was the first instance in which China imported more than half of its oil needs. According to China's National Energy Administration, China's oil dependency rate increased further, to 56.5 per cent, in 2011 (Zhong 2012). According to China's General Administration of Customs, China's oil imports cost the country US$196.7 billion in 2011, accounting for 11.3 per cent of its total import expenditures (J. Ma 2012; Zhong 2012).

China is projected to maintain oil production close to the current level of 4.1 mbpd to 2025, followed by a steady decline as resource depletion sets in (IEA 2011). As a result its oil imports will continue to soar in the decades ahead. The IEA (2011) estimates that by 2035, China will be importing nearly 12.6 mbpd—more than the United States imports today—in order to meet its expected oil demand of 14.9 mbpd. This puts China's oil dependency rate at 84.6 per cent in 2035 (IEA 2011). China will thus become far more exposed to the risk of international supply disruptions than it is today. Energy security has risen to the height of importance in its foreign policy, and is becoming what has been called a 'transforming' factor in relations between China and the Middle East, Russia and energy-rich Central Asian, African and Latin American countries (Yi 2005).

Indeed, China's oil dependency rate is already high and increasing; however, this need not be viewed in a solely negative way. As a country's overall trade intensity (defined as a ratio of the sum of imports plus exports to GDP) suggests, the higher ratio means that country is more integrated with the global economy. It does not necessarily suggest increased economic insecurity in that country. Moreover, many large economies have even higher oil dependency rates than China, although China naturally stands out in terms of the sheer quantity of its requirements. Furthermore, China itself experienced complete dependence on foreign oil prior to discoveries of its own reserves in the 1950s. In the post–civil war period China was geopolitically isolated, and it had to import essentially all of its oil. Taking these points together, the oil dependency rate alone is insufficient to determine the true level of energy security/insecurity of a country. To evaluate the energy security of a country properly, this factor has to be combined with other factors, including sources and routes of oil supply. Specifically, we need to look at

- whether oil imports are concentrated on a few source countries—more diversified sources of supply are obviously preferred
- whether the main oil-exporting countries are politically stable
- whether the transport routes for oil imports are considered vulnerable to physical disruption and how much influence the importer has on these transport lanes.

As shown in Figure 15.1, in 1995, China relied mainly on the Middle East and South-East Asia (mainly Indonesia, which alone accounted for nearly one-third of China's total imports) for 82 per cent of its crude-oil imports. The Middle East was—and is—clearly vital. Thus, China will continue to consolidate its base there. In recent years though, China has also turned its attention to the emerging oil and gas fields of Africa. Top Chinese leaders have paid frequent visits to oil-producing countries in the region. This high-profile, goodwill-based energy diplomacy has helped China make remarkable inroads in striking energy deals with oil-rich African countries (Zhang 2007, 2010b). By 2005, this strategy enabled China to significantly diversify its import mix. As shown in

Figure 15.1, Africa accounted for 30 per cent of China's oil imports in 2005—up from 7 per cent in 1995—while Russia supplied 10 per cent of total imports, up from less than 1 per cent 10 years earlier (Downs 2006).

China became slightly more reliant on the Middle East in 2005 than it had been 10 years ago, with 47 per cent of its imports coming from the Persian Gulf. In addition, because China is now heavily reliant on Africa as well as the Middle East, it now depends more on a single chokepoint—the Strait of Malacca—than it had before, with nearly 77 per cent of its oil imports flowing through the strait. This situation remained unchanged in the following five years: China still imported 78 per cent of its crude from the Middle East and Africa in 2010 (BP 2011; Kennedy 2011).

Figure 15.1 China's Crude-Oil Imports by Region in 1995 (left) and 2005 (right)

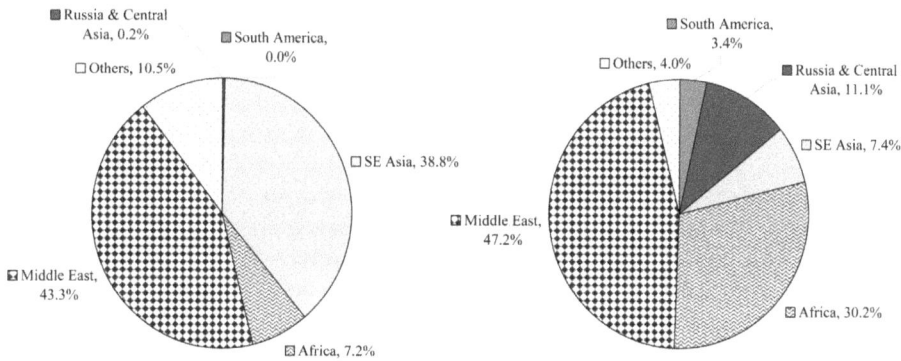

Source: From Chen (2010) and Zhang (2011b).

Foreign trade has become one of the pillars underpinning China's phenomenal economic growth over the past three decades, and oil is intimately related to it. Given that most crude-oil imports from the Middle East and Africa have to pass through the Strait of Malacca, the strait is of immense strategic and economic importance to China's economic and energy security. As a chokepoint, this strait directly affects China's sealane of communications, but China has little direct influence over it. Therefore, China has every reason to be concerned about the safe and smooth passage of its shipments. Beijing feels susceptible to this strategic weakness. Any adverse event in the strait would disrupt its trade flows and particularly oil imports, which could deal a further blow to China's economic development, social stability and military capability (Chen 2010; Zhao 2007).

Clearly, oil poses a unique challenge for China, not only because its oil dependency rate is already high and continues to rise, but also, more importantly, because oil imports come from less politically stable regions and have to be shipped to China via routes that are considered vulnerable to physical disruption but which China has little physical sway over. Viewed in this context, energy security in China to a large extent equates to oil security.

Putting China's Global Search for Energy Security into Perspective

Over the past few years top Chinese leaders have come to view the Strait of Malacca as a strategic vulnerability (Blumenthal 2008; Holmes 2007). In November 2003, President, Hu Jintao, declared that 'certain major powers' were bent on controlling the strait and called for the adoption of new strategies to mitigate the perceived vulnerability. Thereafter, the Chinese press devoted considerable attention to the country's 'Malacca dilemma' (Lanteigne 2008; Storey 2006). The *China Youth Daily*, a leading Chinese newspaper, declared: 'It is no exaggeration to say that whoever controls the Strait of Malacca will also have a stranglehold on the energy route of China' (Shi 2004).

Given the strategic importance of the Strait of Malacca and China's lack of influence on the waterway, China has made great efforts on both the demand and the supply sides to cope with the perceived 'Malacca dilemma' and to enhance its energy security.

On the demand side, China has taken considerable efforts to control the growth of its demand for energy and oil and thus its demand for oil imports. For the first time, China has incorporated an input indicator as a constraint in its five-year economic plan, requiring that energy use per unit of GDP be cut by 20 per cent during the Eleventh Five-Year Plan period, running from 2006 to 2010. This formal acknowledgment is widely considered to be an important step towards building a 'harmonious society' through 'scientific development'. Just prior to the Copenhagen climate change summit, China further pledged to cut its carbon intensity by 40–45 per cent by 2020 relative to its 2005 levels in order to help reach an international climate change agreement at Copenhagen or beyond (for further discussion, see Zhang 2010a, 2011a, 2011c). Meeting these energy and carbon intensity targets will not only help to limit the growth of China's carbon emissions, but also will reduce China's growing hunger for foreign oil, leave more oil on the market and thus help to stabilise world oil prices.

On the supply side, China has instituted a variety of policies to address its growing dependence on imported oil. The country has made considerable efforts to maintain domestic production close to the current level. In the meantime, China has been making significant efforts to support the expansion of its own NOCs (the so-called 'going-out policy'); to diversify both sources of and routes for its oil supply, including setting up a string of refineries in China through joint ventures with partners from energy-rich countries that often come with supply agreements; to develop its own strategic petroleum reserves; and to strengthen its naval capabilities to protect supply lines (Chen 2010; Jiang and Sinton 2011; Kennedy 2011; Wang and Wu 2011; Zhang 2007, 2010b, 2011b). Clearly, China has resorted to these unilateral and bilateral measures to enhance its energy security and cope with the Malacca dilemma.

In this context, China's global quest for resources—in particular, oil and natural gas—has received unprecedented worldwide attention and scrutiny. This is partly because of China's high-profile energy diplomacy and some debatable issues about the management and operation of Chinese NOCs. In my view, this is mainly because of misconceptions and misunderstandings of China's quest for energy security both inside and outside China. Inside China, these relate to the hypothesised US-led oil blockade against China and the role of Chinese investments in oil fields overseas. Outside China, misconceptions and misunderstandings mainly relate to how Chinese policy banks operate and their oil and natural gas-based loans. The following section seeks to clarify each of these points.

An American-Led Oil Blockade Against China?

The strategic importance of the Strait of Malacca to China on the one hand and its lack of influence on the waterway on the other have raised concerns about the threat of a US-led oil blockade against China.

As mentioned in the preceding section, China has made great efforts in both the demand and the supply sides to cope with the perceived Malacca dilemma and to enhance its energy security. One of the significant efforts on the supply side is to support the expansion of its own NOCs abroad through the so-called 'going-out policies' and thus to increase the NOCs' overseas oil production. If Chinese NOCs' overseas oil production is to help to improve China's energy security then oil so produced needs to be shipped back to China. But, if the threat of a US-led blockade is a concern then attempts to send Chinese NOCs' equity oil shares back home will face the same blockade problem.

As the sole superpower, the United States is certainly reluctant to accept the rise of China and is wary of any prospective challenge to its hegemony. Geopolitically, the United States has attempted to contain China's increasing global influence. As the United States withdraws from its two long wars in Iraq and Afghanistan and refocuses on the Asia-Pacific region, its 'strategic pivot' to Asia has so far mainly manifested itself in a shoring up of its 'encircling alliances' with the countries on China's periphery (The Economist 2012a). Auctioning a policy that would inhibit the Chinese economy is, however, highly unlikely, because the world's two largest economies are too integrated and interdependent for one to fail. It would be a policy of self-immolation. The United States' attempt to influence, but not intervene in, the recent Taiwanese presidential election to avoid instability in the Taiwan Strait clearly supports this view. In the last week or so running up to the election in January 2012, the opposition party's presidential candidate was running neck and neck with the ruling party's nominee. The opposition party was against the 1992 consensus that aims for a peaceful unification of Mainland China and Taiwan and if its candidate had been elected to the presidency, the United States believed the outcome could lead to instability. So, at the last moment, current and former top US officials were in Taiwan, disregarding the opposition party's demand to keep political neutrality, which had been the stance the United States took in previous Taiwanese elections. Instead, these US officials explicitly persuaded the voters to treasure the current stability in cross-strait relations, which was clearly viewed as being to the ruling party's advantage.

Some might take the US-led Trans-Pacific Partnership (TPP) free-trade agreement—essentially a free-trade pact currently under negotiation between the United States, Australia, Brunei, Chile, Malaysia, New Zealand, Peru, Singapore and Vietnam—as a counterargument. But I do not share the view that the United States is using the TPP to isolate China economically. Rather, I think the United States wants to use the TPP to press China to observe the rules of the road on trade and intellectual property. The United States also wants to use the TPP to achieve its major goal of levelling the playing field in which private and state-owned enterprises (SOEs) compete.[3] This goal reflects serious US frustration with what it sees as the unfair advantages Chinese SOEs have in world trade (Bussey 2012; Davis 2011).

Even if the United States were to attempt a blockade, it would probably not be very successful (Collins and Murray 2008), and would be extremely difficult to operate in practice. If the blockade operations were undertaken close to China, blockading vessels would be vulnerable to attacks from China. In contrast, if the blockade were implemented far from China's shores, it would be extremely difficult to differentiate oil that was bound for China from oil that was bound for other countries, not only because oil carried in a given tanker can be destined for several countries, but also because ownership of the oil within that tanker can easily change during the course of its journey (Kennedy 2011).

---

3 There is a challenge for the United States to come up with a position on state-owned firms because the US proposal could be used against the US Postal Service, Tennessee Valley Authority and other state-owned or state-controlled entities. The United States also bought a controlling interest in General Motors during the financial crisis. While Democrats on the House Ways and Means Committee in a letter to the White House in June 2011 said that other free-trade agreements had exceptions for 'prudential measures taken to ensure the integrity and stability of the financial system', US trading partners could see an exception of that sort as justifying a variety of aid to their state-owned firms (Davis 2011).

Taking these points together, it is safe to say that the threat of a US-led oil blockade against China is largely a chimera. If this blockade is unlikely to happen—and even if attempted has a low chance of success—then it seems strange that China's energy security policy should take it as such a serious potential threat.

It is undeniable that Western powers have gained control over the best oil fields available and, as a late entrant to the international oil game, China has little choice but to strike deals with so-called rogue states and to take risks to make acquisitions in oil-rich but politically unstable countries or regions (Zhang 2007, 2010b). That explains why Chinese NOCs are actively bidding for assets in West Africa and Latin America. In my view, however, in their course of action and in the expansion of their overseas business, Chinese NOCs exacerbate the extent of potential disruption to oil supply. And in the name of energy security, Chinese NOCs are complicating China's foreign relations in sensitive regions of the world. This could potentially hijack the Chinese Government's going-out policies, as the NOCs prioritise their own profits but at the potential expense of China's overall national interests.

The Operations of Chinese Policy Banks

During the 1994 reforms of the financial sector, the Chinese Government created the China Development Bank (CDB) and the Export–Import Bank of China as 'policy banks' (Bräutigam 2009). Their loans would explicitly support the Government's policy objectives. The creation of designated policy banks would theoretically free commercial banks from policy lending and hold them accountable for rational, market-based lending.

The two policy banks provide lines of credit to Chinese NOCs and foreign entities—mainly NOC counterparts—to support international expansion and secure oil or natural gas deals. As shown in Table 15.1, since 2009, CDB has extended lines of credit totalling almost US$85 billion to national energy companies and government entities in Brazil, Ecuador, Russia, Turkmenistan and Venezuela (Downs 2011a).

There is a widespread perception that the CDB provided these loans exclusively to advance Chinese Government policy objectives without commercial concerns. Contrary to this popular view, the CDB is not a mere puppet of the Chinese Government. It is wholly state owned, but it is not state run.

To be sure, the CDB has a mission to advance the Chinese Government's policy objectives at home and abroad, including securing oil and natural gas supplies, but that mission does not prevent it from pursuing its own agenda to expand its business at home and abroad and pursue profits. In fact, the CDB is successful at balancing commercial and policy priorities so that it has high profits and a balance sheet that is even healthier than all the other major Chinese commercial banks.[4] Its non-performing loans ratio has stood at less than 1 per cent since 2005—lower than that of all other major Chinese commercial banks. It lends at market-based interest rates. The interest rates on the lines of credit totalling US$45.6 billion extended to Petrobras, Rosneft and Transneft in 2009 and to Venezuela's Bank of Economic and Social Development in 2010 are all based on the benchmark London Interbank Offered Rate (LIBOR), although the spread over LIBOR in Table 15.1 might be thinner than what a Western bank would require (Downs 2011a).

The CDB has been vocal in mobilising China's massive foreign reserves to support cross-border energy and natural resource deals. Chen Yuan, its Governor, was quoted as saying that investing in energy and minerals was a good way to hedge against a declining dollar and rising commodity prices, and thus served as a medium for shifting China's foreign exchange reserves away from low-yielding financial instruments (Downs 2011b). So the CDB made huge loans to Russia and resource-rich countries in Central Asia, West Africa and Latin America. China's loan commitments of US$37 billion in 2010 to Latin America were more than those from the World Bank, the Inter-American Development Bank and the US Export–Import Bank combined for that year.

Associated with these loans are the common claims that Chinese loans to Latin America have more favourable terms, impose no policy conditions and have less stringent environmental guidelines than the loans of international financial institutions and Western governments. But Gallagher et al. (2012) find that this is often not the case. They find that the CDB loans carry more stringent terms than World Bank loans. In 2010, the CDB offered Argentina a US$10 billion loan at 600 basis points above LIBOR. In the same year, the World Bank Group's International Bank for Reconstruction and Development (IBRD) granted

---

4 There are at least two factors for its success. Under the leadership of its Governor, Chen Yuan, the CDB brought the lender's risk-management system up to global standards, even rejecting loans to projects approved by the powerful National Development and Reform Commission (Downs 2011b). Jacob Frenkel, Chairman of JP Morgan Chase International and a former governor of the Bank of Israel, was quoted as saying that '[e]ven though it is a government arm, it is really treated by the marketplace as a well-managed and well-run modern financial institution' (Forsythe and Sanderson 2011). Second, unlike debt issued by other state-owned banks in China, the special financing bonds issued by the CDB are classified at the same level as sovereign debt by the Government. This is considered one of its biggest competitive advantages. Banks that buy the bonds can count them at a zero-risk weighting on their balance sheets. The Chinese Prime Minister, Wen Jiabao, plans to reclassify the CDB as a commercial bank instead of a policy lender so that the CDB has to compete on an equal footing with other state-owned banks that now have commercial bank status. That means the CDB would have to pay more to borrow money. With strong resistance from the CDB, the Chinese Government extended its special financial status through the end of 2012 (Forsythe and Sanderson 2011).

Argentina a US$30 million loan with a spread of 85 basis points. In 2009, the CDB gave Brazil a US$10 billion loan at 280 basis points. The IBRD gave Brazil a US$43.4 million loan in 2000 at a variable spread of 30–55 basis points.

Table 15.1 China Development Bank's Energy-Backed Loans

	Borrower	Amount (US$billion)	Term (year)	Interest rate	Oil/gas deliveries to secure loan**
2005	Rosneft, Russia	6*	6	LIBOR + 3.0% (2005) LIBOR + 0.7% (2006–10)	180 kp/d
2008	BANDES, Venezuela	4	3	n.a.	100 kp/d
2009	Rosneft, Russia	15	20	LIBOR + 5.69%	180 kp/d
2009	Transneft, Russia	10	20	LIBOR + 5.69%	120 kp/d
2009	Petrobras, Brazil	10	10	LIBOR + 2.8%	150–200 kp/d
2009	BANDES, Venezuela	4	3	n.a.	107–153 kp/d
2009	Turkmengaz, Turkmenistan	4	n.a.	n.a.	n.a.
2010	BANDES, Venezuela	20.6	10	LIBOR + 0.5–2.85%	200–300 kp/d
2010	Ministry of Finance, Ecuador	1	4	6.0%	36 kp/d
2011	Turkmengaz, Turkmenistan	4.1	n.a.	n.a.	10 bcm
2011	BANDES, Venezuela	4	n.a.	n.a.	n.a.
2011	Ministry of Finance, Ecuador	2	8	6.90%	67.58 kp/d

n.a. = not applicable

* includes funds from Export–Import Bank of China

** kb/d = thousand barrels per day

Source: Downs (2011a).

China's Export–Import Bank, in contrast, generally offers lower interest rates than the US Export–Import Bank. This is mainly because Chinese banks package commercial financing and development aid differently than their foreign counterparts. Instead of giving development aid through the CDB, China channels it through China's Export–Import Bank. The IBRD and other development banks offer concessionary interest rates as an official form of development aid, while the CDB does not. Despite the CDB's 'development bank' label, the Chinese bank generally charges borrowers the full cost of finance.

For this reason, Bräutigam (2009) labels the CDB 'the development bank that doesn't give aid'. It is not surprising, therefore, that the CDB's interest rates are higher (Gallagher et al. 2012).

Given that the CDB offers loans at market-based interest rates on the one hand and that it imposes no policy conditions on the other, to mitigate loan risks, Chinese banks do require equipment purchases and sometimes oil sale agreements with borrowers as a sort of collateral in kind. This method allows China to loan to less creditworthy borrowers. As the CDB founder, Chen Yuan, states, backing loans with oil shipments 'effectively keeps risks to a minimum level' (Forsythe and Sanderson 2011). The risk mitigation of loans-for-oil seems to explain why the CDB was able to offer the US$20 billion loan to Venezuela at a floating rate of 50–285 basis points over LIBOR—only a fraction of its 935 basis point cost in sovereign debt markets (Gallagher et al. 2012). To date, this kind of lending seems to work well for borrowing countries in which they need less costly Chinese inputs and equipment to develop their own energy, mining, infrastructure, transportation and housing sectors. We will discuss this issue further in the next section.

Loans for Oil and Gas Deals

Using loan-for-oil and loan-for-gas deals to secure long-term supplies is not a Chinese invention. Japan gave China loans for its oil as early as the 1970s. This type of deal is not new for China and has been used by Chinese NOCs for some time. In 2004, CNPC loaned the Russian oil producer Rosneft US$6 billion for 180 000 barrels per day of oil supplies through 2010 (Downs 2011a). But such deals are dwarfed by the deal with Russia in 2009. China and Russia had been discussing a cross-border pipeline for crude oil since the early 1990s, but were not able to finalise a deal. Leveraging its relative financial strength at a time when most other big economies were in recession, China eventually struck its long-awaited mega loan-for-oil deal with Russia on 17 February 2009. Under this long-term deal, the CDB lends US$25 billion to Rosneft, Russia's biggest oil producer, and Transneft, its oil pipeline operator. In exchange, Russia will provide China with an additional 15 million tonnes of crude oil a year between 2011 and 2030, which represents about 300 000 barrels per day for 20 years, or nearly 7 per cent of China's volume of oil imports in 2009, through a new pipeline, which began making commercial deliveries on 1 January 2011. The deal not only provides the two Russian oil companies with much needed credit, it also helps Russia to secure customers and reduce its dependence on Western European customers. Another notable deal is a US$10 billion loan agreement with the Brazilian state-owned oil giant Petroleo Brasileiro SA, known as Petrobras—the biggest deal in Central and South America. This loan is to help Petrobras develop newly discovered offshore oil reserves, which promise to convert Brazil into a major world oil exporter. Under the terms of the 10-year loan from CDB, Petrobras was to supply China Petroleum and Chemical Corporation, known as Sinopec, with 150 000 barrels per day in 2009, rising to 200 000 barrels per day for another nine years, from 2010 to 2019 (Ma 2009; The Economist 2010).

It should be pointed out that loan-for-oil and loan-for-gas deals are not without risk. Contracts could be voided with a change of government. Resource-rich countries might fail to supply the promised quantities. Moreover, because the oil is not collateral for the loan, if the borrowers threaten to cut off the supply of oil, lenders cannot seize extra oil or oil revenue to compensate for potential losses (Jacob 2010; Jiang and Sinton 2011). Therefore, loan-for-oil and loan-for-gas deals are not the preferred method of the NOCs to gain foreign supplies. Good-quality assets are, however, rarely for sale these days, and even if they were, Chinese NOCs might not be able to fairly win the bids, as foreign governments have blocked many Chinese NOCs' attempts to buy oil fields. Given these constraints, loan-for-oil and loan-for-gas deals serve as a second-best strategy for China to diversify its oil supply (Arnson and Davidow 2011; Jiang and Sinton 2011; The Economist 2010).

In the midst of the global financial crisis, China further diversified its energy import mix via loan-for-oil and loan-for-gas deals. Chinese state-owned banks made loans worth US$77 billion to nine different oil and gas-producing countries in 2009 and 2010, all of which are located outside the Middle East (Jiang and Sinton 2011). Many outside observers explicitly or implicitly assume that these deals grant Chinese NOCs a discount. Under this assumption, borrowers simply send oil to China at a preset price to pay back the loan, and thus might lose out as oil prices rise. This is a misunderstanding of how this kind of deal works,[5] and is a misreading of the evidence. Chinese NOCs have no bargaining on prices, and all the deals are linked to market prices, not quantities of oil. Russia, Brazil and Venezuela all sell their oil to China at market prices (Downs 2011a; Gallagher et al. 2012; Jiang and Sinton 2011). These market-based arrangements will ensure deliveries of oil, as the temptation to default on supply contracts if the market price were to rise above a negotiated price would be very strong. The difficulties seen in other commodity markets—such as for iron ore—where long-term contracts sit beside spot markets, illustrate this reality.

Chinese NOCs, however, with support from the Chinese Government and backed with Chinese policy banks, did take advantage of stricken foreign companies in the global financial crisis to enable them to reach otherwise

5 In a typical deal involving the CDB, one Chinese NOC and a foreign borrower (say, a foreign oil company), the CDB provides the loan to the foreign borrower and opens an account to the borrower. Then the Chinese NOC buys the oil from the borrower at market prices and deposits its payments into the borrower's designated account at the CDB. In this way, the foreign borrower is obliged to sell oil to the Chinese NOC, and the CDB is guaranteed to receive payments to repay itself for the loan.

unlikely deals and receive long-term oil and gas supplies. Moreover, these deals, backed with the CDB's loans, required the borrowers to buy and hire from China to mitigate loan risks,[6] despite no policy conditions being imposed (Gallagher et al. 2012). The agreement with Petrobras stipulates that US$3 billion of the US$10 billion loan must be used to purchase oil equipment from China. China's US$10 billion loan to Argentina in 2010 is to buy Chinese trains. Thus, this loan is actually a credit line for Chinese railway companies to invest in 10 separate rail projects in Argentina, with the money effectively staying in China. Half of the US$20.6 billion loan the CDB granted to Venezuela's Bank of Economic and Social Development is denominated in Chinese renminbi, which locks Venezuela into buying Chinese equipment and hiring Chinese firms (De Córdoba 2011; Downs 2011b; Hall 2010). Clearly, in addition to securing oil supplies, these deals also serve the Government's goal of creating new export markets for Chinese companies and at the same time reduce their exposure to default risks and the borrowers' potential for misuse and corruption (Bräutigam 2009). These borrowers find purchase requirements attached to Chinese loans less objectionable because they seek to build up their energy, mining, infrastructure, transportation and housing sectors inexpensively using Chinese inputs and equipment.[7]

Chinese NOCs' Equity Oil Shares

In the early 2000s, the Chinese Government adopted its so-called going-out policies to help state-owned companies, including Chinese NOCs, to achieve their ambition to grow and build global businesses. Arguably the Government also sees supporting Chinese NOCs to make oil and natural gas mergers and acquisitions (M&A) overseas as a way to diversify its foreign exchange reserves to higher-yielding assets away from low-yielding financial instruments such as US Treasury Bonds (Downs 2011b). As a result of the going-out policy supported by Chinese policy banks, these NOCs now have equity stakes in production in 20 countries. By the first quarter of 2010, NOCs' overseas equity shares had reached 1.36 mbpd—nearly one-third of China's net imports in 2009 (Jiang and Sinton 2011).

---

6 Western development loans tend to attach transparency and seniority clauses and reform requirements in an effort to reduce loan risks.

7 This depends on the requirements of the borrowers. Mexico, Colombia and Peru—the traditional borrowers of the World Bank and Inter-American Development Bank—are undertaking projects outside the energy, mining, infrastructure, transportation and housing sectors for which Chinese purchase requirements would be a burden. They find the transparency and reform requirements of Western loans less costly than Chinese equipment. Brazil and Argentina accept Western loans where they find it acceptable to comply with Western standards. At the same time, they take on Chinese oil, mining and railway loans because they are willing to use Chinese inputs and have little objection to the purchase requirements (Gallagher et al. 2012).

With oil an internationally traded commodity, China's endeavours to expand its global search and production of oil are constantly confronted with the issue of whether this strategy is superior to simply buying oil in open markets because of concerns about Chinese NOCs' overbidding and making investment losses abroad.

The Chinese oil companies have a history of overpaying for equity positions (Balfour 2002).[8] Because China has viewed paying a higher price than competitors to secure energy resources as more of a national security issue than a pure business decision (Bradsher 2005), such bidding wars between Chinese companies and their rivals have further intensified the tendency of Chinese oil companies to pay far above what competitors offer. Prior to the credit crisis, China had grabbed these deals by overbidding by at least 10 per cent more than its competitor from India did. In January 2006, the CNOOC bought a 45 per cent stake in the Akpo offshore oil and gas field in Nigeria for US$2.27 billion by outbidding the competitor, India's state-owned Oil and Natural Gas Corp (ONGC), which submitted a bid of US$2 billion but withdrew after India's cabinet raised concerns about the risks involved (Aiyar 2006; Masaki 2006). In August 2005, the CNPC paid US$4.18 billion to acquire Canadian oil company PetroKazakhstan, making it China's largest foreign acquisition ever at that time (Bradsher 2005). Originally, the CNPC offered US$3.6 billion. With an Indian consortium (ONGC-Mittal) bid of US$3.8 billion, the CNPC hiked its offer to US$4.18 billion to secure the deal (Basu 2005).

The financial and credit crises and the decline in global oil demand have turned the oil industry into a buyers' market, however temporarily. Should Chinese oil majors be able to make better M&A deals than those prior to the credit crisis? On 24 June 2009, Sinopec made a C$8.27 billion (US$7.22 billion) takeover bid for the international oil and gas exploration company Addax Petroleum, making it the largest overseas takeover by a Chinese company. The takeover would have given Sinopec access to Addax's stakes in oil fields off the coast of West Africa, as well as in Iraq (Zhang 2010b). The Korea National Oil Corporation also bid for Addax, offering USS$6.9 billion (The Chosun Ilbo 2009). Sinopec offered US$7.2 billion to win the deal. So, Sinopec overbid its competitor by only 4.6 per cent—far less than the overbidding of at least 10 per cent it had made in those aforementioned deals prior to the credit crisis. Measured in other ways, however, the story differs. Sinopec's offer is equivalent to US$34

---

8   Overpaying for acquisitions does not apply to China alone. Areva, a French state-owned nuclear energy group, is reported to have overpaid in its US$2.7 billion purchase in 2007 of UraMin, a Canadian start-up firm with mining assets in Namibia, resulting in a huge operating loss for 2011. In the rush to snap up uranium deposits at a time when expectations of a nuclear renaissance caused uranium prices to soar, Areva failed to do enough metallurgical due diligence on UraMin's mines. The reserves in Namibia turned out to be smaller and less easily extractable than expected. This was compounded by a plunging uranium price after the Fukushima nuclear accident, thus further reducing the deposits' value (*The Economist* 2012b).

a barrel of proved reserves and US$14 a barrel of proved and probable reserves. The African transaction average in 2007—when the average crude price was similar to the prices in 2009 at the time this deal was made—was US$14.40 a barrel for proved reserves and US$9.90 for proved and probable reserves, respectively. On a proven basis, the 2007 average suggests US$3.1 billion total value for the deal. Therefore, US$7.2 billion implies a 135 per cent premium (Xu 2009). In December 2008, Sinopec paid C$2.1 billion to acquire Tanganyika Oil, a Canadian company that owned oil fields in Syria. The 95 per cent takeover marked the first time a Chinese company had almost complete ownership of a formerly North American oil and gas firm. The C$2.1 billion deal was initiated when the price of oil was at US$90 a barrel. When the price fell to US$40 a barrel by December of that year, the offer was generally seen as overpriced. The company still went ahead with the purchase (Vaidyanathan 2012). On 8 October 2011, Sinopec bought Daylight Energy, a Canadian oil and natural gas producer, for about C$2.2 billion in cash. Under the terms of the deal, Sinopec offered C$10.08 a share. That is more than double Daylight's closing price of C$4.59 on the last trading day and 43.9 per cent above the 60-day weighted average trading price. China's largest refiner paid a very high premium over its share price to fully acquire Daylight Energy (De La Merced 2011).

It is important to note, however, that the higher bid does not always win in a politically charged industry such as energy. CNOOC in 2005 failed to acquire Unocal for US$18.5 billion, although it topped Chevron's bid of US$16.4 billion. In the end, Chevron won the deal based on other factors. This overpaying could partly reflect a need to overcome the kinds of political difficulties that hampered Chinese state-owned companies' overseas takeover attempts in recent years. Nevertheless, the Chinese NOCs are more reluctant than in the past to overpay for assets for at least two reasons. First, the Chinese NOCs have moved up technology and project management learning curves that the IOCs have dominated and have become increasingly sophisticated and capable internationally. Second, they have been tightening their premiums by examining the financial returns of their bids. CNOOC has started using a financial metric system that allows it to price its bids more accurately. Now even the larger national oil companies like PetroChina and Sinopec have started to follow the CNOOC's path (Vaidyanathan 2012). A recent study by the International Energy Agency uncovered no evidence of systematic or intentional overpayment associated with recent acquisitions (Jiang and Sinton 2011); however, this is still an issue open to debate, and there is still disagreement. Some American analysts, like Herberg (2012), believe that Chinese NOCs continue to pay significant premiums to acquire overseas assets. Derek Scissors of the conservative Heritage Foundation was also quoted as saying that Chinese companies usually pay 20 to 30 per cent more than other companies to secure assets (Vaidyanathan 2012). The premiums were generally seen as necessary to keep shareholders happy and quell any political concerns given anti-China sentiment in certain circles. Eventually, whether assets are worth the premium price in the long run depends on whether and how far the value of oil and gas properties will rise.

Another issue is related to wide concerns about huge losses incurred when investing abroad. A study by China University of Petroleum suggests that China's 'big-three' oil corporations (CNPC, Sinopec and CNOOC) had invested in some 144 overseas projects totalling US$70 billion by the end of 2010, but two-thirds of such overseas investments suffered losses (Fu and Lin 2012; Oxford Analytica 2011). Given that these SOEs may cover overseas losses through their access to capital at home, this has created a perception of these SOEs as irresponsible users of state funds.

It can be argued that economic rationales take the back seat if the NOCs' oil production outside China can help to improve China's energy security. The question is then: are the Chinese NOCs' equity oil shares improving China's energy security?

First, as mentioned above, sending Chinese NOCs' equity oil shares home would mean they faced the same US-led oil blockade problem if it were to emerge—even though this author is sceptical about the effectiveness of any blockade, as argued above.

Second, China's oil imports rapidly outpace the equity oil production of the Chinese NOCs and their ability to acquire oil assets and accumulate investments in equity production abroad, so the equity oil strategy is hopelessly inadequate as a critical energy security strategy (Herberg 2012).

Third, it is widely understood that Chinese NOCs' willingness to overpay is to a large extent because these state-owned oil majors are obliged to guarantee China's energy security. There is little evidence, however, to suggest that the Chinese NOCs necessarily send their equity oil production back to China. Instead, the NOCs apparently prefer to let market conditions decide whether it is shipped back to China or whether it is sold to regional or international markets at the best price, as other IOCs do (Jiang and Sinton 2011; Kennedy 2011). Prior to completion of the Kazakhstan–China oil pipeline in 2009, the Chinese equity oil from the Aktobe field in Kazakhstan was transported via the pipeline to Atyrau to be sold on the international market. Even with the new pipeline in operation, some of CNPC's equity oil from Kazakhstan is still not shipped home. CNPC International, the exploration and production arm for CNPC's overseas production, determines whether it is profitable to sell the oil that it produces to China National United Oil Corporation. This CNPC trading company also evaluates whether buying crude oil locally close to the pipeline starting point (Atasu, prior to 2009) is more economical than buying crude produced at Aktobe by CNPC's exploration and production subsidiary and transporting it to Atasu (Jiang and Sinton 2011). China's equity production in Venezuela has also not been shipped back to China. This is mainly because it is too costly to do that given the long distance involved, and partly because Venezuelan heavy crude was not compatible with the existing Chinese refining capabilities before PetroChina teamed up with the Venezuelan state-owned oil company, PDVSA, to build a refinery to process this type of crude oil in Jieyang, Guangdong (Jiang and Sinton 2011).

Fourth, the available evidence does not suggest that oil produced from the Chinese NOCs would be either cheaper or more available to Chinese consumers in a supply crisis. Indeed, these NOCs have shown little inclination to grant Chinese customers a discount when prices are high (Kennedy 2011). In fact, the NOCs responded to rising crude oil prices prior to 2008 by reducing supplies of refined products to the Chinese market, resulting in widespread shortages at the pump, since the Government's controls over the prices of oil products did not allow them to pass their rising crude costs on to customers (Downs 2010).

In the meantime, Chinese investments in oil fields overseas do help to pump more oil out of the fields and enlarge the overall availability of oil on the world market. But this is seen as beneficial not only for Chinese consumers but also for other global consumers (Zhang 2007, 2010b). Taking these points together, Chinese NOCs' efforts to secure overseas oil and gas supplies are not a threat to US or Western energy security because Chinese investments in oil fields overseas enlarge the overall availability of oil on the world market. But they do not unambiguously improve China's energy security either because the NOCs do not necessarily send their equity oil production back to China (Herberg 2012; Jiang and Sinton 2011; Kennedy 2011).

Concluding Remarks

China is the world's largest energy consumer and the world's largest energy producer. China has relied and will continue to rely heavily on domestic energy resources to fuel its economic development. This makes China different from many other large economies. China is a key player on both the demand and the supply sides. Those who hold the 'China energy threat' view and blame Chinese oil demand and imports for high oil prices often tend to neglect this basic fact.

This is not to deny the fact that China is increasingly dependent on imported oil. Indeed, this, combined with its heavy reliance on the Strait of Malacca to ship imported oil to China, poses distinct security challenges for China. Given the strategic importance of the Strait of Malacca and China's limited influence on the waterway, China has taken great efforts on both the demand and the supply sides to cope with its perceived Malacca dilemma and to enhance its energy security. China's responses on the demand side are well formulated and justified, but the same cannot be said on the supply side. Some measures—for example, developing its own strategic petroleum reserves—are well taken, but others, such as going-out policies and exacerbation of disruption of supply, are open to debate. They might be considered misguided and not well founded.

Needless to say, NOC expansion is a positive development for the companies themselves. If NOCs' deals improve China's energy security then it is reasonable to allow profitability to be sought as a second priority. If, however, that first condition is not met then the entire strategy is questionable because many NOCs' deals are not justified on economic grounds alone.

China's aggressive global expansion to acquire resources is often perceived as a threat. This is a misreading of the evidence because Chinese NOCs' efforts to secure overseas oil and gas supplies do not threaten US or Western energy security. Most oil produced by Chinese NOCs abroad was sold on international markets, benefiting not only Chinese consumers but also other global consumers. This perceived threat could, however, lead the Chinese NOCs to overpay in deals, and drive up the world prices of resources compared with what would otherwise have been the case. Being aggressive and keeping higher profiles than is strictly necessary, in the name of energy security, the Chinese NOCs are complicating China's foreign relations in sensitive regions of the world and they could hijack the Chinese Government's going-out policies to increase their own profits but at the expense of China's overall national interests.

In the context of discussions of China's energy security, there is a tendency to overestimate potential disruptions to oil supply or take a pessimistic view of the stability of energy trade. This largely reflects mistrust of global oil markets; but evidence suggests that market-based energy contracts are long lasting, prevailing over ideological differences, wars or politically motivated action. Evidence suggests that under commercial contracts the former Soviet Union exported natural gas to Western Europe virtually unimpeded even during the Cold War era; however, brothers can be brought into conflicts if one does not follow market rules. This was clearly reflected by natural gas disputes between Russia and the Ukraine in 2005, despite the fact that the latter was a former Soviet republic and they remain close to each other. Russia attempted to halt the supply of natural gas to the Ukraine because of a disagreement over a payment for its natural gas sold to the Ukraine. Russia supplied the natural gas to the Ukraine at a price of US$50 per 1000 cu m at that time while its gas exported to Western Europe was at a price nearly five times that (Mao 2006). Clearly, the root cause of this dispute was politics because this supply of natural gas was not based on a commercial contract but rather on a political deal. Thus, it should not come as a surprise that one side was not going to stick to the deal when it saw changing political conditions on the other side. In this case, Russia viewed the Ukraine's notable trend towards autonomy and political independence away from Russia.

Moreover, the oil embargos led by the Organisation of Petroleum Exporting Countries (OPEC) are most unlikely to be repeated—first, for the sake of OPEC itself. Even if undertaken, they would not be as damaging as in the 1970s because the major energy-consuming economies are much less energy intensive and have diversified their primary energy supply and have built up their emergency oil stockpiles to deal with any physical disruptions to supply. Furthermore, using resources as a political weapon is condemned internationally. Russia has been heavily criticised for its continued differential treatment of the former Soviet republics in terms of the price of its supplied natural gas. It supplies natural gas at a low price to those republics politically close to Russia but at a high price to those politically close to the West. While China denied the embargo threat, it received heavy criticism of its alleged embargo of rare-earth exports to Japan after Japan's arrest of a Chinese trawler captain in the Diaoyu Islands in September 2010.

It thus follows that both China and Western countries need to depoliticise China's global quest for energy security. Western politicians need to recognise that their rhetoric in relation to China's efforts to secure energy supplies overseas—which paints it as a major threat—has done nothing but intensify China's fear that they might seek to deny China's access to the oil it needs for development. China needs to reconsider its stance of distrusting global oil markets and to recognise that reliance on aggressive acquisitions of overseas oil fields and equity oil production has been of little help in strengthening its energy security. Just like other oil importers, China's energy security depends increasingly and deeply on the stability of global oil markets and reliable and growing oil supplies to the market. Thus, China and other major oil-importing countries share profound common interests in maintaining and strengthening the stability of global oil markets and reducing the chance of potential disruptions to oil supply and the resulting damaging oil-price shocks.

Acknowledgments

I would like to dedicate this chapter to my mother, Guo Xié, who passed away on 3 April 2012. The main ideas of the chapter were presented at the Conference on China Energy Issues in the Twelfth Five Year Plan and Beyond, Singapore, 23–24 February 2012. The chapter has benefited from work in this area from The Australian National University, Brookings Institution, Global Development and Environment Institute and the International Energy Agency. That said, the views expressed here are those of the author, and do not reflect the positions of those institutions. The author bears sole responsibility for any errors and omissions that remain.

References

Aiyar, P., 2006, 'No "great game" between India and China', *Asia Times*, 13 January, <http://www.atimes.com/atimes/China_Business/HA13Cb01.html>

Arnson, C. and Davidow, J., 2011, *China, Latin America, and the United States: The new triangle*, Woodrow Wilson International Center for Scholars, Washington, DC.

Balfour, F., 2002, 'A global shopping spree for the Chinese: Mainland companies are snapping up more overseas assets', *Business Week*, 18 November, <http://www.businessweek.com/magazine/content/02_46/b3808162.htm>

Basu, I., 2005, 'India discreet, China bold in oil hunt', *Asia Times*, 29 September, <http://www.atimes.com/atimes/South_Asia/GI29Df01.html>

Blumenthal, D., 2008, 'Concerns with respect to China's energy policy', in G. B. Collins, L. Goldstein, A. S. Erickson and W. S. Murray (eds), *China's Energy Strategy: The impact of Beijing's maritime policies*, Naval Institute Press, Annapolis, Md, pp. 418–36.

Bradsher, K., 2005, 'Chinese company to buy Kazakh oil interests for $4 billion', *The New York Times*, 22 August.

Bräutigam, D., 2009, *The Dragon's Gift: The real story of China in Africa*, Oxford University Press, Oxford.

British Petroleum (BP), 2011, *BP Statistical Review of World Energy 2011*, British Petroleum, London.

Bussey, J., 2012, 'US attacks China Inc.', *Wall Street Journal*, 3 February.

Chen, S., 2010, 'China's self-extrication from the "Malacca dilemma" and implications', *International Journal of Chinese Studies*, vol. 1, no. 1, pp. 1–24.

Collins, G. and Murray, W., 2008, 'No oil for the lamps of China?', in G. Collins, L. J. Goldstein and A. S. Erickson (eds), *China's Energy Strategy: The impact of Beijing's maritime policies*, Naval Institute Press, Annapolis, Md, pp. 387–407.

Davis, B., 2011, 'US targets state firms, eyeing China', *Wall Street Journal*, 25 October.

De Córdoba, J., 2011, 'China—oil deal gives Chávez a leg up', *Wall Street Journal*, 9 November, <http://online.wsj.com/article/SB10001424052970203733504577026073413045462.html>

De La Merced, M. J., 2011, 'Sinopec to buy Daylight Energy for $2.1 billion', *The New York Times*, 9 October, <http://dealbook.nytimes.com/2011/10/09/sinopec-to-buy-daylight-energy-for-2-1-billion/>

Downs, E., 2006, *China*, Foreign Policy Studies Energy Security Series, Brookings Institution, Washington, DC.

Downs, E., 2010, 'China's energy rise', in B. Womack (ed.), *China's Rise in Historical Perspective*, Rowman & Littlefield, Lanham, Md.

Downs, E., 2011a, 'China Development Bank's oil loans: pursuing policy—and profit', *China Economic Quarterly*, vol. 15, no. 4, pp. 43–7.

Downs, E., 2011b, *Inside China Inc.: China Development Bank's cross-border energy deals*, John L. Thornton China Center Monograph Series No. 3, Brookings Institution, Washington, DC.

Forsythe, M. and Sanderson, H., 2011, 'Financing China costs poised to rise with CDB losing sovereign-debt status', *Bloomberg*, 2 May, <http://www.bloomberg.com/news/2011-05-02/financing-china-costs-poised-to-rise-with-decision-on-cdb-debt.html>

Fu, M. M. and Lin, X., 2012, 'Overseas investment of Chinese enterprises suffers losses of nearly US$100 billion, 70% of the investment does not make money', *China Times*, 11 February, <http://finance.sina.com.cn/china/hgjj/20120211/081311358170.shtml>

Gallagher, K. P., Irwin, A. and Koleski, K., 2012, *The New Banks in Town: Chinese finance in Latin America*, Inter-American Dialogue, Washington, DC.

Hall, S., 2010, 'China to invest in Argentine railways', *Wall Street Journal*, 13 July, <http://online.wsj.com/article/SB100014240527487045189045753645238 11330964.html>

Herberg, M., 2012, China's global quest for resources and implications for the United States, Testimony before the US–China Economic and Security Review Commission, Washington, DC, 26 January, <http://www.uscc.gov/hearings/2012hearings/written_testimonies/12_01_26/12_1_26_herberg_testimony.pdf>

Holmes, J., 2007, China's energy consumption and opportunities for US–China cooperation to address the effects of China's energy use, Testimony before the US–China Economic and Security Review Commission, Washington, DC, 14 June, <http://www.uscc.gov/hearings/2007hearings/transcripts/june_14_15/holmes_prepared_remarks.pdf>

Hua, Y., 2011, 'China leads the world in energy production during the 11th five-year period', *Sina Finance*, 6 January, <http://finance.sina.com.cn/g/20110106/10009212106.shtml>

International Energy Agency (IEA), 2000, *World Energy Outlook 2000*, International Energy Agency, Paris.

International Energy Agency (IEA), 2010, *World Energy Outlook 2010*, International Energy Agency, Paris.

International Energy Agency (IEA), 2011, *World Energy Outlook 2011*, International Energy Agency, Paris.

Jacob, J., 2010, 'Ecuador, China sign $1 billion cash-for-crude loan deal', *International Business Times*, 1 September, <http://www.ibtimes.com/articles/48140/20100901/ecuador-china-energy-crude-latinamerica-petrochina-petroecuador-opec-loan.htm>

Jiang, J. and Sinton, J., 2011, *Overseas investments by Chinese national oil companies: assessing the drivers and impacts*, February, Information Paper prepared for the Standing Group for Global Energy Dialogue of the International Energy Agency, Paris.

Kennedy, A., 2011, 'China's petroleum predicament: challenges and opportunities in Beijing's search for energy security', in J. Golley and L. Song (eds), *Rising China: Global challenges and opportunities*, ANU E Press, Canberra, pp. 121–35.

Lanteigne, M., 2008, 'China's maritime security and the "Malacca dilemma"', *Asian Survey*, vol. 4, no. 2, pp. 143–61.

Ma, J. T., 2012, The national economy maintained steady and rapid development in 2011, 17 January, National Bureau of Statistics, Beijing, <http://www.stats.gov.cn/tjfx/jdfx/t20120117_402779443.htm>

Ma, W., 2012, 'Shell reaches Chinese shale-gas deal', *Wall Street Journal*, 21 March.

Ma, Y. D., 2009, 'China and Brazil signed US$10 billion loan-for-oil for a period of 10 years', *Oriental Morning Post*, 20 May, <http://www.dfdaily.com/node2/node23/node220/userobject1ai169877.shtml>

Mao, Y. S., 2006, 'Politics vs market', *China Security*, no. 3, pp. 106–15.

Masaki, H., 2006, 'Japan takes on China in Africa', *Asia Times*, 15 August, <http://www.atimes.com/atimes/Japan/HH15Dh01.html>

National Bureau of Statistics of China (NBS), 2009, *China Statistical Yearbook 2009*, China Statistics Press, Beijing.

National Development and Reform Commission (NDRC), Ministry of Finance, Ministry of Land and Resources and National Energy Administration, 2012, *Development Plan for Shale Gas*, 13 March, National Development and Reform Commission, Ministry of Finance, Ministry of Land and Resources and National Energy Administration, Beijing, <http://zfxxgk.nea.gov.cn/auto86/201203/P020120316383507834234.pdf>

Oxford Analytica, 2011, 'China: state firms face scrutiny for overseas losses', *Oxford Analytica*, 20 October.

Oxford Analytica, 2012, 'China: gas consumption set to soar', *Oxford Analytica*, 7 February.

Shi, H. T., 2004, 'China's "Malacca dilemma"', *China Youth Daily*, 15 June, <http://zqb.cyol.com/content/2004-06/15/content_888233.htm>

Storey, I., 2006, 'China's "Malacca dilemma"', *China Brief*, vol. 6, no. 8 (12 April), <http://www.jamestown.org/single/?no_cache=1&tx_ttnews%5Btt_news%5D=31575>

The Chosun IIbo, 2009, 'South Korea fought against China for natural resources despite repeated losses', *IFeng*, 10 August, <http://finance.ifeng.com/news/hqcj/20090811/1071120.shtml>

The Economist, 2010, 'Brazil/China economy: deeper inroads—Latin America', *The Economist*, 16 August, <http://latinamerica.economist.com/news/brazilchina-economy-deeper-inroads/200>

The Economist, 2012a, 'Lexington: buttering-up and scolding', *The Economist*, 18 February, p. 36.

The Economist, 2012b, 'Nuclear energy in France: fallout', *The Economist*, 18 February, p. 67.

Tsukimori, O., 2012, 'China overtakes Japan as world's top coal importer', *Reuters*, 26 January, <http://www.reuters.com/article/2012/01/26/us-coal-china-japan-idUSTRE80P08R20120126>

United States Energy Information Administration (USEIA), 2004, *International Energy Outlook 2004*, Energy Information Administration, Washington, DC.

United States Energy Information Administration (USEIA), 2011a, *International Energy Outlook 2011*, DOE/EIA-0484(2011), Energy Information Administration, Washington, DC, <http://205.254.135.24/forecasts/ieo/pdf/0484(2011).pdf>

United States Energy Information Administration (USEIA), 2011b, *World Shale Gas Resources: An initial assessment of 14 regions outside the United States*, Energy Information Administration, Washington, DC, <http://www.eia.gov/analysis/studies/worldshalegas/pdf/fullreport.pdf>

Vaidyanathan, G., 2012, 'China: with energy investments rising, vice president heads to US', *Greenwire*, 14 February.

Wang, X. and Wu, P., 2011, 'China's strategic oil reserves in 2020 will increase to about 85 million tons', *China Economic Weekly*, 18 January, <http://news.sina.com.cn/c/sd/2011-01-18/001821830415.shtml>

Welsch, E. and Lee, Y., 2012, 'China fuels its global energy supply', *Wall Street Journal*, 3 February.

Xinhua, 2012, 'Sinopec buys shale interest from Devon for US$2.2b', *Xinhua*, 4 January, <http://www.china.org.cn/business/2012-01/04/content_24316460.htm>

Xu, J., 2009, 'Is China Inc. overpaying in its merger deals?', *Wall Street Journal*, 25 June, <http://blogs.wsj.com/deals/2009/06/25/is-china-inc-overpaying-in-its-merger-deals/>

Yi, X., 2005, 'Chinese foreign policy in transition: understanding China's "peaceful development"', *Journal of East Asian Affairs*, vol. 19, no. 1, pp. 74–112.

Zhang, Z. X., 1990, *Evolution of Future Energy Demands and CO_2 Emissions up to the Year 2030 in China*, ECN-I--91-038, The Energy Research Centre of the Netherlands, The Hague.

Zhang, Z. X., 1998, *The Economics of Energy Policy in China: Implications for global climate change*, New Horizons in Environmental Economics Series, Edward Elgar, Cheltenham, UK.

Zhang, Z. X., 2007, 'China's hunt for oil in Africa in perspective', *Energy and Environment*, vol. 18, no. 1, pp. 87–92.

Zhang, Z. X., 2010a, 'China in the transition to a low-carbon economy', *Energy Policy*, vol. 38, pp. 6638–53.

Zhang, Z. X., 2010b, 'Energy policy in China in the transition to a low-carbon economy', in F. Fesharaki, N. Y. Kim and Y. H. Kim (eds), *Fossil Fuels to Green Energy: Policy schemes in transition for the North Pacific*, Korean Energy Economics Institute Press, Seoul, pp. 176–225.

Zhang, Z. X., 2011a, 'Assessing China's carbon intensity pledge for 2020: stringency and credibility issues and their implications', *Environmental Economics and Policy Studies*, vol. 13, no. 3, pp. 219–35.

Zhang, Z. X., 2011b, 'China's energy security, the Malacca dilemma and responses', *Energy Policy*, vol. 39, pp. 7612–15.

Zhang, Z. X., 2011c, *Energy and Environmental Policy in China: Towards a low-carbon economy*, New Horizons in Environmental Economics Series, Edward Elgar, Cheltenham, UK.

Zhao, H., 2007, 'Rethinking the Malacca dilemma and China's energy security', *Contemporary International Relations*, no. 6, pp. 36–42.

Zhong, J. J., 2012, 'Crude oil imports rose by 6% year-on-year, dependence rate reached 56.5% in 2011', *China News Net*, 13 January, <http://finance.chinanews.com/ny/2012/01-13/3601502.shtml>

Index

TOTAL 332
total factor productivity (TFP) 33, 99,
112, 135, 139, 145, 146
Transneft 340, 341, 342
Trans-Pacific Partnership (TPP) 338
Turkmenistan 339, 341

Ukraine 349, 350
unemployment 19, 23
benefits 265, 267, 269
insurance 9, 281
see also employment, labour
United Nations 160, 267
United States 11, 19n.2, 23, 38, 52, 59,
71, 82, 87, 88, 97, 123, 124, 129,
143, 151, 155, 157, 169, 293, 311,
329–34, 337–9, 344, 346, 347, 348,
349
Unocal 346
US dollar 23, 79, 80, 81, 82, 83, 86, 87,
123, 135, 161, 340
see also currency, dollar peg
US Export–Import Bank 340, 341

Venezuela 339, 340, 341, 342, 343, 344,
348
Vietnam 157, 338

water 16, 83, 158, 309–27
Wen Jiabao 8n.6, 52, 268, 273, 282,
340n.4
Western Development Strategy 262
World Bank 46n.2, 53, 54, 160, 161, 269,
340, 344n.7
World Trade Organisation (WTO) 70, 72,
74, 77, 118, 141, 291
Wuxi 119, 121

Xiamen 116, 119, 120, 121
Xinjiang 98n.1, 184, 193, 324
Xuzhou 119

Yangtze River 117, 119, 193, 311, 312,
313
Yantai 119, 122
Yellow (Huang) River 311, 312, 315, 325

Yellow River Conservancy Commission
(YRCC) 325
Yunnan 98n.1, 184, 196, 324

Zhanjiagang 121
Zhejiang 98n.1, 119, 183, 193, 211, 229,
324
Zhuhai 116, 119, 120, 121